Marketing Research
with SAS Enterprise Guide

DATE DUE

Demco, Inc. 38-293

Marketing Research with SAS Enterprise Guide

KRISTOF COUSSEMENT

NATHALIE DEMOULIN

KARINE CHARRY

GOWER

Published by
Gower Publishing Limited
Wey Court East
Union Road
Farnham
Surrey, GU9 7PT
England
www.gowerpublishing.com

Ashgate Publishing Company
Suite 420
101 Cherry Street
Burlington,
VT 05401-4405
USA

SAS ®, SAS® Enterprise Guide® are trademarks or registered trademarks of SAS in the USA and other countries. ® indicates USA registration.

Created with SAS® software. Copyright 2011, SAS Institute Inc., Cary, NC, USA. All Rights Reserved. Reproduced with permission of SAS Institute Inc., Cary, NC, USA.

Data Request Code KCNDKC11

British Library Cataloguing in Publication Data
Coussement, Kristof.
  Marketing research with SAS Enterprise Guide.
  1. SAS (Computer file) 2. Enterprise guide. 3. Marketing
  research--Data processing.
  I. Title II. Demoulin, Nathalie. III. Charry, Karine.
  658.8'3'028555-dc22

Library of Congress Cataloging-in-Publication Data
Coussement, Kristof.
  Marketing research with SAS enterprise guide / by Kristof Coussement, Nathalie Demoulin and Karine Charry.
      p. cm.
  Includes bibliographical references and index.
  ISBN 978-1-4094-2676-9 (paperback) -- ISBN 978-1-4094-2677-6
(ebook) 1. Marketing research--Data processing. 2. Business--Data processing. 3. Enterprise guide.
4. SAS (Computer file) I. Demoulin, Nathalie. II. Charry, Karine. III. Title.
  HF5415.2.C645 2011
  658.8'3028553--dc23

2011031227

ISBN   978-1-4094-2676-9 (pbk)
ISBN   978-1-4094-2677-6 (ebk)

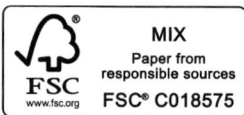

Contents

Foreword

It is an honour to share this book with you. It fills an important need for our customers, both in academia and in industry.

This book makes the fundamental marketing research methods accessible to students and researchers through a practical approach illustrated with marketing management examples. After the first chapter, which presents the SAS Enterprise Guide environment for creating a project to access and manipulate data, the other chapters mainly introduce descriptive analysis, multivariate analysis such as factor or cluster analysis, analysis of variance and regression. Thus it provides, step by step, all the most important analyses required for marketing research.

Marketing is not simply *feeling* and *communicating*. The essential cornerstone of robust, successful modern marketing is statistical analysis to understand needs, markets and trends. This book introduces the reader to basic marketing statistics by using an easy point-and-click tool, that is, SAS Enterprise Guide.

SAS, through its analytical strength, is historically strongly used in marketing departments. Its offerings cover many business needs: customer knowledge (segmentation, scoring, analysis of customer behaviour, loyalty, churn, customer life time value, and so on), multichannel marketing campaign management and optimization, event-driven marketing, social media analysis or e-reputation. Beyond the SAS software solutions, it is a question of the business defining optimized multichannel strategies, integrating existing and new customer knowledge, and so on. The key to success lies in the analysis of data.

The SAS Global Academic Program works closely with universities, engineering schools and business schools to develop skills for tomorrow's organization. The partnership with IÉSEG School of Management is one of our best examples of success in France. This book is the outcome of a very fruitful collaboration during the last few years. Working with IÉSEG School of Management is a pleasure: from our perspective IÉSEG

School of Management is one of the rare business schools which really focuses on decision making based on analytics. SAS is confident that tomorrow's management leaders will need to focus increasingly on the dimension of *analytics*.

The core business of SAS is analytics. SAS Enterprise Guide reduces the gap between marketers and statisticians, and this analytical power provides a real value-add for marketing professionals.

Beyond these business needs, SAS Enterprise Guide provides marketing professionals, as well as teachers and researchers, with guidance on typical issues such as survey analysis, or more specific matters such as campaign simulations (repetitive or not).

This practical book is characterized by a very good pedagogical approach, and provides an overview of objectives that can be achieved with SAS Enterprise Guide for marketing research. Each case is illustrated with a business problem, its translation into statistical terms, a theoretical review, a dataset description, a guided analysis with screenshots and interpretations of the results. It concludes with advice on managerial decisions.

Basic statistical knowledge, the mastery of SAS and the strong marketing experience of the authors are gathered here in a book of high quality.

So it is with great pleasure that I recommend this easy-to-read book to everyone engaged in, or interested in, marketing research.

Ariane Sioufi, Academic Director, SAS France
Grégoire de Lassence, Teaching and Research Manager, SAS France

Preface

Nowadays a lot of researchers involved in marketing face the problem of correctly using statistical procedures and accurately interpreting the outputs. Usually these people are scared off by the statistics behind the different analyses procedures and thus often rely on external sources to come up with sound answers to the proposed research questions. This book has the intention to show its readers how to select the right statistical procedures and how to put these methods into practice by always starting from a real managerial problem. It shows its readers, through a step-by-step approach, which procedures to use in which particular situation and how to practically execute it in a SAS Enterprise Guide environment. SAS is the largest statistical software provider worldwide and it offers a very user-friendly environment called SAS Enterprise Guide. This software uses a simple drag-and-drop menu interface, also suitable for non-experienced SAS users. It is widely employed by companies, many universities and business schools. SAS OnDemand for Academics is a free-of-charge service offering professors from degree-granting institutions the opportunity to use SAS Enterprise Guide for teaching. Professors can simply register on the SAS support website in order to create a course and invite students to participate. Once set up, the professor and their students can download the SAS Enterprise Guide interface and install the software. SAS files and other file types (Excel, txt, cvs, SPSS and so on) can be opened from the user's local computer and analysis run on them from the SAS servers. Additionally, SAS OnDemand for Professionals is a service offering a learning version of SAS Enterprise Guide for professionals, with licences available for six or twelve months. More information can be found on the book website http://www.MarketingResearchwithSASEnterpriseGuide.com.

The purpose of this book is straightforward: it offers a pragmatic approach based on real-life marketing research examples to help the reader solve their day-to-day (business) problems. Furthermore a complete section is dedicated to the managerial interpretation of the results.

This book is aimed at several target audiences, all of whom need robust answers to existing business problems.

- This book intends to be a reference manual for all professional marketers who would like to use statistical procedures in SAS Enterprise Guide. Consequently, the manual does not only give an overview of the basic options for the statistical tests used, but it also digs deeper into more specific and detailed options.

- This book is suitable for all undergraduate and postgraduate academic programmes in which 'Marketing research' and 'Research methodology' are taught.

- This book is also suitable for all researchers analyzing survey-based data in a wide range of frontier domains such as psychology, finance, accountancy, negotiation, communication, sociology, criminology, management, management information systems and so on.

The statistical procedures considered in this book refer to the most common marketing issues encountered by the various target audiences listed above. But in order to enable the non-familiar users of SAS Enterprise Guide to feel empowered, the first chapter is devoted to a thorough description of the SAS Enterprise Guide software. First, we propose a tour of the environment. Then, we show how to create a project. Last, we focus on the data structure (data characteristics and manipulation such as creating, sorting and filtering variables). The second chapter is devoted to descriptive statistics and their usefulness. The third and fourth chapters consider exploratory procedures: Exploratory Factor Analysis and Cluster Analysis respectively. The next chapters discuss the confirmative statistical tests. Chapter 5 is devoted to hypothesis testing for parametric and non-parametric data, Chapter 6 explains the relevancy of correlations, Chapter 7 shows how to run regression analyses (linear and logistic), and Chapter 8 presents discriminant analysis.

Chapters referring to the various statistical procedures (Chapters 4, 5, 6, 7 and 8) could be independently read from each other. According to the type of analysis one has to consider, one may limit the reading to the relevant chapter. However, the first two chapters should probably be studied by readers with less knowledge about SAS Enterprise Guide and/or statistics.

All the statistical procedures mentioned above are explained using the same pedagogical scheme. As such, the reader will become familiar with the methodological and mental process of solving a particular marketing research problem. For most analyses, the following structure is used within the book.

Fundamentals

Managerial Problem

Translation of the Managerial Problem into Statistical Notions

Hypotheses

Dataset Description

Data Analysis

Interpretation

Managerial Recommendations

In the *Fundamentals* section, the objective of the statistical procedure is explained. The managerial situations in which the analysis can be used are presented. This section also communicates the important steps to conduct to successfully lead the analysis. Further, the managerial problem describes a real-life managerial problem with which every researcher or manager could be confronted (*Managerial Problem*). The reader is guided on how to solve the problem him/herself. Once the managerial problem is clearly defined, it is translated into the description of the statistical purpose of the analysis without formally using symbols or statistical formulas (*Translation of the Managerial Problem into Statistical Notions*). In other words, the research question is translated using a statistical terminology. This is a necessary step that enables choosing the appropriate statistical procedure, but it is kept very simple to facilitate understanding. Providing in-depth theoretical explanations of statistical issues is beyond the scope of this book (nevertheless, some references are provided at the end of each chapter for the diggers). Furthermore, a statistical representation of the statistical problem is proposed by translating it into a null and an alternative hypothesis (*Hypotheses*). Then, a detailed overview of the data delivered is given the name of the file, number of observations, descriptions of the variables and the measurement scale of the variables used (*Dataset Description*). All datasets are freely available via the official book website http://www.MarketingResearchwithSASEnterpriseGuide.com. At this stage, the readers should completely comprehend all elements, giving them a complete understanding of the business problem and the way one should solve it. The next step is data analysis. This book will employ a step-by-step approach to show how to perform the statistical procedure in SAS Enterprise Guide (*Data Analysis*). Readers of this book will be taken by the hand and shown how to run a procedure through the use of multiple screenshots of the software environment. This will drastically enhance the readability of the book. Based on the outputs of the statistical program, guidance is proposed to facilitate interpretation of the results. The interpretation is done in a fragmented approach in which the title of each table or the header of each figure is stated, followed by the corresponding SAS output (*Interpretation*). In the last stage, the statistical output is converted into a detailed answer on the managerial problem (*Managerial Recommendations*).

We would like to thank the various people and institutions that directly or indirectly contributed to this book project: Tristan Crombet, Koen De Bock, Grégoire de Lassence, Bart Larivière, Christophe Majois, Raluca Mogos-Descotes, SAS France, Ariane Sioufi, Anneleen Van Kerckhove, Griet Verhaert, and our students, who we had constantly in mind when working on this book.

Kristof Coussement
Nathalie Demoulin
Karine Charry

Author Biographies

Kristof Coussement (PhD) is Professor of Marketing at IÉSEG School of Management (LEM-CNRS) of the Catholic University of Lille in France. Dr Coussement teaches several marketing-related courses including *Strategic Marketing Research*, *Customer Relationship Management* and *Database Marketing* in which students are taught the theoretical principles of all aspects of marketing research, operational and analytical CRM and the methodological foundations of predictive marketing modelling.

Dr Coussement has had papers published in international peer-reviewed journals and his works have been presented at various conferences around the world. His main research interests are all aspects in customer intelligence, B-to-B intelligence, direct marketing and analytical CRM. Improving his 'practical' experience over the years by doing several real-life research projects in a different number of industries, his main focus is on doing profound academic research with a high added value to business.

Dr Coussement is founder and a committee member of BAQMaR, the largest online European Association for Quantitative and Qualitative Marketing Research.

More information about his work can be found at http://www.KristofCoussement.com.

Nathalie Demoulin (PhD) is Professor of Marketing and head of the Marketing track at IÉSEG School of Management (LEM-CNRS) of the Catholic University of Lille in France. Dr Demoulin teaches several courses related to marketing strategy such as *Marketing Strategy and Company Observation, Retail Marketing Strategy* and *Markstrat: A Marketing Strategy Simulation.*

Dr Demoulin's primary research interests were the marketing managers' decision-making process and the impact of marketing decision support systems on managers. She currently conducts research linked to customers' loyalty, waiting time and sensorial marketing in service and retailing sectors. She has published in international and French peer-reviewed journals such as *Decision Support Systems, Journal of Retailing, Journal of Retailing and Consumer Services* and *Systèmes d'information et Management.*

Karine Charry (PhD) is Professor of Marketing at IÉSEG School of Management (LEM-CNRS) of the Catholic University of Lille in France. Dr Charry's research focuses on consumer behaviour – and namely children as consumers – as well as persuasion mechanisms in marketing and health prevention communications. Her ten years of experience in marketing departments of diverse companies and sectors in B-to-B and B-to-C contributes to the pragmatic approach of her publications and teaching (*Consumer Behaviour, Persuasion in Marketing Communication* and *Social Marketing*).

Chapter 1

Getting Started with SAS Enterprise Guide

Objectives

1. Introduce the SAS Enterprise Guide software and its requirements.

2. Understand the structure of the SAS Enterprise Guide work space.

3. Understand the usefulness of creating projects.

4. Learn how to create and add data sources to the SAS Enterprise Guide environment.

5. Describe the different types of data one can use.

6. Learn basic data manipulation tasks like filtering data, creating new variables by using an expression, recoding variables and sorting data.

1.1. What is SAS Enterprise Guide?

SAS is the leader in business and statistical analytics software and services, and it is the largest independent vendor in the business intelligence market. Through innovative solutions delivered within an integrated framework, SAS helps customers at more than 45,000 sites improve performance and deliver value by making better decisions faster. Since 1976, SAS has been giving customers around the world THE POWER TO KNOW®.

SAS Enterprise Guide provides a SAS graphical interface that helps the marketer exploit the power of SAS and publish dynamic results in a Microsoft Windows client application. This solution is the preferred SAS interface for business analysts, programmers and statisticians and it is the key application in SAS Business Intelligence offerings.

The benefits of using SAS Enterprise Guide are threefold:

1. *Provide a self-service environment for analysts and statisticians*. Only SAS Enterprise Guide integrates the extensive array of analytics with the power of SAS software in an efficient, friendly graphical user interface application. Business analysts can produce the analyses and distribute reports they need, freeing IT to focus on other strategic projects.

2. *Provide easy access to data sources through a SAS graphical interface*. SAS Enterprise Guide is the only front end that provides a guided mechanism to access data across multiple platforms, operating systems and databases. A centralized system for managing access to corporate data ensures that users have appropriate access privileges while empowering them to react quickly to evolving business conditions.

3. *Make reporting and analytics available to everyone*. The ability to develop and deploy customized tasks enables users to extend the core functionality to create custom wizards, which can be distributed easily as needed. Information can be delivered through an established publishing framework with the ability to publish dynamic, interactive content to Microsoft Office and Web users.

1.2. Software Requirements

The computer on which the SAS software runs is referred to as the SAS server. Usually the SAS server will be the same computer as the SAS software is installed on, referred to as the Local Computer. This book assumes that the technical environment has already been set up. Below you will find a short overview of the different IT requirements necessary to install SAS Enterprise Guide. The SAS Enterprise Guide software can run on different operating systems such as Windows (x86-32): Windows 2000 Professional, Windows XP Professional, Windows Server 2003, Windows Vista, Windows 7 (Enterprise, Business, Ultimate and Home editions supported). Additional SAS software, that is, Base SAS, is required to get SAS Enterprise Guide installed. More detailed information can be found at http://support.sas.com/documentation/installcenter/.

The examples in this book are shown using SAS Enterprise Guide 4.3, running SAS 9.2 under Windows 7 Professional. Slight differences could be observed compared to previous and future releases of SAS Enterprise Guide.

If you have any additional questions or remarks concerning the technical requirements of running SAS Enterprise Guide on your computer, we advise you to contact your local SAS representative or to visit http://support.sas.com.

1.3. Touring the Environment

When one launches SAS Enterprise Guide, the software opens with the **Welcome to SAS Enterprise Guide** window. At this step, an existing project can be opened or a new task (project, SAS program or data) can be created.

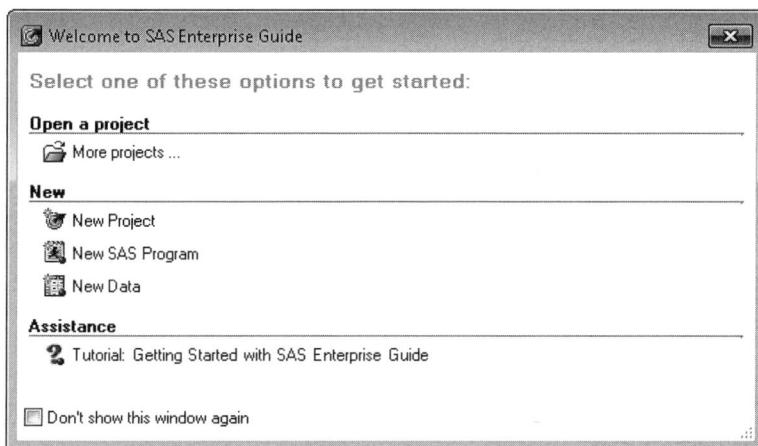

The SAS Enterprise Guide environment stores all relevant information about a specific analysis in a *Project* (.egp extension), which bundles the different data sources, the different analyses or *Tasks* that were run and the results output to the user. It contains further user-specific information on how and why particular decisions are made at a given point in the analysis flow. The authors suggest creating a separate project answering a specific research question. This habit will facilitate the analyses by delivering a better project structure to the marketing analyst. Project files can be saved, copied, reopened and adapted if necessary.

The default SAS Enterprise Guide interface as shown below consists of three different parts, that is, Project Tree, Process Flow, Server List, and an easy-to-use Help Facility that is accessible via the main toolbar by clicking on the **Help** button.

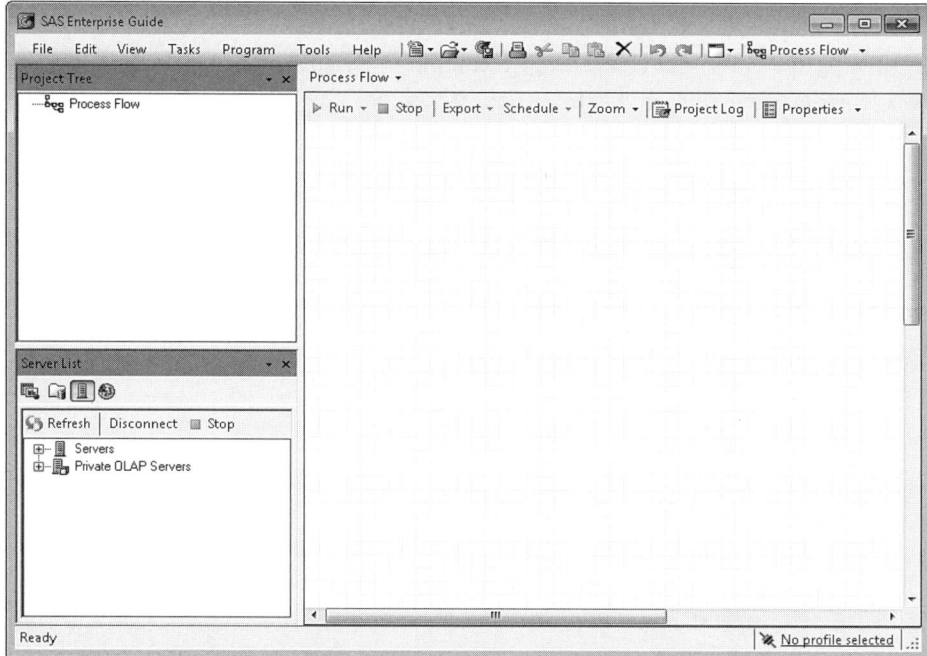

For instance, an example project called *Retail Project* is given opposite. It shows that the user read in a SAS dataset *RETAIL.sas7bdat*, that she calculated some summary statistics using the **Summary Statistics** task, while in the end the output is converted to a .pdf file using the Export possibility in the **Output Data** tab.

Below, a more detailed overview is given for the functionalities for each of the three parts of the SAS Enterprise Guide environment, that is, Project Tree, Process Flow, Server List, and the Help Facility.

1.3.1. PROJECT TREE

The project tree summarizes the different elements of the project in a structured way using the shape of a traditional project tree. The default name of a project is *Process Flow*, but this can easily be changed by right-clicking the project name and clicking on **Rename**.

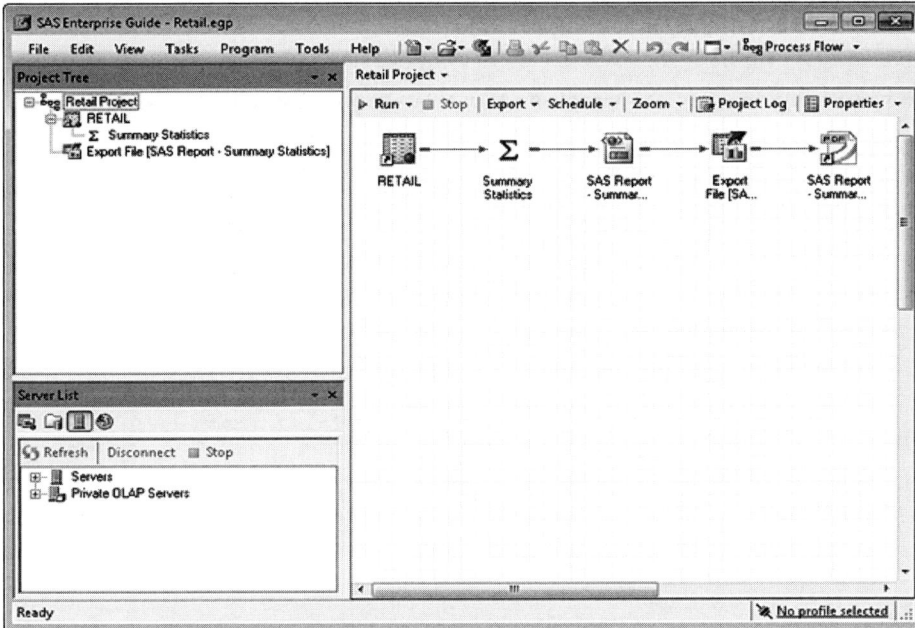

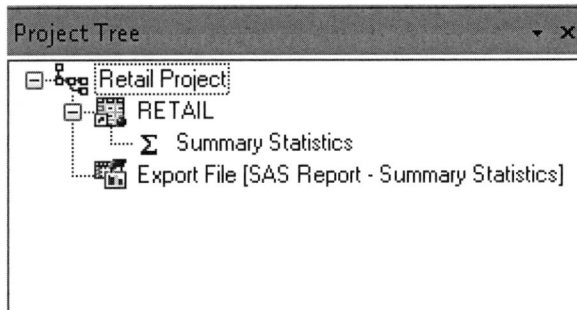

The above figure shows an example of a project called *Retail Project* and it shows that:

- the name of the project is *Retail Project*;

- the name of the imported SAS data file is *RETAIL*;

- the analysis task asked by the analyst is called **Summary Statistics**;

- an export file is generated from the default **Output Data** tab by using the Export possibility.

1.3.2. PROCESS FLOW

The process flow diagram visualizes the sequence of the different decisions and analyses a researcher took. It consists of icons that could represent datasets, tasks and outputs that are employed within a project. It visualizes the different contents and their follow-ups during the project. The default name for a diagram is *Process Flow* and it is automatically changed when the project name is changed. The figure below visualizes the different stages of the *Retail Project*.

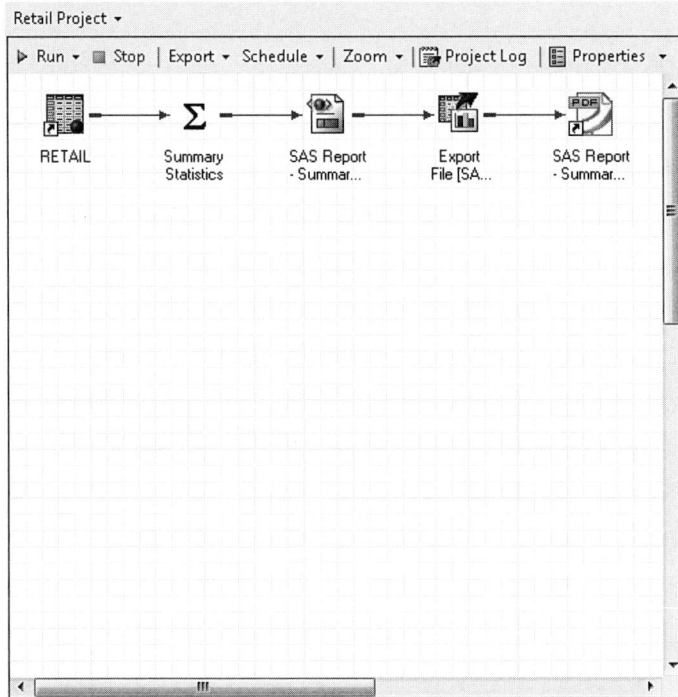

1.3.3. SERVER LIST

The server list gives the analyst an overview of the different servers available, while pinpointing the server which is currently active. The area under *Server List* is known as the resources pane. Here one can select any of the four displayed icons to view the *Task List*, *SAS Folders*, *Server List* or *Prompt Manager*.

- The *Task List* represents the different tasks or analyses available within the SAS Enterprise Guide environment.

- The *SAS Folders* show the meta-data folder structure available to the user.

- The *Server List* summarizes the availability and connectivity to the SAS servers.

- The *Prompt Manager* allows the SAS Enterprise Guide user to introduce prompts during the task processing. This enables the analyst to add flexibility during the analysis phase, because based on the user's input in the prompt, the analysis results will differ.

1.3.4. HELP FACILITY

If you want additional information about a particular operation or task in SAS Enterprise Guide, one can access the **Help Facility** through the menu bar by clicking the **Help** button.

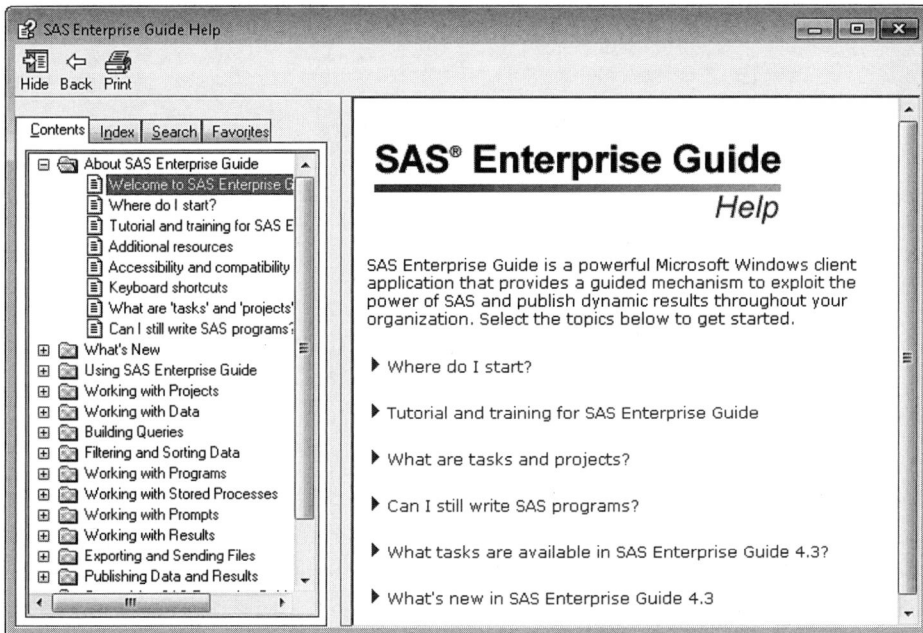

1.4. Creating Projects

1.4.1. PROJECT DEFINITION

The first step in working with the SAS Enterprise Guide environment is the creation of a new project. Selecting **File** → **New** provides the user with different options. Creating a new project can be done by directly producing a new project (*Project*), by creating a new SAS dataset (*Data*) or by creating a new SAS program (*Program*).

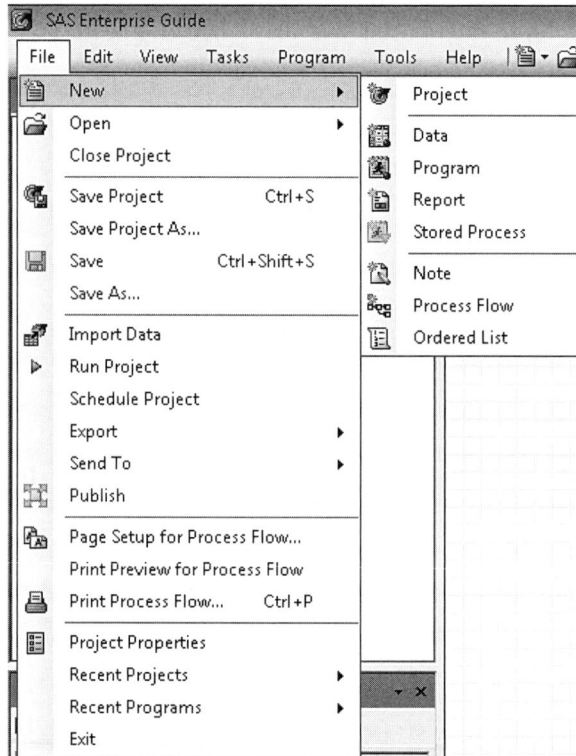

1.4.2. CREATING DATA SOURCES

The SAS Enterprise Guide environment facilitates the creation of SAS data files by manual encoding. This feature is very useful because the encoding of a survey could be performed directly in the SAS Enterprise Guide environment. More specifically, it is possible to manually input different values for different variables that correspond, for instance, to the answers of respondents on a particular survey.

Suppose that a marketing researcher collected gender information on the first 20 customers entering a store of the furniture company Belco. After collecting these data, the marketing researcher wants to get these data into the SAS Enterprise Guide environment. The researcher would like to create a SAS dataset containing two columns or variables, an *ID* variable representing the customer's identifier and a *Gender* variable containing the gender information. The following procedure is used:

1. Go to **File** → **New** → **Data** to open the new data creation window.

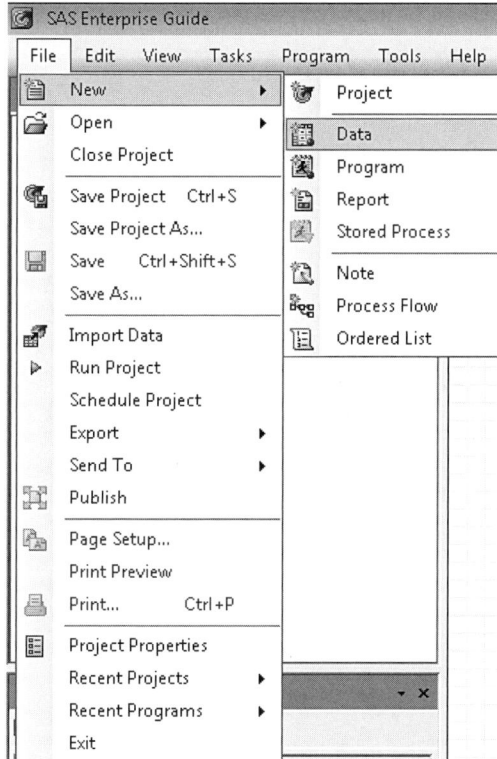

2. The **New Data** pane opens, and the name of the encoded dataset and the location where one would like to save the new dataset should be specified. In our setting, the name of the new SAS dataset is specified as *Create_DSN* and the *WORK* library is selected to save file into the temporary SAS environment. Click **Next** to proceed.

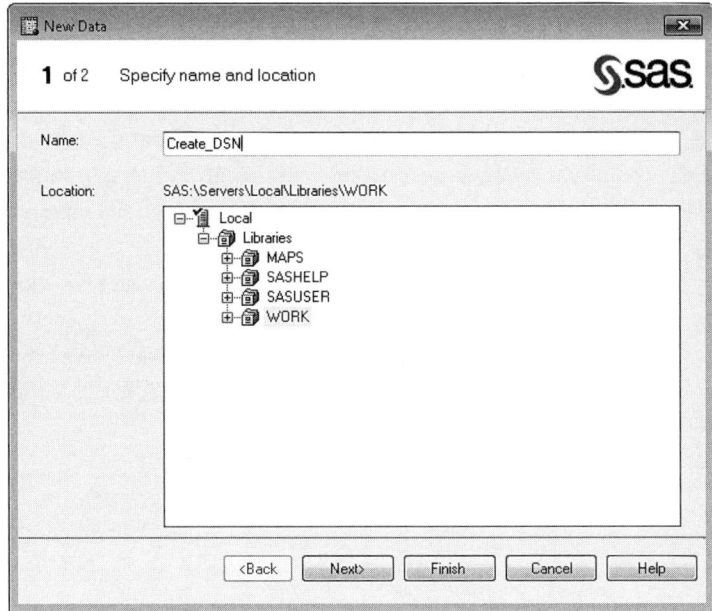

3. A new pop-up window appears that enables the marketing analyst to define the columns or variables to be included in the new dataset, together with the corresponding column properties.

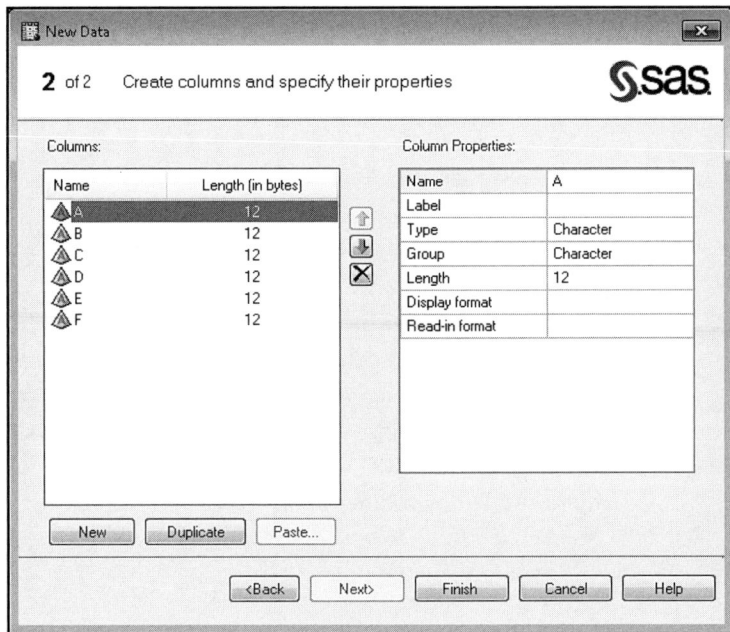

4. Different column properties could be specified; the column name (**Name**), the label that identifies the column (**Label**), and the data type of the column, that is, *Character* or *Numeric* (**Type**). The data group (**Group**) depends on the option selected under **Type**. If **Type** is *Numeric* than the value of **Group** can be numeric, date, time or currency, otherwise the value of **Group** can only be *Character* for character types. The length of the column (**Length**), the format to be used to display the column (**Display format**) and the informat that is used to read in the column (**Read-in format**). In our setting, a two column table is created with a variable *ID* and a variable *GENDER*. The *ID* variable indicates the respondent's identifier number and the *Gender* variable contains the gender of the respondent with *M* for males and *F* for females. Both variables have the same characteristics as specified for the *ID* variable shown in the figure below. Click <u>**Finish**</u> to proceed to the SAS Enterprise Guide input table.

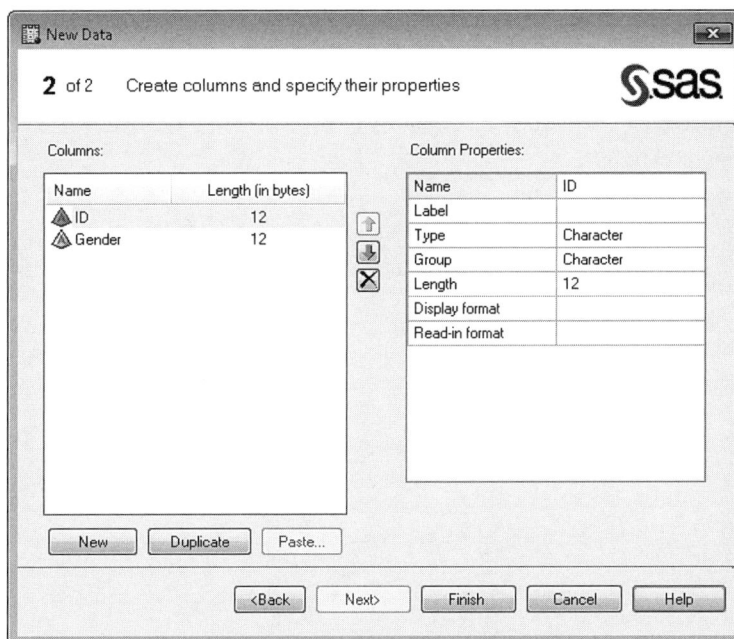

5. The input table appears and this enables the marketing researcher to add the values of both variables by clicking on a particular cell of the table and typing the correct value.

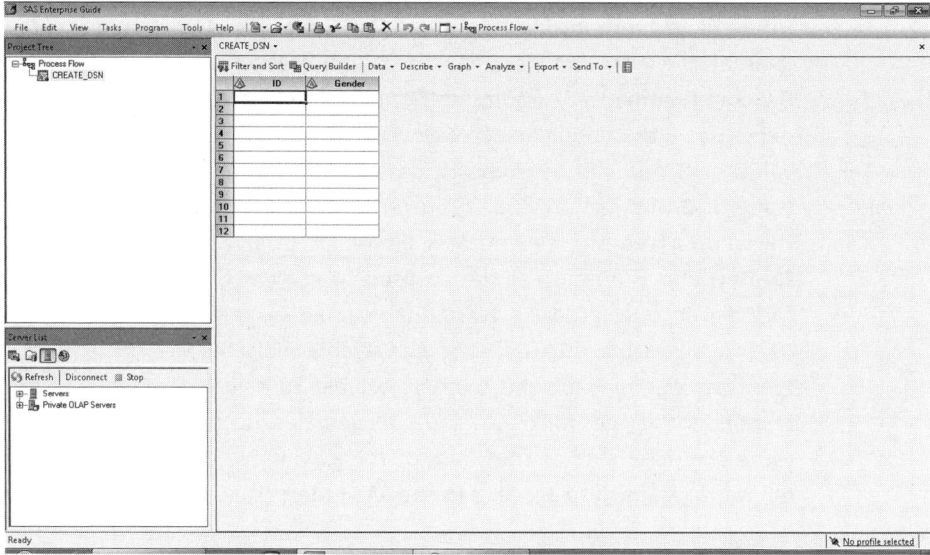

The final *Create_DSN* table looks as follows. Notice that SAS Enterprise Guide automatically changed the format of *ID* to *Numeric*, because this best fits the values of the *ID* variable.

	ID	Gender
1	1	M
2	2	M
3	3	F
4	4	M
5	5	F
6	6	M
7	7	F
8	8	F
9	9	F
10	10	M
11	11	M
12	12	M
13	13	F
14	14	F
15	15	F
16	16	M
17	17	M
18	18	M
19	19	F
20	20	F

1.4.3. ADDING DATA SOURCES

In order to add SAS datasets (*.sas7bdat, *.sas7bvew or *.sd2), Microsoft Excel files (*.xls, *.xlsx, *.xlsm and *.xlsb), Microsoft Access files (*.mdb and *.accdb), Dbase files (*.dbf), Lotus 1-2-3 files (*.wk?) and Paradox files (*.db) to a project, select **File** → **Open** → **Data...**

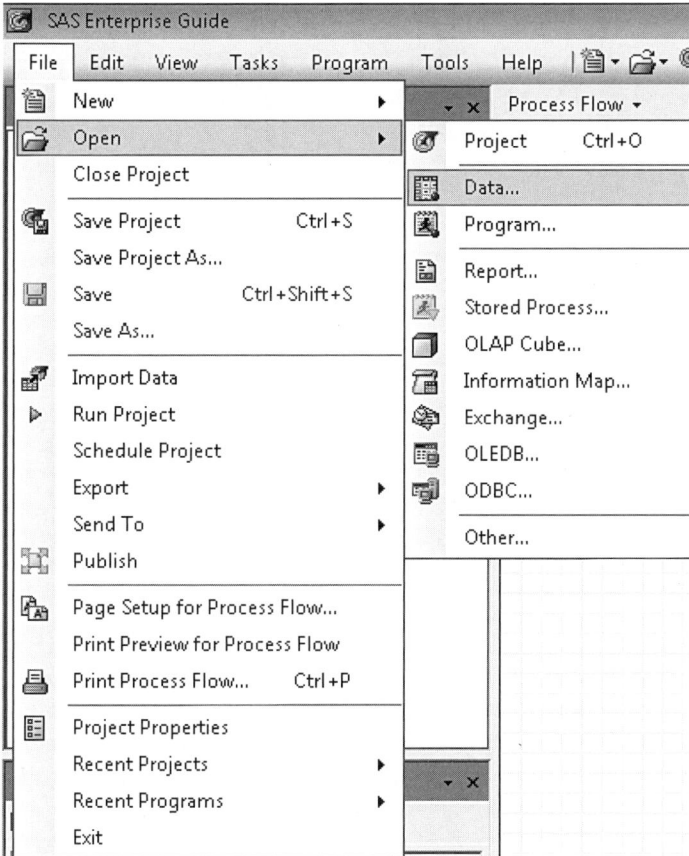

If you would like to open a SAS dataset, a pop-up window appears as shown in the figure below and prompts for the location on your computer to open the data files. Search the data file, open it and one will see that it will directly be imported into the current project.

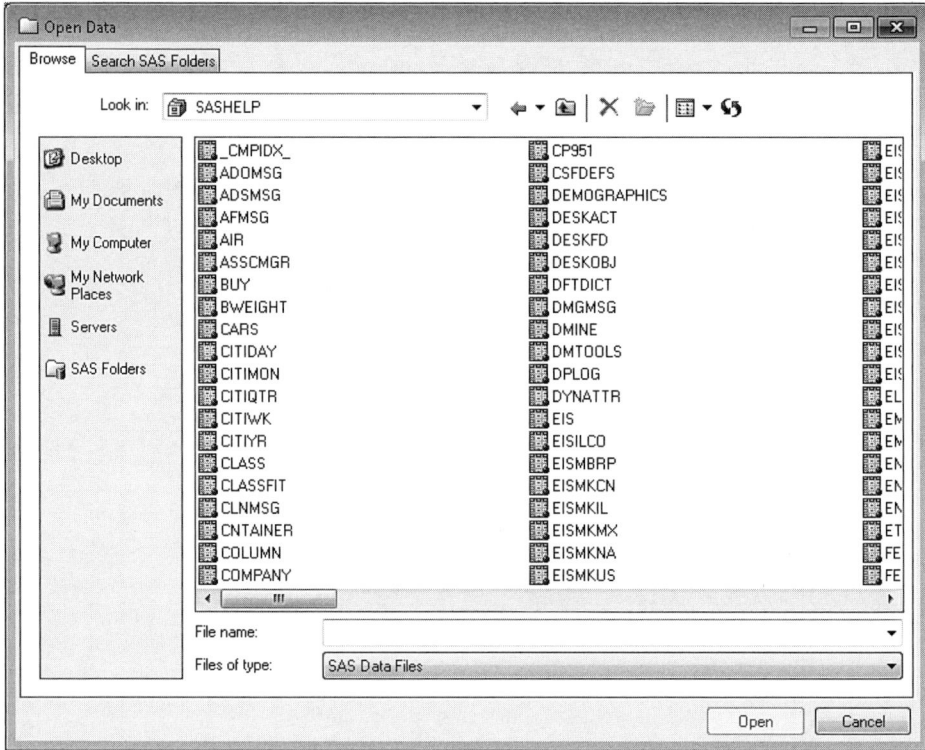

If you would like to open a <u>Microsoft Office</u> file, the SAS Enterprise Guide environment will open a four-step import wizard task. Finishing the different steps of the import wizard task, the Microsoft Office file will be added to your SAS Enterprise Guide environment. Below you will find an example of how to import the *Descriptive_ Analysis.xlsx* Excel file into the SAS Enterprise Guide environment.

1.   Go to **File** → **Open** → **Data...**

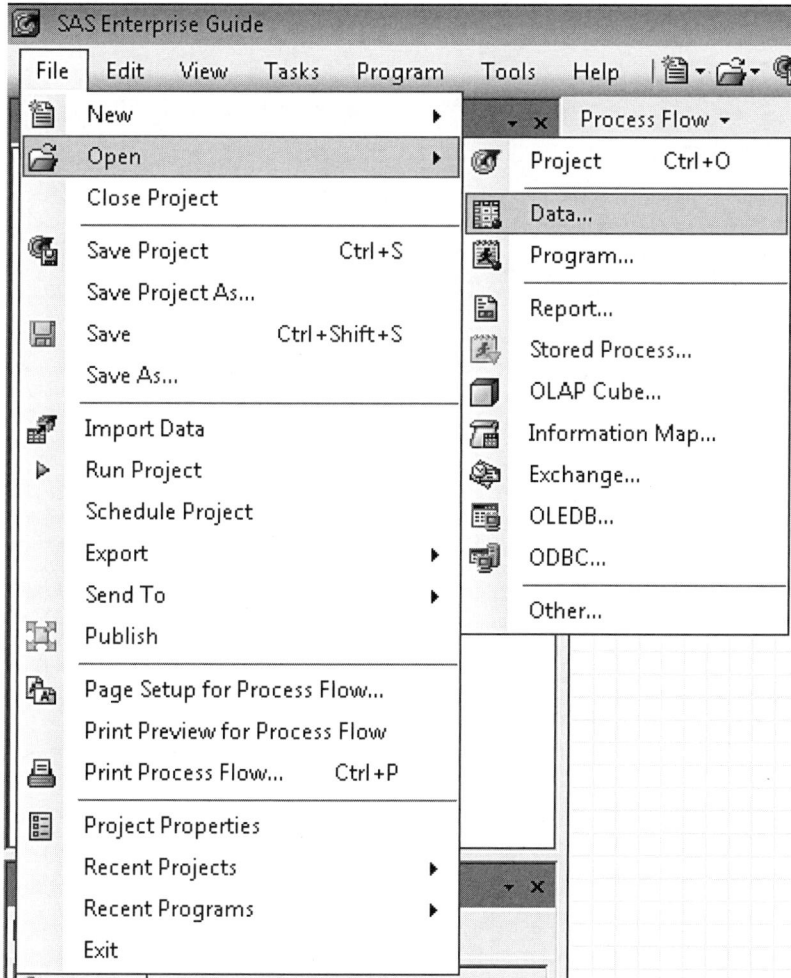

2. Search on your local computer for the dataset *Descriptive_Analysis.xlsx* and open it.

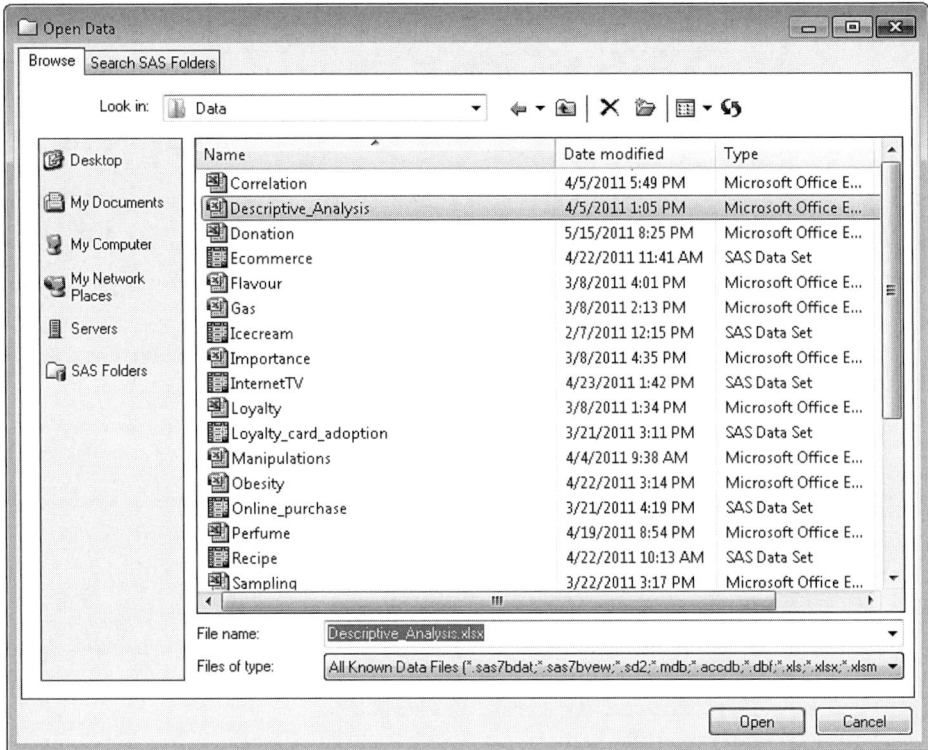

3. A new window appears that asks where to output the imported data file. In our example, the dataset is imported in the library *WORK* under the name *Descriptive_Analysis*. Click **Next** to proceed.

4. In step 2 of the import data wizard, one should pay attention to import the correct worksheet, while specifying whether the variables' names could be found in the first row of the Excel file by (un)ticking the option **First row of range contains field names**. Click **Next** to proceed to step 3.

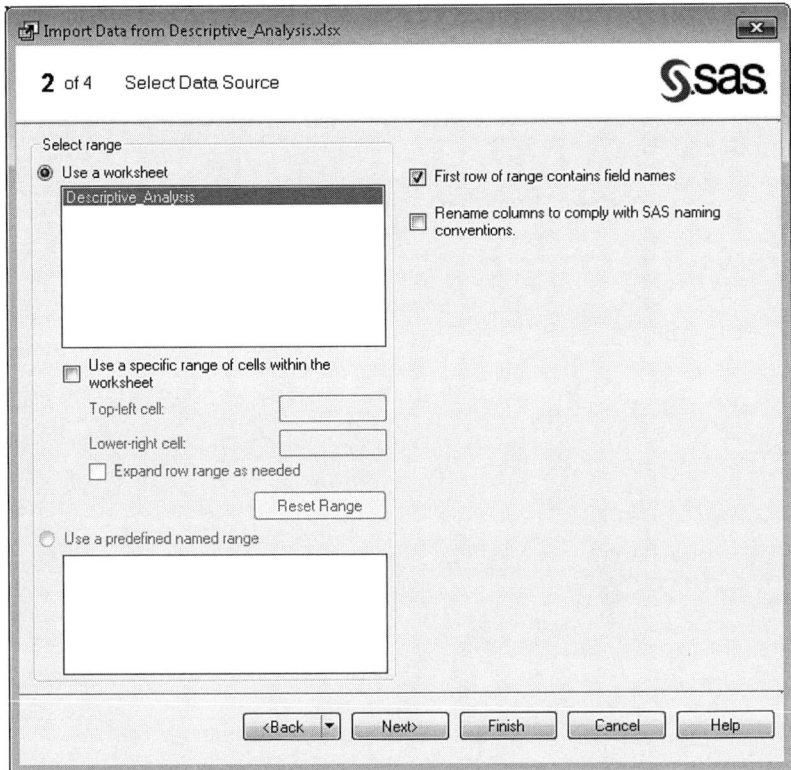

5. Step 3 of the wizard lets you decide which variables to import into the SAS Enterprise Guide environment by (un)ticking the box before the variable names in the column *Source Name*, while the values of the different variable characteristics can be changed by clicking the button **Modify**. If one clicks **Next**, more advanced options are proposed by the SAS Enterprise Guide system, if needed. At this stage, simply click **Finish** to import the Excel file into the SAS Enterprise Guide environment.

If one wants to open an <u>IBM SPSS</u> file (*.sav), two different options exist. Either run a SAS code program, or use the **Import SPSS File** task.

First, you will find the procedure to import IBM SPSS datasets using SAS code.

    1.   Go to **File** → **Open** → **Program...**

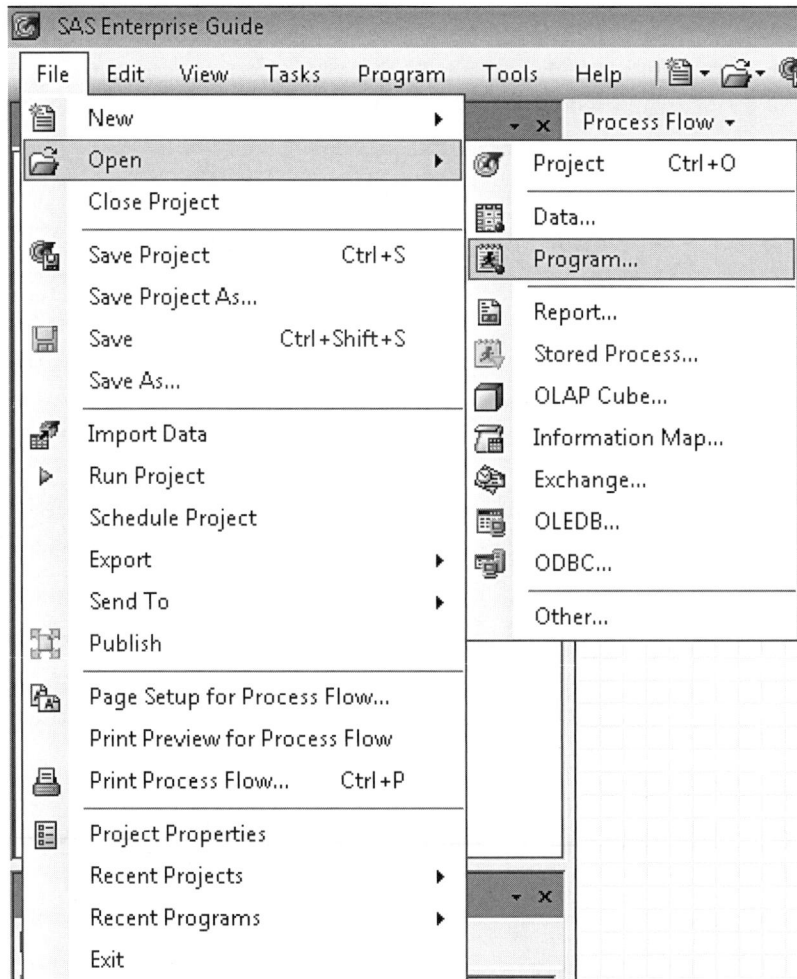

    2.   Search on your local computer for the *SPSS_Import.sas* code file and open it. A new SAS Enterprise Guide window appears showing you the SAS code to be used to import the IBM SPSS file (.sav extension).

This code needs to be adapted in order to import your IBM SPSS file (*.sav) into the SAS Enterprise Guide system. This example code shows you how to read an IBM SPSS file called *sfile1.sav* located in the folder *C:\Data*. The SAS output file is called *spss_file* in this example. In order to import your own .sav file, you need to change the code in two places:

- after *%let dsn_name =*, fill in the required output dataset name by replacing *spss_file*;

- after *%let path =*, you fill in the path where the SAS system finds your .sav file.

Once you have changed the code, you click **Run** and the SAS Enterprise Guide environment imports your IBM SPSS .sav file as a SAS dataset called *spss_file* into the current environment.

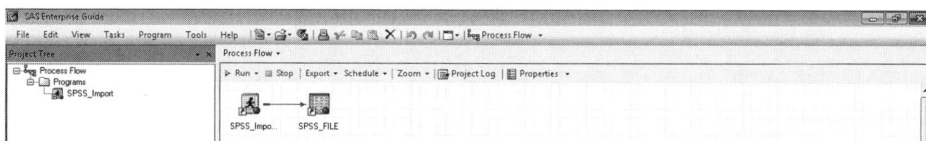

The second option to import SPSS files is to make use of the **Import SPSS file** task that can be reached via **Tasks** → **Data** → **Import SPSS file...** A pop-up window will appear that makes it possible to search on your computer for the SPSS file to be imported.

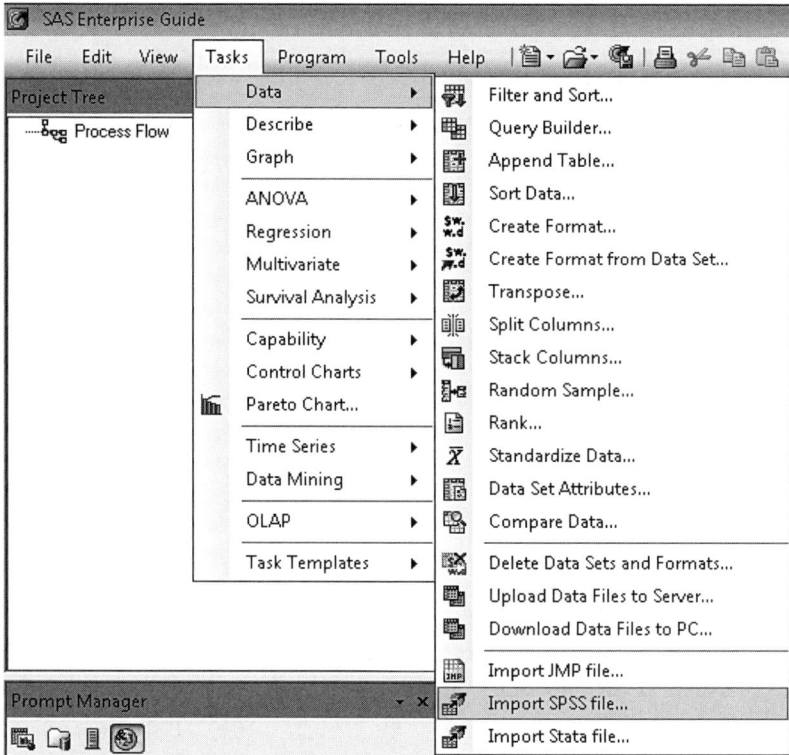

1.4.4. STORING SAS DATASETS

SAS Enterprise Guide saves SAS data files from default Windows folders or SAS data libraries.

- SAS Enterprise Guide is a Microsoft Windows client application. Consequently, the procedure of saving data files can be done in the default Windows manner, meaning that data files can be saved in whichever location you choose on your personal computer. This is the most common way of storing SAS datasets when working in the SAS Enterprise Guide environment.

- SAS data libraries are locations defined within the SAS software. A SAS library is a collection of SAS files identified by a library reference or a shortcut name. The SAS libraries are accessible via the *Server List* under *Servers* and then *Local*.

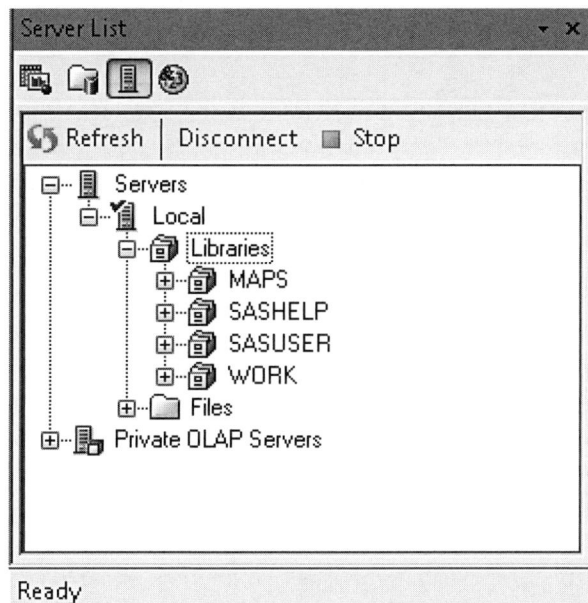

Default SAS libraries are created by SAS Enterprise Guide like *WORK*, *SASHELP*, *SASUSER* and *MAPS*.

- The *MAPS* library is a library that contains a dataset per country with all information necessary to visualize the country borders in SAS.

- The *SASHELP* library is a permanent folder containing all datasets used in the SAS help facility. A SAS user can consult this library for exercising a particular technique. This library is permanent meaning that the datasets in this library are not automatically deleted when the SAS software is closed.

- The *SASUSER* library is a permanent folder that stores files which are necessary for the SAS Enterprise Guide environment. Many tasks automatically produce intermediary datasets in this library.

- The *WORK* library is a temporary folder in which SAS Enterprise Guide stores all files needed for a SAS Enterprise Guide session. Once SAS Enterprise Guide is closed, all data files in the *WORK* library are deleted.

⚠ *Changing the physical location of your data files on your computer will result in the fact that saved projects cannot be reopened and rerun!*

1.5. Exploring Dataset Characteristics

A SAS dataset is the keystone within every SAS Enterprise Guide project. It is the starting point for data analysis. It can contain measurements, frequencies, characteristics and categorizations of individuals or observations. A SAS dataset has the shape of a matrix with the rows corresponding to respondents or observations and the columns of the matrix corresponding to the different variables that contain respondent or observation data.

A SAS dataset has the following characteristics: the maximum length for the dataset name is 32 characters and the name should begin with a character or an underscore. No blanks are allowed in dataset names. The dataset names can be written in lowercase, uppercase or a combination of both, but SAS processes the dataset names in uppercase.

A SAS variable has specific properties on how the variable is processed through the SAS system. Below you will find a short overview of the SAS variables properties.

- Name
  The name of a variable identifies the variable within the whole dataset. The variable names are restricted to 32 characters in length. They can start with any character, while blanks are allowed in the variable naming. Names have to be unique and the purpose is to differentiate between the variables. The names can be lowercase, uppercase or a combination of both, but the letter cases are for representation only and for instance a variable named *Sales*, *sales* or *SALES* would refer to the same variable.

- Label
  A variable label identifies the variables within the whole dataset, but compared to the name of the variable, the label is often much more informative. The maximum length of a label can be up to 256 characters.

  Variable labels can be displayed instead of the variable names as follows:
  1. Go to **Tools** → **Options**.
  2. Select **Data** → **Data General** from the selection pane and tick the option **Use labels for column names**.
  3. Click **OK.**

  To inverse the option, repeat the above steps but uncheck the box **Use labels for column names**.

For the dataset *SNACKS* in the *SASHELP* library, the dataset with the variable names is listed in the figure below.

	QtySold	Price	Advertised	Holiday	Date	Product
1	0	1.99	0	0	01JAN2002	Baked potato chi...
2	0	1.99	0	0	02JAN2002	Baked potato chi...
3	0	1.99	0	0	03JAN2002	Baked potato chi...
4	0	1.99	0	0	04JAN2002	Baked potato chi...
5	0	1.99	0	0	05JAN2002	Baked potato chi...
6	0	1.99	0	0	06JAN2002	Baked potato chi...
7	0	1.99	0	0	07JAN2002	Baked potato chi...

Furthermore, the same dataset showing the variable labels is given below.

	Quantity sold	Retail price of product	Advertised (1=yes)	Holiday (1=yes)	Date of sale	Product name
1	0	1.99	0	0	01JAN2002	Baked potato chi...
2	0	1.99	0	0	02JAN2002	Baked potato chi...
3	0	1.99	0	0	03JAN2002	Baked potato chi...
4	0	1.99	0	0	04JAN2002	Baked potato chi...
5	0	1.99	0	0	05JAN2002	Baked potato chi...
6	0	1.99	0	0	06JAN2002	Baked potato chi...
7	0	1.99	0	0	07JAN2002	Baked potato chi...

- Type

  SAS stores the variables in two different ways: numeric and character types. Numeric types are indicated by a blue ball, while character variables are indicate by a red triangle. However, special numeric types exist within the SAS Enterprise Guide environment: dates indicated by a calendar, currency indicated by currency signs and time indicated by a clock.

  A missing numeric value is indicated by a dot in the dataset, while a missing character value is represented by a blank.

- Length

  The length of a variable value refers to the way SAS stores the values into the system in number of bytes. The default length for a numeric type ranges between 3 and 8, while the default length for a character variable can range from 1 up till 32,767.

- Formats
  A format of a variable determines how the user will see the variable displayed. *Numerical formats* come in the form of *Xw.d* where *X* stands for the type of format to be displayed, the *w* stands for the maximum number of characters, while *d* equals the number of decimal places. The default numeric format is called *BEST12.0* and this format has following characteristics:
  1. the values are displayed with at most 12 characters;
  2. the zero in *BEST12.0* is ignored;
  3. the format writes integers without decimal points, that is, 5 instead of 5.00;
  4. unnecessary decimal points are neglected, that is, 5.01 instead of 5.0100.

  Character formats always start with a dollar sign and the default form is *$w.* where *w* stands for the maximum width of the character field. The default character format is *$12.* where character values are displayed at most with 12 characters.

- Informats
  An informat refers to how SAS stores the values of a particular variable in the system. The default formats and informats for the different data types are given below.

Data type	Format	Informat
Character	*$w.*	*$w.*
Numeric	*BESTw.d*	*w.d*
Date	*MMDDYYw.d*	*MMDDYYw.d*
Time	*TIMEw.d*	*TIMEw.d*
Currency	*DOLLARw.d*	none

1.6. Dataset Manipulations

This section deals with various dataset manipulation tasks that are often required in a traditional marketing research project. Four different manipulations are proposed in this section: filtering datasets, the creation of new variables using an advanced expression, the recoding of variables and the sorting of data. This section makes use of the *Manipulations.xlsx* dataset that contains data issued from an experiment conducted on children on the influence of using different types of cartoons in advertising on their attitude towards the advertising. The following variables are used within this study:

- Customer identifier (*ID*).

- Experimental condition representing the cartoon to which children are exposed to (such as *Garfield, Obelix, Chef Ratatouille* and *Ursula*) (*Condition*).

- Gender with *B* equal to Boy and *G* equal to Girl (*Gender*).

- Age expressed in years (*Age*).

- Attitude towards the cartoon measured by six items on a four-point scale (*Aad1-Aad6*).

1.6.1. FILTERING DATA

Creating subsets of data is a crucial element in traditional marketing research projects. It is the process of selecting the observations that satisfy one or more conditions. Suppose that one would like to include only boys in a particular analysis. To subset this data, the **Filter and Sort** task is used.

1. Add the *Manipulations.xlsx* to your project environment.

2. Open the **Filter and Sort** task by clicking **Tasks** → **Data** → **Filter and Sort...**

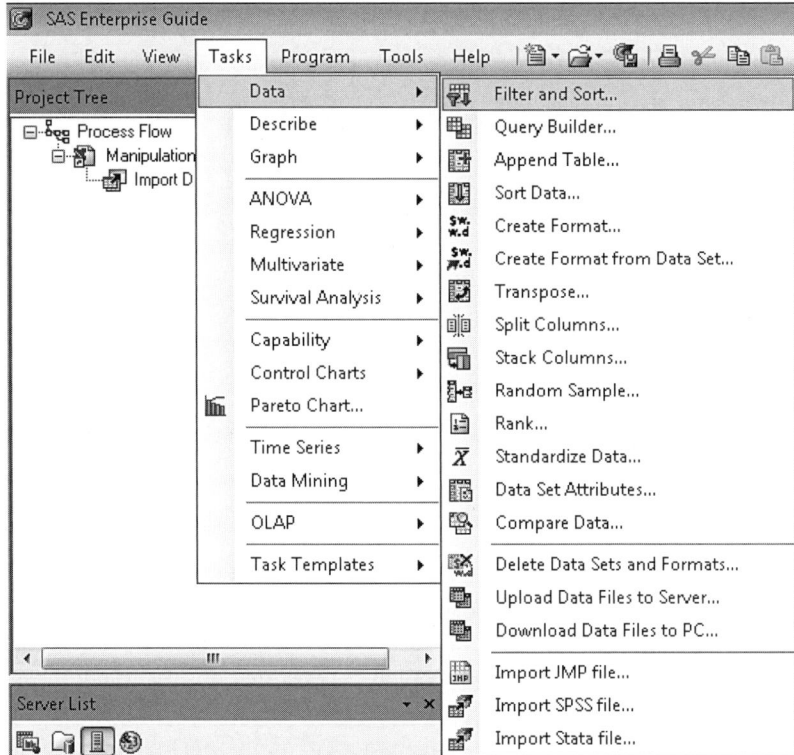

*When you are in the **Output Data** tab, an alternative way to filter data is available by clicking on the **Filter and Sort** button. Furthermore, in each and every SAS Enterprise Guide task in the **Data** tab, a possibility exists to filter data by clicking on the **Edit...** button.*

3. The pane opens at the **Variables** tab. Here one drags and drops the variables to be included in the final output table from the left to the right box. Here, we would like to add all original variables to the new dataset.

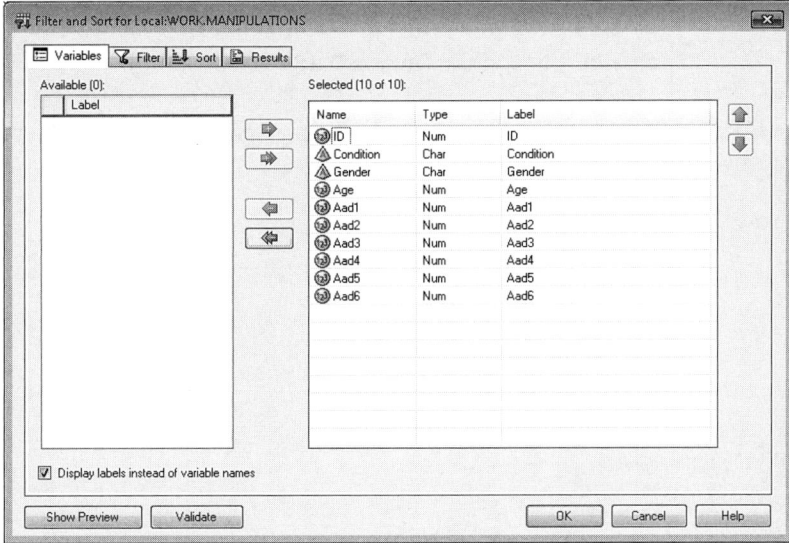

4. In order to filter the current dataset, the **Filter** tab is clicked. Under the **Filter description** label, one specifies the filter criterion (or criteria). As shown in the figure below, all observations that meet the *Gender* equal to *B* criterion will be included in the new dataset.

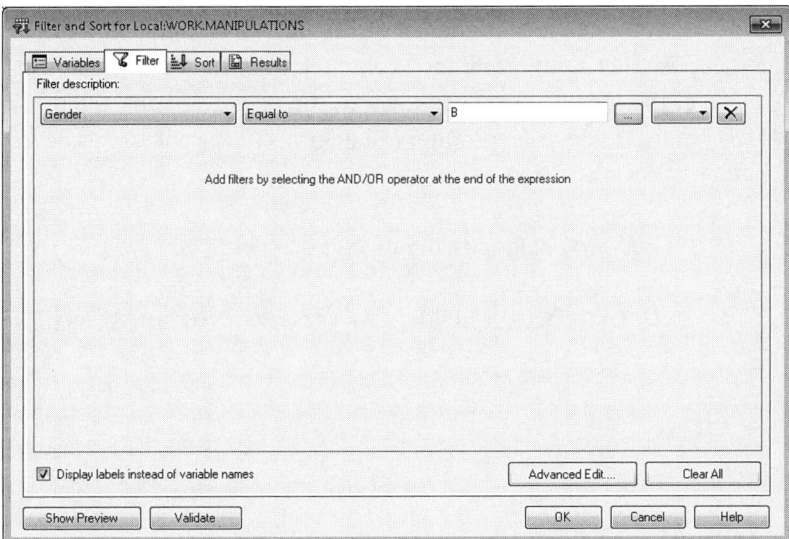

5.   Click **OK** and you verify that only the boys are included in the output dataset found in the **Output Data** tab.

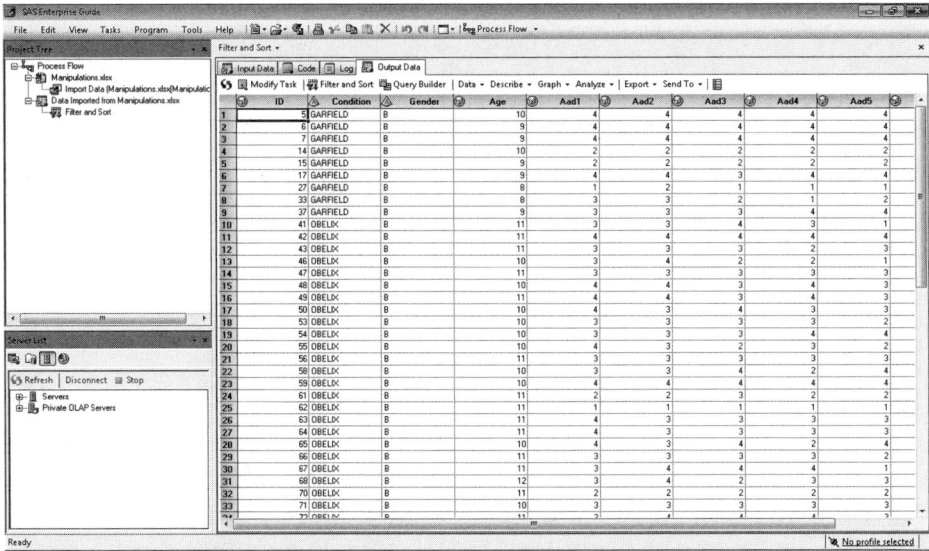

1.6.2. CREATING NEW VARIABLES USING EXPRESSIONS

The creation of new variables based on regrouping existing variables is an important task. Suppose that a new computed column is needed that represents the average of all items of the construct attitude towards the advertisement, that is, *Aad1* till *Aad6*. SAS Enterprise Guide uses the **Query Builder** task to calculate this new variable using a mathematical expression.

1.   Add *Manipulations.xlsx* to your process flow.

2.   Open the **Query Builder** task via **Tasks** → **Data** → **Query Builder...**

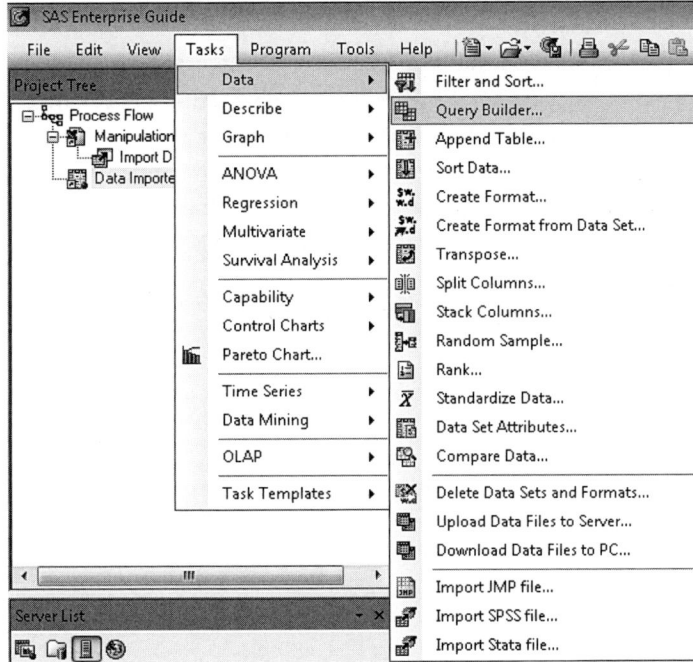

3. The query builder pane opens. First, one drags and drops all variables to be incorporated in the final output table from the left to the **Select Data** tab.

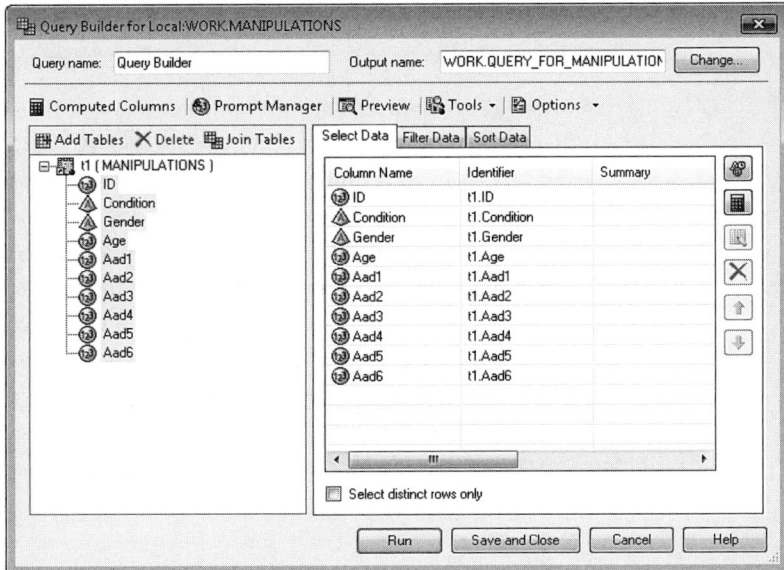

4. Adding the new computed column into the dataset is accomplished by clicking on the little calculator on the right-hand side of the pane. A new window opens and different alternatives (**Summarized column, Recode Column** and **Advanced expression**) are proposed to create a new column. Here, we are interested to create the mean value of *Aad1* till *Aad6*. Mathematical operations on one or more variables are executed by means of the **Advanced expression** option. Click **<u>Next</u>** to proceed.

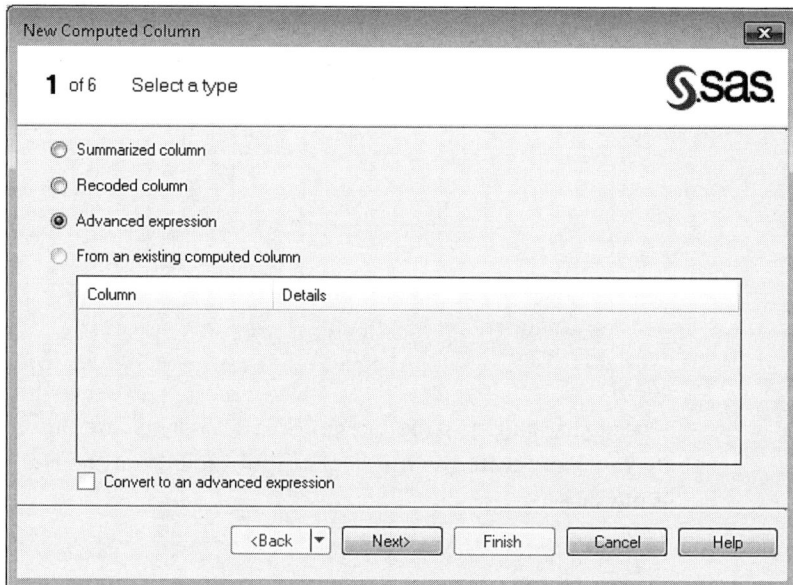

5. In the pop-up window, one is now able to write down the expression in the expression box. In order to facilitate the formulation of your expression, predefined functions are available in the **Functions** folder, while the table names and the corresponding variables are listed in the **Tables** folder. By double-clicking the **Tables** folder, and afterwards the corresponding table name, one is able to see each and every variable included in that table. In order to calculate the mean for the *Aad1* till *Aad6*, the mean function is used. Again, to select the specific variables to consider in the mean function, one may double-click the corresponding variables in the **Tables** folder. Make sure to put a comma between each variable included in the mean function. Click **<u>Next</u>** to proceed.

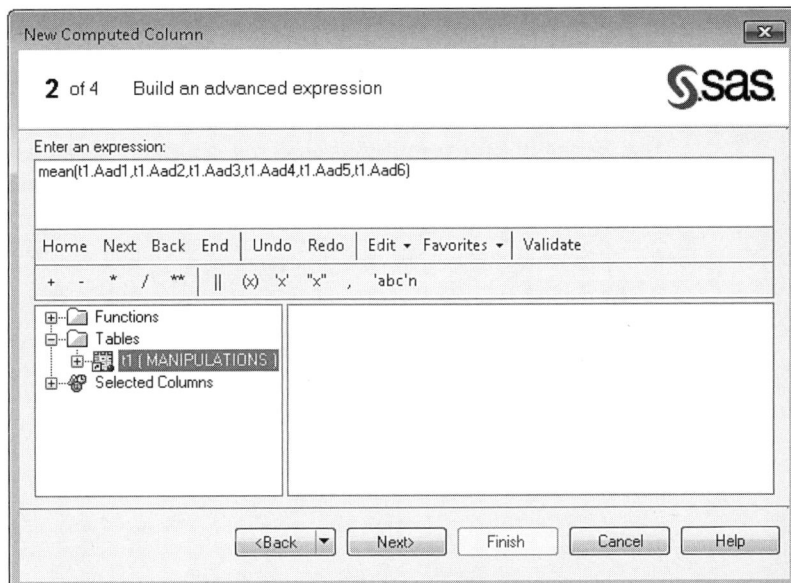

6.   In a next step, there is a possibility to change the name of the new column (**Identifier**), and the name of the new column output by the SAS Enterprise Guide environment (**Column Name**). Furthermore, if needed, a column heading that is more informative and that is used in your report output can be specified (**Label**). Here the **Identifier** and **Column Name** are changed to *Mean_Aad*. Click **Next** to proceed to the final step of the process.

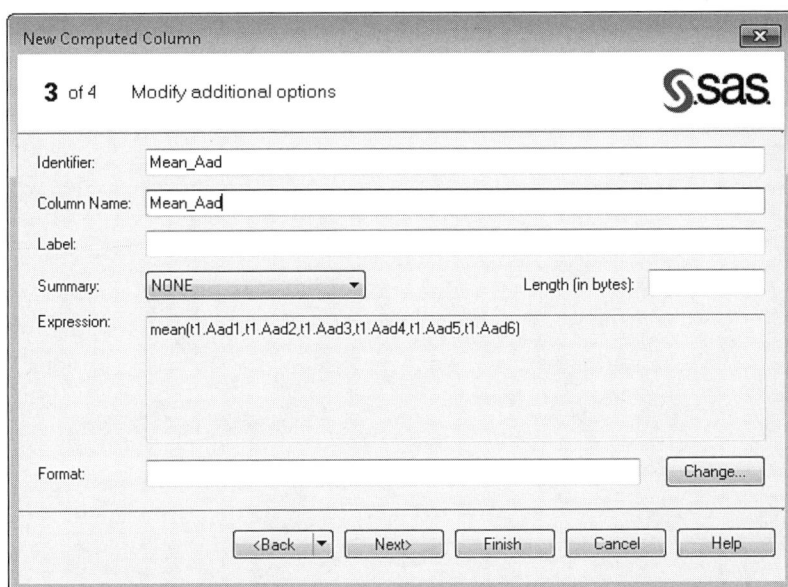

7.   A new pop-up window appears that summarizes your previous decisions. Just click **Finish** to end the creation of the new variable using an advanced expression.

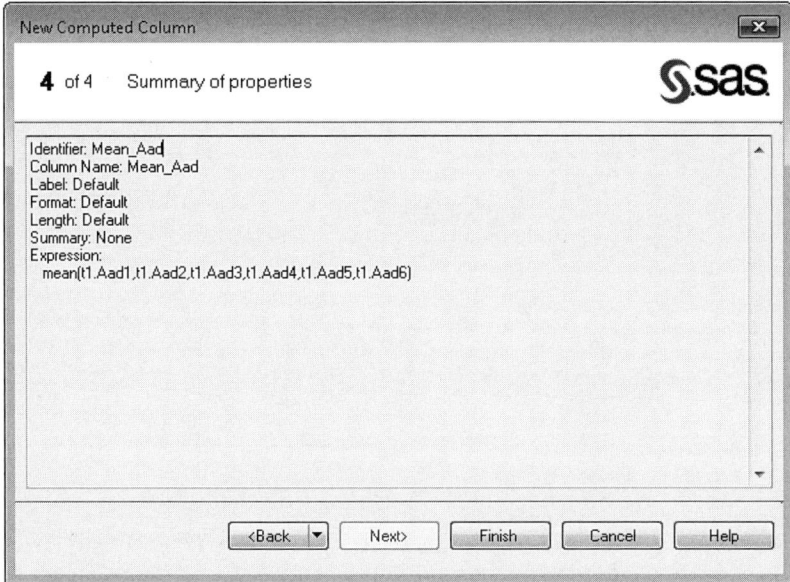

8.   By now, one is traced back to the initial **Query Builder** screen, where one sees the new variable *Mean_Aad* appearing in the variables to be included in the final output table.

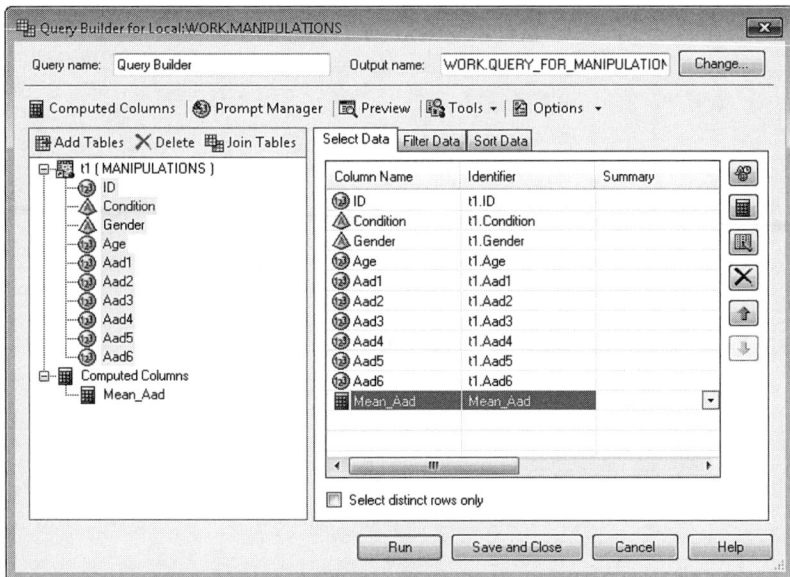

9.   Click **Run** to finish this task and you find the new computed column in the **Output Data** tab.

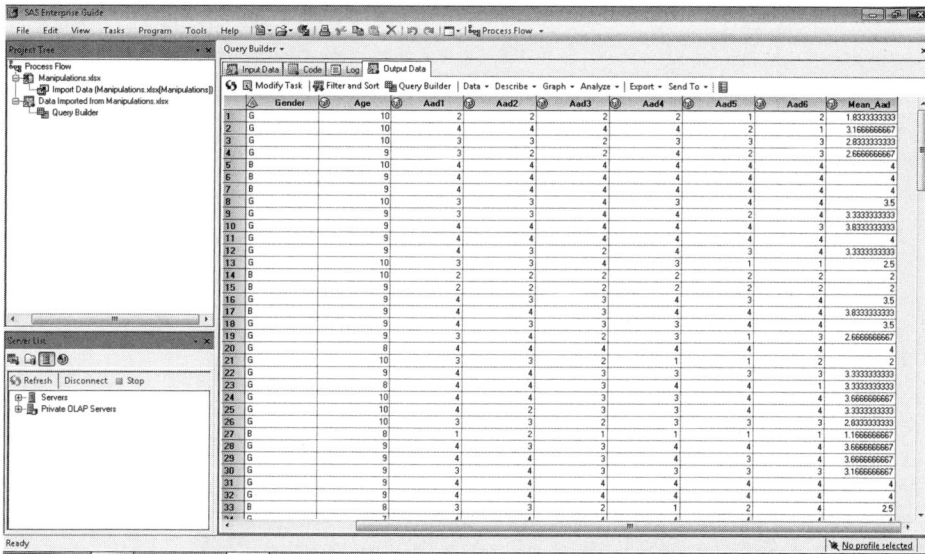

1.6.3. RECODING VARIABLES

Recoding variables is a useful task, especially if you would like to create dummy variables, that is, variables containing only two unique values, from a variable or if you would like to merge categories for a variable. Suppose that the variable *Gender* needs to be recoded into a dummy variable that takes the value of 1 when the respondent is a boy, and 0 otherwise. To recode variables, the **Query Builder** task is used.

1.   Add *Manipulations.xlsx* to your process flow.

2.   Recoding variables is done via **Tasks** → **Data** → **Query Builder...**

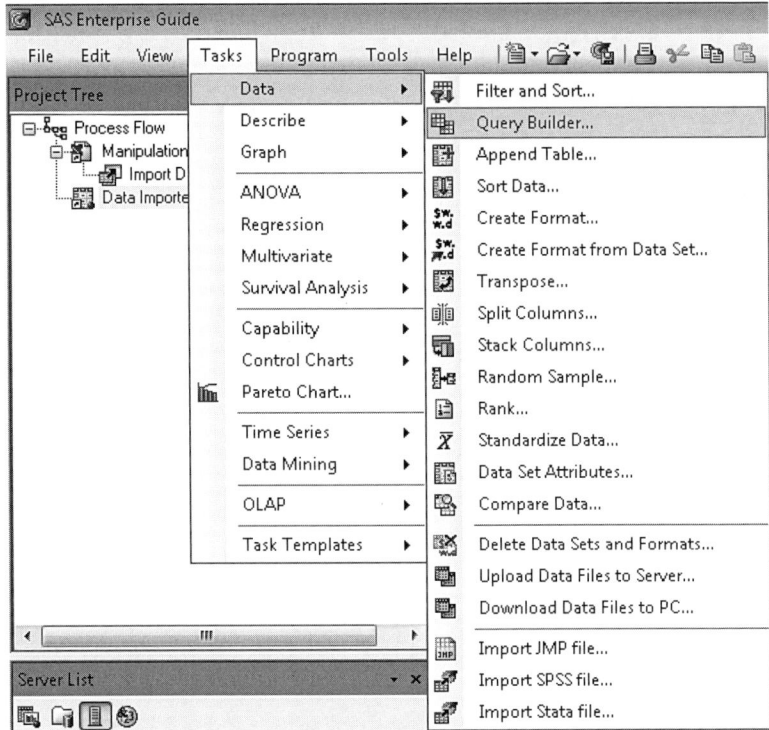

3. A new pop-up window appears and one drags and drops all variables to be included in the final output table under the **Select Data** tab.

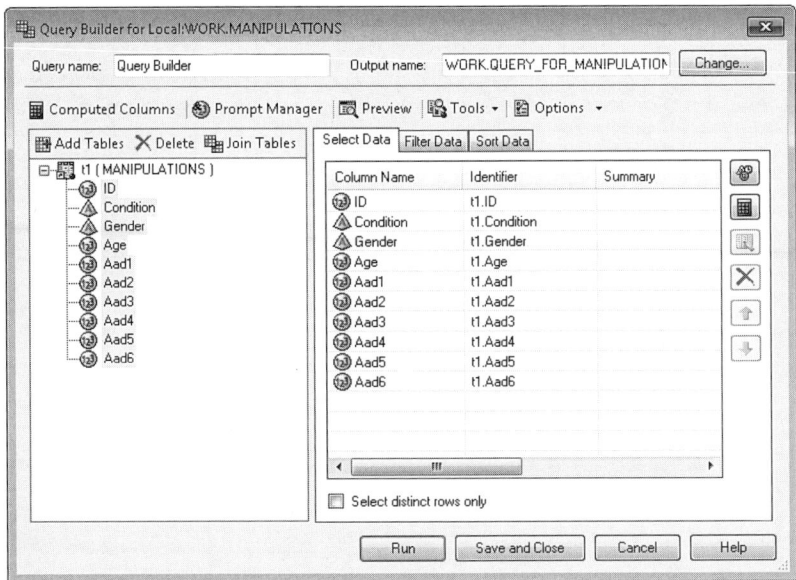

4. Click on the little calculator on the right and the **New Computed Column** pop-up window appears. To recode a variable, tick the option **Recoded column**.

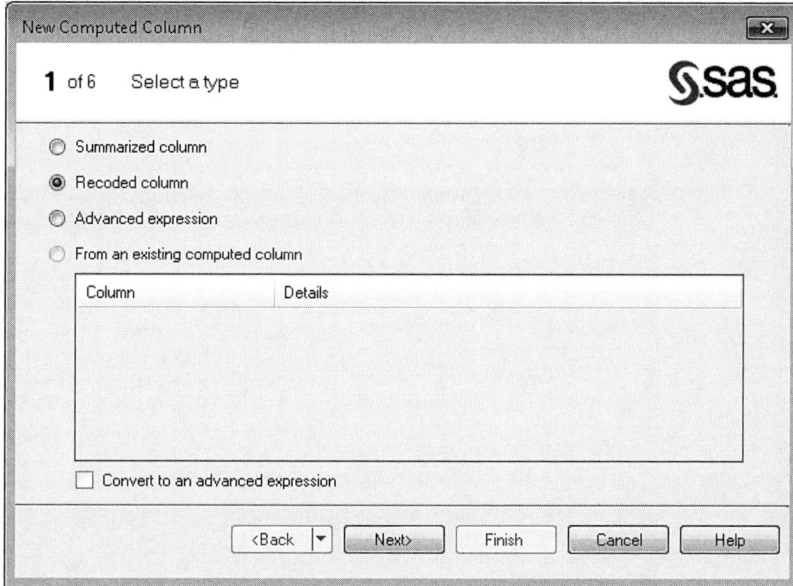

5. A new window appears and you select the variable to be recoded, in our case *Gender*. Click **Next** to proceed.

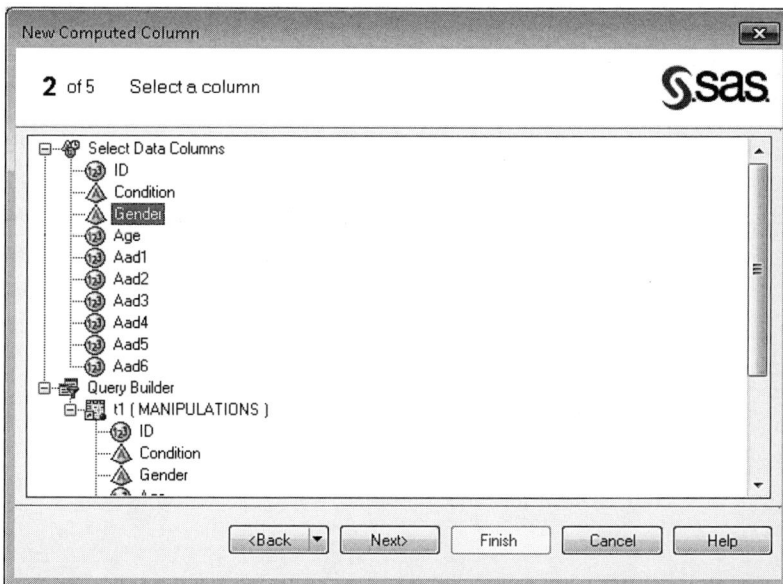

6.   The replacement window consisting of three parts appears. A **Replacement** area where one specifies the recoding schemes, an **Other values** area to specify what SAS Enterprise Guide should do with values not considered in the replacement schemes and a **Column type** area that specifies which format the new variable will have.

To add a recoding scheme to the SAS Enterprise Guide environment, one clicks on **Add...**

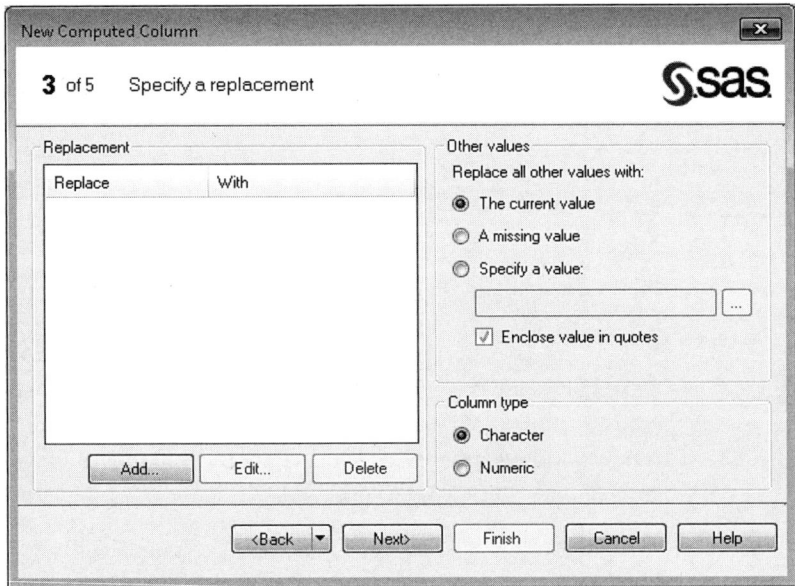

7.   A new pop-up window appears where one specifies exactly how the old value should be replaced by a new value. For instance, the old value *B* should be replaced by a value *1*. Moreover, the new value will be enclosed in quotes, because the option **Enclose this value in quotes** is ticked. Values enclosed in quotes always represent character type values. Click **OK** to add the recoding scheme to the SAS Enterprise Guide environment.

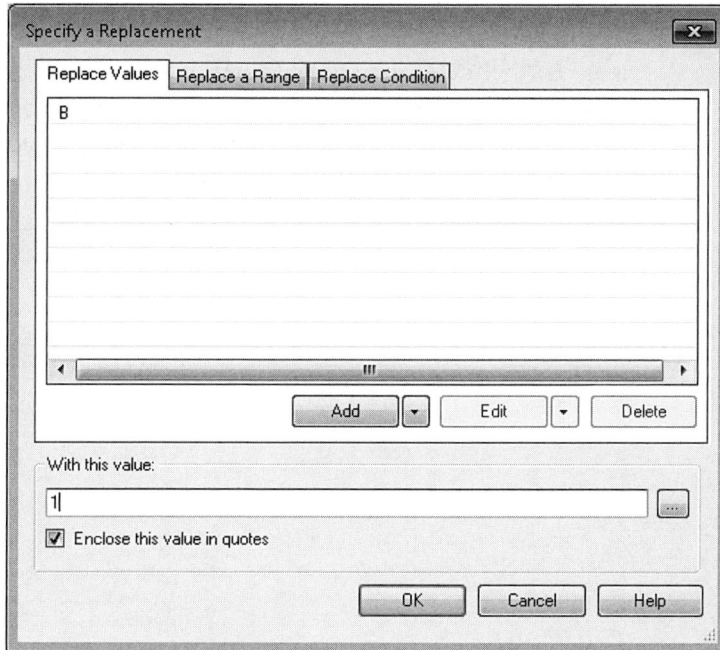

Repeat steps 6 and 7 to add a recoding scheme for the girls where the value *G* should be replaced by *0*.

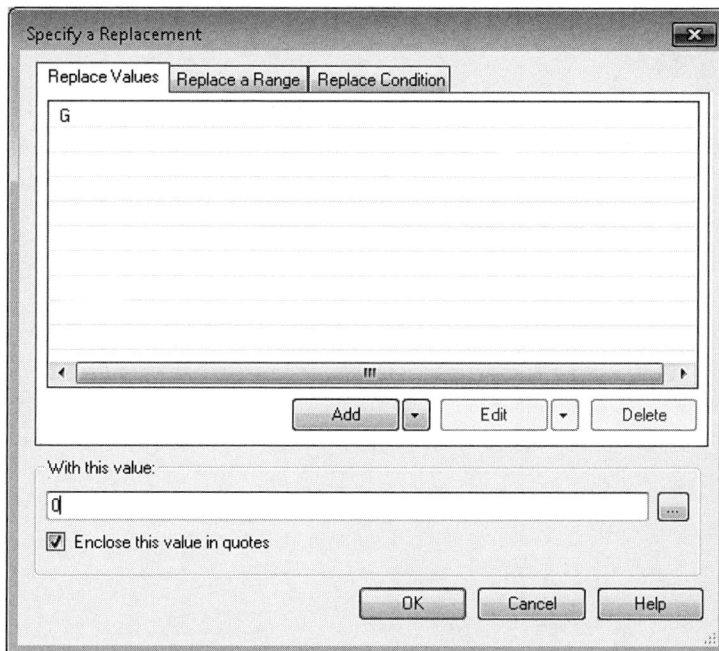

8. By now one sees that the recoding schemes are added to the **Replacement** area. Furthermore, the **Other values** are set to the option **A missing value**. This means that other than *B* or *G* values in the original variable *Gender* will be replaced by a missing value. Furthermore, the **Column type** is considered as **Character**. Click **Next** to advance.

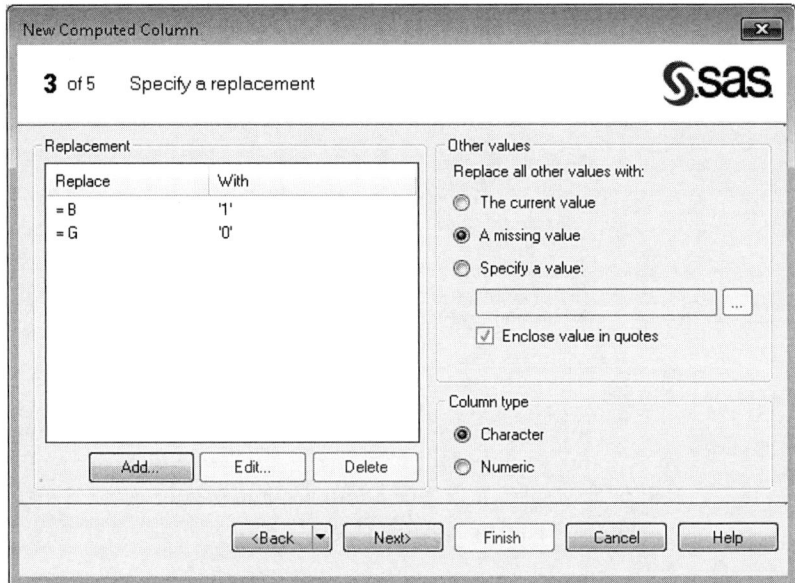

9. In the next choice window, the marketing analyst chooses the way the variable will look in the dataset and the way it will be represented in the SAS Enterprise Guide output. The **Identifier** and the **Column Name** are set to *Dummy_Gender*. Click **Next** to go on.

10. The following window summarizes the properties of your recoding scheme. If everything looks fine, you click **Finish**.

11. The new recoded variable, *Dummy_Gender*, is now incorporated in the main Query Builder interface. You click **Run** to run the task.

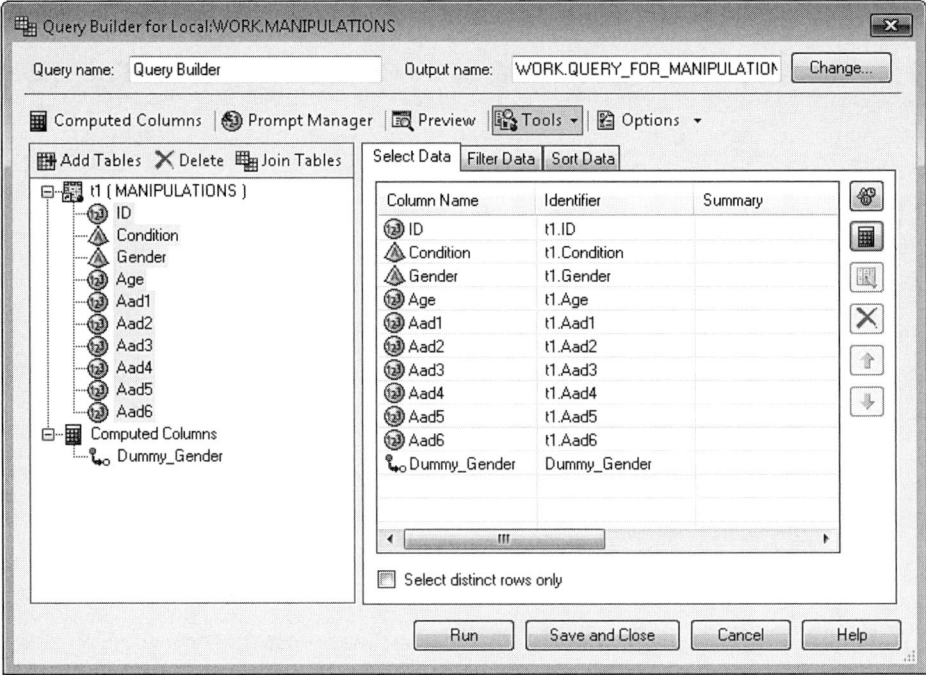

12. Finally, the recoded variable is incorporated in the new output dataset in the **Output Data** tab.

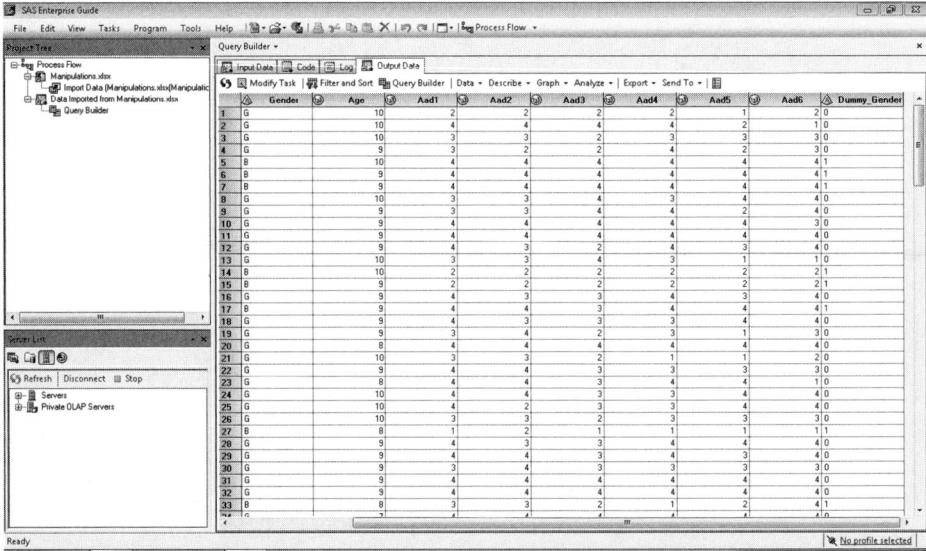

1.6.4. SORTING DATA

This section shows the reader how to sort a particular dataset. Suppose that the customers in *Manipulations.xlsx* need to be sorted from oldest to youngest. This is done in the SAS Enterprise Guide environment by making use of the **Sort Data** task.

1.   Add *Manipulations.xlsx* to your SAS Enterprise Guide environment.

2.   Go to **Tasks** → **Data** → **Sort Data...**

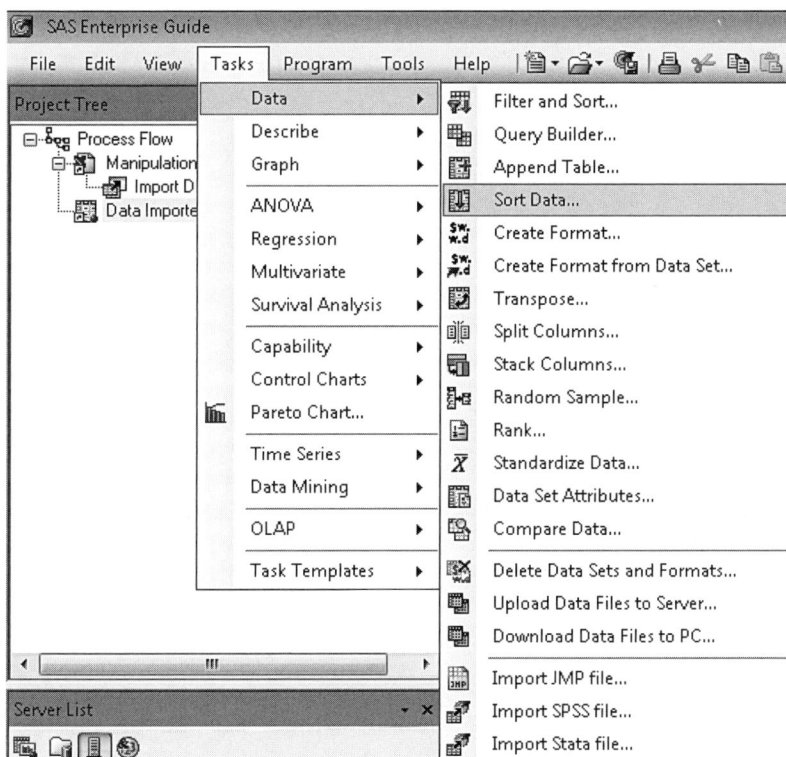

3.   The **Data** pane opens, and you drag and drop the variable by which you would like to sort your dataset to the **Sort by** role, in our setting the *Age* variable. Afterwards, you choose whether you would like to sort in ascending or descending order. As we are interested to sort the dataset from oldest to youngest, the **Age sort order** option is set to **Descending**.

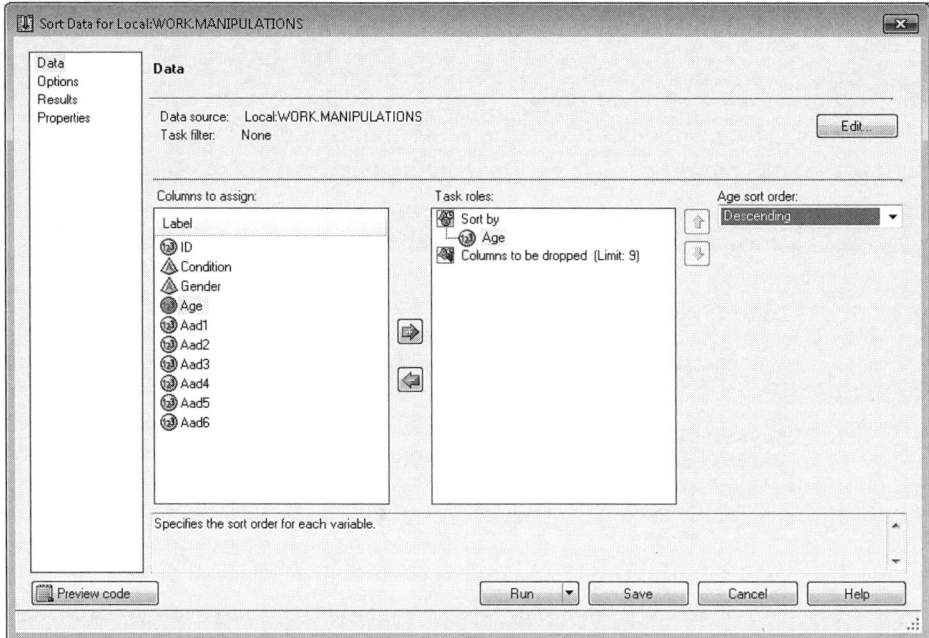

4. Click **Run** and the sorted dataset can be inspected via the **Output Data** tab.

⚠️ *When you are in the **Output Data** tab, an alternative way to sort the data is available by clicking on the **Filter and Sort** button.*

Chapter 2

Descriptive Analysis

Objectives

1. Discuss descriptive statistics, including measures of location, variability and shape.

2. Learn how to interpret frequency tables for categorical variables.

3. Describe data analysis linked with the distribution analysis for continuous variables including formal normality testing.

Fundamentals

A descriptive analysis is the starting point of a traditional marketing research project. Exploring and describing the characteristics of a dataset is inevitable! Delivering preliminary insights gives researchers a first indication of the success of the data collection and consequently the data quality concerned. The type of descriptive analysis depends on whether the variable is continuous or categorical. Indeed, two different types of variables exist depending on the measurement level of the variable. If the measurement level of the variable is interval- or ratio-scaled and the variable is normally distributed, the variable is considered as continuous. An interval-or ratio-scaled variable is said to be normally distributed when the distribution follows a bell and symmetrical shape, while the mean, median and mode are almost similar to one another. A statistical test can be applied to formally test the normality (see infra). For instance, the variable net monthly salary expressed in euros, *Monthly_salary*, is considered as a continuous variable when its distribution is normal. Furthermore, nominal and ordinal variables are considered as categorical variables. Nominal variables are variables containing categories which cannot be given any order. For instance, the variable *Gender* is a nominal variable because it has two categories, male or female, and these two categories cannot be ordered. Ordinal variables are categorical variables where the categories can be ordered. The variable

Age_group, consisting of three age categories: young (less than 25 years), middle-age (between 26 and 64 years old) and old (more than 65 years) is an example of an ordinal variable. Furthermore, continuous variables, that is, interval-scaled or ratio-scaled variables, which do not satisfy the normality assumption, are also considered as ordinal variables in the remainder of this book. Finally, Likert-scales (having five or more than five points) are statistically considered as ordinal scales. However, previous research studies showed that using these Likert-scales as interval variables does not necessary results in unreliable results. In the remainder of the book, Likert-scales with five or more points are considered as interval variables.

This chapter is split in two large blocks, section 2.1. Descriptive Statistics and section 2.2. Distribution Analysis.

Dataset Description

Throughout this chapter the dataset *Descriptive_Analysis.xlsx* is used. The dataset contains the following information:

- A respondent identifier (*ID*).

- Gender with *1* being male and *2* being female (*Gender*).

- Age groups (*Age*):
  1. <= 20 years
  2. between 21 and 30 years
  3. between 31 and 45 years
  4. between 46 and 60 years
  5. > 60 years.

- A categorical variable indicating the retail store (*Retailer*).

- A composite measure for attitudinal loyalty measured on a 5-point Likert-scale (*AttitudinalLoyalty*).

- A composite measure for behavioural loyalty measured on a 5-point Likert-scale (*BehaviouralLoyalty*).

- A composite measure for the satisfaction level of the customer measured on a 5-point Likert-scale (*Satisfaction*).

2.1. Descriptive Statistics

This section explains how to extract descriptive statistics like the mean, the standard deviation, and so on using SAS Enterprise Guide. Suppose that you want to get some descriptive statistics for *AttitudinalLoyalty*, *BehaviouralLoyalty* and *Satisfaction* separately for men and women (*Gender*). SAS Enterprise Guide uses the **Summary Statistics** task to output the basic descriptive statistics.

1.   Add the *Descriptive_Analysis.xlsx* dataset to your process flow.

2.   Go to **Tasks** → **Describe** → **Summary Statistics...**

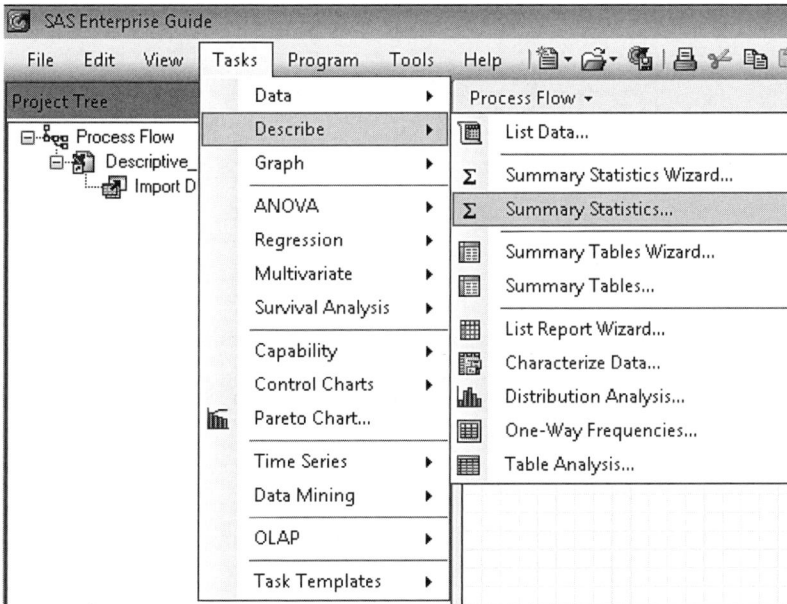

3.   In the **Data** pane, drag and drop the variables for which you want descriptive statistics for under the **Analysis variables** task role. Furthermore, one can drag and drop a categorical variable under the **Classification variables** task role. This will lead to separate descriptive statistics analyses per category of this categorical variable. In our example, drag and drop *AttitudinalLoyalty*, *BehaviouralLoyalty* and *Satisfaction* under the **Analysis variables** task role, while *Gender* is put under **Classification variables** to get different analyses for males and females.

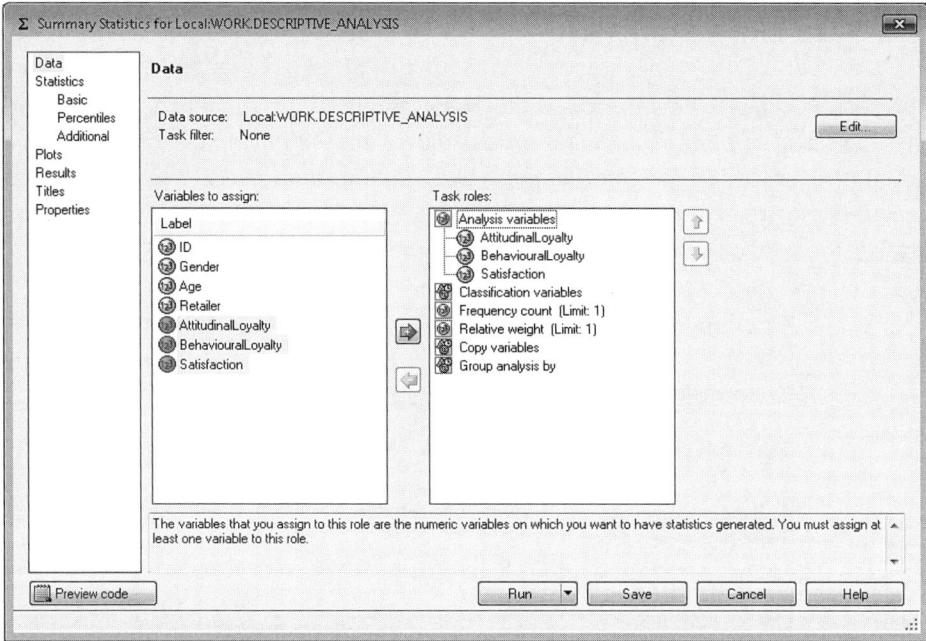

4.   In the **Statistics** pane under **Basic**, a variety of different descriptive statistics can be chosen. Here the **Mean**, **Standard deviation**, **Minimum**, **Maximum**, **Range** and the **Number of observations** are asked.

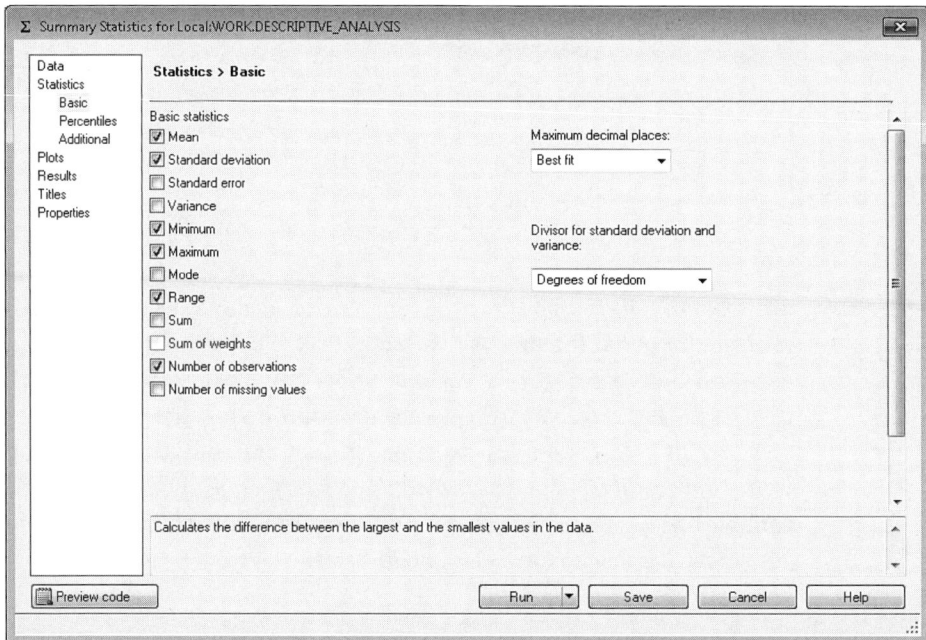

5.   In the **Statistics** pane under **Percentiles**, different percentile statistics are available. In the current example, the **Median** is chosen.

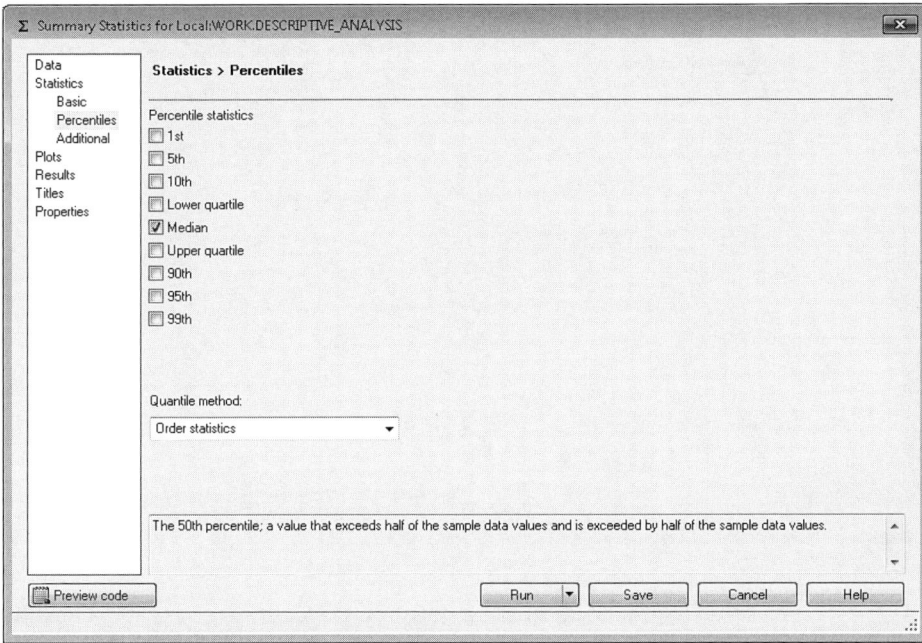

6.   In the **Plots** pane, **Histogram** and **Box and Whisker** plots are asked by ticking the boxes next to the corresponding options.

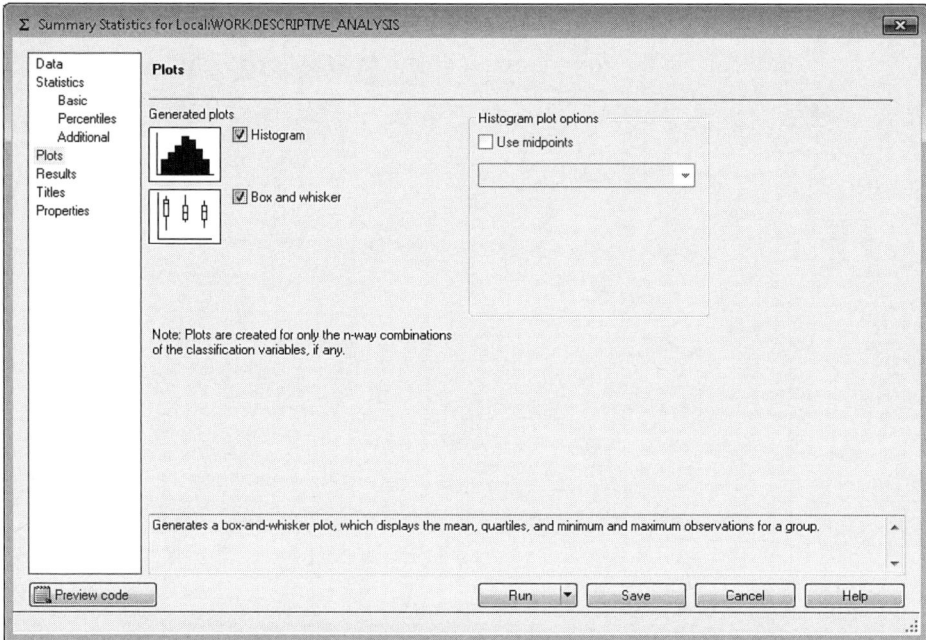

7. Click **Run** to get the descriptive statistics. Explore the results in the **Results** tab.

Interpretation

- **Gender N Obs Variable Mean Std Dev Minimum Maximum Range N Median**

Gender	N Obs	Variable	Mean	Std Dev	Minimum	Maximum	Range	N	Median
1	63	AttitudinalLoyalty	1.8214286	0.7885631	1.0000000	4.0000000	3.0000000	63	1.7500000
		BehaviouralLoyalty	2.5370370	0.9729516	1.0000000	5.0000000	4.0000000	63	2.5000000
		Satisfaction	3.2962963	0.9930062	1.0000000	5.0000000	4.0000000	63	3.3333333
2	137	AttitudinalLoyalty	2.0675182	0.8831051	1.0000000	5.0000000	4.0000000	137	2.0000000
		BehaviouralLoyalty	2.4744526	0.8335516	1.0000000	4.8333333	3.8333333	137	2.5000000
		Satisfaction	3.3892944	0.8580352	1.0000000	5.0000000	4.0000000	137	3.6666667

This table gives an overview of the basic summary statistics for each variable in the analysis, that is, *AttitudinalLoyalty*, *BehaviouralLoyalty* and *Satisfaction*, split up for the two values of the *Gender* variable. Besides the mean, the minimum and maximum value, this table reports the standard deviation for each variable. The standard deviation is the most widely used measure of variability, as it shows how much variation there is from the mean value. Together with the range and the median, these summary statistics lead to a decision on the quality of the data For instance, suppose that one discovers abnormal high values for the summary statistics for the variable *AttitudinalLoyalty*, this could mean that a typo occurred during survey encoding, for instance a value of *59* typed instead of *5*.

- **Histograms**

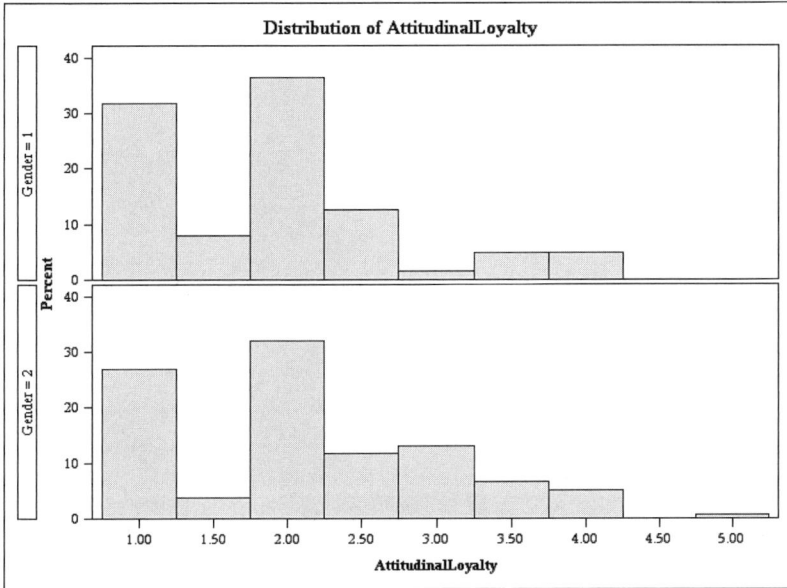

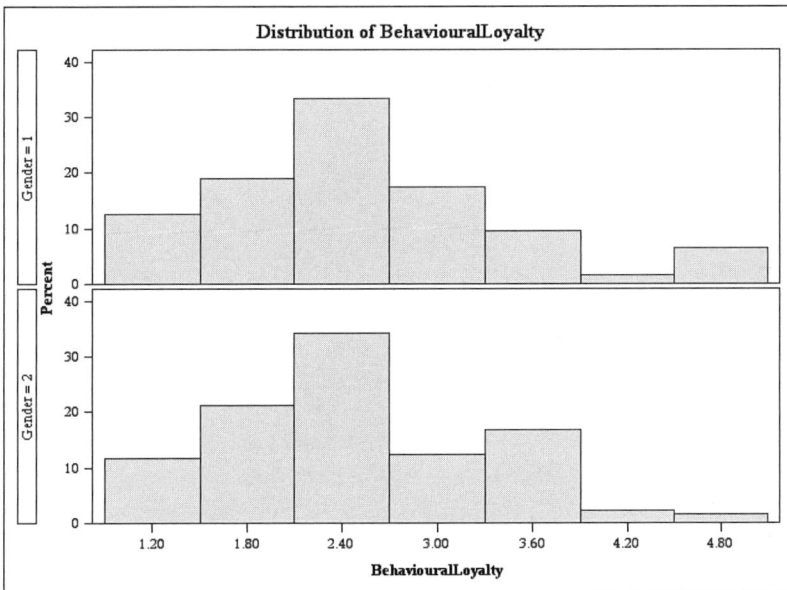

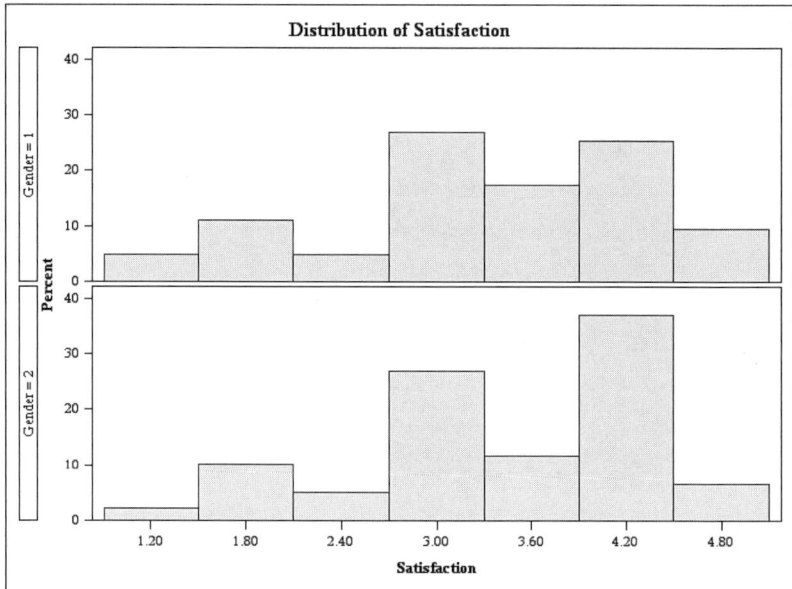

The histograms of *AttitudinalLoyalty*, *BehaviouralLoyalty* and *Satisfaction* summarize their frequency distribution. On the X-axis, one finds the value of the variable, while the Y-axis gives the percentage of cases belonging to the corresponding variable value. In detail, the histograms for males and females for the variables *AttitudinalLoyalty*, *BehaviouralLoyalty* and *Satisfaction* look very similar and there are no specific trends that could draw the attention of the marketing researcher.

- **Box and Whisker Plots**

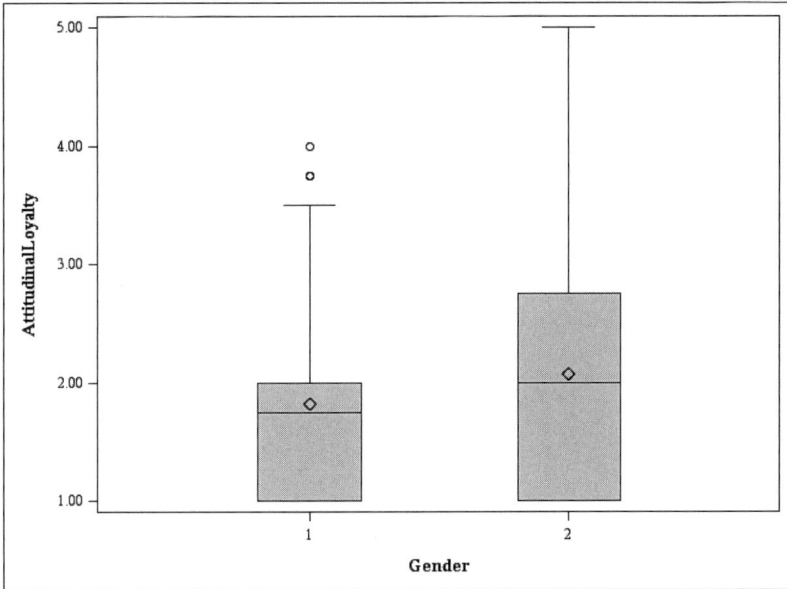

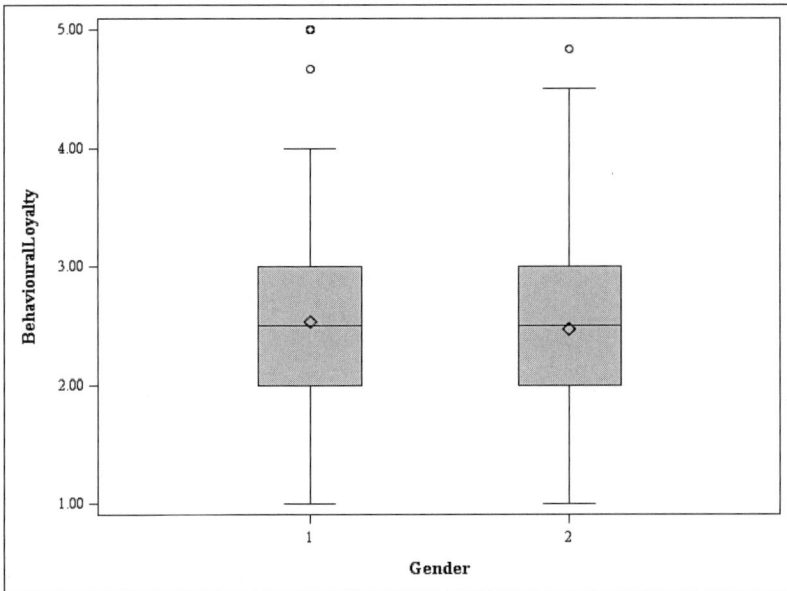

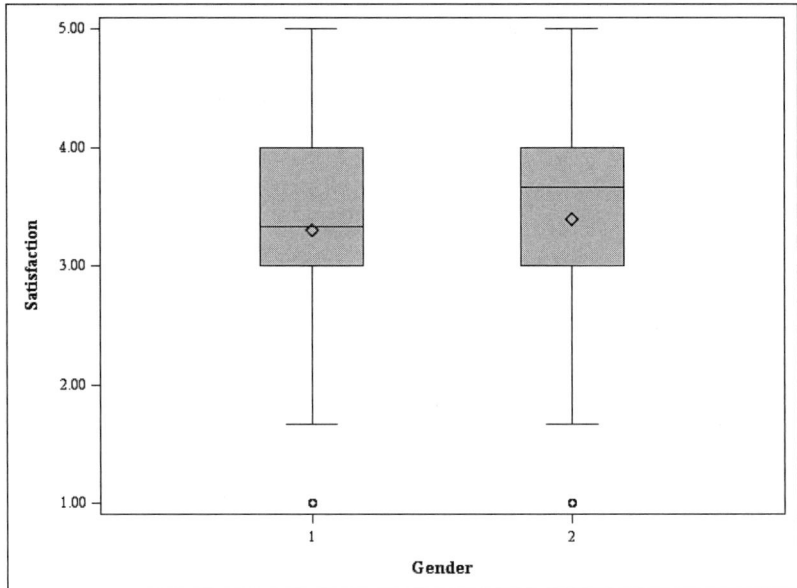

The box and whisker plots summarize the different summary statistics into one graph, that is, the mean, the median, the 25th and 75th percentile and the outliers. The lower and upper edges of the box are located at the 25th and 75th percentiles. Thus, the box contains roughly half of the observations. The horizontal line drawn within the box marks the 50th percentile or the median. The diamond (◊) sign marks the mean value. The vertical lines, also called whiskers, extend from the box as far as the data extend to a maximum distance of 1.5 times the interquartile range, that is, the difference between the 75th percentile and the 25th percentile. Any value more extreme than the whiskers is called an outlier and these are marked with a circle (o).

2.2. Distribution Analysis

In this section, we examine how SAS Enterprise Guide deals with distribution analysis. Distribution analysis is the process by which the pattern of data points for a particular type of variable is summarized. Distribution analysis is another important step in discovering the quality and the characteristics of your data. For instance, it is an ideal tool to discover extreme variable values or outliers, or to verify whether a variable is normally distributed. This chapter shows how to visualize and summarize the distribution of categorical variables (section 2.2.1. Categorical Variables) and continuous variables (section 2.2.2. Continuous Variables).

2.2.1. CATEGORICAL VARIABLES

To inspect the distribution of categorical variables, marketing analysts use frequency tables. A frequency table is a matrix summarizing the total number of observations per level in the categorical variable. Suppose that the marketing analyst wants to get an indication on the age distribution of the respondents surveyed. Are there more youngsters surveyed? Or are there more older people in the survey sample? The solution to this question is the creation of a frequency table for the variable *Age*. SAS Enterprise Guide outputs frequency tables for categorical variables by using the **One-Way Frequencies** task.

1. Add *Descriptive_Analysis.xlsx* to your SAS Enterprise Guide environment.

2. Go to **Tasks** → **Describe** → **One-Way Frequencies...**

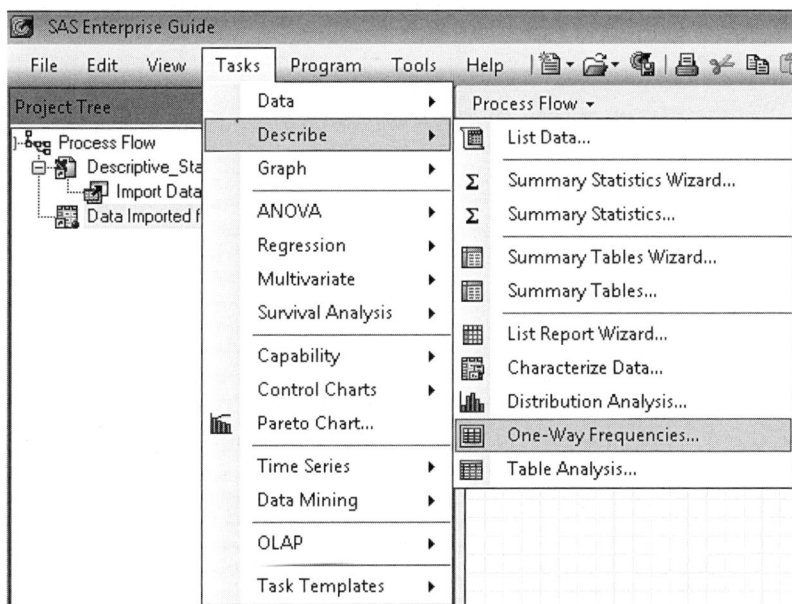

3. In the **Data** pane, drag and drop the variable of interest, that is, *Age*, to the **Analysis variables** role.

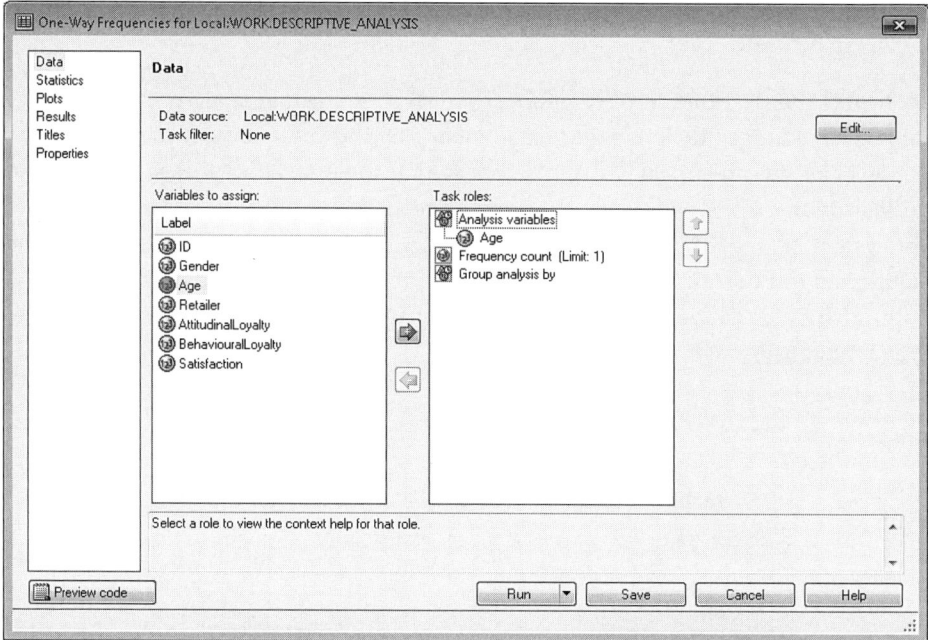

4. In the **Statistics** pane under the option **Frequency table options**, you might ask various frequency statistics. You could ask for raw frequencies or percentages per level of your categorical variable, while the cumulative indicators could be added to the output table as well. In our example, raw frequencies and percentages with cumulatives (the default option) are asked by ticking the option **Frequencies and percentages with cumulatives**.

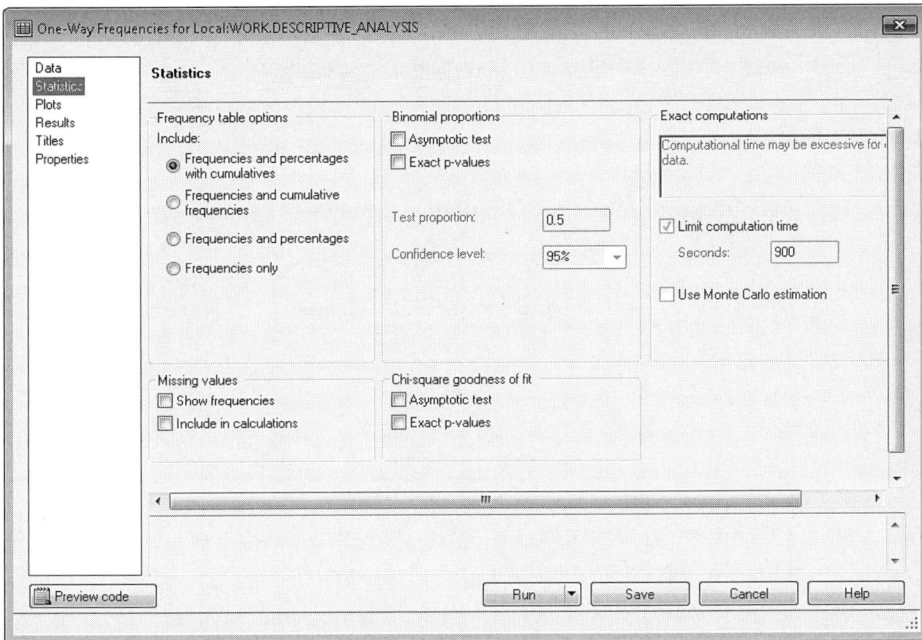

5.   In the **Plots** pane, one can ask for horizontal or vertical bar charts. In the current example, tick the option **Horizontal** to obtain a horizontal bar chart.

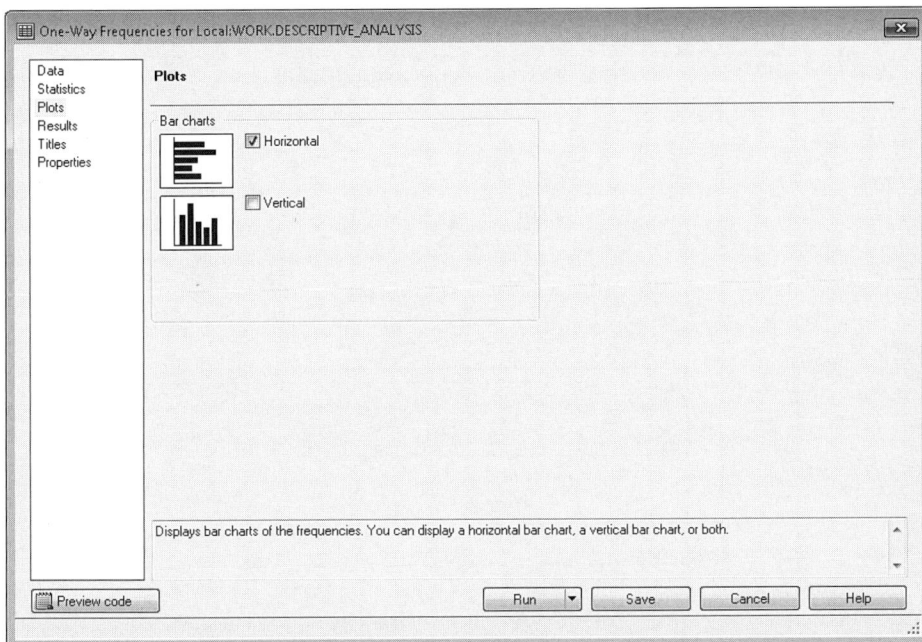

6. Click **Run** to proceed with the creation of the frequency table. Below you will find the output of the **One-Way Frequencies** task.

Interpretation

- **Age Frequency Per cent Cumulative Frequency Cumulative Per cent**

Age	Frequency	Per cent	Cumulative Frequency	Cumulative Per cent
1	2	1.00	2	1.00
2	73	36.50	75	37.50
3	44	22.00	119	59.50
4	68	34.00	187	93.50
5	13	6.50	200	100.00

This table summarizes the frequency distribution of the categorical variable *Age*. For each of the five age categories, the number of observations (*Frequency*), the percentage of observations (*Per cent*) and the corresponding cumulative indicators (*Cumulative Frequency* and *Cumulative Per cent*) are given. Based on this table, one knows that 59.50 per cent of the respondents are younger than 46 years old (cumulative percentage of categories of age, from 1 to 3).

- **Distribution of Age**

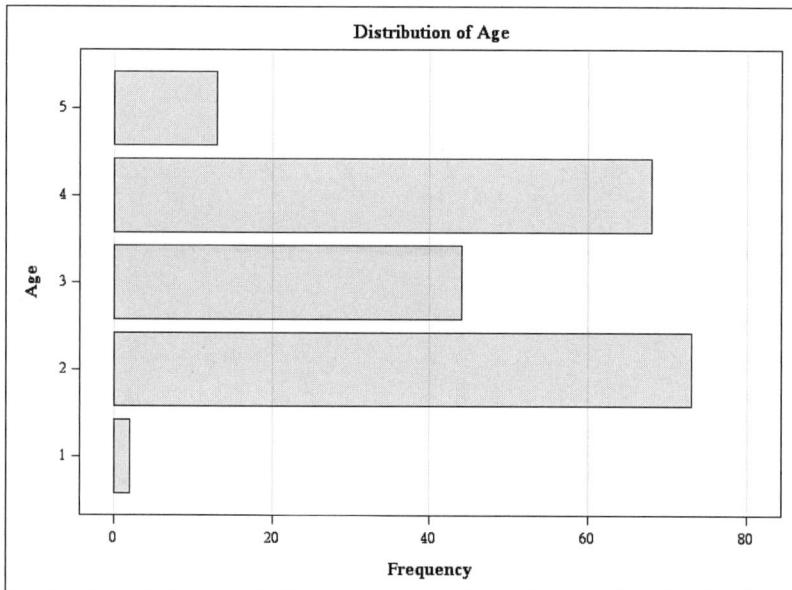

Distribution of Age

The horizontal bar chart gives a visual representation of the frequency table. On the X-axis the absolute number of observations belonging to a particular age group as specified on the Y-axis is given.

Both outputs lead to the same result that most of the respondents surveyed are people between 21 and 60 year (age groups 2, 3 and 4), while there is an underrepresentation of young people (age group 1) and older people (age group 5).

2.2.2. CONTINUOUS VARIABLES

This section explains how to visualize and contrast the distribution of a continuous variable against a predefined distribution. It shows how one is able to test whether a variable follows a normal distribution. In marketing research, it is crucial to verify whether a continuous variable is normally distributed or not. Depending on the normality of your dependent variable, the hypothesis process is different (see Chapter 5 Hypothesis Testing). The normality of a continuous variable is formally tested using the Kolmogorov–Smirnov test. The following hypotheses are considered:

H_0:   The distribution follows a normal distribution.

H_1:   The distribution does not follow a normal distribution.

Below we describe the procedure that visualizes the distribution of *Satisfaction*, and the explanation how to verify whether *Satisfaction* follows a normal distribution. A distribution analysis for a continuous variable is run via the **Distribution Analysis** task.

1.   Add *Description_Analysis.xlsx* to the SAS Enterprise Guide working environment.

2.   Go to **Tasks** → **Describe** → **Distribution Analysis...**

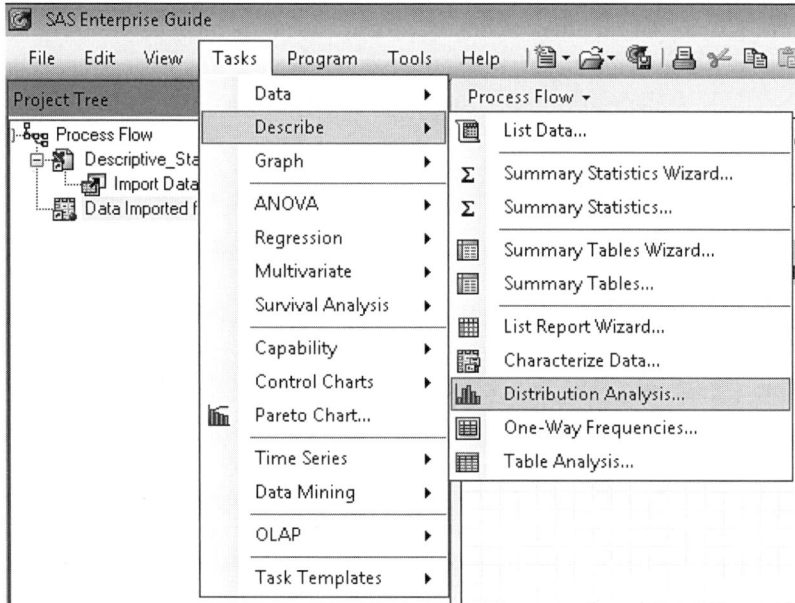

3. In the **Data** pane, drag and drop the continuous variable of interest, *Satisfaction*, under the **Analysis variables** task role.

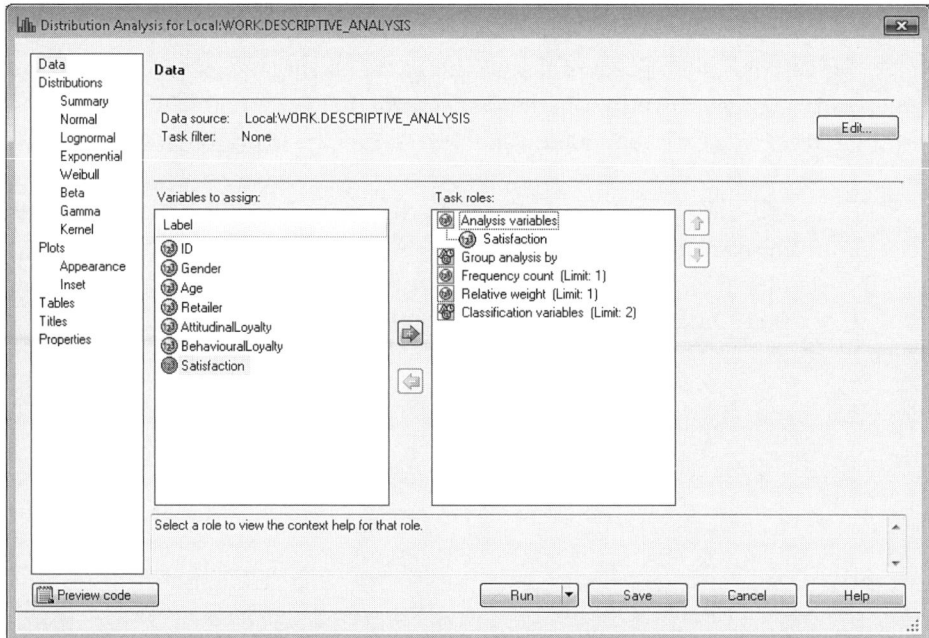

4.   In the **Distributions** pane under **Summary**, the theoretical distribution is chosen to which the empirical distribution of the continuous variable *Satisfaction* is compared. Different options exist, but in our setting the option **Normal** is ticked to make a comparison with the theoretical normal distribution.

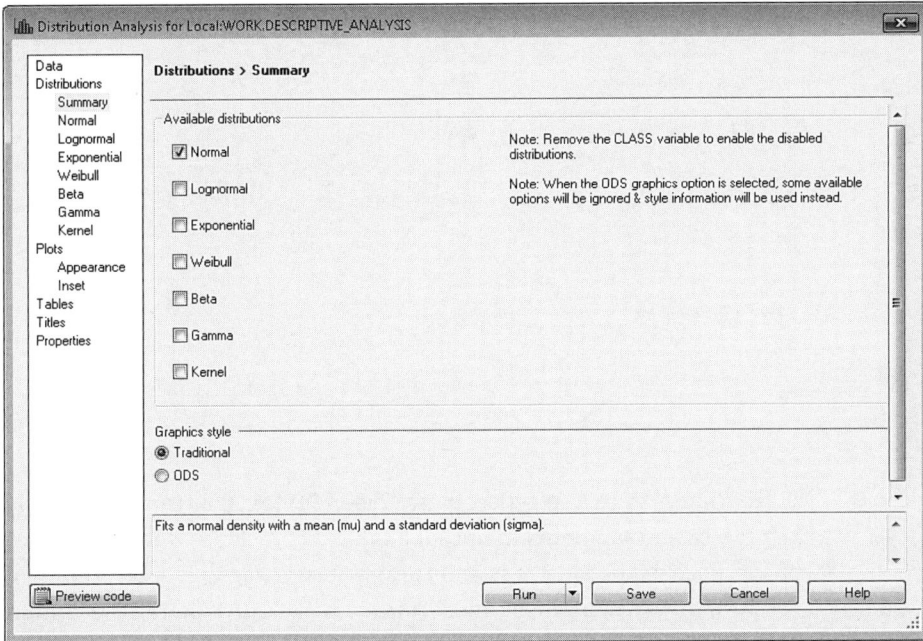

5.   In the **Plots** pane under **Appearance**, different ways of visualizing the distribution of the variable under consideration are available. Commonly-used distribution analysis plots are asked by ticking the options **Histogram Plot**, **Probability Plot**, **Quantiles plot** and **Box plot** to get the corresponding plots. Furthermore, if needed, the axis colour, the background colour and the axis width are changeable.

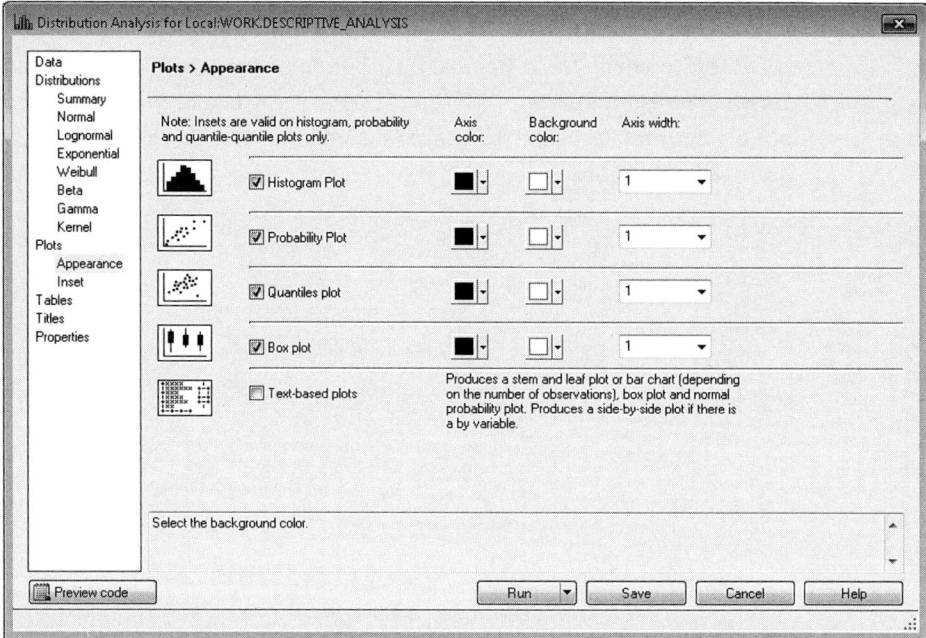

6. Furthermore in the selection pane under **Tables**, you can additionally tick the option **Moments** to output a table that includes the measures of shape, such as the skewness and kurtosis (see paragraph 'Interpretation' for further explanation of these measures). Furthermore, the option **Tests for normality** is ticked in order to output a table with the results of the Kolmogorov–Smirnov test.

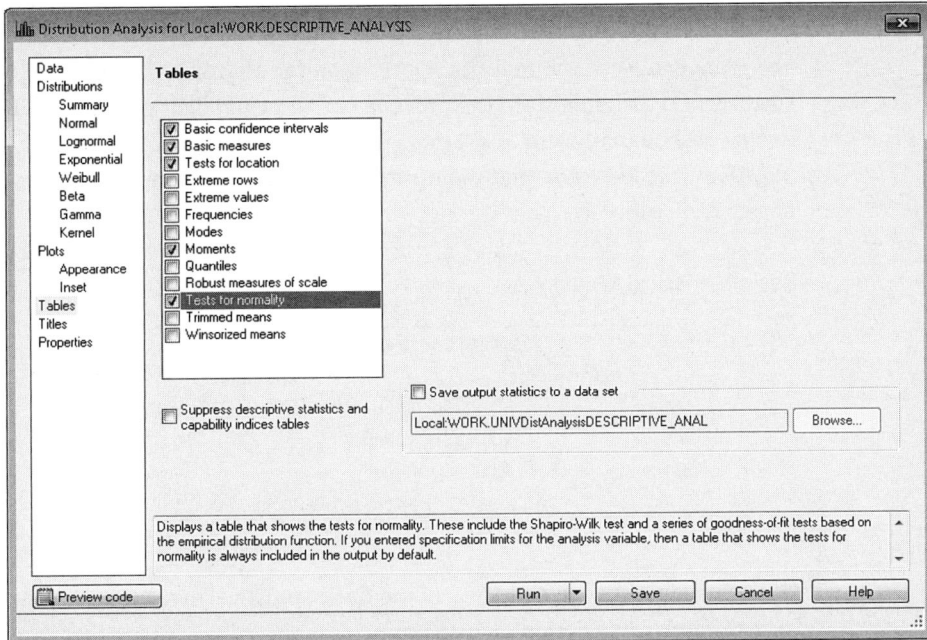

7.   Click **Run** to inspect the results and draw your conclusions for the *Satisfaction* variable.

Interpretation

- **Moments**

Moments			
N	200	Sum Weights	200
Mean	3.36	Sum Observations	672
Std Deviation	0.90124302	Variance	0.81223897
Skewness	-0.4831315	Kurtosis	0.09990182
Uncorrected SS	2419.55556	Corrected SS	161.635556
Coeff Variation	26.8227088	Std Error Mean	0.0637275

This table contains statistical measures amongst the measures of shape like the skewness and kurtosis. The skewness gives an indication about the (a)symmetry of the distribution. A skewness around 0 could indicate a symmetrical, normal distribution. A positive (negative) skewed distribution is a distribution with a long right (left) tail and having the mass of the distribution to the left (right), that is, a right- (left-) skewed distribution. The kurtosis is a figure representing the peakedness of the data. The kurtosis is positive if the tails are heavier than for a normal distribution and it is negative if the tails are lighter than for a normal distribution. A kurtosis of 0 could indicate the presence of a normal distribution. In our setting, although the kurtosis is close to 0, the skewness figure is (slightly) negative. This indicates that the distribution of *Satisfaction* is maybe not normally distributed.

- **Basic Statistical Measures**

Basic Statistical Measures			
Location		**Variability**	
Mean	3.360000	Std Deviation	0.90124
Median	3.333333	Variance	0.81224
Mode	4.000000	Range	4.00000
		Interquartile Range	1.00000

This table gives you an overview of the basic statistical measures, like the mean, standard deviation, and so on.

- **Tests for Normality**

Tests for Normality				
Test		**Statistic**		**p Value**
Shapiro–Wilk	W	0.927625	Pr < W	<0.0001
Kolmogorov–Smirnov	D	0.171188	Pr > D	<0.0100
Cramer–von Mises	W-Sq	1.068218	Pr > W-Sq	<0.0050
Anderson–Darling	A-Sq	5.919437	Pr > A-Sq	<0.0050

This table shows the results of the formal statistical normality test, Kolmogorov–Smirnov. In the row *Kolmogorov–Smirnov*, you find a p-value that is smaller than 0.0100, and thus smaller than 0.05, that is, the threshold for the p-value when considering a 95 per cent confidence level. This means that the null hypothesis is rejected and that the *Satisfaction* variable is not normally distributed.

- **Histogram**

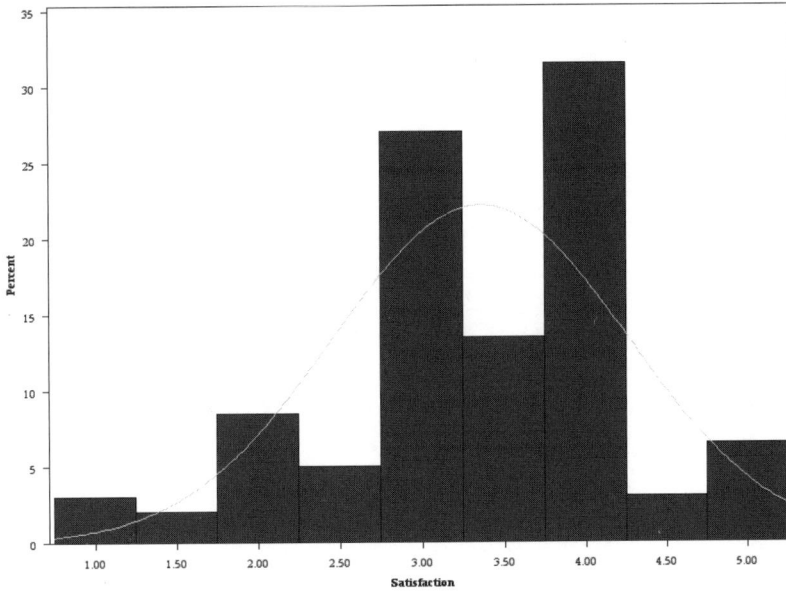

The histogram gives an overview of the distribution of the *Satisfaction* variable. For each and every value of *Satisfaction*, the corresponding percentage of observations is given in the bars. The curved line represents the theoretical normal distribution. The histogram of *Satisfaction* does not follow a symmetrical, bell-shaped distribution, and thus there is no indication that *Satisfaction* is normally distributed.

- **Quantiles Plot**

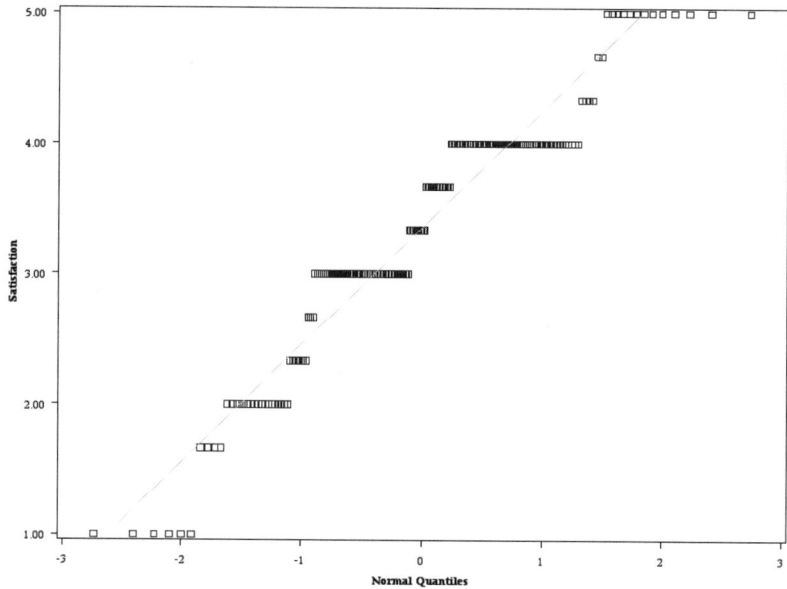

A quantiles plot is a graph that plots the theoretical normal quantiles on the X-axis and the empirical quantile distribution of *Satisfaction* on the Y-axis. Quantiles are defined as equally-sized subsets obtained by dividing the ordered values of the variable. When considering a normal distribution, the quantiles plot should follow the 45-degree line. This means that the empirical distribution follows the theoretical normal distribution. In our setting, the quantiles plot of *Satisfaction* does not clearly suggest that *Satisfaction* follows a normal distribution, because the empirical distribution does not closely follow the 45-degree line meaning that the empirical distribution of *Satisfaction* on the Y-axis does not follow the theoretical normal distribution on the X-axis.

- **Probability Plot**

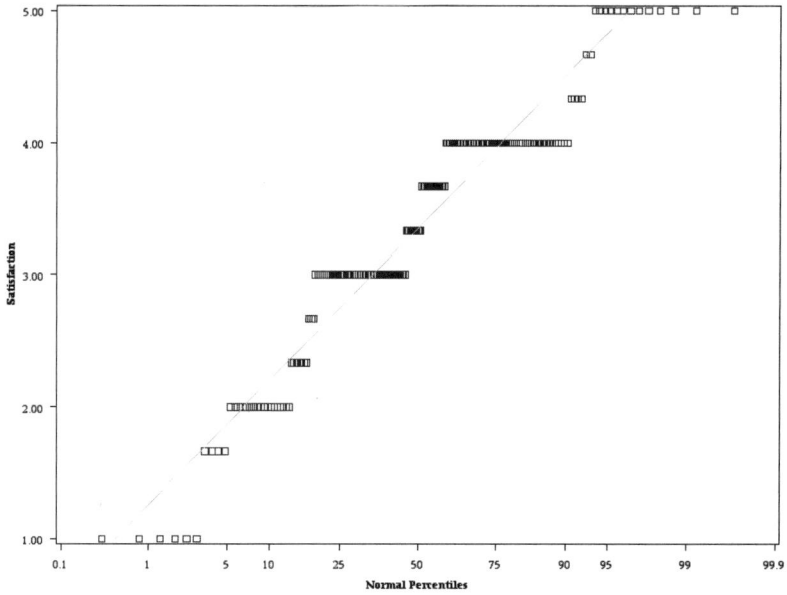

The interpretation of the probability plot follows the same philosophy as the quantiles plot. The only difference is that percentiles instead of quantiles are used to compare the empirical distribution of *Satisfaction* with the theoretical normal distribution. Identical to the quantiles plot, the probability plot does not suggest a normal distribution of *Satisfaction*.

• **Box and Whisker Plot**

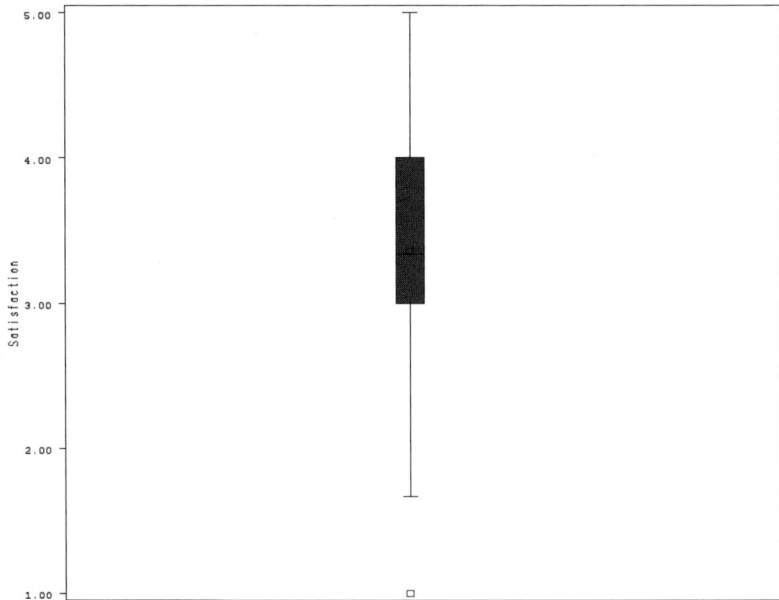

The box and whisker plot summarizes the different summary statistics into one single visual, that is, the mean, the median, the 25th and 75th percentile and the outliers. The lower and upper edges of the box are located at the 25th and 75th percentiles. Thus, the box contains roughly half of the observations. The horizontal line drawn within the box marks the 50th percentile or the median. The little box at the bottom of the graph marks the mean value. The vertical lines, also called whiskers, extend from the box as far as the data extend to a maximum distance of 1.5 times the interquartile range, that is, the difference between the 75th percentile and the 25th percentile. Any value more extreme than the whiskers is called an outlier and these are marked with a little box sign. Here the box and whisker plot turns out not to suggest a normal distribution as well, because in order to indicate a normal distribution, the markers of the box plot (mean, median, the 25th and the 75th percentile) need to be well spread.

Further Reading

Slaughter, S.J. and Delwiche, L.D. (2010), *The Little SAS Book for Enterprise Guide 4.2*, 1st edition, SAS Publishing.

Chapter 3

Exploratory Factor Analysis

Objectives

1. Describe the concept of exploratory factor analysis.

2. Understand the decisions that are needed to conduct an exploratory factor analysis, including the determination of the adequacy of the analysis, the choice of the factoring method, the rotation method, the choice of the number of factors and the interpretation of the factors.

3. Understand and learn the process of a reliability analysis.

4. Understand the choice of the factor representation options like factor score coefficients, surrogate variables and summated scales.

Fundamentals

The purpose of a factor analysis is to reduce the number of variables or items in the dataset. This results in a lower dimensional dataset in which the new dimensions or factors represent unobservable latent concepts. The factors are formed based on the mutual correlation of the initial variables in the dataset. With factor analysis, one aims at representing the current dataset in a lower dimensional dataset that gives the best approximation to the original one. The new factors could then be described by the original variables in the dataset.

The necessary assumption for running a factor analysis is that the level of measurement of the variables is *at least* interval-scaled and that the measurement level between the variables under consideration is comparable. For instance, Likert-scales (having five or more than five points) are statistically considered as ordinal scales, and this would mean that they could not be used within an exploratory factor analysis setting. However, previous research studies showed that using these Likert-scales as interval variables does not necessary results in unreliable results. Furthermore, if you have variables with different measurement scales, it is possible to use them in the same exploratory factor analysis by first standardizing the variables. Standardizing variables means that you convert each and every variable in your analysis to have a mean of 0 and a standard deviation of 1 to make sure they are on the same measurement scale.

The different analytical decisions that can be used when running a factor analysis are listed below:

1. *The usefulness of an exploratory factor analysis* should be tested because if the variables are highly uncorrelated, it will be very hard to find a robust factor analysis outcome. SAS Enterprise Guide outputs the Kaiser's Measure of Sampling Adequacy (MSA) that gives the analyst an indication about the usefulness of an exploratory factor analysis. The global MSA measure always lies between 0 and 1, and it should be higher than 0.5 to decide that the factor analysis is useful.

2. *The choice of the factoring method* is another important decision to make. Several options are available in SAS Enterprise Guide (see SAS Enterprise Guide Help for more details). The options differ in terms of the calculation of the weighting coefficients they apply to calculate the factor scores. This book employs the most commonly-used principal components analysis method that extracts the most variance out of the initial dataset, while making sure that the first factor explains the biggest part of the variance, the second factor the second biggest part of the variance, and so on.

3. *Whether choosing a rotation method or not.* If yes, when applying an orthogonal rotation or an oblique rotation? The ideal exploratory factor analysis is a factor analysis in which all items loading high on a particular factor are close to 1, while all other items for that factor are close to 0. The unrotated factor solution is certainly not close to this ideal situation, because the factors are correlated with a lot of items. Consequently, a solution is available by rotating the factors in order to approach the ideal situation. Two types of rotation methods are available in SAS Enterprise Guide: (i) orthogonal rotations and (ii) oblique rotations. The orthogonal rotations rotate the factors in such a way that they are uncorrelated,

while trying to increase the interpretability by reducing the number of items with high loadings on a particular factor. The oblique rotations allow some correlations between the different factors. In practice, the varimax rotation is often used as an orthogonal rotation, while the oblique promax rotation is a common oblique rotation scheme.

4.   Furthermore, *the number of factors to be retained* is a crucial step while running an exploratory factor analysis. Several common options are available in the marketing research world, depending on whether the researcher has a prior knowledge of the number of factors to expect. If no prior knowledge on the number of factors is available (i) the Kaiser's criterion; (ii) the Scree plot; and (iii) the common variance accounted by a factor should be considered. Otherwise the researcher can fix the number of factors to obtain in correspondence with the theoretical guidelines (iv). The four options are explained below. (i) Kaiser's criterion is the criterion for which the factors are retained with an eigenvalue bigger than 1. The eigenvalue represents the total variance explained by a factor. Consequently, those factors with an eigenvalue larger than 1 explain a large part of the variance in the dataset. (ii) The Scree plot gives a visual representation of the number of factors, given their eigenvalues on the Y-axis and the number of factors on the X-axis. The Scree plot criterion suggests retaining the number of factors equal to the 'knick' or elbow in the curve minus 1. (iii) Furthermore, it is possible to specify a threshold on the common variance accounted by a retained factor. As such, it is possible to only retain these factors with a variance larger than the threshold set by the analyst. (iv) Frequently, researchers know in advance how many factors to retain and they set the number of factors straight from the beginning equal to that number.

5.   Finally, once the researcher is satisfied with the factor solution, a decision needs to be taken *on how to represent the different factors* for further analysis. Three possible aggregation methods exist.

1. Factor score coefficients

    The final factor score of a respondent is calculated as being a linear combination of the original scores of the input variables. The factor score F_k is then calculated by

    $$F_k = w_{1k} X_1 + w_{2k} X_2 + w_{3k} X_3 + \ldots w_{zk} X_z$$

with w_{ik} the factor weighting coefficient for a particular variable i on a particular factor k and X_i the respondent's value of the variable.

2. Surrogate variable

   Another possible solution to represent the factor is to take the highest-loading item on that factor as a surrogate for the full factor. However, this option is seldom used in practice because it throws away a lot of valuable information from the other items.

3. Summated scale

   The last and most-commonly used solution is to take into account all variables loading high on a particular factor. By calculating the mean of the values on these variables, one gets a summated scale that represents the factor. Before summarizing the different variables into a summated scale variable, a reliability analysis is needed to validate the internal consistency of the different variables (see infra).

Managerial Problem

The purpose of this factor analysis example is to detect the underlying structure in the relationship between several loyalty items measured in a survey. The dataset used within this section is called *Loyalty.xls* and it describes the following managerial problem. The sports company Shoetas wishes to assess the degree of consumers' loyalty towards Shoetas' trainers. They interviewed 189 consumers in a sports store through the medium of a questionnaire. Two dimensions of loyalty are taken into consideration, namely the cognitive loyalty and the affective loyalty.

Cognitive loyalty was measured by rating six statements on 5-point Likert-scale, ranging from 1 = completely disagree to 5 = completely agree. The statements used in the questionnaire are the following:

- It's preferable to use Shoetas' trainers (*CLOY1*).

- The characteristics of Shoetas' trainers globally correspond to my expectations (*CLOY2*).

- If someone proposes that I use another trainers' brand, I will continue using Shoetas for their design (*CLOY3*).

- If someone proposes that I use another trainers' brand, I will continue using Shoetas for their durability (*CLOY4*).

- If someone proposes that I use another trainers' brand, I will continue using Shoetas for their quality (*CLOY5*).

- If someone proposes that I use another trainers' brand, I will continue using Shoetas for their price (*CLOY6*).

Affective loyalty was measured by rating three statements on 5-point Likert-scale, ranging from 1 = completely disagree to 5 = completely agree. The statements used in the questionnaire are the following:

- I like Shoetas' trainers more than the other trainers (*ALOY1*).

- I like the characteristics of my Shoetas trainers (*ALOY2*).

- I have a positive attitude towards Shoetas trainers (*ALOY3*).

Data Analysis

A factor analysis makes use of the **Factor Analysis** task to generate the report.

1. Add the *Loyalty.xls* dataset to your SAS Enterprise Guide project.

2. To open the **Factor Analysis** task, select **Tasks** → **Multivariate** → **Factor Analysis...**

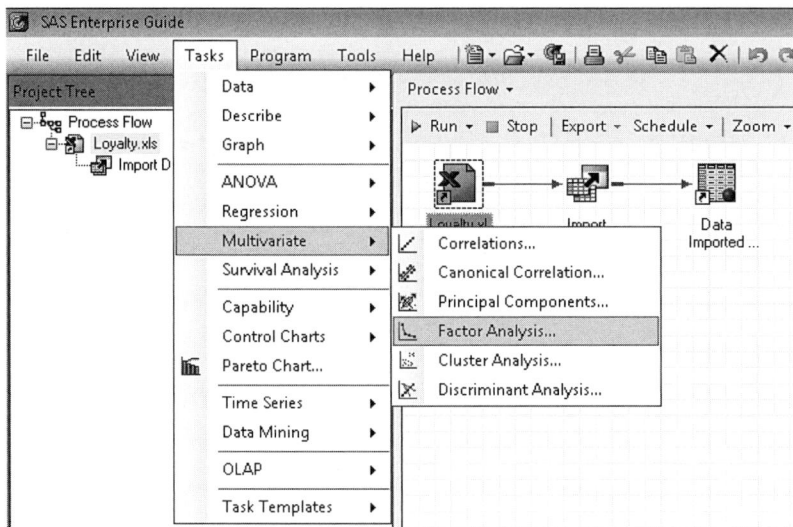

You can also double-click on the imported dataset in the Process Flow to open the dataset. If you select **_Analyze_** → **_Multivariate_** → **_Factor Analysis...,_** the factor analysis pane opens.

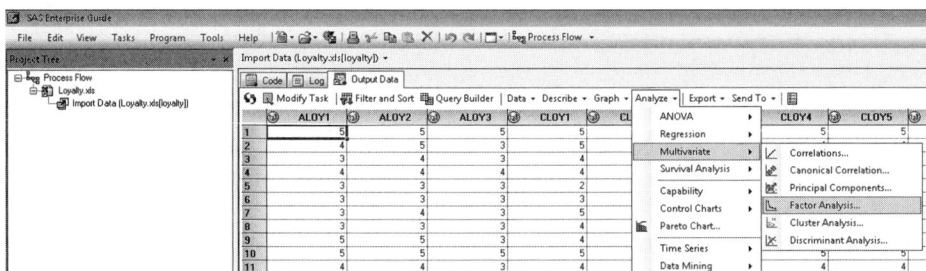

3. In the **Data** pane, drag and drop the relevant variables, *ALOY1–ALOY3* and *CLOY1–CLOY6*, to the **Analysis variables** role.

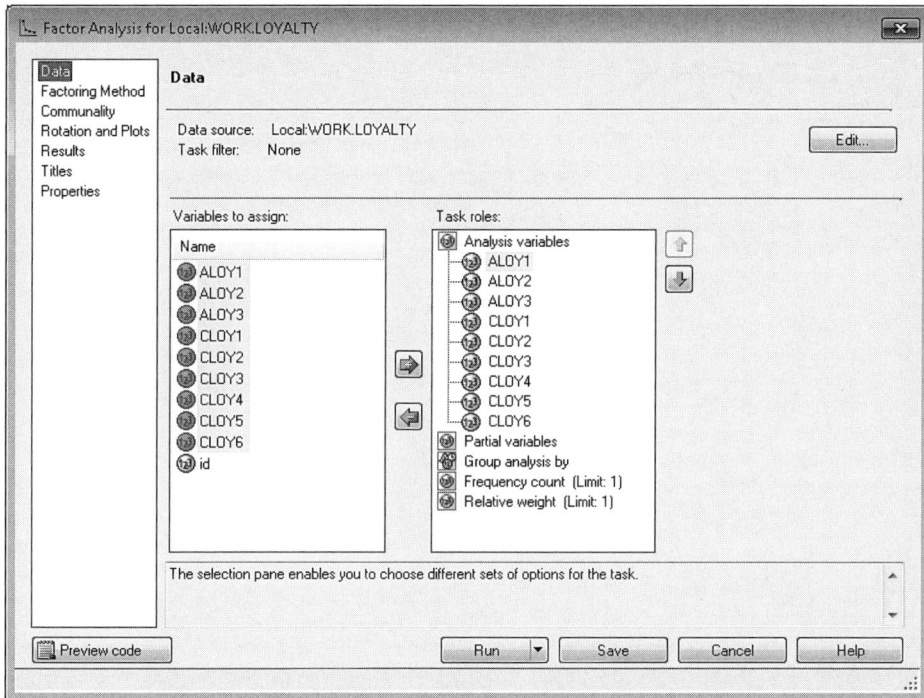

4. In the **Factoring Method** pane, the factoring method is set to the commonly-used **Principal components analysis**. Moreover in the pane, one chooses the option to retain the number of factors based on several criteria:

- smallest eigenvalue for which a factor is retained;
- number of factors to retain;
- per cent of common variance accounted for by retained factor.

In this example, the **Smallest eigenvalue for which a factor is retained** option and the **Per cent of common variance accounted for by retained factor** option are kept to their default settings, thus allowing all factors to be retained. However, as the final factor solution should have two factors, a two-factor solution is directly asked to the SAS Enterprise Guide software. This is done by setting the **Number of factors to retain** equal to *2*.

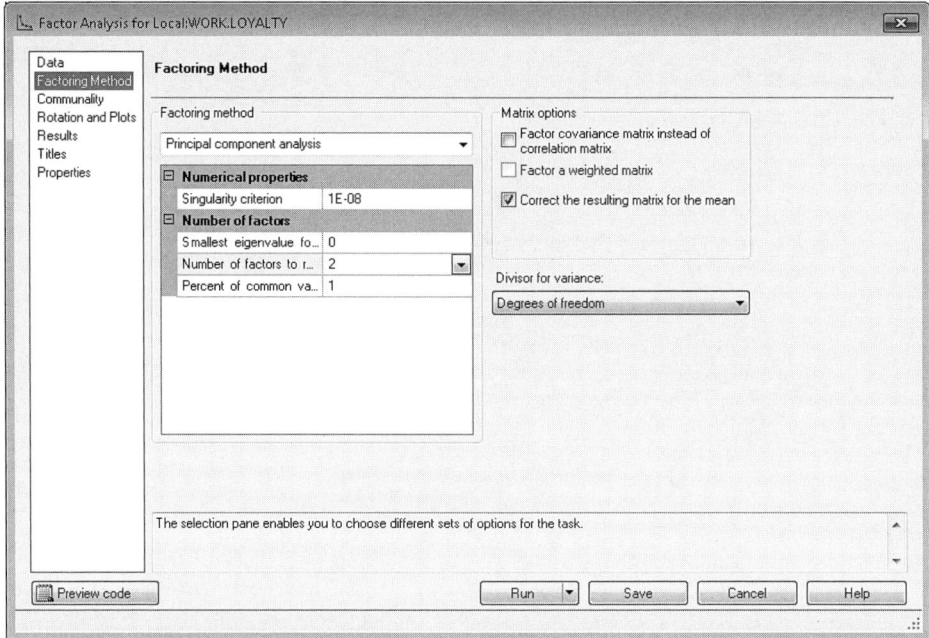

5. Select **Rotation and Plots** from the selection pane. Here one chooses the rotation method for the factor analysis. When one assumes that the factors should be uncorrelated, an orthogonal rotation is applied, otherwise the researcher allows some correlation between the different factors and an oblique rotation is employed. In this case, the affective and cognitive loyalty constructs should be uncorrelated and thus the **Orthogonal varimax** option is selected as the Rotation method. Moreover, a plot of the rotated factor pattern is requested by ticking the option **Plot the factor pattern (after rotation)**. Finally, a Scree plot of the eigenvalues of the factors is requested by ticking the **Show a scree plot of the eigenvalues** option.

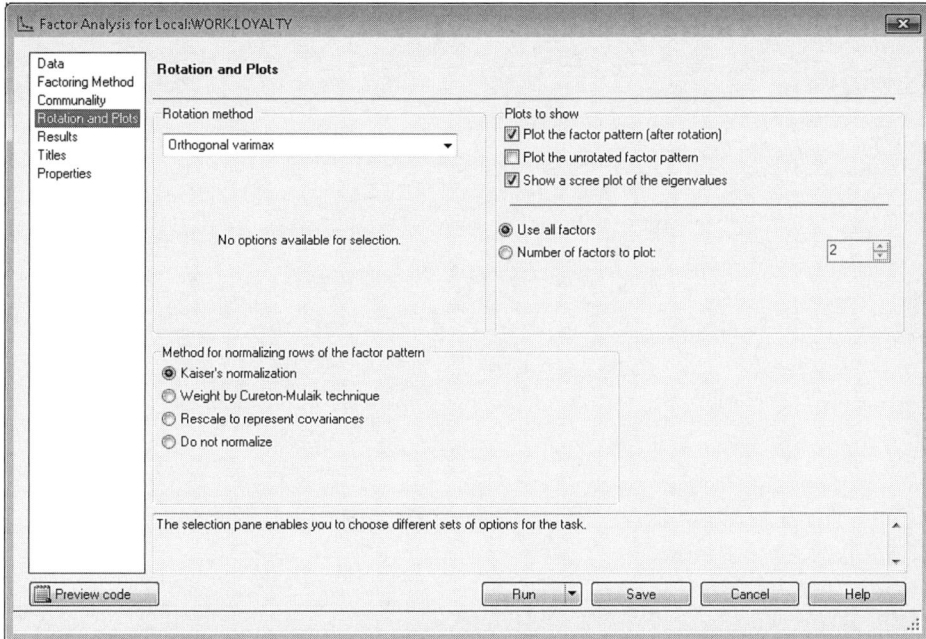

6.   In the selection pane **Results**, two output datasets are asked; one with the factor scores done by ticking the box **Factors** and one with the factor analysis statistics asked by ticking the box **Statistics**. Moreover, to generate the factor scores for every individual in the dataset, the option **Factor scoring coefficients** is ticked. Furthermore, the options **Correlation matrix of input columns** and the **Kaiser's measure of sampling adequacy** is requested to give the additional statistics respectively.

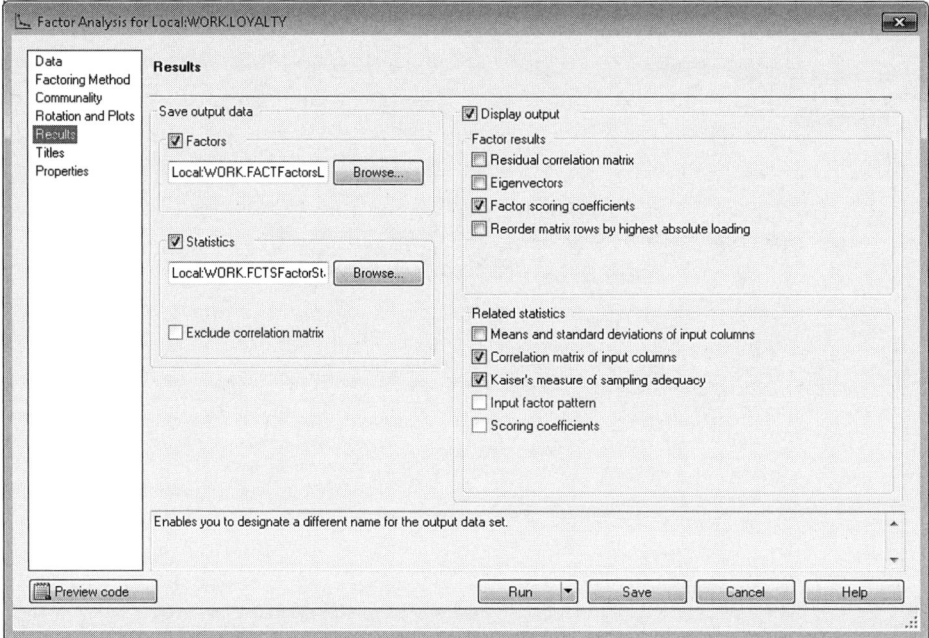

7.   Click **Run** to generate the report and examine the results. View the report in the **Results** tab or select the **Output Data** tab to view the dataset.

Interpretation

The interpretation of a factor analysis consists of several steps.

- **Partial Correlations Controlling all other Variables**

Partial Correlations Controlling all other Variables								
	ALOY1	ALOY2	ALOY3	CLOY1	CLOY2	CLOY3	CLOY4	CLOY5	CLOY6
ALOY1	1.00000	0.66004	0.11037	0.07263	-0.01271	-0.04600	0.05185	0.05437	0.01886
ALOY2	0.66004	1.00000	0.10141	-0.16382	0.00343	0.15308	-0.04433	0.07890	0.30360
ALOY3	0.11037	0.10141	1.00000	-0.05667	0.08845	-0.03529	-0.02377	-0.02571	0.55450
CLOY1	0.07263	-0.16382	-0.05667	1.00000	0.12975	0.15131	0.11676	0.34313	0.19052
CLOY2	-0.01271	0.00343	0.08845	0.12975	1.00000	0.59943	0.05896	0.17077	0.00348
CLOY3	-0.04600	0.15308	-0.03529	0.15131	0.59943	1.00000	0.24401	-0.12941	-0.03376
CLOY4	0.05185	-0.04433	-0.02377	0.11676	0.05896	0.24401	1.00000	0.54709	0.05777
CLOY5	0.05437	0.07890	-0.02571	0.34313	0.17077	-0.12941	0.54709	1.00000	-0.06341
CLOY6	0.01886	0.30360	0.55450	0.19052	0.00348	-0.03376	0.05777	-0.06341	1.00000

This table represents the partial correlations matrix. The higher the absolute value of the partial correlation coefficients, the stronger the relationship between the variables. In order to make factor analysis meaningful, the partial correlations should indicate some correlation between the different variables. The table shows that several variables are correlated to another resulting in the assumption that factor analysis *could be* beneficial to find underlying patterns in the data.

• **Kaiser's Measure of Sampling Adequacy: Overall MSA = 0.86464761**

Kaiser's Measure of Sampling Adequacy: Overall MSA = 0.86464761								
ALOY1	ALOY2	ALOY3	CLOY1	CLOY2	CLOY3	CLOY4	CLOY5	CLOY6
0.85356290	0.82484679	0.86385117	0.91559289	0.87737210	0.85272912	0.88554852	0.85713229	0.85725955

In order to formalize the hypothesis that factor analysis is beneficial, we look at the Kaiser's measure of sampling adequacy index. It measures whether the strength between the variables is large enough and thus this index should be at least 0.5 for a satisfactory factor analysis to proceed. The Kaiser's measure of sampling adequacy in this loyalty case is 0.8646 which is larger than 0.5. The factor analysis is useful.

• **Eigenvalues of the Correlation Matrix: Total = 9 Average = 1**

	Eigenvalues of the Correlation Matrix: Total = 9 Average = 1			
	Eigenvalue	Difference	Proportion	Cumulative
1	5.50988144	3.88615288	0.6122	0.6122
2	1.62372856	1.14164265	0.1804	0.7926
3	0.48208592	0.04190658	0.0536	0.8462
4	0.44017933	0.15079773	0.0489	0.8951
5	0.28938160	0.08342780	0.0322	0.9273
6	0.20595380	0.02562237	0.0229	0.9501
7	0.18033143	0.03353311	0.0200	0.9702
8	0.14679832	0.02513872	0.0163	0.9865
9	0.12165959		0.0135	1.0000

Although the number of factors is fixed to 2 for theoretical reasons, the Kaiser's criterion gives an indication of how many factors to expect, namely the factors with an eigenvalue larger than 1. This table indicates that there would have been two factors (eigenvalue larger than 1) retained, together explaining 79.26 per cent of the total variance in the dataset (to be found in column *Cumulative*).

• **Scree Plot**

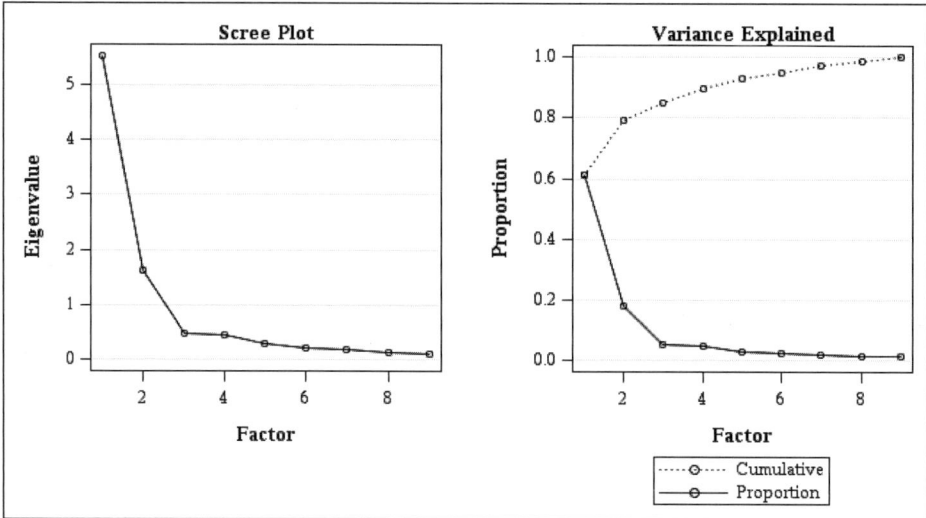

This graph represents the Scree plot for the current factor solution. It is a visual representation of the number of factors on the X-axis and the eigenvalue on the Y-axis. Based on the Kaiser's eigenvalue criterion (see supra), one would retain two factors. Using the Scree plot criterion to determine the optimal number of factors, one picks the number of factors equal to the elbow of the Scree plot minus 1. In our case, the Scree plot criterion would suggest a two-factor solution. Indeed, the elbow is found at the three-factors solution (3-1 = 2 factors). This result is in line with the Kaiser's criterion.

Note that in this example, whatever the solution obtained, we would stick to a two-factor solution for theoretical reasons.

Under the assumption that no prior knowledge is available on the number of factors to retain, the general decision rule is that the Kaiser's criterion, the Scree plot and the minimum common variance rule are put in the balance and that the simplest factor solution is retained suggested by the majority of the criteria.

- **Factor Pattern**

	Factor Pattern	
	Factor1	Factor2
ALOY1	0.77489	0.43466
ALOY2	0.78418	0.48165
ALOY3	0.68701	0.55637
CLOY1	0.77402	-0.39212
CLOY2	0.82269	-0.33379
CLOY3	0.80197	-0.32909
CLOY4	0.81751	-0.38700
CLOY5	0.80328	-0.37852
CLOY6	0.76802	0.47619

This table summarizes the unrotated factor solution and therefore this solution should not be examined because it does not facilitate interpretation.

- **Final Communality Estimates: Total = 7.133610**

Final Communality Estimates: Total = 7.133610								
ALOY1	ALOY2	ALOY3	CLOY1	CLOY2	CLOY3	CLOY4	CLOY5	CLOY6
0.78937787	0.84692995	0.78153024	0.75286719	0.78823512	0.75144796	0.81809042	0.78852761	0.81660364

This table represents the communalities of the different variables. The communality of a particular variable tells us how much of the variance of that variable is explained by the proposed factor solution. We argue that at least 60 per cent of the variance should be explained by the factor solution in order to retain the variable for subsequent analysis. For instance for *ALOY1*, the two-factor solution accounts for 78.94 per cent of the variation in that variable.

- **Rotated Factor Pattern**

Rotated Factor Pattern		
	Factor1	Factor2
ALOY1	0.30560	0.83426
ALOY2	0.28208	0.87599
ALOY3	0.15967	0.86950
CLOY1	0.84290	0.20588
CLOY2	0.84191	0.28183
CLOY3	0.82311	0.27192
CLOY4	0.87259	0.23806
CLOY5	0.85627	0.23524
CLOY6	0.27336	0.86132

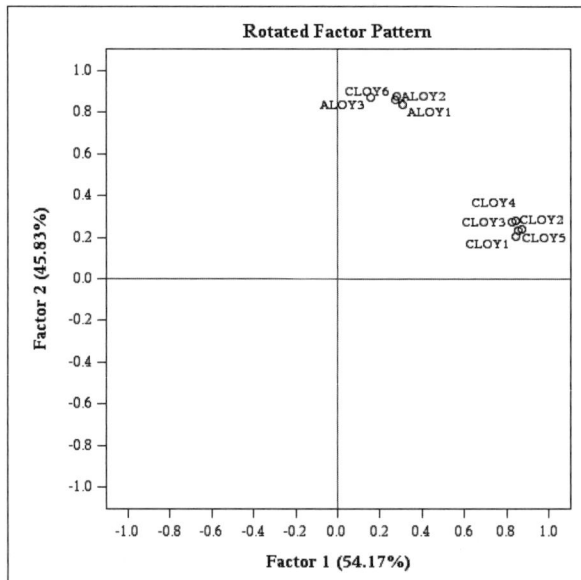

The next step is to identify which items load on the corresponding factors or constructs. One should always look at the rotated factor pattern matrix and/or at the rotated factor pattern plot in order to facilitate interpretation of the solution. An item is deleted from the factor analysis:

(i)   when it does not achieve a *high* loading (on the correct factor); or

(ii)   when the item has multiple *high* loadings on different factors.

A factor loading is considered high when exceeding 0.55 for a sample size of around 100 respondents, exceeding 0.40 for a sample size of around 200 respondents and exceeding 0.30 for a sample size larger than 300 respondents. It is clear from both the matrix and the graph that all items of the loyalty construct load high on the same factor, except item *CLOY6* that loads high on factor 2, the wrong construct, that is, the affective loyalty construct. This is unacceptable, thus one should rerun the factor analysis by withdrawing *CLOY6* from the analysis.

8. Go to the **Process Flow** pane and right-click the Factor Analysis icon and select the **Modify Factor Analysis** option.

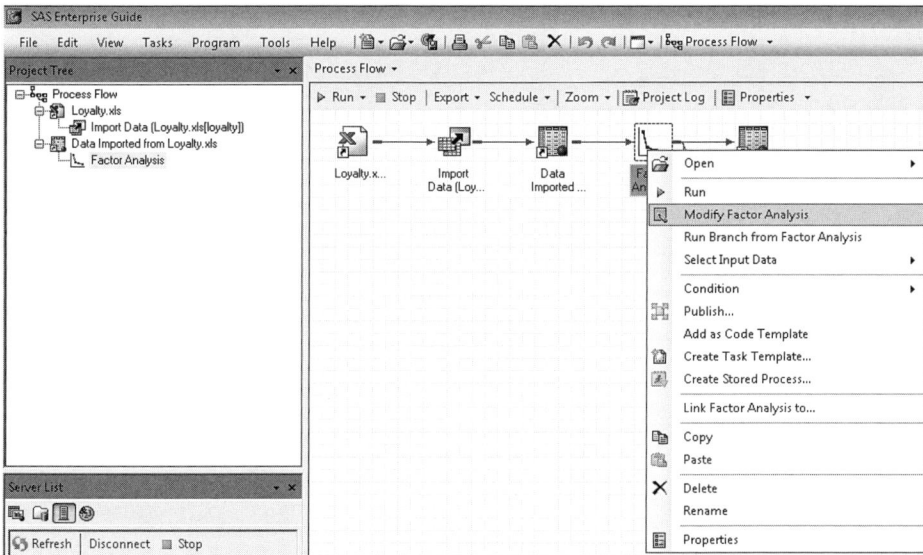

9. Withdraw the item *CLOY6* by removing it from the **Analysis variables** role.

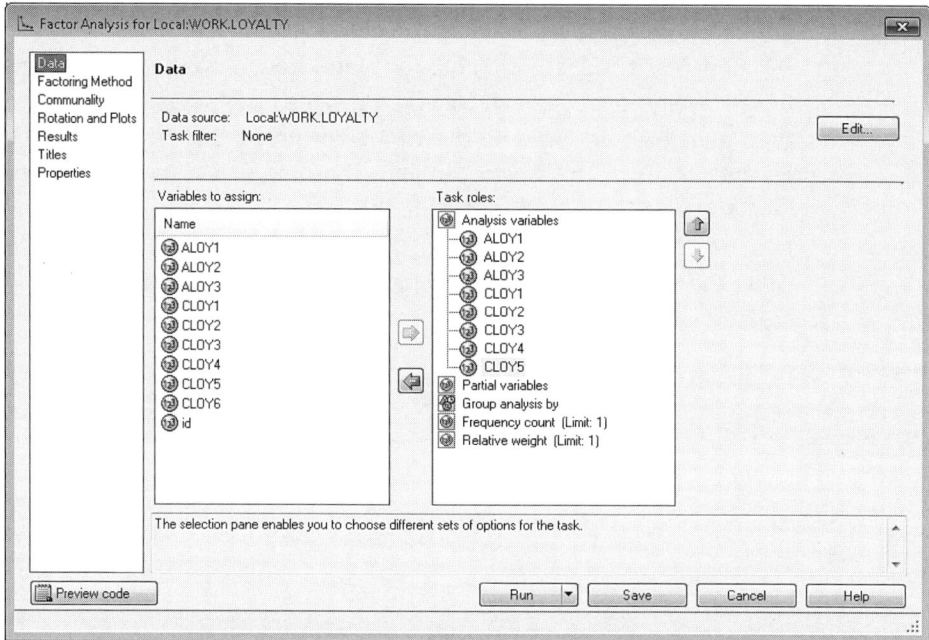

10. Select **Run** and save the results in another node by clicking **No** in the pop-up window. View the report in the **Results** tab and explore the new Rotated Factor Pattern matrix and graph.

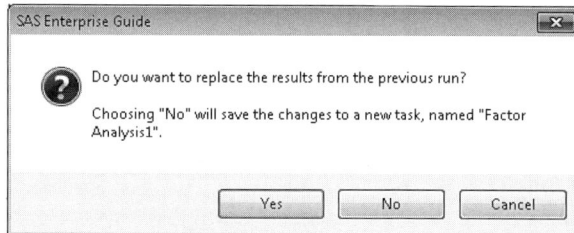

Interpretation

- **Rotated Factor Pattern**

Rotated Factor Pattern		
	Factor1	Factor2
ALOY1	0.29814	0.87058
ALOY2	0.27967	0.89644
ALOY3	0.17252	0.84747
CLOY1	0.85074	0.18105
CLOY2	0.84232	0.28100
CLOY3	0.82190	0.27554
CLOY4	0.87376	0.23324
CLOY5	0.85593	0.23584

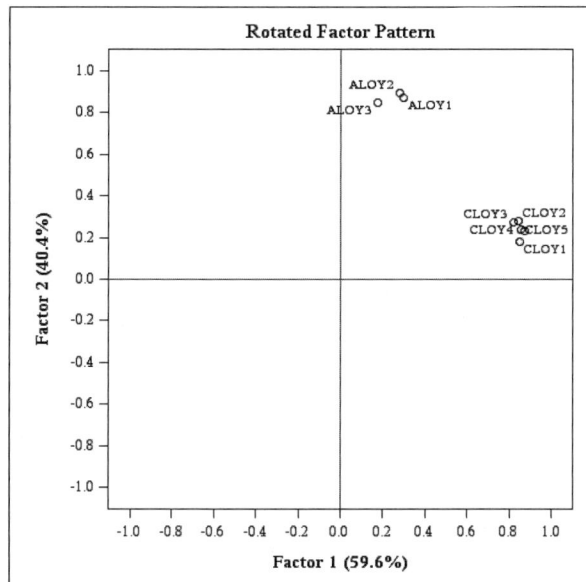

Inspecting the new rotated factor pattern matrix and/or the new rotated factor pattern plot, one can see that the final result of the new factor analysis looks good, because all items load high on the correct factor. In sum, the items *CLOY1–CLOY5* form the cognitive loyalty construct and items *ALOY1–ALOY3* represent the affective loyalty construct.

Exploratory factor analysis gives us an insight into which items load on which construct. However, the researcher should always check whether the items that load on the same construct are internally consistent. In other words, are these items correlated enough to be put together into one construct measure? We should check the reliability of the different items loading on the same construct by calculating a measure that checks the internal consistency. This measure is called the Cronbach's alpha. The Cronbach's alpha is calculated using the **Correlations** task. The calculation of the Cronbach's alpha for the cognitive loyalty construct is shown below.

1.   Open the **Correlations** task by clicking **Tasks** → **Multivariate** → **Correlations...**

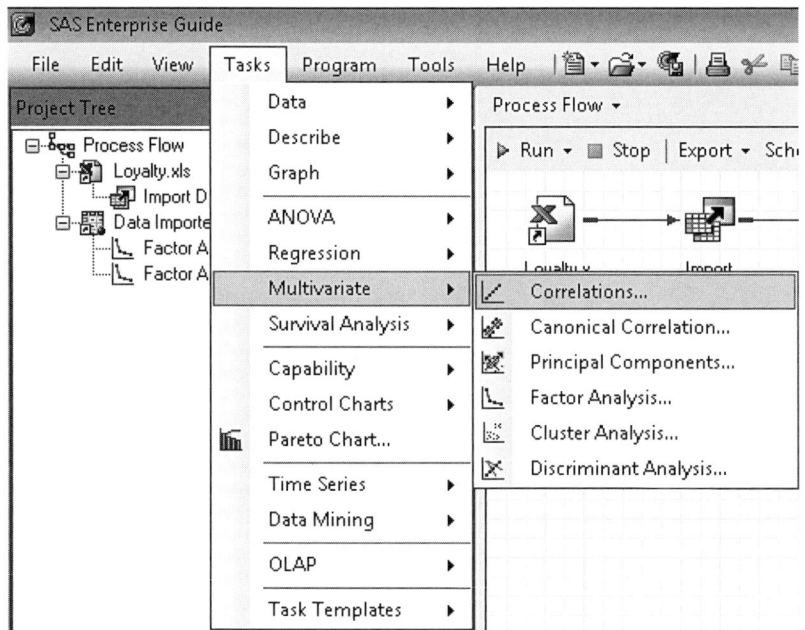

2.   In the **Data** pane, drag and drop the relevant variables, here *CLOY1–CLOY5* into the **Analysis variables** role.

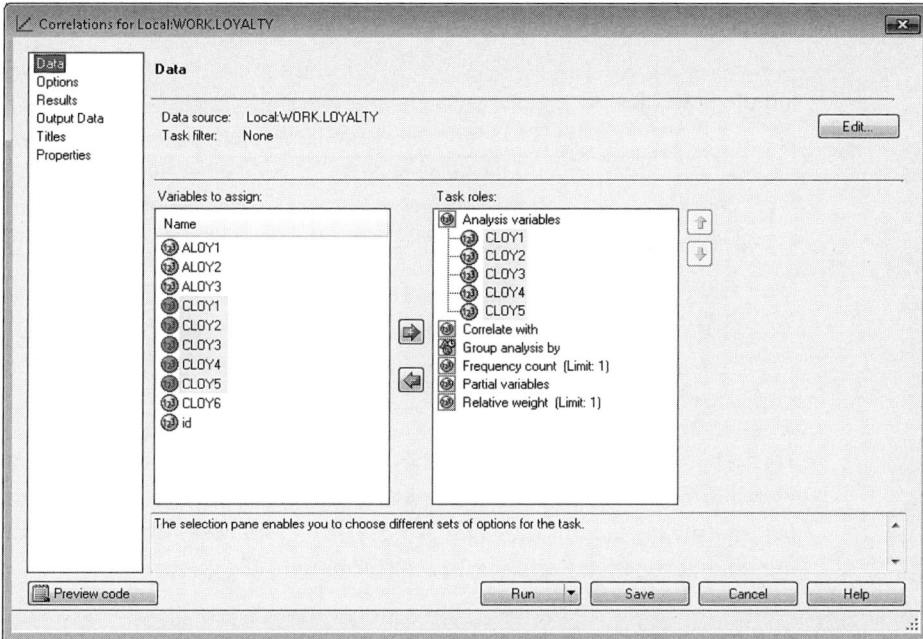

3. In the **Options** pane, select the **Cronbach's coefficient alpha** option.

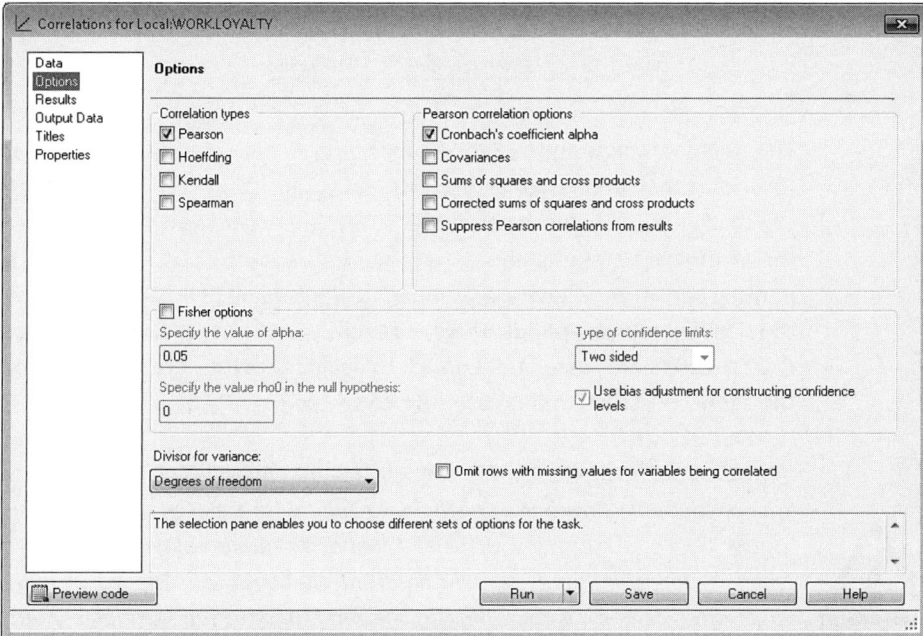

4. Select <u>**Run**</u>. View the report in the **Results** tab.

Interpretation

- ### Simple Statistics

			Simple Statistics			
Variable	N	Mean	Std Dev	Sum	Minimum	Maximum
CLOY1	189	4.27513	0.72086	808.00000	2.00000	5.00000
CLOY2	189	4.09524	0.79321	774.00000	1.00000	5.00000
CLOY3	189	4.17460	0.78969	789.00000	1.00000	5.00000
CLOY4	189	4.07407	0.82823	770.00000	1.00000	5.00000
CLOY5	189	4.16931	0.82055	788.00000	1.00000	5.00000

This table gives an overview of the different statistics for the different variables under consideration. For instance, the number of observations (*N*), the mean (*Mean*), the standard deviation (*Std Dev*), the sum (*Sum*), minimum (*Minimum*) and maximum (*Maximum*) are given.

- ### Cronbach Coefficient Alpha

Cronbach Coefficient Alpha	
Variables	Alpha
Raw	0.928839
Standardized	0.929159

This table contains the reliability measure, Cronbach's alpha. In order to decide that the variables are internally consistent, the standardized Cronbach's alpha value must exceed 0.80. It is clear from the output of the Cronbach's alpha analysis that the items *CLOY1–CLOY5* show a high internal consistency having a Cronbach's alpha value of 0.9291 exceeding the 0.80 (in column *Alpha*). This result tells the analyst that the variables *CLOY1–CLOY5* are correlated enough to decide that they are measures for the same construct. In this case, the items can directly be summarized.

*If the Cronbach's alpha value is not sufficient (lower than 0.80), one should look at the table **Cronbach Coefficient Alpha with Deleted Variable**. This matrix tells you by how much the Cronbach's alpha value will increase when a particular item is deleted from the analysis. The new alpha value after deletion is found in the column Standardized Variables under Alpha. As such, one could increase the Cronbach's alpha or the internal consistency of the construct items. The deletion of items can be repeated*

taking into account the balance between the increase in Cronbach's alpha value and the number of items left. Two options could occur after this process: either the Cronbach's alpha cannot be increased above 0.60, this means that the items cannot be summarized. Or the Cronbach's alpha falls between 0.60 and 0.80 after item deletion, meaning that one could proceed with the items aggregation.

You can repeat steps 1 to 4 of the reliability analysis to check whether the *ALOY1– ALOY3* variables are internally consistent.

The next step is to decide how the different variables *CLOY1–CLOY5* and *ALOY1–ALOY3* can be summarized in the dataset to represent the general cognitive loyalty construct. Three possible aggregation options are available to the analyst:

1. factor score coefficients;

2. surrogate variable;

3. summated scale.

The <u>factor scores</u> for every respondent for each factor are automatically calculated, because the output dataset **Factors** was ticked, while the option **Factor scoring coefficients** was selected in the **Results** pane. You will find the factor scores variables, *Factor1* and *Factor2*, in the **Output Data (2)** tab.

Another option to construct a factor is the use of a <u>surrogate variable</u>. This means that the item that loads the highest on a particular construct in the Rotated Factor Pattern matrix is used to represent the construct. In this case, this would be item *CLOY4* for the cognitive loyalty construct and *ALOY2* for the affective loyalty construct.

A last option to represent a construct is to calculate the <u>summated scale</u>. This means that we will aggregate all high-loading items for a particular construct by calculating their mean. The mean of the original item values represents the new construct value. Suppose that *CLOY_scale* is the summated scale variable for the cognitive loyalty construct. Practically, one has to calculate the mean for the items *CLOY1* till *CLOY5*. In order to do so, open the **Query Builder** task.

1.   Right-click the loyalty dataset in the **Process Flow** and select **<u>Query Builder...</u>**

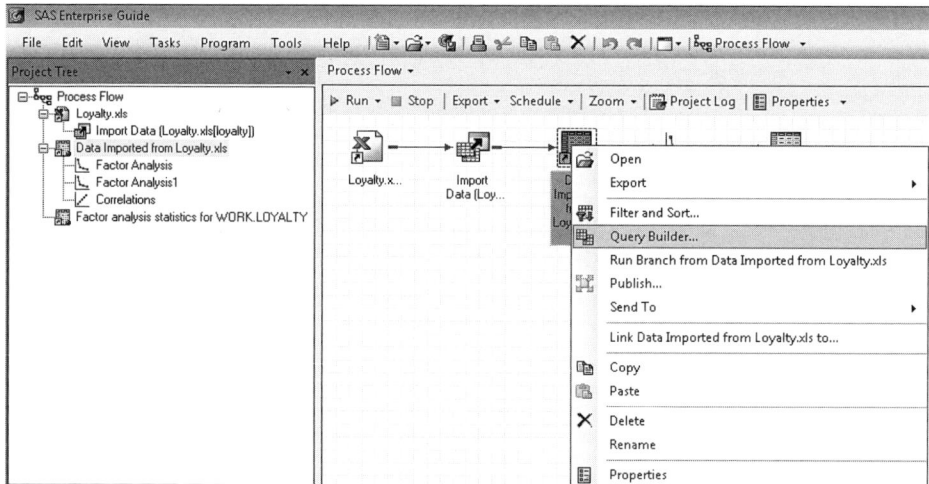

2.   Add all variables including the *CLOY1–CLOY5* variables to the **Select Data** pane, and rename the query to *CLOY_Scale_Query*. Click on the little calculator on the right-hand side to add a new computed variable to the output dataset.

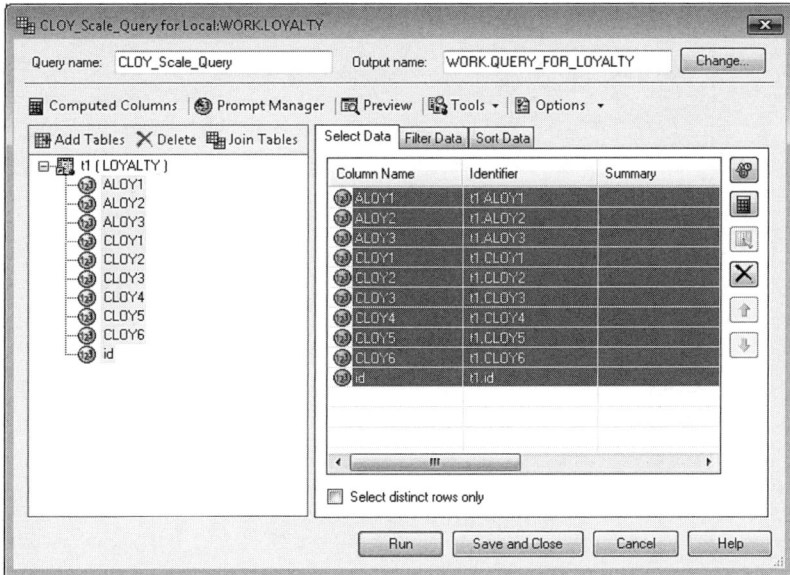

3. Tick the option **Advanced expression** and click on **Next**.

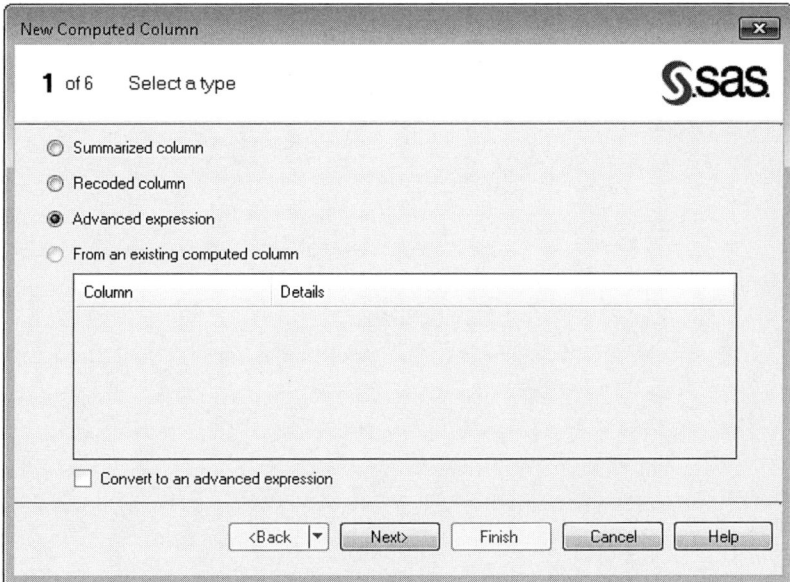

4. Create the summated scale by averaging the values of *CLOY1–CLOY5* and click on **Next**.

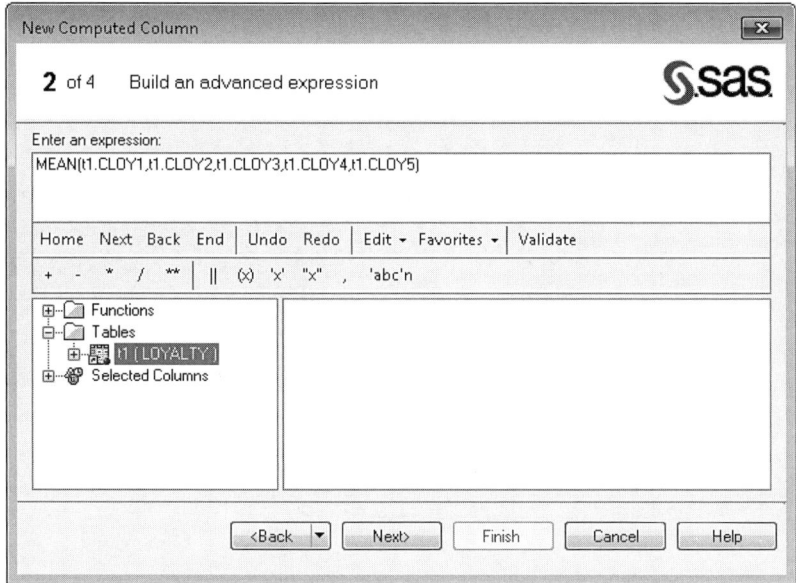

5.   Rename the **Identifier** and **Column Name** option to your new variable name *CLOY_Scale* and click on **Finish**.

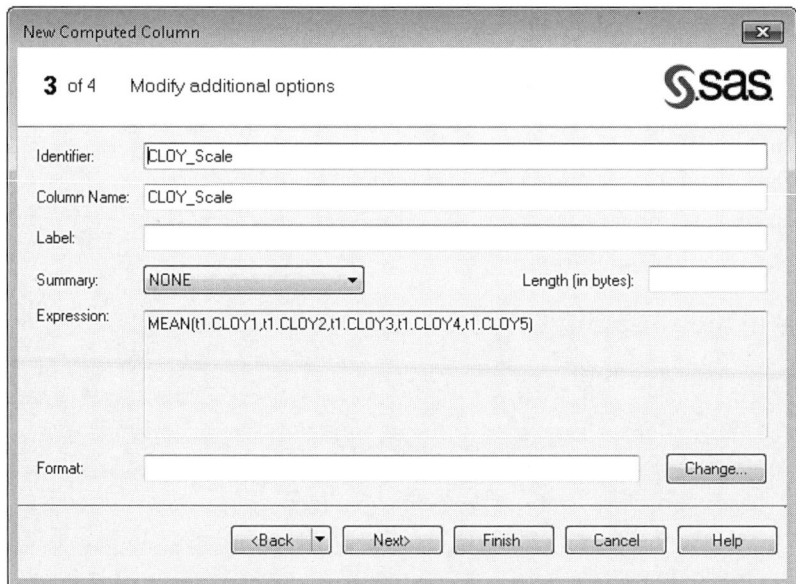

6.   Now you will see that the new variable *CLOY_Scale* is added to the variables to be included in the new dataset. When you click on **Finish**, the **Query Builder** task is run and a new dataset is created with the new

CLOY_Scale variable that represents the summated scale for the cognitive loyalty construct.

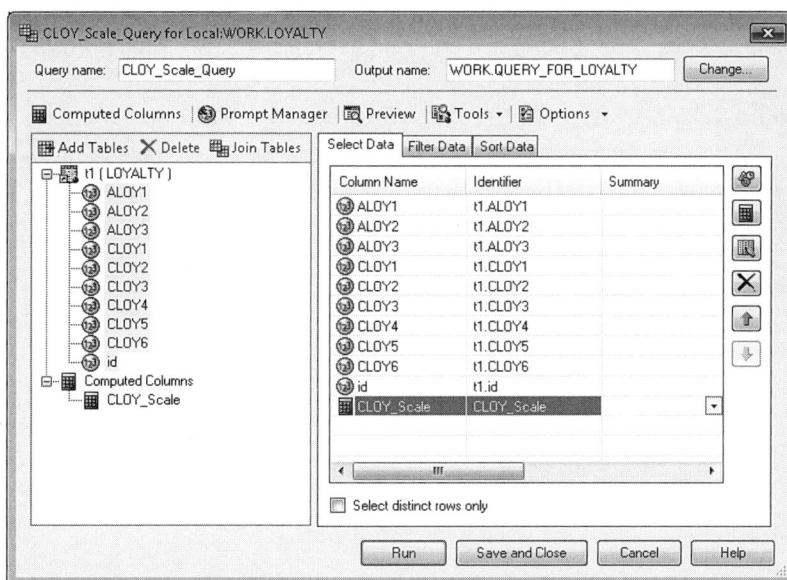

Steps 1 till 6 must be repeated to create the *ALOY_Scale* summated scale variable that represents the affective loyalty construct.

In the end, the researcher creates two new variables representing the cognitive loyalty and the affective loyalty of the respondents. These new variables could be further used in other analyses.

Further Reading

Carmines, E.G. and Zeller, R.A. (1979), *Reliability and Validity Assessment*, Quantitative Applications in the Social Sciences, Sage Publications, Inc.

Cronbach, L.J. (1951), 'Coefficient alpha and the internal structure of tests', *Psychometrika*, 16 3, pp. 297–334.

Diamantopoulos A. (2005), 'The C-OAR-SE procedure for scale development in marketing: a comment', *International Journal of Research in Marketing*, 22 1, pp. 1–9.

Gerbing, D.W. and Anderson, J.C. (1988), 'An updated paradigm for scale development incorporating undimensionality and its assessment', *Journal of Marketing Research*, 25 2, pp. 186–192.

Gerbing, D.W. and Hamilton J.G. (1996), 'Viability of exploratory factor analysis as a precursor to confirmatory factor analysis', *Structural Equation Modeling: A Multidisciplinary Journal*, 3 1, pp. 62–72.

Hair, J., Black, W.C., Babin, B.J. and Anderson R.E. (2009), *Multivariate Data Analysis*, 7th edition, Prentice Hall.

Kim, J.-O. and Mueller, C.W. (1978), *Factor Analysis: Statistical Methods and Practical Issues*, Quantitative Applications in the Social Sciences, Sage Publications, Inc.

Rossiter J.R. (2002), 'The C-OAR-SE procedure for scale development in marketing', *International Journal of Research in Marketing*, 19 4, pp. 305–335.

Chapter 4

Cluster Analysis

Objectives

1. Describe the basic concepts of cluster analysis.

2. Explain the difference between the different clustering methods.

3. Describe the methods for evaluating the quality and robustness of a clustering solution.

4. Learn how to profile a cluster solution.

Fundamentals

Cluster analysis is used to separate objects or individuals into several homogeneous groups or clusters. The clustering is based on variables that characterize these objects or individuals. Clusters are formed so that the homogeneity is maximized within the clusters, while the heterogeneity is maximized between the clusters. Therefore, members of the same cluster share common characteristics. The cluster analysis groups together observations (or individuals) based on characteristics measured for each observation. In marketing, variables used to group consumers into segments are demographical variables (for example, age, gender and so on), behavioural variables (for example, purchase frequency, level of loyalty and so on), benefits sought or lifestyle variables. These variables enable the identification of different groups of consumers so that customers are most similar within the group, whereas groups must be as different as possible.

Let us imagine that we use two variables X_1 and X_2 to characterize the customers of a retail chain. X_1 is the average shopping frequency (number of visits per week) and X_2 is the average amount of their shopping basket per visit (in euros). The figure below represents these two dimensions considering that the values for the variables X_1 and X_2 are the coordinates for each individual.

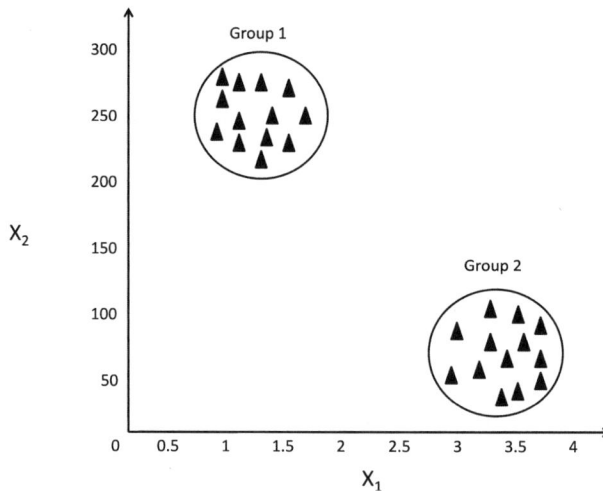

We can identify two groups of customers: the first one has a low shopping frequency but spends a high amount of money whereas the second one has a high shopping frequency but the size of their shopping basket is lower than the first group. Customers have similar profiles within a group. The cluster analysis enables the identification of groups of individuals or objects for which the homogeneity within the group and the heterogeneity between groups are maximized.

There are two types of clustering methods: hierarchical and non-hierarchical methods. The figure below shows that the **Cluster Analysis** task in SAS Enterprise Guide allows a choice between these two methods.

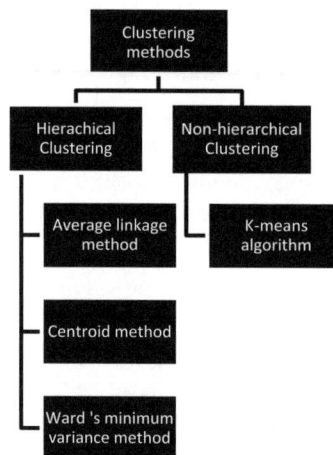

Hierarchical clustering methods allow different types of data, including coordinate data or distance data. A dataset including coordinate data is composed of observations and their characteristics (rows include observations and columns represent observations' characteristics). Distance data includes distance measures between observations. One finds observations in rows and columns whereas the intersection includes the distance between two given observations. If the dataset contains coordinate data, the task computes Euclidean distances before applying clustering methods. The result of the hierarchical clustering is visualized in the form of a tree diagram, also called a dendrogram. At the bottom of the dendrogram, one finds all the observations, each observation being considered as a cluster. There are as many clusters as observations. Then, two groups that are considered the most similar (based on the smallest distance measured) are joined to form a cluster. This step is repeated until all individuals belong to the same cluster. One will choose a solution (number of clusters to be retained) so that the homogeneity within groups is optimal.

Among hierarchical methods (see section 4.1. Hierarchical Clustering), SAS Enterprise Guide proposes three distance measures: the average linkage method, the centroid method and the Ward's minimum variance method. These three methods are explained below.

- The average linkage method is based on arithmetic averages, and the distance between two clusters is computed as the average distance between all pairs of observations or individuals in the two clusters.

- The centroid method uses the distance between the centroid of two clusters to evaluate the cluster solution. The centroid is the centre for a particular cluster. It is the vector of means in the multidimensional space defined by the clustering variables. The distance between two clusters is calculated as a difference between the centroids.

- The Ward's minimum variance method creates clusters that minimize the variance within each cluster. For each cluster, the mean for each variable is calculated. In each cluster, observations are compared with the mean for each variable. Observations or/and clusters are combined so that the variance within the final cluster solution is minimized. The Ward's minimum variance method is the most commonly used in marketing.

The non-hierarchical clustering method or the K-means method is a clustering algorithm that partitions the observations into a predefined number of clusters based on the nearest mean (see section 4.2. Non-hierarchical K-means Clustering). This method is therefore also called a partitioning cluster method. The non-hierarchical clustering method or the K-means method in SAS Enterprise Guide can handle different types of data, including coordinate data. However, one cannot use the K-means method with distance data.

With the K-means method, K individuals are randomly selected from the dataset to be the initial centroids of the K clusters. The other individuals are assigned to their nearest cluster so that the squared distance between each individual and the centroid of the cluster is minimized. The centroid of the cluster is computed in the multidimensional space defined by the clustering variables, and this calculation is done after the assignment of the individuals. During the optimization process of K-means, individuals are reassigned to other clusters based on their nearest centroid. Each iteration aims at reducing the least squared Euclidean distance. This process is iterative until all individuals are in the optimal cluster and no reassignment is necessary.

The main advantage of the K-means method is that it is a faster method than the hierarchical method particularly when the sample size is large (more than 100 observations). The K-means method can be used when the research problem may include an indication on the exact number of clusters to expect. However with smaller datasets, K-means results are sensitive to the order of the observations in the dataset. Furthermore, the number of clusters (K) must be decided beforehand in a K-means clustering setting. If the number of clusters cannot be set beforehand, a two-stage clustering approach is frequently proposed. Practically, the Ward's minimum variance method is used to identify the number of clusters in a first stage. In a second stage, a K-means clustering with the number of clusters identified by the Ward's minimum variance method is run to assign a cluster number to each and every individual in the dataset.

After the cluster analysis, one must further investigate the clusters' profile. Indeed, cluster analysis assigns individuals to groups. The next step is to understand how clusters differ from each other. To do so, one must use descriptive statistics to evaluate the profile of each cluster based on clustering variables (see section 4.3. Profiling Clusters).

4.1. Hierarchical Clustering

Managerial Problem

A company selling tablet computers investigates customers' usage of computers and smartphones to find customers willing to buy tablet computers. The marketing manager wants to segment its customers according to the usage frequency of features such as: Office software, phone, messages, e-book, music, searching for information on the web, video, email, social networking, instant messenger, photos, as well as the importance of having a high quality display, the price that they are willing to spend monthly for their Internet connection as well as the purchase of applications, and the price at which they are willing to purchase the device. An online survey has been conducted. Customers should then be grouped according to these variables to identify segments of customers with the same usage preferences. The marketing manager will choose the group(s) that is (are) the most interested by the proposed features. Finally, the marketing manager will judge whether the size of this (these) segment(s) is large enough to ensure a sufficient market potential.

Translation of the Managerial Problem into Statistical Notions

The objective is to group customers (individuals) into segments (clusters) according to their similarities in terms of usage of tablet features. Customers should be grouped into several clusters. Before running the cluster analysis, we need to standardize the clustering variables, given that all variables are measured on different scales. Standardizing is necessary to account for an equal contribution of each variable in the calculation of the distances during the clustering process. The clustering process proceeds in the following steps:

The first step is to select a clustering procedure together with a distance measure. In this setting, the Ward's minimum variance method is chosen as the hierarchical clustering algorithm. We choose a hierarchical method because the number of clusters is unknown in advance.

The second step is to choose/identify the number of clusters. We must find a relevant cluster solution on the basis of several criteria such as the Cubic Clustering Criterion (CCC), the Pseudo F and the Pseudo T-Squared statistics as well as the tree diagram or dendrogram.

- The CCC value must be greater than 2 or 3 to indicate a good cluster solution. CCC values between 0 and 2 show potential clusters, and thus these clusters should be considered with caution. The larger the positive values of the CCC are, the better the solution is.

- Additionally, the Pseudo F statistic helps to identify the number of clusters. The Pseudo F is the ratio of the mean sum of squares between the clusters to the mean sum of squares within the clusters. Large values of the Pseudo F statistic indicate a stopping point.

- Furthermore, a general rule for interpreting the values of the Pseudo T-Square statistic is to search for the elbow in the curve. At that point, the ideal cluster solution is found.

- Finally, the dendrogram indicates the optimal number of clusters based on the trade-off between the number of clusters identified and the height of the Semi-Partial R-Squared. The Semi-Partial R-Squared measures the loss of homogeneity due to joining two clusters to form a new one. It must be minimized while considering an acceptable number of clusters. A low Semi-Partial R-Squared shows that two homogeneous clusters have been joined to form a new cluster. On the contrary, if the value is high, it suggests that the cluster solution is obtained by merging two heterogeneous clusters. In the vertical dendrogram, individual observations are put at the bottom. In the initialization phase, each observation is considered as a separate cluster. In the beginning of the process, the observations are very similar when they are joined together to form a cluster, and thus the Semi-Partial R-Squared is very low. This process continues until all individuals are joined together into one big cluster. The more you go up, the higher the Semi-Partial R-Squared will be. The Semi-Partial R-Squared is (usually) maximized at the last step meaning that the cluster solution includes only one heterogeneous cluster.

The third step is to interpret the results of the clustering solution based on the clusters' profile. Practically, mean values for each original clustering variable are calculated per cluster and this enables the marketing researcher to compare the different clusters (see section 4.3. Profiling Clusters for more information).

Dataset Description

The SAS dataset *Tablet.sas7bdat* describes customers' usage frequency of electronic device features. 160 customers answered the online survey. The dataset includes 16 columns (variables) and 160 rows (individuals). The variables are the following:

- The respondent identifier (*ID*).

- The extent to which they perceive themselves as innovator (*INNOVATOR*).

- The usage intensity of Office software (*OFFICE SOFTWARE*).

- The usage intensity of their phone (*PHONE*).

- The usage intensity of SMS (*MESSAGES*).

- The reading frequency of e-books on their mobile device (*E-BOOK*).

- The listening frequency of music on their mobile device (*MUSIC*).

- The frequency at which they search for information on the Web (*INFORMATION*).

- The frequency of video watching on their mobile devices (*VIDEO*).

- The extent to which they use emails to communicate with others (*EMAILS*).

- The usage frequency of social networks (*SOCIAL NETWORK*).

- The usage frequency of instant messenger (*INSTANT MESSENGER*).

- The frequency at which they view photos on mobile devices (*PHOTOS*).

- The importance of a high quality display for their mobile devices (*HIGH QUALITY DISPLAY*).

- The price they are ready to pay monthly for their Internet connection as well as the purchase of applications (*MONTHLY PRICE*).

- The price they are willing to pay to purchase the device (*PRICE*).

The usage frequency variables and the perceived importance of high quality display have been measured on 7-point Likert-scales (ranging from 1 = low usage frequency to 7 = high usage frequency). The survey also includes a question about whether they perceive themselves as innovator (7-point Likert-scale). Moreover, the price questions, that is, *MONTHLY PRICE* and *PRICE*, are expressed in euros.

Data Analysis

The cluster analysis is done via the **Cluster Analysis** task. Before starting the clustering process, it is important that the variables used during clustering are standardized. Standardizing is necessary to make sure that all variables are put on the same scale, that is, in our case a mean of 0 and a standard deviation of 1, because cluster analysis is based on calculating distances which implicitly imply equal measurement units to be valid. Standardizing variables in SAS Enterprise Guide is done via the **Standardize Data** task.

1. Add the *Tablet.sas7bdat* dataset to your SAS Enterprise Guide environment.

2. Standardizing the clustering variables is done by clicking **Tasks** → **Data** → **Standardize Data...**

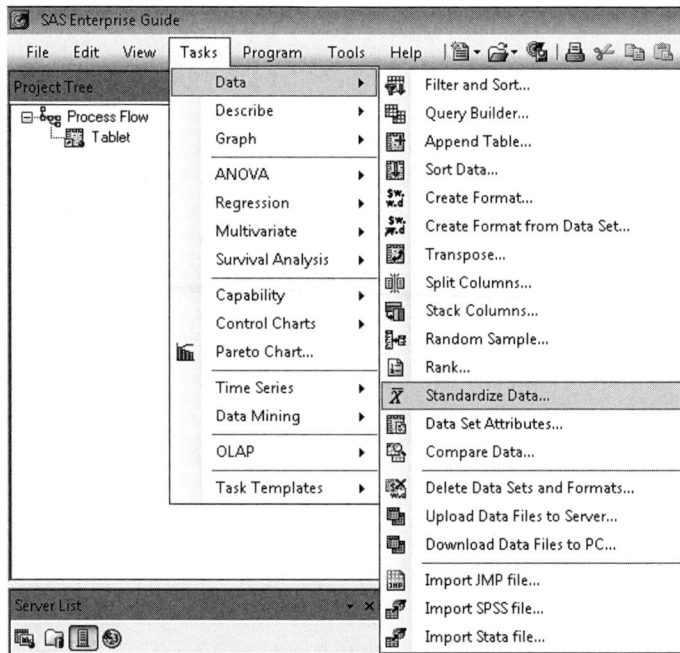

3. The selection pane opens at **Data** and you drag and drop all clustering variables under the **Analysis variables** role.

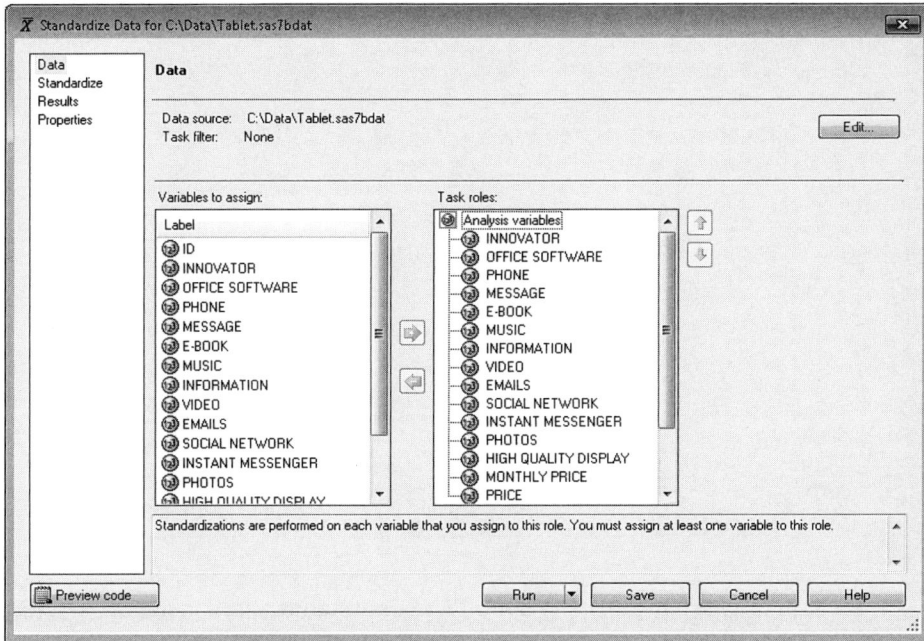

4. Go to the **Standardize** pane and make sure to standardize all variables to the new mean of 0 and the new standard deviation of 1 by setting the correct option accordingly.

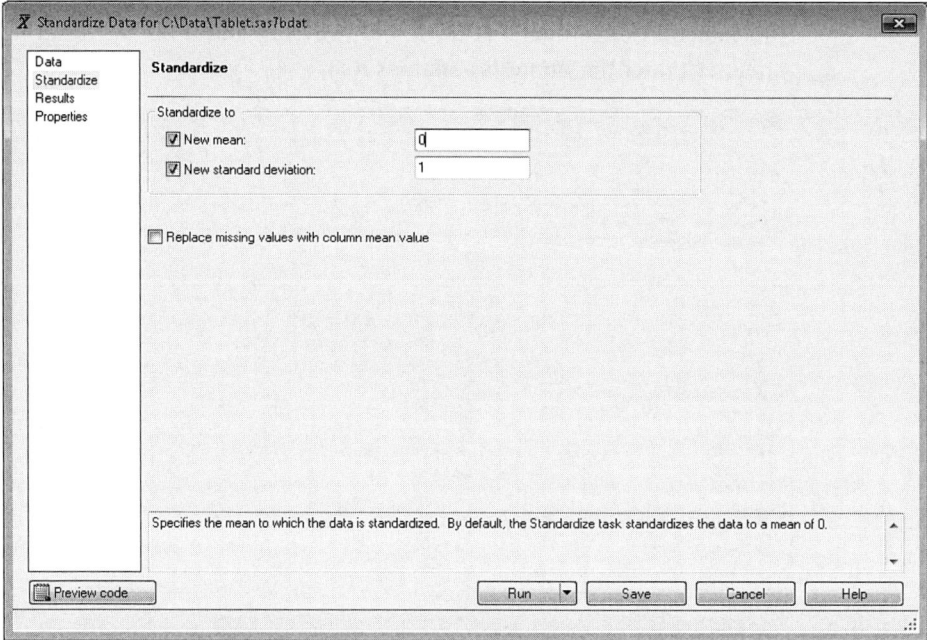

5. In the **Results** pane, the option **Add new standardized variables** is ticked by default. It will output the standardized variables as new additional variables in the new output dataset.

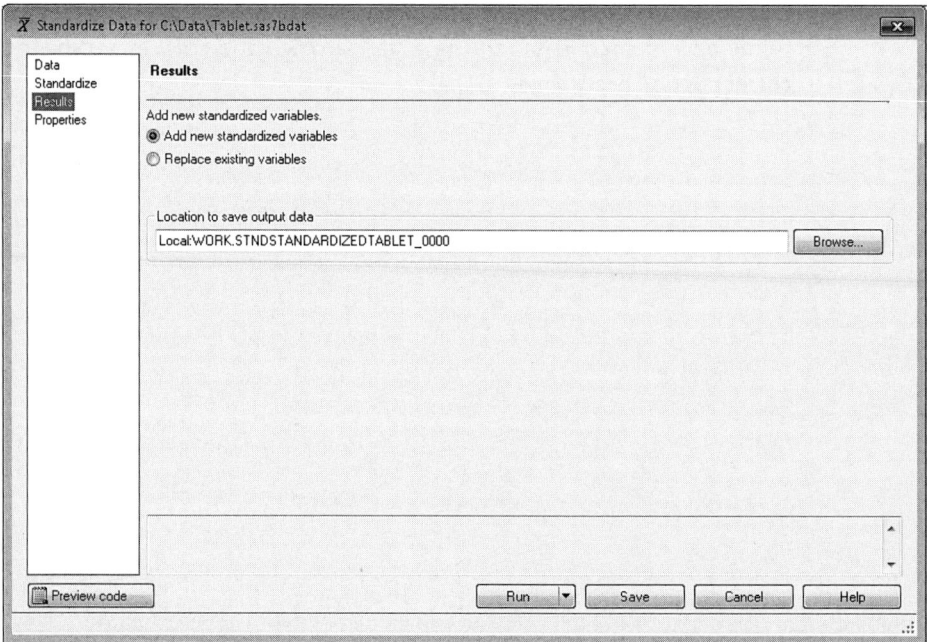

6.   Click **Run** and a new dataset with the standardized variables included is added to the SAS Enterprise Guide working environment.

At this stage, all clustering variables are scaled to the same unit, that is, mean 0 and standard deviation 1, and now the clustering analysis process can start. The Ward's minimum variance method is employed as a hierarchical clustering algorithm in this section.

7.   To start the cluster analysis, select the dataset output by the **Standardize Data** task and open the **Cluster Analysis** task via **Tasks** → **Multivariate** → **Cluster Analysis...**

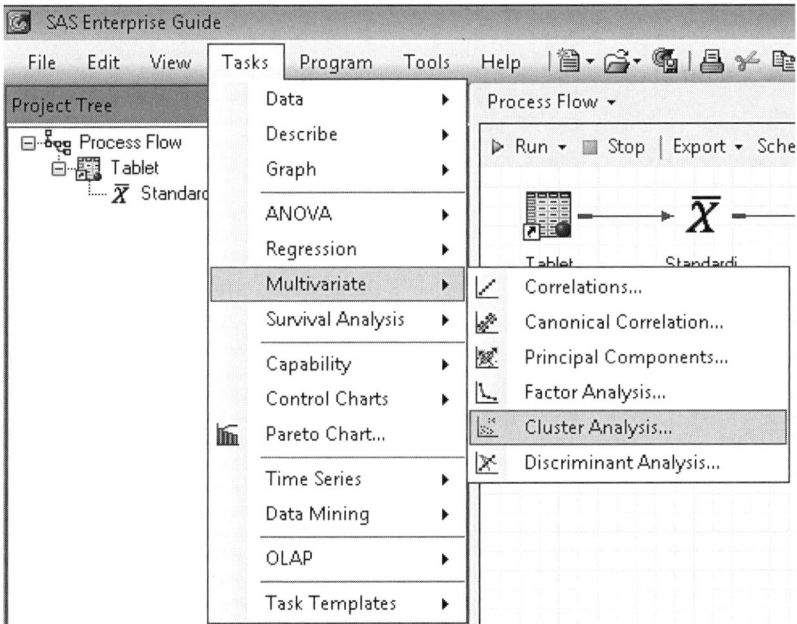

8.   Drag and drop all standardized clustering variables under the **Analysis variables** role in the **Data** pane. In order to add the original, non-standardized variables to the output dataset of the Ward's minimum variance method, drag and drop them under the **Copy variables** task role.

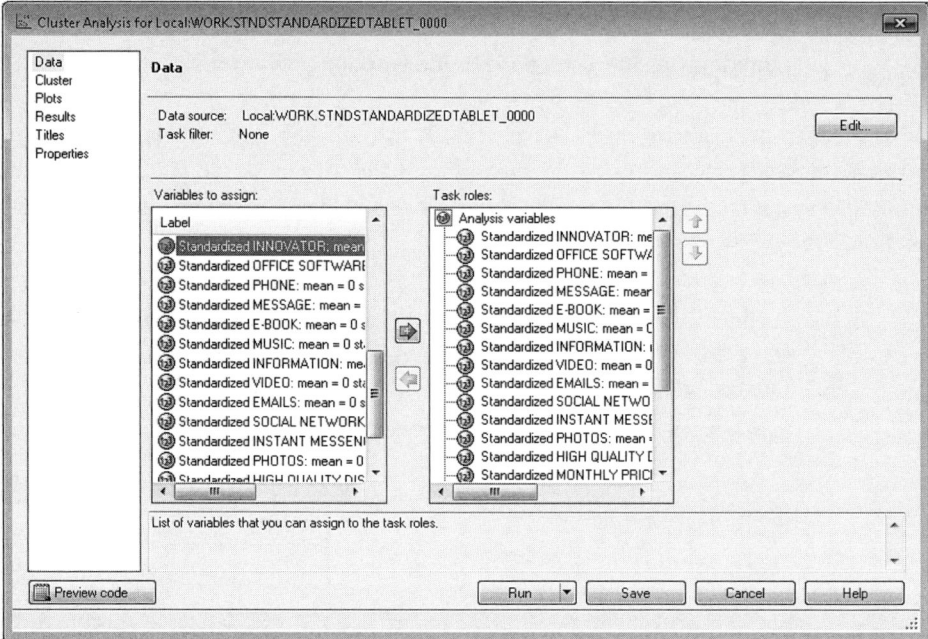

9. Run the Ward's clustering method by clicking the option **Ward's minimum variance method** in the **Cluster** pane.

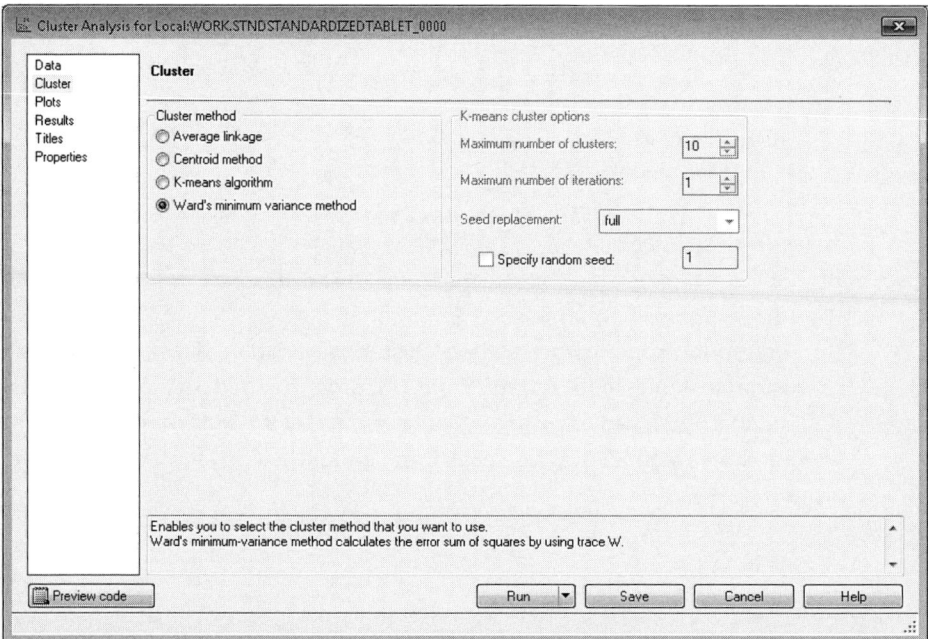

10. Click **Run** to obtain the results of the Ward's minimum variance method. Verify the results by clicking the **Results** tab.

Interpretation

- **Criteria for the Number of Clusters**

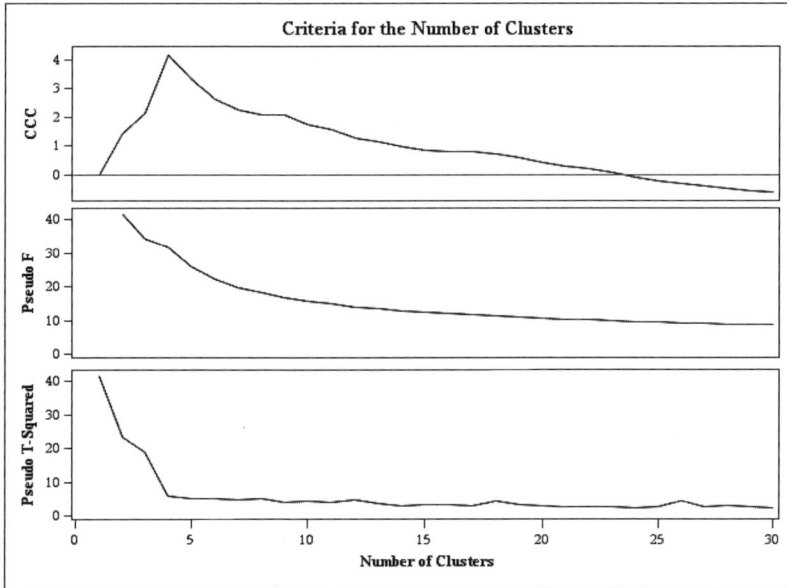

Criteria for the Number of Clusters

This graph gives a visual representation of the different criteria (CCC, Pseudo F and Pseudo T-Squared) that give an indication of how many clusters to expect. One notices that the CCC value is maximum at a four clusters solution, while the knick in the Pseudo F and the Pseudo T-Squared curves is also found around four clusters. These results indicate that the marketing analyst should strive towards a four clusters solution.

- **Cluster tree data for WORK.STNDSTANDARDIZEDTABLET_0000**

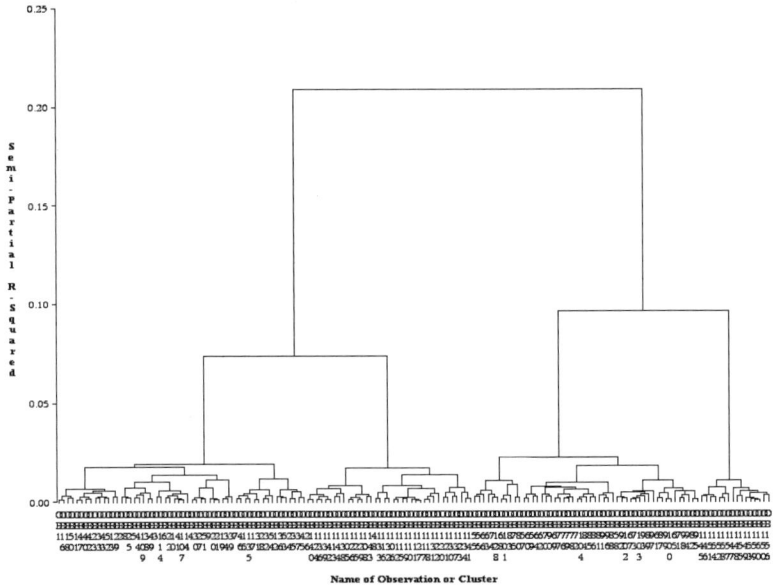

The dendrogram can also be used to decide how many segments to be retained. A dendrogram contains the name of the individuals or clusters on the X-axis and the Semi-Partial R-Squared on the Y-axis. In the bottom, one finds each single individual belonging to the original dataset, while at the top, one finds all individuals grouped together into one cluster. In the dendrogram, an individual or cluster is represented by a vertical line. The individuals who share the same characteristics are grouped together in the same cluster. This step is represented with a horizontal line. The clustering procedure stops when all individuals are assigned to the same cluster which is represented by the top horizontal line. One will choose a solution with a low Semi-Partial R-Squared while having an acceptable number of clusters. In our case, you will see that the four cluster solution has a low Semi-Partial R-Squared of 0.0226, while it is a workable solution in a segmentation setting. Moving to more clusters is not worthwhile because the Semi-Partial R-Squared will not drop significantly, while one only adds complexity, that is, more clusters.

- **Cluster History**

Cluster History

NCL	Clusters Joined		FREQ	SPRSQ	RSQ	ERSQ	CCC	PSF	PST2	Tie
30	CL54	CL38	10	0.0065	.659	.664	-.61	8.7	2.3	
29	CL71	CL37	14	0.0065	.653	.657	-.55	8.8	2.6	
28	CL60	CL52	9	0.0066	.646	.650	-.49	8.9	2.9	
27	OB147	CL41	9	0.0067	.640	.643	-.41	9.1	2.6	
26	CL97	CL117	7	0.0068	.633	.635	-.33	9.2	4.3	
25	CL69	CL59	7	0.0068	.626	.628	-.22	9.4	2.7	
24	CL45	CL43	7	0.0068	.619	.620	-.09	9.6	2.3	
23	CL81	CL44	8	0.0069	.612	.612	0.06	9.8	2.5	
22	CL66	CL33	13	0.0071	.605	.604	0.21	10.1	2.7	
21	CL63	CL22	17	0.0077	.598	.595	0.31	10.3	2.7	
20	CL28	CL61	15	0.0079	.590	.586	0.43	10.6	3.1	
19	CL48	CL31	15	0.0079	.582	.577	0.58	10.9	3.3	
18	CL72	CL109	5	0.0083	.573	.567	0.73	11.2	4.4	
17	CL21	CL55	21	0.0095	.564	.558	0.78	11.6	3.0	
16	CL23	CL35	16	0.0102	.554	.547	0.80	11.9	3.3	
15	CL25	CL27	16	0.0104	.543	.536	0.86	12.3	3.3	
14	CL36	CL18	11	0.0106	.533	.525	0.96	12.8	3.1	
13	CL39	CL30	19	0.0107	.522	.513	1.14	13.4	3.6	
12	CL26	CL78	10	0.0112	.511	.500	1.27	14.1	4.8	
11	CL34	CL32	16	0.0114	.500	.486	1.56	14.9	3.9	
10	CL19	CL24	22	0.0135	.486	.472	1.73	15.8	4.5	
9	CL16	CL12	26	0.0136	.472	.455	2.06	16.9	3.9	
8	CL20	CL10	37	0.0169	.456	.438	2.05	18.2	5.1	
7	CL29	CL9	40	0.0173	.438	.418	2.23	19.9	4.9	
6	CL17	CL13	40	0.0180	.420	.395	2.63	22.3	5.3	
5	CL7	CL11	56	0.0189	.401	.367	3.29	26.0	5.0	
4	CL14	CL6	51	0.0226	.379	.332	4.16	31.7	5.8	
3	CL5	CL8	93	0.0738	.305	.279	2.12	34.4	18.9	
2	CL4	CL15	67	0.0964	.209	.191	1.42	41.6	23.5	
1	CL3	CL2	160	0.2086	.000	.000	0.00	.	41.6	

This table summarizes the graphs **Criteria for the Number of Clusters** and **Cluster tree data for WORK.STNDSTANDARDIZEDTABLET_0000**. It represents the history of the clustering process and the relevant statistical figures in that table are the number of clusters (*NCL*), the clusters that joined the solution (*Clusters Joined*), the number of observation added per step (*FREQ*), the Semi-partial R-Squared (*SPRSQ*), the Cubic Clustering Criterion (*CCC*), the Pseudo F-statistic (*PFS*) and the Pseudo T-Squared statistic (*PST2*). The four cluster solution statistics are found in the row where *NCL* is 4.

4.2. Non-Hierarchical K-means Clustering

Managerial Problem and Dataset Description

The managerial problem and the dataset are the same as in the section 4.1. Hierarchical Clustering. Given that the Ward's minimum variance method identified four clusters as being the best clustering solution, four clusters are set during the K-means clustering method. The Data Analysis part of this section starts from the final output of section 4.1. Hierarchical Clustering.

Data Analysis

1. Right-click the previous **Cluster Analysis** task node in the process flow and select the **Modify Cluster Analysis** option.

2. In the **Cluster** pane, change the Cluster method to the **K-means algorithm** option to run a K-means clustering. Make sure to set the **Maximum number of clusters** option to 4 and to allow a reasonable amount of iterations of clustering optimization by setting the option **Maximum number of iterations** to 100.

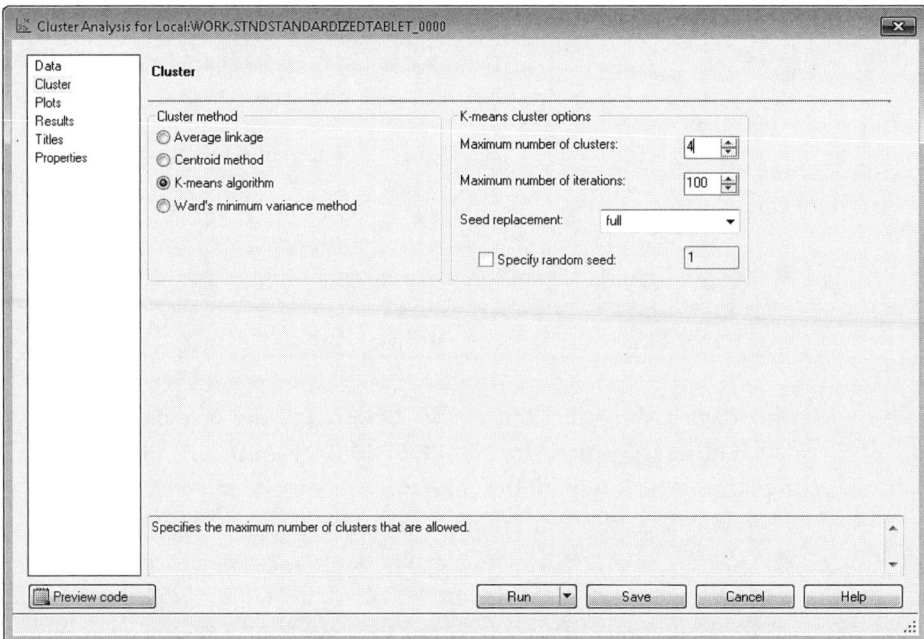

3. In the **Results** pane, make sure you tick **K-means clusters** option to output a new dataset that will contain two new variables, that is, a *Cluster* variable that indicates to which cluster a particular individual belongs, and a *Distance* variable that shows the distance from that individual to the cluster centre.

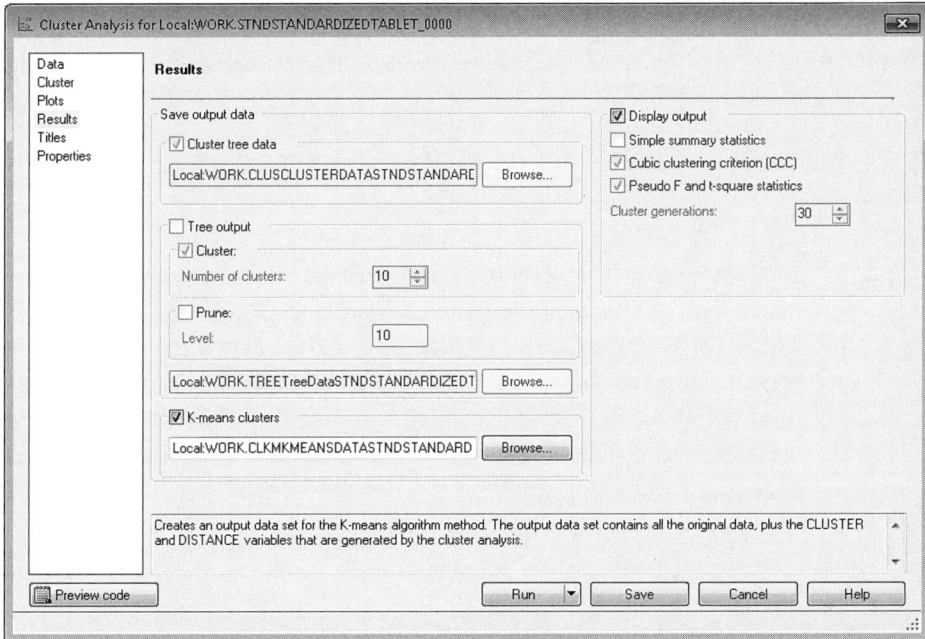

4. Click **Run** to run the modified **Cluster Analysis** task. A pop-up window appears that asks you whether you want to replace the results from the previous clustering. You click **No** and you will see that a new **Cluster Analysis** task node appears in the process flow, together with the output of the new modified clustering solution.

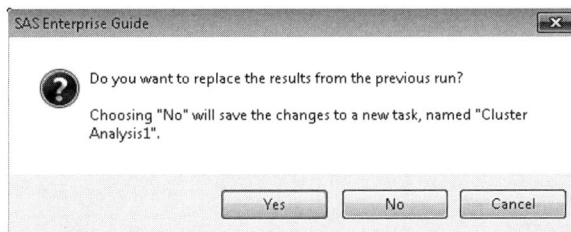

Interpretation

- **Cluster Summary**

			Cluster Summary			
Cluster	Frequency	RMS Std Deviation	Maximum Distance from Seed to Observation	Radius Exceeded	Nearest Cluster	Distance Between Cluster Centroids
1	60	0.8132	4.4873		4	2.7471
2	45	0.7959	3.8906		1	3.7354
3	17	0.7740	4.0151		2	4.3810
4	38	0.7675	4.0414		1	2.7471

The table shows the number of observations in each cluster (*Frequency*) and the root of the mean squared standard deviation (*RMS Std Deviation*). Other columns display the nearest cluster (*Nearest Cluster*) and the last column (*Distance Between Cluster Centroids*) shows the distance between the cluster centroid and the nearest cluster centroid. It enables us to evaluate the distance between the cluster and the nearest cluster. For instance, clusters one and four are the closest with a distance between the cluster centroids of 2.7471.

- **Statistics for Variables**

	Statistics for Variables			
Variable	Total STD	Within STD	R-Square	RSQ/(1-RSQ)
stnd_INNOVATOR	1.00000	0.73826	0.465252	0.870041
stnd_OFFICE SOFTWARE	1.00000	0.86838	0.260143	0.351613
stnd_PHONE	1.00000	0.92827	0.154582	0.182847
stnd_MESSAGE	1.00000	0.66138	0.570825	1.330054
stnd_E-BOOK	1.00000	0.86408	0.267456	0.365106
stnd_MUSIC	1.00000	0.80866	0.358403	0.558610
stnd_INFORMATION	1.00000	0.77189	0.415432	0.710665
stnd_VIDEO	1.00000	0.86355	0.268351	0.366775
stnd_EMAILS	1.00000	0.93407	0.143984	0.168202
stnd_SOCIAL NETWORK	1.00000	0.69394	0.527533	1.116549
stnd_INSTANT MESSENGER	1.00000	0.63675	0.602198	1.513815
stnd_PHOTOS	1.00000	0.68238	0.543147	1.188888
stnd_HIGH QUALITY DISPLAY	1.00000	0.86914	0.258857	0.349267
stnd_MONTHLY PRICE	1.00000	0.75568	0.439728	0.784847
stnd_PRICE	1.00000	0.74625	0.453616	0.830213
OVER-ALL	1.00000	0.79367	0.381967	0.618037

Pseudo F Statistic = 32.14
Approximate Expected Over-All R-Squared = 0.15157
Cubic Clustering Criterion = 46.860

This table displays statistics for the clustering variables. For each variable, the table lists the total standard deviation (*Total STD*), the pooled within-cluster standard deviation (*Within STD*) and the R-square value for predicting the variable from the cluster (*R-Square*). The higher the R-square, the higher the variable contributes to the cluster formation. In the last column (*RSQ/(1-RSQ)*), one finds the ratio of the between-cluster variance to the within-cluster variance. A high ratio means that the variable is important in differentiating between the clusters. In this case, the variables that discriminate the most clusters are *INSTANT MESSENGER, MESSAGE, PHOTOS, SOCIAL NETWORK, INNOVATOR* and *PRICE*.

Below, one can read the value for the Pseudo F statistic, the approximate expected overall R-squared and the CCC. The explanation of these statistics is presented in the section *Fundamentals* at the beginning of this chapter. One can use these statistics to compare solutions with different number of clusters. Nevertheless, the CCC must be greater than 2 or 3 to achieve a good clustering solution. One should be cautious if the CCC values are between 0 and 2. Large negative values can indicate that the dataset includes outliers. In this example, the CCC is equal to 46.860 which indicates that the solution obtained is good.

The tables **Cluster Means** and **Cluster Standard Deviation** cannot be interpreted because the variables are standardized. However, the next section (section 4.3. Profiling Clusters) explains how to obtain means for each variable and how to interpret the cluster profiles.

4.3. Profiling Clusters

The most important aspect during clustering from a marketing research perspective is to profile each cluster based on the average values of the original, non-standardized clustering variables. Practically, this is done by starting from the output dataset from the clustering algorithm. This dataset contains the original clustering variables and a variable *Cluster* that contains the cluster number per individual in the dataset. The purpose in the profiling phase of a clustering analysis is to calculate the mean value for each clustering variable per cluster. Afterwards, this output is used to profile the clusters based on the clustering variables. This profiling task is done using the **Summary Statistics** task. Here, the example is given for the K-means cluster solution.

1. Select the output dataset of the K-means clustering procedure and open the **Summary Statistics** task by clicking **Tasks** → **Describe** → **Summary Statistics...**

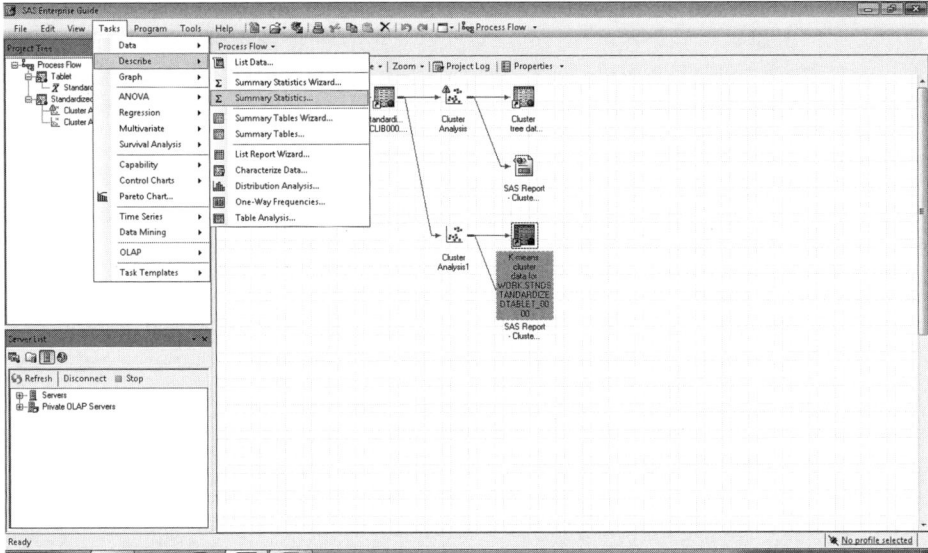

2. The selection pane opens at **Data**. Drag and drop all original non-standardized clustering variables under the **Analysis variables** role, then drag and drop the *Cluster* variable under the **Group analysis by** role to ask separated summaries per cluster.

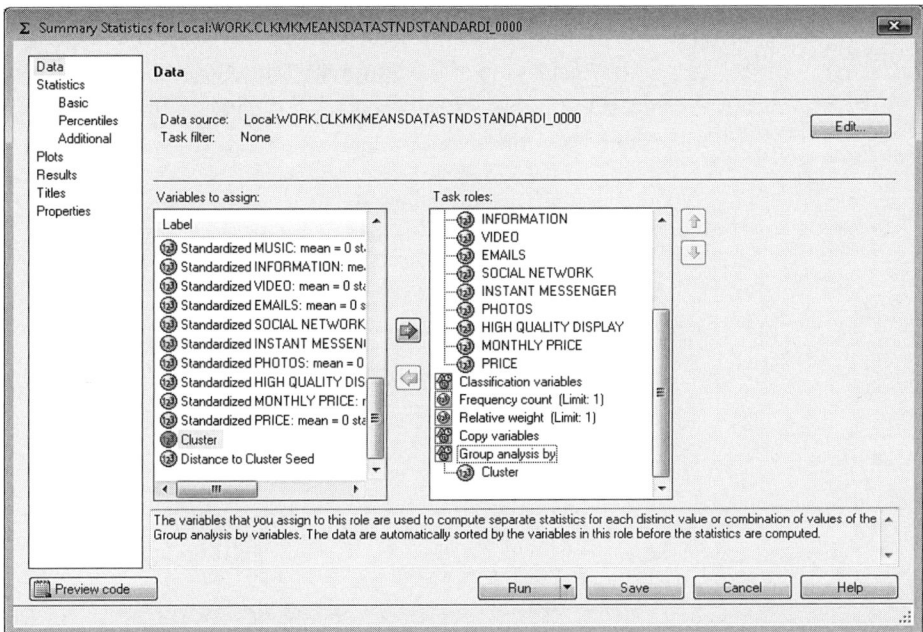

3. In the **Statistics** pane under **Basic**, make sure that the option **Mean** is ticked to ask the mean values of the clustering variables, and that the option **Number of observations** is selected to show the number of customers in the clusters.

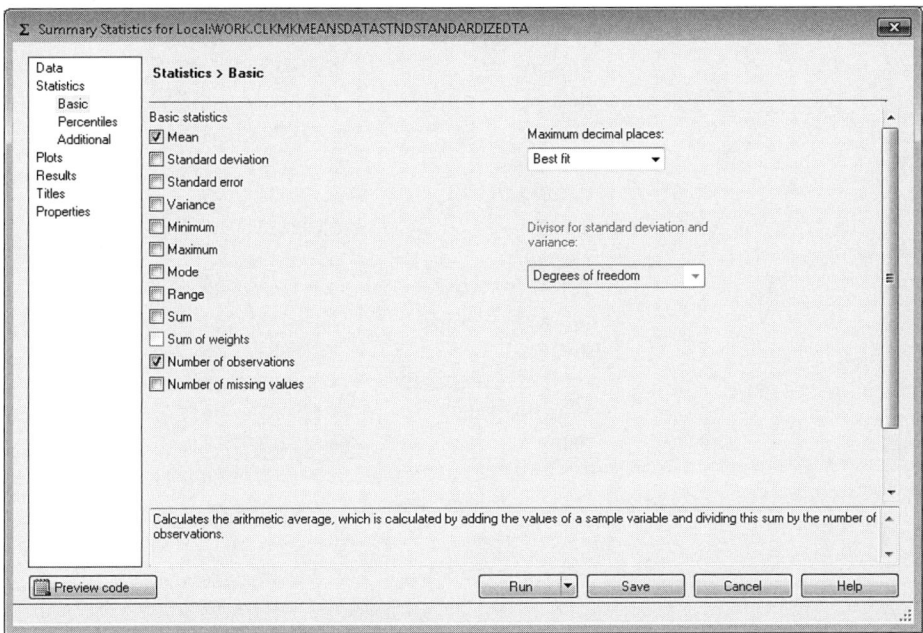

4. Click **Run** to finalize the cluster profiling process and check the profiles of the clusters in the **Results** tab of the **Summary Statistics** task. The profiling output is given below, while its interpretation is given in the **Managerial Recommendations** section.

Cluster=1

Variable	Mean	N
INNOVATOR	3.6333333	60
OFFICE SOFTWARE	3.8500000	60
PHONE	5.7833333	60
MESSAGE	5.8000000	60
E-BOOK	5.0666667	60
MUSIC	5.2333333	60
INFORMATION	3.7000000	60
VIDEO	3.4333333	60
EMAILS	4.3333333	60
SOCIAL NETWORK	5.9000000	60
INSTANT MESSENGER	5.4000000	60
PHOTOS	5.1166667	60
HIGH QUALITY DISPLAY	4.1000000	60
MONTHLY PRICE	24.9166667	60
PRICE	587.8333333	60

Cluster=2

Variable	Mean	N
INNOVATOR	2.2666667	45
OFFICE SOFTWARE	5.5555556	45
PHONE	5.4666667	45
MESSAGE	2.0888889	45
E-BOOK	3.7333333	45
MUSIC	3.7111111	45
INFORMATION	5.3333333	45
VIDEO	3.6222222	45
EMAILS	5.6444444	45
SOCIAL NETWORK	3.1555556	45
INSTANT MESSENGER	3.1111111	45
PHOTOS	2.2888889	45
HIGH QUALITY DISPLAY	4.0000000	45
MONTHLY PRICE	24.5555556	45
PRICE	568.2222222	45

Cluster=3		
Variable	Mean	N
INNOVATOR	2.4117647	17
OFFICE SOFTWARE	3.3529412	17
PHONE	4.2941176	17
MESSAGE	3.0000000	17
E-BOOK	6.0000000	17
MUSIC	6.1764706	17
INFORMATION	5.2941176	17
VIDEO	6.1176471	17
EMAILS	5.0000000	17
SOCIAL NETWORK	2.8823529	17
INSTANT MESSENGER	1.4117647	17
PHOTOS	1.9411765	17
HIGH QUALITY DISPLAY	5.3529412	17
MONTHLY PRICE	44.7058824	17
PRICE	783.5294118	17

Cluster=4		
Variable	Mean	N
INNOVATOR	5.1315789	38
OFFICE SOFTWARE	3.5526316	38
PHONE	5.8684211	38
MESSAGE	3.8947368	38
E-BOOK	3.6315789	38
MUSIC	3.5263158	38
INFORMATION	2.2631579	38
VIDEO	3.1842105	38
EMAILS	4.4210526	38
SOCIAL NETWORK	5.5526316	38
INSTANT MESSENGER	6.0000000	38
PHOTOS	5.2368421	38
HIGH QUALITY DISPLAY	5.8947368	38
MONTHLY PRICE	32.6315789	38
PRICE	710.5263158	38

Managerial Recommendations

The cluster analysis groups customers into four segments having divergent profiles regarding their usage frequency of computers and mobile device's features. The first cluster contains customers who are heavy users of their phone, message, e-book, social network, instant messenger and photo feature, but they have a low willingness to pay (*PRICE*=587.83 euros) compared to other segments, and thus maybe not that interesting to target. The second segment's usage habits fit more with a traditional laptop user. They have a high usage frequency for office software, phone, information and email. Moreover, their willingness to pay is also quite low. The third segment is the smallest one with only 17 customers, but has usage habits that fit with tablet computers. Indeed, they heavily use e-books, music, information, video and email. They care about a high quality display and their willingness to pay is high (*PRICE*=783.52 euros). The fourth segment has a high usage of phone, social network, instant messenger and photos. They like a high quality display and their willingness to pay is high (*PRICE*=710.53 euros). Moreover, they consider themselves as innovators. These features apply to smartphone users. Therefore, the two segments that are more willing to purchase a tablet computer are the third and the fourth segments. Their sizes are 10.63 per cent and 23.75 per cent respectively of the total sample size. If we consider that the sample is representative of the population under study, the company can target 34.35 per cent of the market. The features to be emphasized in the communication campaign must be adapted to each segment according to their usage habits.

Further Reading

Aldenderfer, M.S. and Blashfield, R.K. (1984), *Cluster Analysis*, Series: Quantitative Applications in the Social Sciences, Sage Publications.

Everitt B.S., Landau S., Leese, M. and Stahl, D. (2011), *Cluster Analysis*, 5th edition, Wiley Series in Probability and Statistics, Wiley-Interscience.

Kaufman, K. and Rousseeuw, P.J. (2005), *Finding Groups in Data: An Introduction to Cluster Analysis*, Wiley Series in Probability and Statistics, 1st edition, Wiley-Interscience.

Punj, G. and Steward, D.W. (1983), Cluster Analysis in Marketing Research: Review and Suggestions for Application, *Journal of Marketing Research*, 20 2, pp. 134–148.

Chapter 5

Hypothesis Testing

Objectives

1. Understand the purpose of statistical hypothesis testing.

2. Describe the difference between parametric tests and non-parametric tests.

3. Understand parametric hypothesis testing and the associated statistics.

4. Describe the non-parametric hypothesis testing process and the associated statistics.

Fundamentals

This chapter explains the different types of tests one should use when confronted with managerial situations that require statistical hypothesis testing. Hypothesis testing is a statistical decision-making method that makes use of data from an experimental set-up, surveys or pure observational data collection. The phenomenon is said to be statistically significant if the researcher is sure that the phenomenon is unlikely to happen by chance alone, given a predefined confidence level on the results (usually set at 95 per cent, a rule that we will follow throughout this chapter). Statistical hypothesis testing makes use of two different types of hypotheses, the null hypothesis (H_0) and the alternative hypothesis (H_1). The null hypothesis is the hypothesis that is currently true and deals with equalities. The alternative hypothesis is the hypothesis that the researcher tries to get confirmed by the survey if he searches for differences.

Hypothesis testing is divided in two types of tests, that is, parametric tests and non-parametric tests. The criteria that differentiate the two different types of tests are the level of measurement of the data and the normality assumption of the dependent variable. In order to apply a parametric test to the dataset, the measurement level of the dependent variable must be interval- or ratio-scaled, while the distribution of the dependent variable must be normal. These variables are defined as continuous variables. Non-parametric tests are applied to lower-level measured variables, that is, nominal or ordinal variables. Both nominal and ordinal variables are considered as categorical variables in the remainder of this chapter. Furthermore, continuous variables, that is, interval-scaled or ratio-scaled variables, which do not satisfy the normality assumption, are also considered as ordinal variables. Although parametric tests are statistically speaking more powerful than non-parametric tests, it is possible to employ a non-parametric test to a continuous variable.

Strictly statistically speaking, a variable measured with a Likert-scale is considered as an ordinal variable. However, research literature considers variables measured with 5 or more points Likert-scales to be normally distributed and consequently, as continuous variables.

Furthermore, the selection of the appropriate (non-)parametric test is made according to two main conditions:

- *The number of samples considered in the independent variable*
  The number of samples to be compared during hypothesis testing is a criterion to be taken into consideration when choosing the correct statistical test. The options are one sample, two samples or more than two samples. If you have only one sample, the characteristics of that sample are compared to a predefined threshold or standard. However, when one has at least two samples, the problem often refers to comparing samples to one other.

- *The dependency of the samples considered in the independent variable*
  If the number of samples is at least two, the dependency of the samples is considered as an additional criterion for statistical test choice. Two different types of samples exist, that is, *independent* and *paired* samples. The samples are considered to be independent when the data is randomly drawn from different non-overlapping populations. For instance, if you survey males and females, you are sure that the sample of males is independent of the sample of females. On the other hand, samples are considered to be paired or dependent when the samples are the same. For instance, if you survey people before experiencing an event and after experiencing it, these two samples (before and after) are dependent because they contain the same group of respondents.

In order to facilitate the reading of this chapter, these two elements are listed as keywords under the header of each hypothesis test.

5.1. Parametric Tests

In marketing research, parametric tests are used during hypothesis testing in situations where the dependent variable is continuous. In other words, the dependent variable needs to be interval- or ratio-scaled and it should have a normal distribution. An overview of the different parametric tests explored in this book is given below.

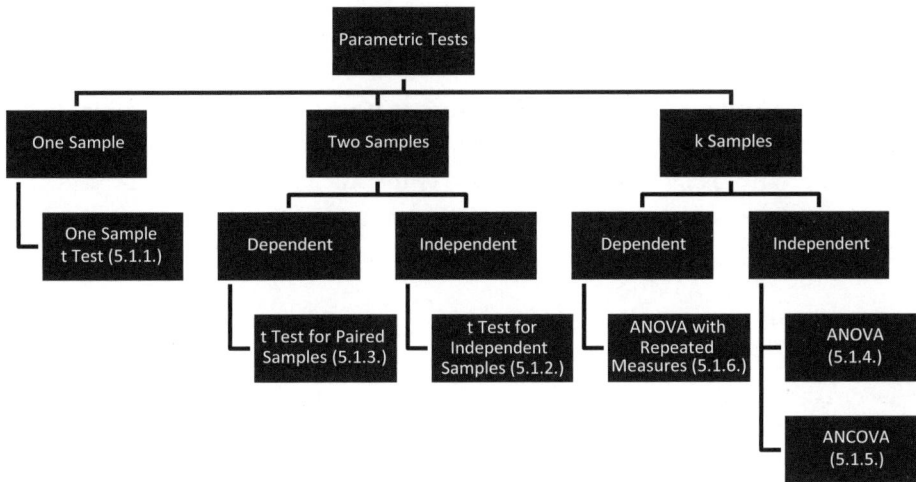

5.1.1. ONE SAMPLE T TEST

Keywords: one sample, standard

> A one sample t Test is a parametric statistical hypothesis test that compares whether the mean of a normally distributed variable is equal to a predefined standard.

Managerial Problem

Suppose that a gas station owner wonders whether he may increase the price of fuel, knowing that the neighbouring tanking stations will remain at the official price. Given that his clients are acclaiming the good quality of the tanking service he provides, he believes that the customers are willing to pay more for the fuel. Based upon experience and considering that all prices are comparable, the manager knows that, on a normal weekday, the average amount of fuel served at his station is 37.12 litres. Practically, he decides to increase the prices for the tanking service and, after a couple of weeks, he wants to check whether the average fuel served during a normal weekday diverges from his reference point of 37.12 litres.

Translation of the Managerial Problem into Statistical Notions

In this context, the problem refers to finding out whether there is a statistically significant difference between the standard (the average fuel served before the price increase) and the mean fuel tanked on any day after the price increase.

A one sample t Test is appropriate in this situation. One sample of observations taken on a normal weekday after the price increase is collected and its corresponding mean fuel quantity tanked on that day is compared to the standard, that is, the average fuel served before the price increase.

Hypotheses

The managerial problem is translated into the following hypotheses:

H_0: There is no significant difference between the mean tanked quantity after the price increase and the standard of 37.12 litres.

H_1: There is a significant difference between the mean tanked quantity after the price increase and the standard of 37.12 litres.

Dataset Description

The SAS data file to consider is named *Tanking.sas7bdat*. It contains 481 observations relative to 481 customers who tanked at the gas station a couple of weeks after the price increase. The variables to consider are:

• The identification of customers (*cust*).

• The dependent variable which corresponds to the amount of litres bought by each consumer after the price increase (*serving*).

Data Analysis

A one sample t Test is carried out using the **t Test** task.

1. Add the *Tanking.sas7bdat* dataset to the SAS Enterprise Guide environment.

2. Go to **Tasks** → **ANOVA** → **t Test...**

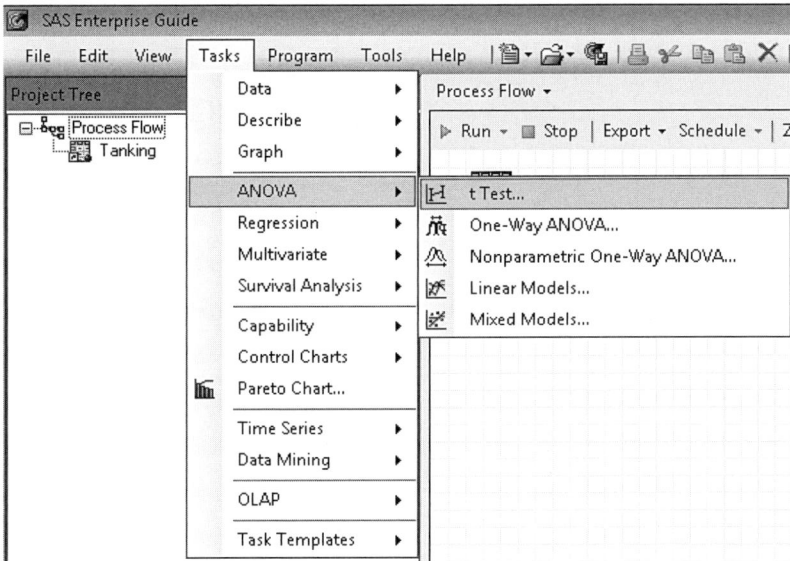

3. The option pane **t Test type** becomes available. In the **Choose t Test type** section of the pane, select the option **One Sample**.

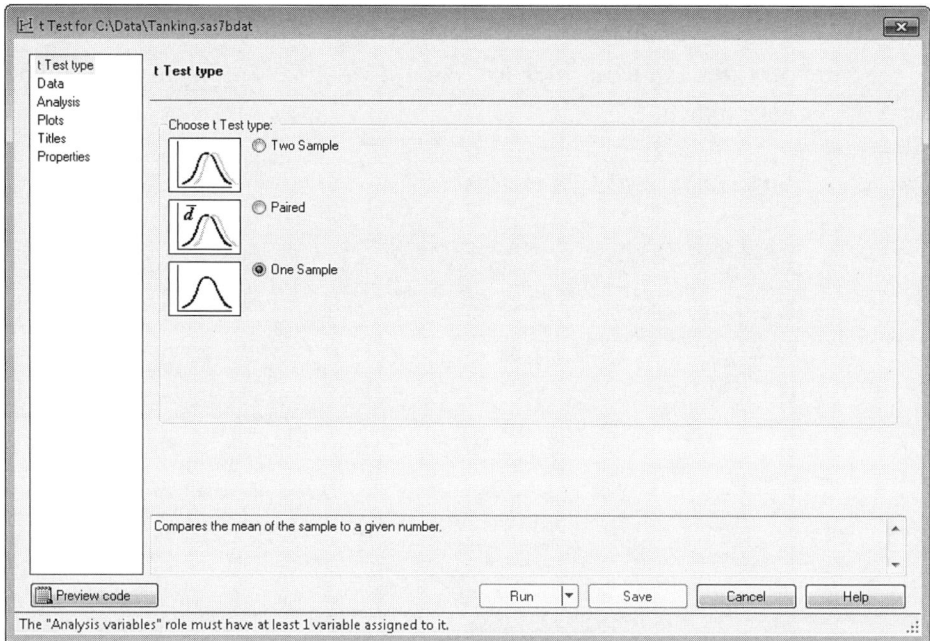

4.   Select **Data** from the selection pane and drop the *serving* variable to the **Analysis variables** role as it is the variable to be analyzed.

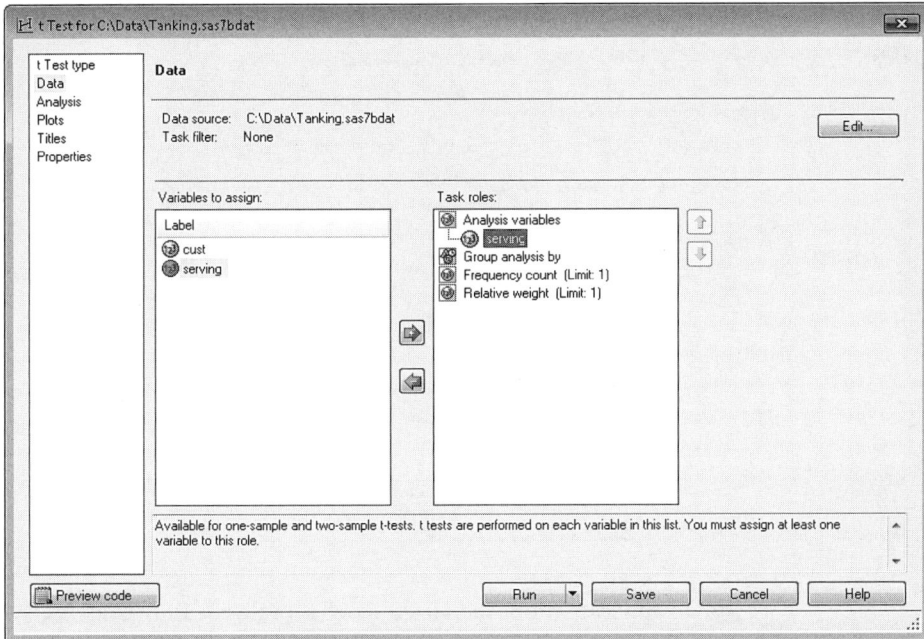

5.   The next step is to indicate the value to which the mean consumption should be compared to (or the standard of 37.12 litres). Select **Analysis** in the selection pane. In the new window under the **Null hypothesis** section, you indicate the value of the standard or 37.12 in this case.

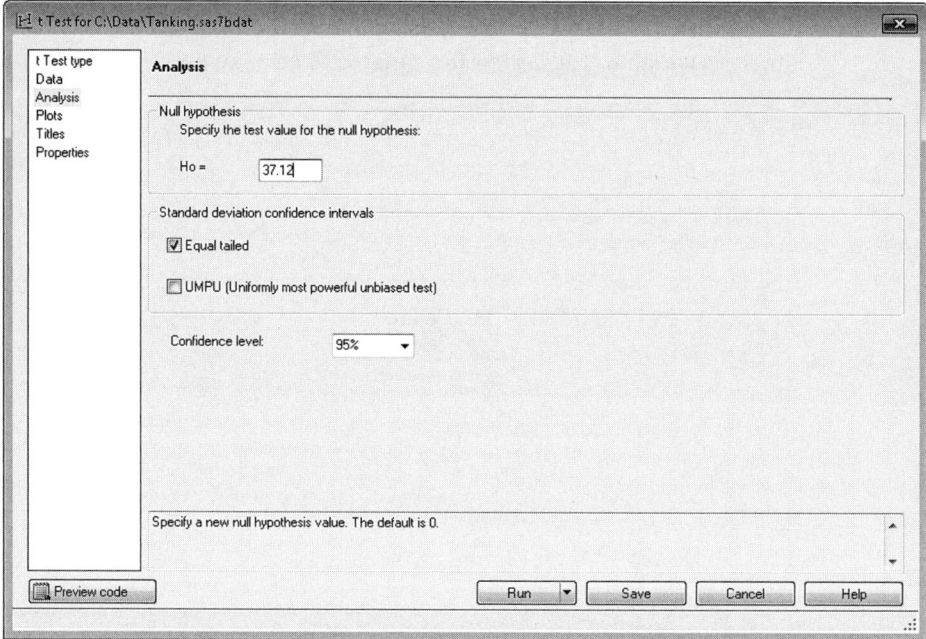

6.   Click **Run** to generate the results for the one sample t Test. The results are shown in the **Results** tab.

Interpretation

*   **N Mean Std Dev Std Error Minium Maximum**

N	Mean	Std Dev	Std Err	Minimum	Maximum
481	36.9986	8.2410	0.3758	14.5000	57.8800

The first output table informs us that the average tanking is 36.9986 litres and that the standard deviation is equal to 8.241 litres. The minimum and maximum quantities tanked are 14.5 litres and 57.88 litres.

*   **DF t Value Pr > |t|**

DF	t Value	Pr > |t|
480	-0.32	0.7469

There is no significant difference between the average fuel quantity sold on the normal weekday after the price increase and the standard of 37.12

litres. The t-value is -0.32 and the associated p-value is 0.7469 and larger than 0.05. This means that the null hypothesis H_0 cannot be rejected.

Nevertheless, it is sometimes not merely a hypothesis of difference but a hypothesis of superiority or inferiority towards the standard. In this case, one could expect that a price increase would lead to inferior sales of fuels. A hypothesis of inferiority would then be stated. When interpreting the results, one should then divide the p-value by two. In the tanking setting, the p-value is 0.7469. Divided by two, the new p-value remains bigger than 0.05. In sum, the owner does not have to worry, because the difference is still not significant at a 95 per cent confidence level and thus the price increase does not affect his sales. More concretely, the mean of fuel served on the day after the price increase, 36.999 litres, is statistically equal to the standard of 37.12 litres.

Managerial Recommendations

Based on the statistical findings, it appears that clients are willing to pay more to tank in the gas station, because there is no significant difference between the average quantity sold before and after the price increase. The change in price has not affected clients' willingness to tank at the station. The manager's decision to ask for a higher price seems fair and smart!

5.1.2. T TEST FOR INDEPENDENT SAMPLES

Keywords: two samples, independent samples

A t Test for two independent samples is a parametric statistical hypothesis test that compares whether the means of two normally distributed independent samples are equal.

Managerial Problem

Suppose that public authorities, who are aware of the obesity epidemic, decide to invest in a new promotion campaign to stimulate the eating of healthy food. Knowing that public funds are limited, the effectiveness of the foreseen campaign needs to be demonstrated before the budgets are granted. A competition between two advertising agencies proposing each a different advertisement is therefore organized in order to identify the most effective campaign. Considering the campaign's objective of trying to increase healthy food consumption, it was decided that the quantity of fruit eaten after exposure to the advertisements was the most appropriate effectiveness indicator. Individuals taking part in the controlled experiment are randomly assigned to one of the two advertisements and the average group fruit consumptions are compared. It is expected that the advertisement that persuades people to consume more fruits will give the best return on investment. This advertisement will be the one broadcast on all national television channels.

Translation of the Managerial Problem into Statistical Notions

This managerial problem is translated to identify whether or not there is a significant difference between the average quantities of fruit consumed in the two different groups. If so, one should identify in which group and thus for which advertisement the average strawberry quantity is significantly higher.

In this context, a t Test for independent samples is appropriate, because two means of independent samples are considered. The two samples are independent, since each individual in the controlled experiment is exposed to only one advertisement. In sum, the group of individuals exposed to the first advertisement did not see the second advertisement and vice versa. They are therefore considered independent from each other.

Hypotheses

The managerial problem is translated and the following hypotheses are presented:

H_0: There is no significant difference in the mean strawberry consumption between the respondents exposed to advertisement 1 and those exposed to advertisement 2.

H_1: There is a significant difference in the mean strawberry consumption between the respondents exposed to advertisement 1 and those exposed to advertisement 2.

Dataset Description

The data file to consider is the Excel 2007 file *Obesity.xlsx*. It contains 199 observations. This means that in total 199 individuals have taken part in the comparison process. The variables to consider are the following:

- The respondent's identification number (*ID*).

- The respondent's gender (*Gender*).

- The advertisements to which individuals are exposed (*Type_of_ad*). 100 adults have been exposed to advert number 1 identified as *'Action'*, 99 individuals to advert number 2, called *'Threat'*.

- The dependent variable representing the weight expressed in grams of the number of strawberries eaten by the respondent (*Cstrawberries*).

Data Analysis

In order to run a t Test on independent samples, the **t Test** task is applied.

1. Add the *Obesity.xlsx* to your SAS Enterprise Guide project.

2. To open the **t Test** task, select **Tasks** → **ANOVA** → **t Test...**

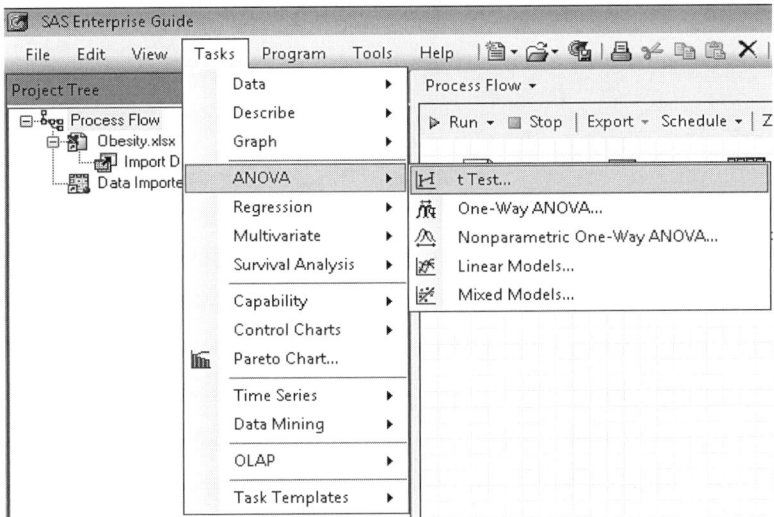

3. The selection pane opens and the option pane **t Test type** is available. In the **Choose t Test type** section, select the option **Two Sample**.

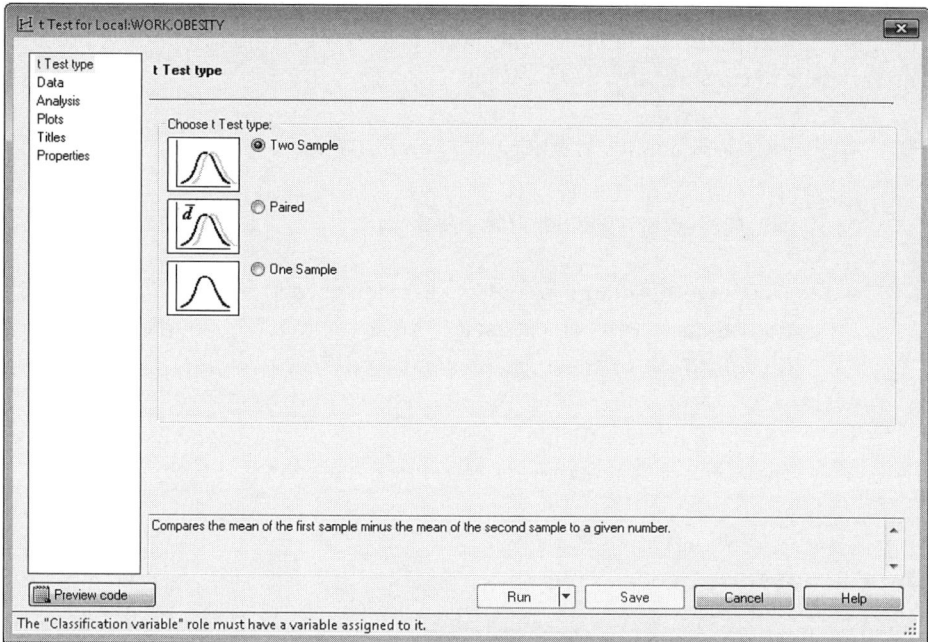

4. Select **Data** in the selection pane to incorporate the relevant variables in the t Test. Drag and drop the variable that indicates to which of the two groups a respondent belongs, the *Type_of_ad* variable, to the **Classification variable** role, while you add the variable of interest, the *Cstrawberries* variable, to the **Analysis variables** role.

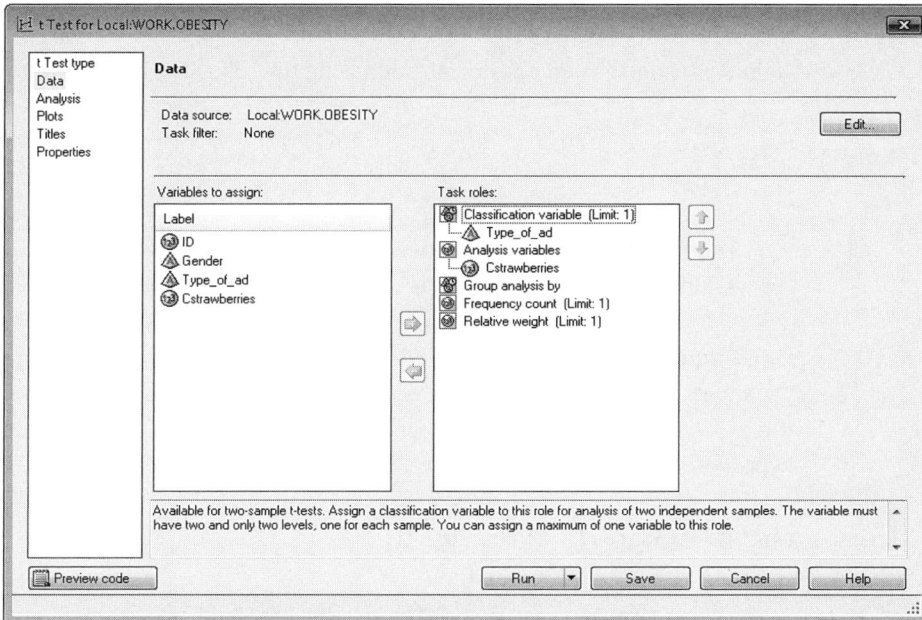

5. Now, click **Run** to get the results for the independent sample t Test. The results are shown in the Results tab.

Interpretation

The interpretation of the t Test for independent samples proceeds in several steps.

- **Equality of Variances**

	Equality of Variances			
Method	Num DF	Den DF	F Value	Pr > F
Folded F	99	98	1.12	0.5676

An assumption in interpreting an independent sample t Test is to verify whether the variances between the different samples are equal. Knowing whether or not the variances are equal impacts the comparison of the means between the different samples. If the variances are equal and one is sure that the variances of the samples are comparable, one is allowed to compare the means. If the variances are unequal, a statistical correction is needed (and automatically operated by SAS Enterprise Guide) to make the means between the groups comparable. The test of equality of variances is performed on the dataset having the following hypotheses:

H_0:   There is no statistical difference between the variances of the two samples.

H_1:   There is a statistical difference between the variances of the two samples.

If the **Equality of Variances** table is explored, one concludes that the variances of the two samples are equal because the F-value is 1.12 and the associated p-value is 0.5676, and is thus larger than 0.05. The null hypothesis is accepted.

- **Method Variances DF t Value Pr > |t|**

Method	Variances	DF	t Value	Pr > |t|
Pooled	Equal	197	-5.92	<.0001
Satterthwaite	Unequal	196.55	-5.92	<.0001

Depending on the equality of the variances, the researcher finds the results of the t Test on different lines in the **Method Variances DF t Value Pr > |t|** table. If the variances are not significantly different, the result of the t Test is read in the row where the column *Variances* equals *Equal*. If the variances are significantly different, the p-value of the t Test is read in the row where the column *Variances* is *Unequal*.

Given that the variances between the two groups are equal, the p-value is checked in the row where the column *Variances* is *Equal*. The null hypothesis (H_0) of the independent t Test is rejected. Its t-value is -5.92 and the associated p-value is smaller than 0.0001 and thus smaller than the threshold probability of 0.05. In sum, the average number of strawberries consumed between the two groups after being exposed to the different advertisements is significantly different. The following question arises: which type of advertisement, *Action* or *Threat,* influences the individuals the most in consuming strawberries?

- **Type_of_ad N Mean Std Dev Std Err Minimum Maximum**

Type_of_ad	N	Mean	Std Dev	Std Err	Minimum	Maximum
Action	100	87.9754	29.6927	2.9693	16.7900	157.3
Threat	99	112.2	28.0252	2.8166	73.6900	179.9
Diff (1-2)		-24.2274	28.8752	4.0939		

This table offers the analyst the answer on which advertisement influences more individuals to consume strawberries. To identify the most effective advertisement, one looks at the *Mean* column containing the mean strawberry consumption for the *Action* and the *Threat* advertisements. We see that the mean consumption of individuals exposed to the *Action* advertisement is 87.9754 grams, while the mean consumption increases to 112.2 grams when people watched the *Threat* advertisement.

Managerial Recommendations

The t Test identifies a significant difference in terms of fruit consumption between the groups exposed to two different types of advertisement. We notice that the threat advertisement induces a higher consumption on average. Therefore, we recommend that the health authorities fund the agency that has proposed the threat advertisement. The public authority should invest in broadcasting the threat type of message in order to increase the healthy consumptions amongst its citizens.

5.1.3. T TEST FOR PAIRED SAMPLES

Keywords: two samples, dependent samples

A t Test for paired samples is a parametric statistical hypothesis test that compares whether the means of the two dependent samples are equal given that the difference between the two samples is normally distributed.

Managerial Problem

Before massively investing into a new recipe for lasagne, a food company wants to evaluate its impact upon the purchase intentions of its consumers. More specifically, the company would like to be sure that the new formula is not going to be negatively perceived by the current consumer. The company would certainly not like to lose customers! Furthermore, they would like to identify whether or not the new recipe is appreciated differently amongst women and men in order to personalize their communication strategy accordingly. For instance, they consider either insisting on the recipe change in women's magazines and/or in the commercial breaks around men's television programmes depending on who really likes the new recipe. Therefore, a survey is conducted whereby 200 people, 100 women and 100 men, are involved to give their opinion on the new lasagne recipe. The experimental set-up is conducted as follows: before tasting the new lasagne, current customers are asked to evaluate their intentions to buy the old recipe lasagne. Afterwards, the new formula lasagne is given to these 200 people in order to get them taste the new flavour. Finally, after the product trial, the same purchase intention question is asked again. By contrasting the answers on these two purchase intention questions, that is, before and after tasting the new lasagne, the company should be able to verify whether the new recipe could attract the current customers or whether there would be a negative effect on future sales by introducing this new lasagne type. Finally, the company is able to analyze the impact of trying the product on the purchase intentions separately for men and women.

Translation of the Managerial Problem into Statistical Notions

Here one wants to explore whether a significant difference exists between the means of the purchase intention questions (before and after trial) asked on dependent samples of individuals. In this setting, the intentions to buy the old recipe product are compared with the intentions to buy the new recipe one. The two samples, before and after trying the product, are dependent, because the people in the two samples are exactly the same individuals. Furthermore, this statistical test is run twice, once for the men and once for the women, to check whether the impact of trying the product is different for males and females.

Paired sample t Tests are typical hypothesis tests for managerial problems that involve a before event question and after event question asked to the same respondents.

Hypotheses

This managerial problem is converted into the following null and alternative hypothesis:

H_0: There is no significant difference between the mean purchase intentions measured before and after the new product trial.

H_1: There is a significant difference between the mean purchase intentions measured before and after the new product trial.

The above hypotheses are now further split, as the company wants to know whether the difference in purchase intention before and after trying the new lasagne is significantly different among respondents from the same gender. For (wo)men the following hypotheses are obtained:

H_0: There is no significant difference between the mean purchase intentions measured before and after the new product trial amongst (wo)men.

H_1: There is a significant difference between the mean purchase intentions measured before and after the new product trial amongst (wo)men.

Dataset Description

The data to use is to be found under *Recipe.sas7bdat*. It contains 200 observations of which 100 females (*F*) and 100 males (*M*). Three variables are considered here:

- The consumers' gender (*gender*).

- The purchase intentions before the product trial (*purchase_intention_before*).

- The purchase intentions after the product trial (*purchase_intention_after*).

These purchase intention variables are measured via various items on a 7-point Likert-scale (with 1 = very low intention to purchase to 7 = very high intention to purchase) and the average score is represented by the variables *purchase_intention_before* and *purchase_intention_after*.

Data Analysis

In order to run a t Test on dependent samples, you use the **t Test** task. This task is run as follows:

1. Add the dataset *Recipe.sas7bdat* to the SAS Enterprise Guide environment.

2. Go to **Task** → **ANOVA** → **t Test...**

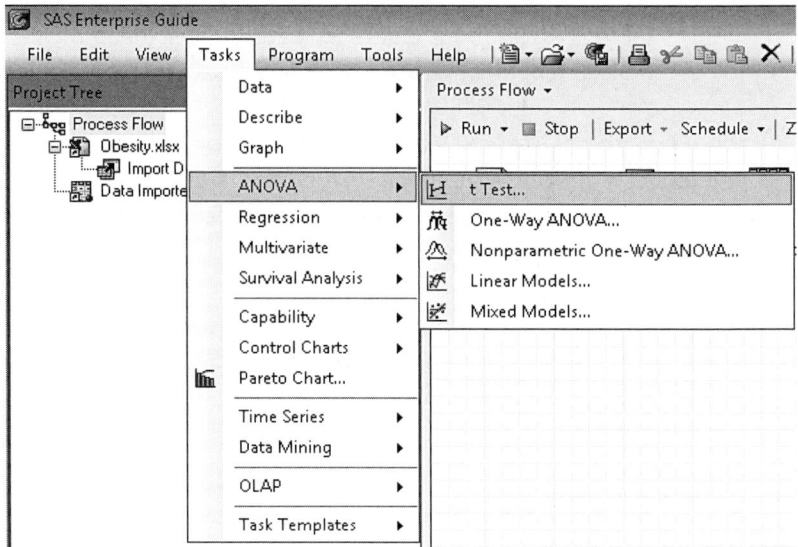

3.   The option pane **t Test type** appears. In the **Choose t Test type** pane, select the option **Paired**.

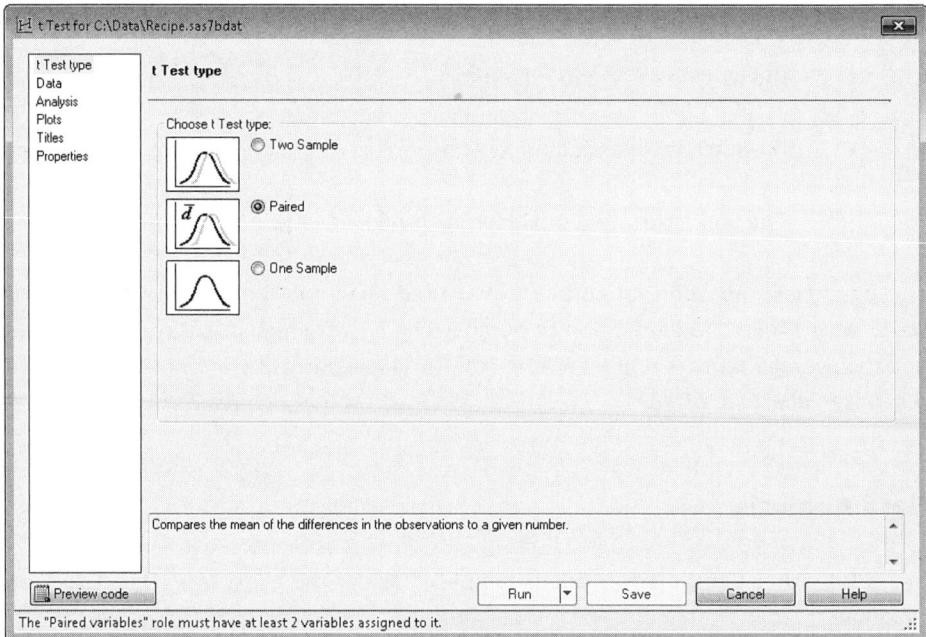

4.   Now go to **Data**. Under the **Task roles** option two variables have to be assigned to the **Paired variables** role. In other words, these variables must

come from the same sample and they contain the answers on the before and after event question. The means of these two variables are compared during statistical hypothesis testing. In our case, the *purchase_intention_after* and the *purchase_intention_before* variables are assigned to it.

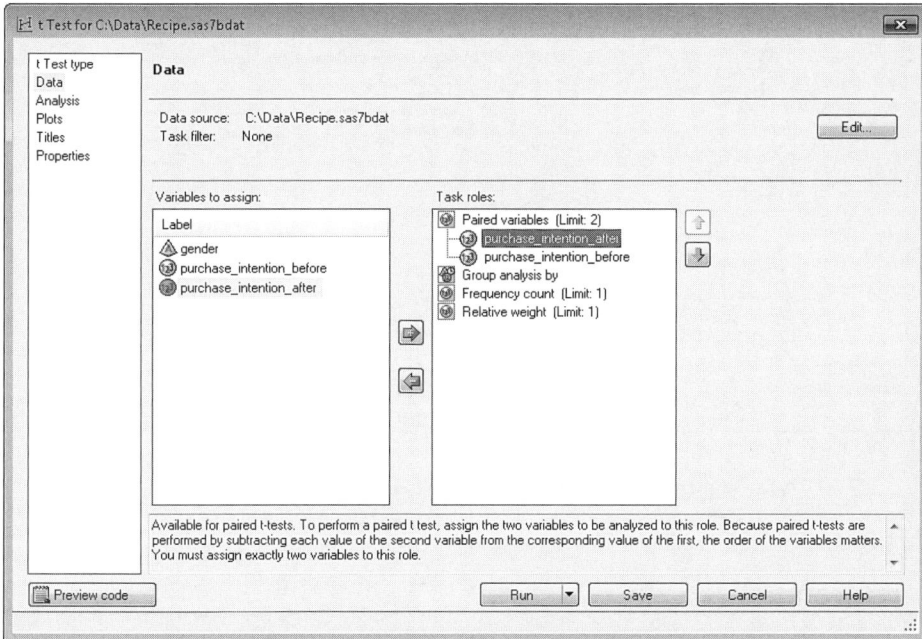

At this stage, we could already ask SAS Enterprise Guide to provide results by clicking on **Run**. They would tell whether for the total sample, that is, women and men taken altogether, a difference exists between the prior- and post-purchase intentions. However, remember that the company wants to know whether there is a positive reaction towards the new recipe within each gender group. We have to tell SAS Enterprise Guide to provide this information per gender. In order to do so, drag and drop the variable *gender* to the **Group analysis by** role so that SAS Enterprise Guide knows for which sub-groups it should run separate paired sample t Tests.

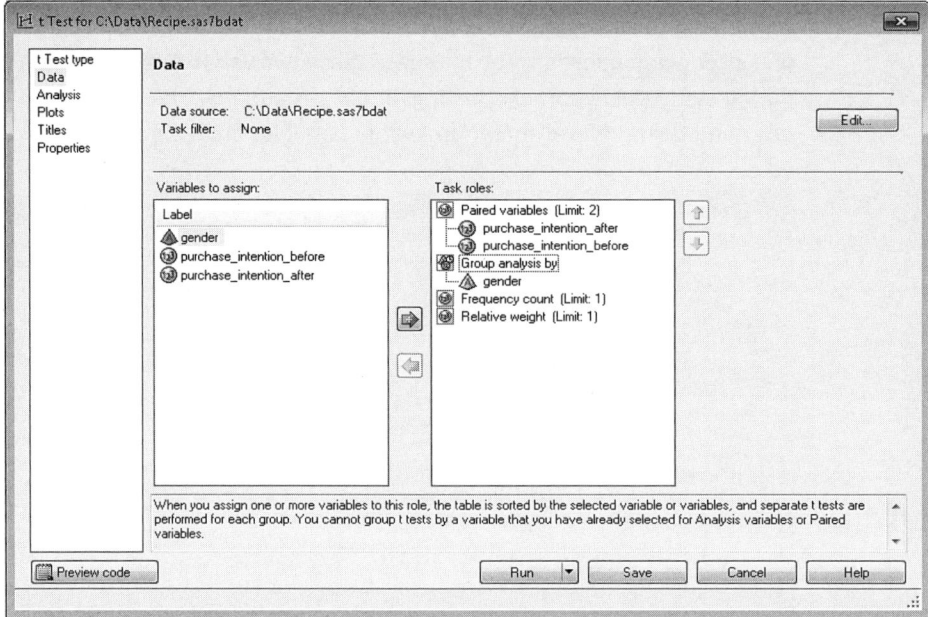

5.   Now click **Run** and check the results in the **Results** tab.

Interpretation

The t Test for dependent samples provides different sets of tables according to the different levels in the **Group analysis by** variable. In this setting, two sets of tables are produced, one set for the males and one for the females. The paired sample t Test does not impose an equal variance testing between the two groups (before and after trying the new product) because the characteristics of the individuals are inherently the same and the mean difference between the two groups (before and after trying the product) is exclusively dedicated to the trial.

- **gender = F**

  Difference: purchase_intention_after – purchase_intention_before

  gender=F

N	Mean	Std Dev	Std Err	Minimum	Maximum
100	0.7960	1.9147	0.1915	-5.7000	4.3800

Mean	95% CL Mean		Std Dev	95% CL Std Dev	
0.7960	0.4161	1.1759	1.9147	1.6811	2.2243

DF	t Value	Pr > |t|	DF	t Value	Pr > |t|
99	4.16	<.0001	99	4.16	<.0001

This table shows the results for the paired sample t Test for the female group. By exploring the p-value under the *DF t Value Pr > |t|* header, we can see that the t-value is equal to 4.16 and that the p-value is smaller than 0.0001, and smaller than 0.05. The null hypothesis (H_0) is rejected. This means that that there is a significant difference for women between the purchase intentions before tasting the new lasagne and after tasting it.

- **gender = M**

  Difference: purchase_intention_after – purchase_intention_before

  gender=M

N	Mean	Std Dev	Std Err	Minimum	Maximum
100	0.0275	2.0947	0.2095	-5.8900	4.3300

Mean		95% CL Mean	Std Dev	95% CL Std Dev	
0.0275	-0.3881	0.4431	2.0947	1.8391	2.4333

DF	t Value	Pr > |t|
99	0.13	0.8958

This table shows the results for the paired sample t Test for the male group. The t-value is 0.13 and the p-value of this test are found under the *DF t Value Pr > |t|* header and it indicates that for men the null hypothesis (H_0) cannot be rejected; the p-value is 0.8958 and thus larger than 0.05.

At this stage, it should be stressed that although we know that men are not sensitive to the new recipe while women are in terms of purchase intentions, we still do not know whether the change in women's intentions to purchase the new lasagne is positive or not. This is easily checked by looking at the mean difference in the corresponding tables under **gender = F** and **gender = M**. The mean difference is defined in the overall title **Difference: purchase_intention_after – purchase_intention_before**, while the value of the mean difference is found in the *Mean* column under the header *N Mean Std Dev Std Err Minimum Maximum*. If the mean difference is positive, this means that the mean of variable *purchase_intention_after* is higher than the mean value of *purchase_intention_before* and vice versa.

As women tend to have significant different purchase intentions as a result of trying the product, we check this value in the **gender = F** table. There you see that the mean difference value is 0.7960. This indicates that women are satisfied by the new recipe resulting in increased average purchase intentions after trying it.

However, men's intentions to buy show a very small mean difference (0.0275 under *Mean* in **gender=M**). This means that the difference between the intentions to purchase before and after trying the new recipe is so small that is not statistically significant.

Managerial Recommendations

The t Test for paired data shows that the intentions to purchase the lasagne before and after the trial of the new recipe differ significantly for women, while men tend to be insensitive to the recipe change. Furthermore, women tend to have an increased purchase intention after the product trial. In sum, the company should invest in this new formula, because the influence identified on purchase intentions is never negative. Concerning their promotion campaigns, the company should realize that investing in the creation of new television advertisements emphasizing the new recipe is not worthwhile when broadcasted before, during or after men's programmes. Communication on the recipe change for men is useless as men do not seem to be sensitive to this recipe change. However, the company would certainly gain from print advertisements for the new lasagne which address women.

5.1.4. ANALYSIS OF VARIANCE (ANOVA)

5.1.4.1. One-way ANOVA

Keywords: k samples, independent samples

> A one-way ANOVA is a parametric statistical hypothesis test that compares whether the means of more than two independent samples described by one factor are equal.

Managerial Problem

An Internet clothing company, aware of the advantages of consumer segmentation, has been segmenting its customers for the last few years. Based upon behavioural segmentation, four customer segments have been identified: heavy users, medium users, light users and ad-hoc users. Furthermore, the company recently issued a satisfaction survey and it wants to evaluate if satisfaction differences exist among the customer segments. More specifically, they would like to identify which segment(s) of consumers is (are) the least happy with the service provided. The idea is then to develop a specific marketing plan with special rewards in order to increase the level of satisfaction among these consumers with low satisfaction.

Translation of the Managerial Problem into Statistical Notions

The managerial context intends to compare the average satisfaction levels amongst the four consumer segments. In other words, we have to determine whether or not there is a significant difference between the various mean levels of satisfaction across the four segments. The type of segment an individual belongs to represents the independent variable (also called the factor).

Consequently, a one-way ANOVA is the appropriate test in this situation, because it compares the means when more than two groups are considered. Furthermore, this test assumes independent samples. In our case, each customer is only part of one segment at the time, that is, the consumer belongs to the heavy, medium, light or ad-hoc user segment for the e-commerce website. This results in the fulfilment of the independency assumption.

Running separate independent two sample t Tests that compare the mean satisfaction levels of two segments at a time is not appropriate, because this would lead to the underestimation of the real error rate, that is, the probability of making a mistake when rejecting the null hypothesis (H_0). The error rate indeed cumulates every time a statistical test is performed on the same data. This phenomenon is known as the family-wise or experiment-wise error rate. Since no prior expectations relative to the differences in satisfaction levels between the different segments are expected, post-hoc tests as part of the one-way ANOVA test help us find out where the differences among the segments are, that is, which segments differ significantly in terms of satisfaction. In other words, a post-hoc test compares the relative satisfaction level between two segments taking into account the family-wise error.

Hypotheses

The null and alternative hypothesis for the one-way ANOVA are expressed as follows:

H_0: There are no significant differences in mean satisfaction level between the four segments.

H_1: There is at least one segment that shows a significant difference with the others in mean satisfaction level.

Dataset Description

The SAS data file to consider is the *Ecommerce.sas7bdat*. It contains 200 observations. The variables to consider are the following:

- An indicator representing one of the four behavioural segments, that is, *Heavy Users*, *Medium Users*, *Light Users* or *Ad-hoc Users* is considered as the independent variable (*segment*).

- The average satisfaction level evaluated on various items using a 10-point scale represents the dependent variable (*satisfaction_score*). The more satisfied the customer, the higher the score on this variable.

Data Analysis

A one-way ANOVA is run using the **One-Way ANOVA** task and the following steps are needed to successfully run it:

1. Add the dataset *Ecommerce.sas7bdat* to your SAS Enterprise Guide environment.

2. Run the one-way ANOVA task by selecting **Tasks** → **ANOVA** → **One-Way ANOVA...**

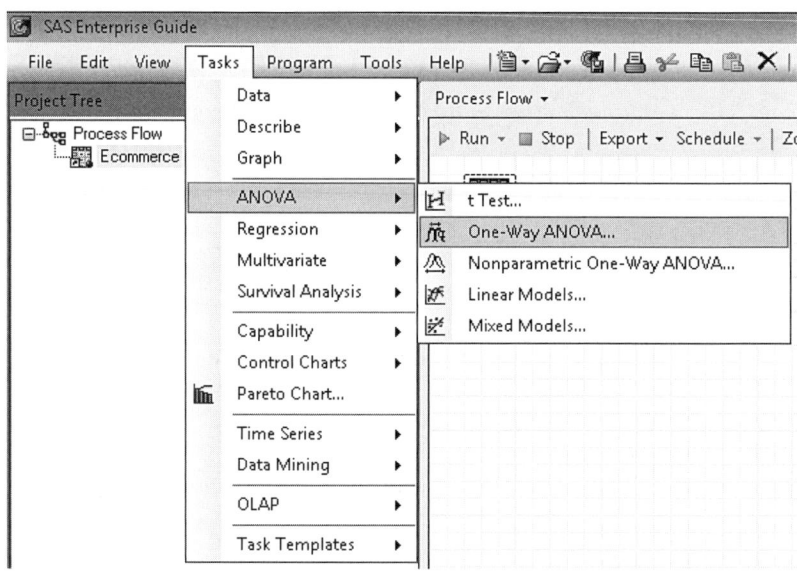

3. The selection pane pops up and the **Data** pane option becomes available. Add the dependent variable, *satisfaction_score*, to the **Dependent variables** role, while the variable that indicates to which segment a particular consumer belongs, the *segment* variable, is added to the **Independent variable** role.

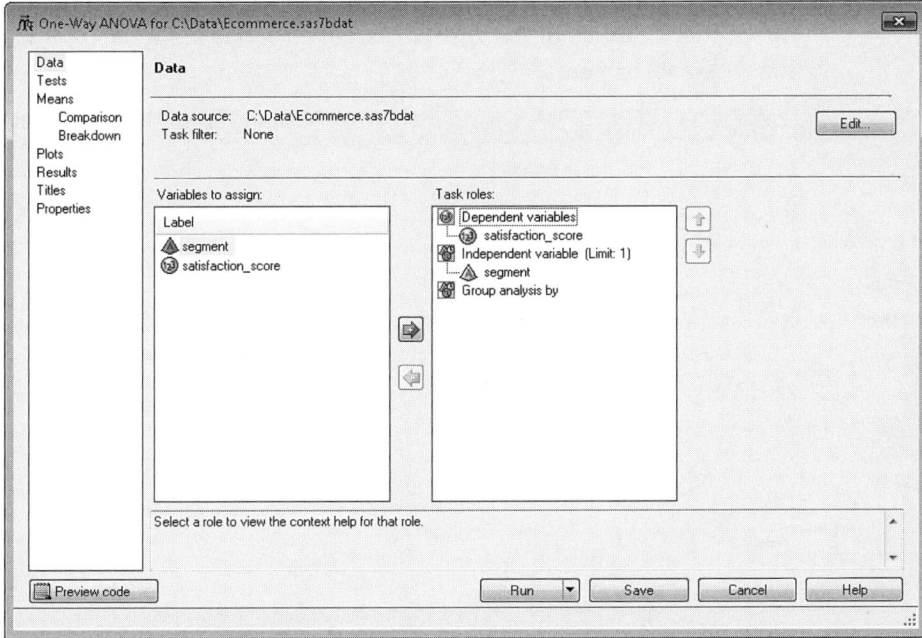

*The independent variable and the dependent variable need to be identified at this stage of the one-way ANOVA process. Furthermore, the independent variable can have all data types as indicated by the different types of symbols under the **Independent variable** role, while the dependent variable must have a numeric format (see the **Dependent variables** role). When one-way ANOVA is considered, many dependent variables can be evaluated at the same time, while only one independent variable can be taken into consideration. However, when more than one independent variable is considered, the ANOVA model is called a two-way ANOVA (with two independent variables), three-way ANOVA (with three independent variables), and so on. In SAS Enterprise Guide, these ANOVA models are run using the **_Linear Models_** task as explained in the subsequent section (section 5.1.4.2).*

4. As a next step, go to the **Tests** pane and select the option **Welch's variance-weighted ANOVA.** By doing this, a special type of one-way ANOVA that takes into consideration the inequality of variances between the levels of the independent variable is run. The procedure indeed recalculates the probabilities with this inequality in sight. Furthermore, select the option **Levene's test** which is a statistical test to verify whether or not the variances of the *satisfaction_score* variable are different for the different segments.

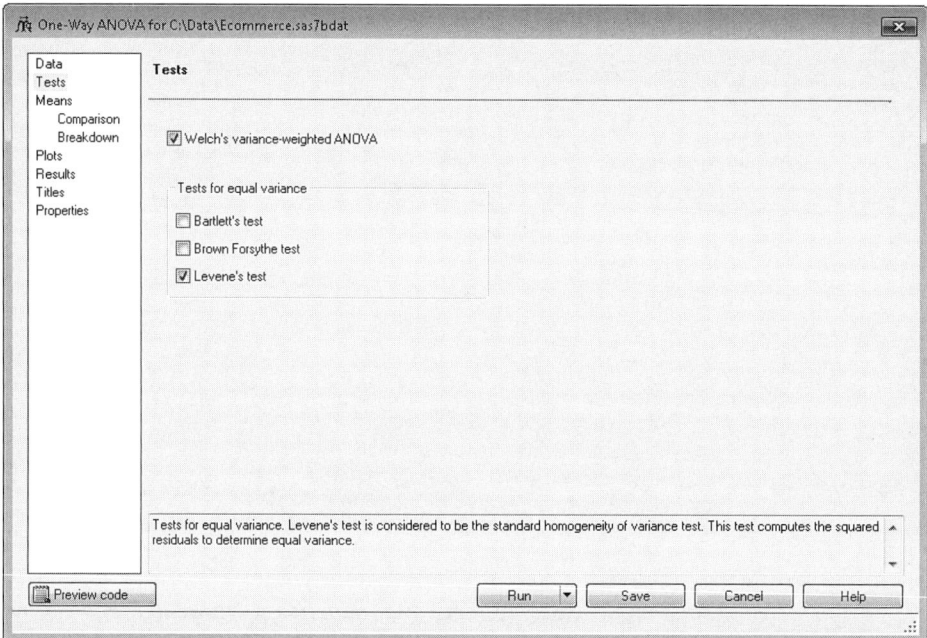

5. Next, go to **Means** and under **Comparison** select the appropriate post-hoc test. This section employs the **Bonferroni t test** to verify whether two segments have significantly different satisfaction levels.

*A post-hoc test is a test that makes a pairwise comparison whether two levels of the independent variable have statistically different levels of the dependent variable. We recommend that you consider the **Bonferroni t test, Tukey's studentized range test (HDS)** or **Fisher's least significant difference test**. One can say that these post-hoc tests are the most commonly used in practice. It is the context of your research setting that will lead you to prefer one over the other post-hoc test. Generally speaking, it is agreed that **Bonferroni's t test** and **Tukey's studentized***

range test (HDS) are more conservative than the ***Fisher's least significant difference test***, although they lack more statistical power (in other words, they are more conservative and may not detect an effect that is existing). ***Bonferronis t test*** performs, however, better on a small number of comparisons. For instance, if the objective is only to compare a control condition to several experimental ones, this is the appropriate test. However, ***Tukey's studentized range test (HDS)*** tends to perform better on large datasets. If the total set of pairwise comparisons (compare every group 2 by 2) is large, we recommend you to use the Tukey's test.

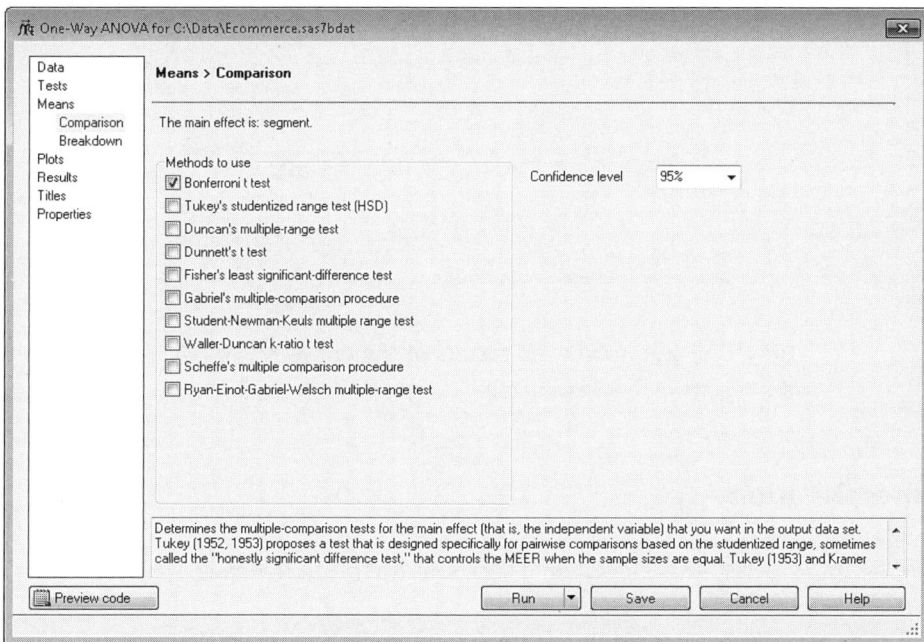

6. Additionally, we suggest selecting the **Mean**, the **Standard deviation** and the **Variance** option in the **Means** pane under **Breakdown.** This will provide the respective statistics for the *satisfaction_score* variable for each level of the independent variable.

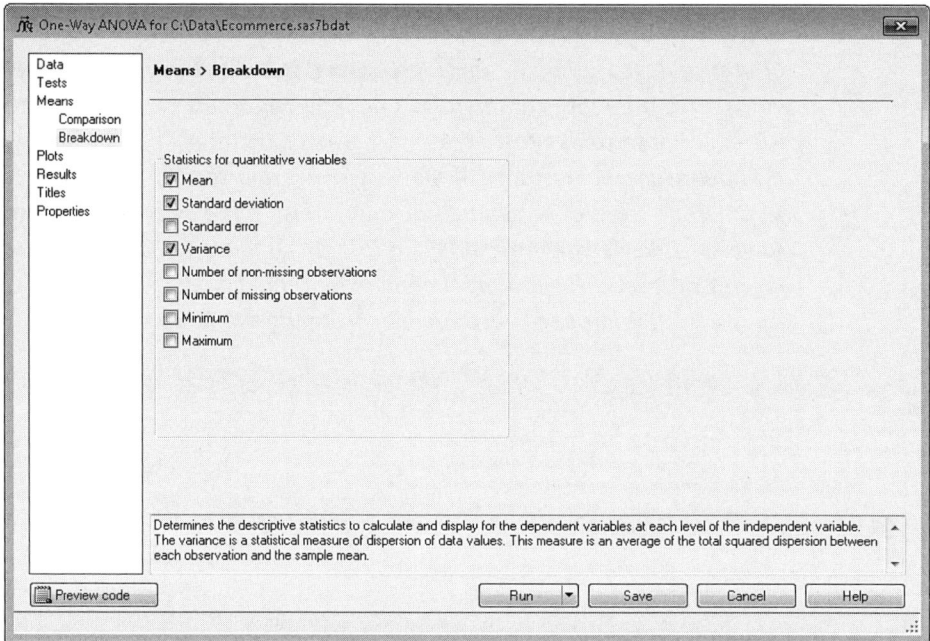

7. Now, click **Run** to get the results of the one-way ANOVA. You can verify the results in the **Results** tab.

Interpretation

The following decisions are needed to correctly interpret a one-way ANOVA test:

- **Levene's Test for Homogeneity of satisfaction_score Variance**

Levene's Test for Homogeneity of satisfaction_score Variance ANOVA of Squared Deviations from Group Means					
Source	DF	Sum of Squares	Mean Square	F Value	Pr > F
segment	3	4.0719	1.3573	0.34	0.7948
Error	196	777.3	3.9657		

Firstly, one must concentrate on the equality of variances of the satisfaction between the four segments. In order to make sure that the mean satisfaction levels of the four segments are statistically comparable, the Levene's test of equality of variance is checked. If the variances among the four segments are equal, one is sure that the means between the groups are comparable. If the variances are unequal, the Welch correction is needed to make the means between the groups comparable (this is why one should tick the **Welch's variance-weighted ANOVA**). The test of equality of variances is performed on the dataset with the following hypotheses:

H_0: The variances of *satisfaction_score* between the four segments are equal.

H_1: The variances of *satisfaction_score* between the four segments are not equal.

When the **Levene's Test for Homogeneity of satisfaction_score Variance** table is explored, one concludes that the variances between the four segments are not statistically different, because the F-value is 0.34 and the associated p-value of 0.7948 is larger than 0.05. Therefore the null hypothesis (H_0) is accepted.

- **Dependent Variable: satisfaction_score**

Source	DF	Sum of Squares	Mean Square	F Value	Pr > F
Model	3	410.3363600	136.7787867	66.93	<.0001
Error	196	400.5180080	2.0434592		
Corrected Total	199	810.8543680			

R-Square	Coeff Var	Root MSE	satisfaction_score Mean
0.506054	21.87312	1.429496	6.535400

Source	DF	Anova SS	Mean Square	F Value	Pr > F
segment	3	410.3363600	136.7787867	66.93	<.0001

As the variances between the groups are equal, the overall one-way ANOVA p-value is considered to verify whether or not at least one segment is statistically different in terms of satisfaction level. In our e-commerce situation, the null hypothesis (H_0) is rejected because the one-way ANOVA F-value is 66.93 and the p-value is smaller than 0.0001, and thus smaller than 0.05 (see the *Source DF Anova SS Mean Square F Value Pr > F* header). In sum, there is at least one segment that shows a significant difference with the others in its mean satisfaction level.

Suppose that the results of the Levene's test showed no homogeneity of the variances across the segments (or the variances are not equal), one should then check the results obtained in the **Welch's ANOVA for satisfaction_score** table.

Welch's ANOVA for satisfaction_score			
Source	DF	F Value	Pr > F
segment	3.0000	62.17	<.0001
Error	108.8		

As mentioned earlier, this one-way ANOVA procedure corrects for the non-homogeneity of the variances between the different levels of the independent variable. The p-value in the table enables us to infer whether there is at least one segment that is significantly different in terms of the dependent variable considered.

- **Bonferroni (Dunn) t Tests for satisfaction_score**

Alpha	0.05
Error Degrees of Freedom	196
Error Mean Square	2.043459
Critical Value of t	2.66530
Minimum Significant Difference	0.762

Means with the same letter are not significantly different.			
Bon Grouping	Mean	N	segment
A	8.2336	50	Medium User
B	7.0428	50	Light User
B			
B	6.5800	50	Heavy User
C	4.2852	50	Ad Hoc User

Note: This test controls the Type I experimentwise error rate, but it generally has a higher Type II error rate than REGWQ.

As the overall one-way ANOVA p-value indicates that at least some significant satisfaction differences exist across the four segments, the post-hoc test will unravel between which two segments different satisfaction levels occur. The results of the Bonferonni's post-hoc tests identify where the differences between the segments are found. In this table, under the header *Mean with the same letter are not significantly different*, satisfaction levels with the same letter are not statistically different. In detail, ad-hoc users experience a different satisfaction level than the other three segments, because the ad-hoc user segment is preceded by a letter C, while all other segments are preceded by a letter A or B. It is clear that the ad-hoc users with a mean satisfaction level of 4.285 are less satisfied than the other segments (that is, the segments identified with the letters A and B). Furthermore, it is clear from the table that the medium users are the most satisfied and their satisfaction level is statistically different from the other segments.

Managerial Recommendations

In conclusion, a significant difference exists in the level of satisfaction between the four segments of consumers. This difference is traced back to the difference in satisfaction level of the ad-hoc users and the other segments, and the difference in satisfaction level between the medium users and the other segments. The ad-hoc users have a statistically lower satisfaction level than the other three user segments, while the medium users are the most satisfied ones. The light users show the same level of satisfaction as the heavy users. Setting these findings in the context of our managerial problem, we suggest that the e-commerce platform primarily focuses their marketing and service efforts on the ad-hoc consumers group. A probable suggestion would be to stimulate the ad-hoc users to do more regular purchases with the e-commerce company in order to let them discover the extended consumer service the company offers to its clients. Nevertheless, a further investigation is needed to discover why people tend to become less satisfied when they are becoming heavy users. This pattern is of great interest to the company, because heavy users are highly involved by spreading the word of mouth on the company's service.

5.1.4.2. Two-way ANOVA

Keywords: k samples, independent samples

> A two-way ANOVA is a parametric statistical hypothesis test that compares whether the means of more than two independent samples described by two factors are equal.

Managerial Problem

A non-profit organization wants to test the effectiveness of various promotion campaigns. This organization is currently working on a new communication campaign with the objective of increasing the overall donation amount. The members of the organization hesitate between two ways of framing the promotion message on two dimensions. The first dimension concerns the different types of norms one may use to motivate people to donate money. Two types of norms are considered. The first one shows what other people do in terms of donation to non-profit organizations (also known as the descriptive norm). The second option insists on what families ought to do, that is, the injunctive norm. The second dimension is related to the closing line of the promotion message that refers to the amount of money donated in previous campaigns. The non-profit organization is not sure whether they should refer to the maximum amount ever donated by the donator or to the average amount usually collected in order to encourage donation. Based on their archives, the information gathered on previous campaigns and the amounts donated, the organization wants to study the impact of both options of the two dimensions (norm: descriptive vs. injunctive and donation amount: average vs. maximum) on donations. Based on the results, they are able to choose the correct communication message.

Translation of the Managerial Problem into Statistical Notions

The problem consists of identifying to what extent the two levels of the two framing dimensions, two types of norms (descriptive versus injunctive) and the two types of donation amount references (maximum versus average), impact the donation behaviour. This setup is called a 2x2 factorial design. In a 2x2 factorial design, the researcher wants to know what the impact is of a particular dimension on the real donation amount when controlling for the other dimension. This is called a main effect. In our setting, two main effects can be explored, that is, the impact of the norm issue and the impact of the donation amount issue on the future donation behaviour. Furthermore, the researcher is also interested to verify whether the two main effects, that is, the types of norm and the references to the donation amount, interact with each other. This is called an interaction effect.

In this setting, a two-way ANOVA is needed because the impact of two variables, that is, the norm dimension and the reference donation amount dimension, is verified on the real donation amount, the dependent variable. As the respondents are only exposed to one of the four levels of the 2x2 factorial design, there is no overlap between the samples; and they are thus independent.

Hypotheses

The null and alternative hypothesis are formulated below:

H$_0$:   There is no significant impact of the types of norm on the amount effectively donated.

H_1: There is a significant impact of the types of norm on the amount effectively donated.

H_0: There is no significant impact of the types of reference to the past donation amount on the amount effectively donated.

H_1: There is a significant impact of the types of reference to the past donation amount on the amount effectively donated.

H_0: The impact of the types of reference to the past donation amount on the amount effectively donated does not vary according to the type of norm.

H_1: The impact of the types of reference to the past donation amount on the amount effectively donated varies according to the type of norm.

Dataset Description

Under *Donation.xls*, you will find the Excel data file to use. It contains all the information collected from the organization's previous campaigns, representing 40 observations. The variables to consider are the following:

- The type of norm used during framing the mailing, that is, *injunctive* or *descriptive*, represents the first independent variable (*norm*).

- The indicator of the past donation amount of the donator, that is, the *maximum* or the *average amount*, to be used in the direct mailing is considered as the second independent variable (*donation_amount*).

- The amount expressed in euros effectively donated after receiving the direct mailing is the dependent variable (*response*).

Data Analysis

In order to run a two-way ANOVA, that is, an ANOVA with two independent variables, the **Linear Models** task is used.

1. Open the dataset *Donation.xls* and add it to your SAS Enterprise Guide environment.

2. Select the **Linear Models** task by **Tasks** → **ANOVA** → **Linear Models…**

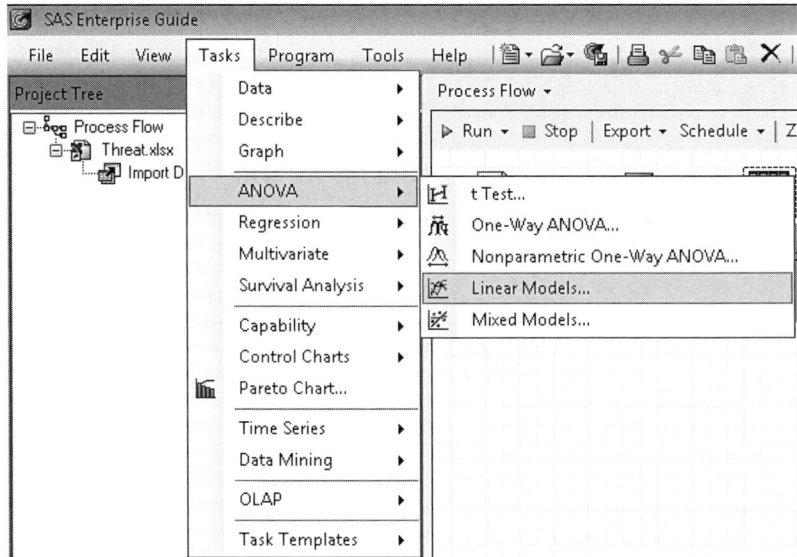

3. The selection pane appears and in the option pane **Data**, you assign the two independent variables, that is, the variable *norm* and *donation_amount*, under the **Classification variables** role. The variable of interest, the *response* variable, is dropped under the **Dependent variable** role.

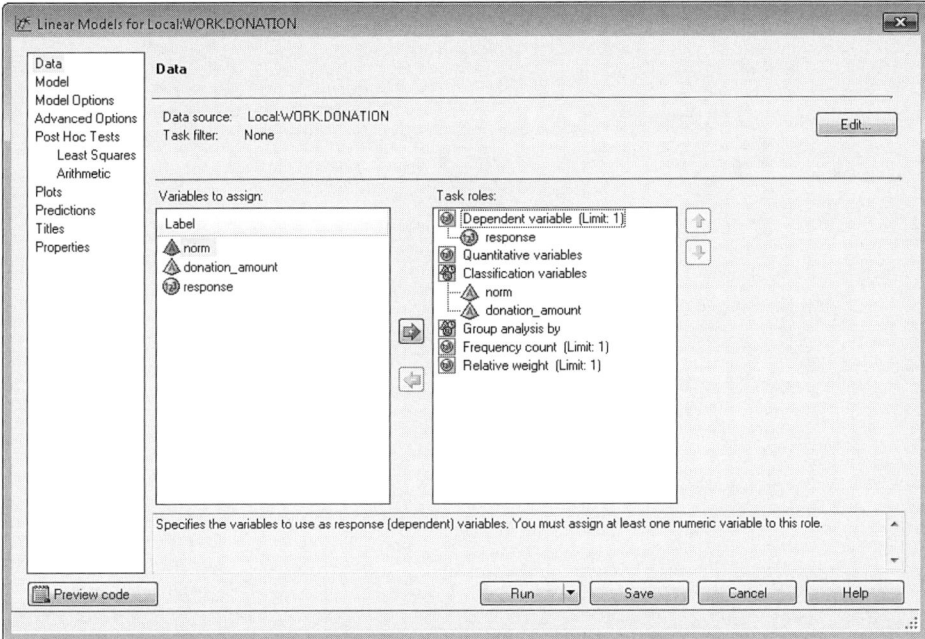

Compared to a traditional one-way ANOVA, more information on the statistical model should now be provided to SAS Enterprise Guide.

4.   In the selection pane, select **Model**. The two independent variables appear here. Select both variables and click on the button **Factorial** as you want to check the main effect for each independent variable and the corresponding interaction effect.

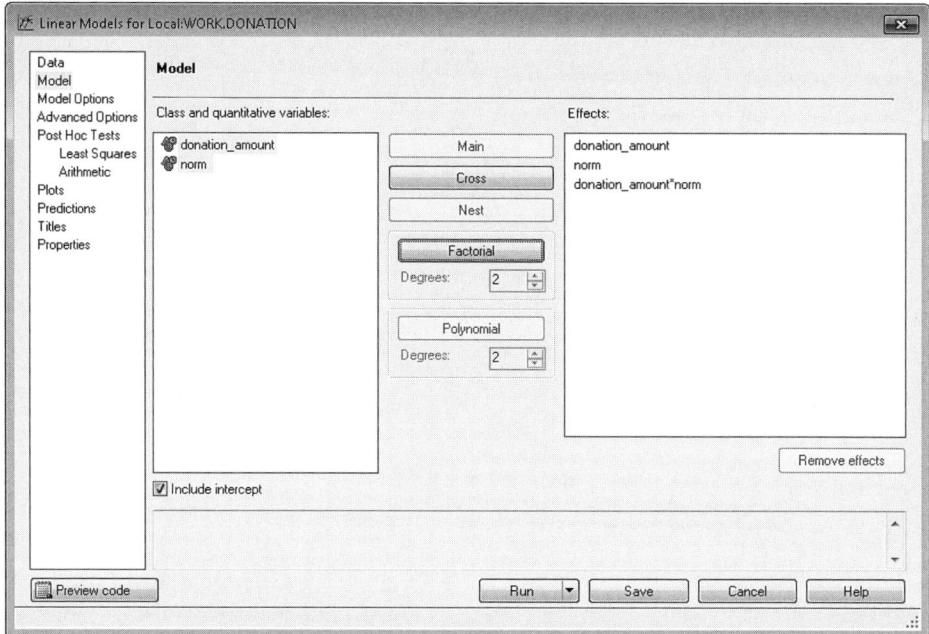

*Clicking on **Factorial** is the quickest way to integrate all main and interaction effects of the independent variables. This is very helpful when there are three or more independent variables. By selecting the corresponding degree of the interaction factor, you decide on the level of interaction(s), that is, how many variables should SAS Enterprise Guide include in the same interaction. For instance, interactions with two variables at the most, that is, degree equals 2 means that although more than two independent variables are selected in the **Class and quantitative variables** role, all interactions of only two variables will be considered. However, you could also proceed step by step, by first selecting your variables, and then by clicking on **Main**, you get the main effects into the model and click then on **Cross**, to obtain the interaction of the variables you selected.*

5. Finally, in the pane **Post Hoc Tests** under **Least Squares,** click on the button **Add** if you want to know (i) whether differences exist across the levels of your independent variables and (ii) where these differences are found. Select the option **True** for all class effects under the option **Class effects to use** for which you would like to test the mean for. Change the **Show p-values for differences** option under the **Comparisons** header in the scrolling pane to **All pairwise differences** to show the p-values for all mutual comparisons on the independent variables.

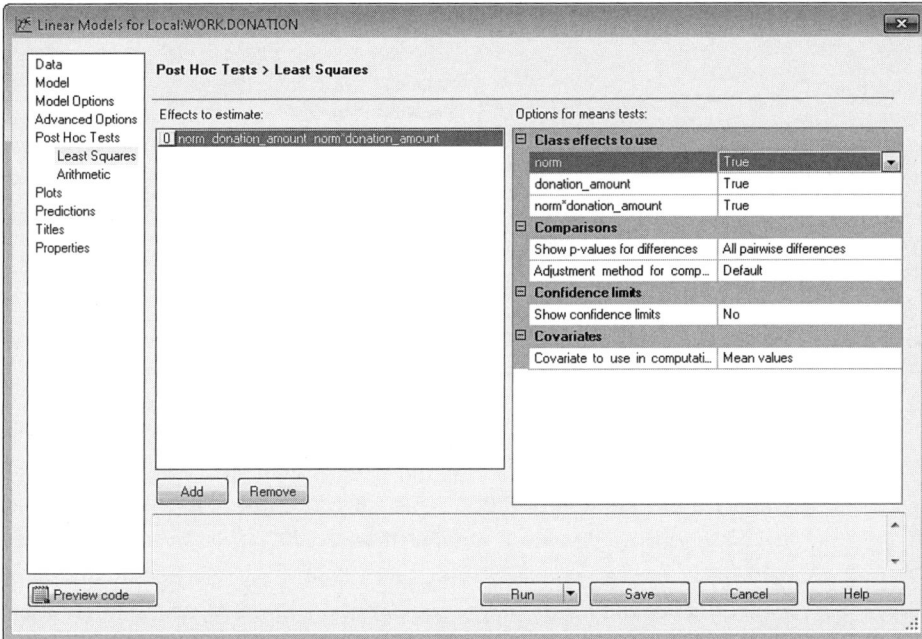

6. Click **Run** to execute the model and to start interpreting the results from the **Results** tab.

Interpretation

• **Dependent Variable: Response**

Source	DF	Sum of Squares	Mean Square	F Value	Pr > F
Model	3	2500.768000	833.589333	16.10	<.0001
Error	36	1863.952000	51.776444		
Corrected Total	39	4364.720000			

R-Square	Coeff Var	Root MSE	response Mean
0.572950	7.448846	7.195585	96.60000

Source	DF	Type I SS	Mean Square	F Value	Pr > F
norm	1	1183.744000	1183.744000	22.86	<.0001
donation_amount	1	1299.600000	1299.600000	25.10	<.0001
norm*donation_amount	1	17.424000	17.424000	0.34	0.5655

Source	DF	Type III SS	Mean Square	F Value	Pr > F
norm	1	1183.744000	1183.744000	22.86	<.0001
donation_amount	1	1299.600000	1299.600000	25.10	<.0001
norm*donation_amount	1	17.424000	17.424000	0.34	0.5655

Parameter	Estimate		Standard Error	t Value	Pr > |t|
Intercept	97.52000000	B	2.27544379	42.86	<.0001
norm descriptive	9.56000000	B	3.21796347	2.97	0.0053
norm injunctive	0.00000000	B	.	.	.
donation_amount average	-12.72000000	B	3.21796347	-3.95	0.0003
donation_amount maximum	0.00000000	B	.	.	.
norm*donation_amount descriptive average	2.64000000	B	4.55088758	0.58	0.5655
norm*donation_amount descriptive maximum	0.00000000	B	.	.	.
norm*donation_amount injunctive average	0.00000000	B	.	.	.
norm*donation_amount injunctive maximum	0.00000000	B	.	.	.

Note: The X'X matrix has been found to be singular, and a generalized inverse was used to solve the normal equations. Terms whose estimates are followed by the letter 'B' are not uniquely estimable.

This table contains the model p-value for this two-way ANOVA model. The model F-value and p-value are found under the header *Source DF Sum of Squares Mean Square F Value Pr > F* in the *Model* row. The F-value is equal to 16.10 and the p-value is smaller than 0.0001. This p-value is smaller than 0.05. We can conclude that there is at least one effect, that is, a main effect of the *norm* and/or the *donation_amount*, or the interaction effect between the two variables on the dependent variable *response*. Under the header *Source DF Type III SS Mean Square F Value Pr > F*, one finds the p-values for the main effects, *norm* and *donation_amount* and the interaction effect *norm*donation_amount*. The F-values and p-values associated indicate that both main effects have a significant impact on the real donation behaviour, that is, both p-values of *norm* (with F-value = 22.86) and *donation_amount* (with F-value = 25.10) are smaller than 0.0001. The interaction effect *norm*donation_amount* is not significant with a p-value of 0.5655 (F-value = 0.34).

If the interaction effect had been significant, one would have concluded that depending on the type of norm, the type of donation will influence significantly the future amount donated.

- **Adjustment for Multiple Comparisons: Tukey**

These tables give you an insight into the direction of the significant effect of your two-way ANOVA. First, the main effects of *norm* and *donation_amount* are discussed, while finally the interaction effect between *norm* and *donation_amount* is interpreted.

Adjustment for Multiple Comparisons: Tukey

norm	response LSMEAN	H0:LSMean1=LSMean2 Pr > |t|
descriptive	102.040000	<.0001
injunctive	91.160000	

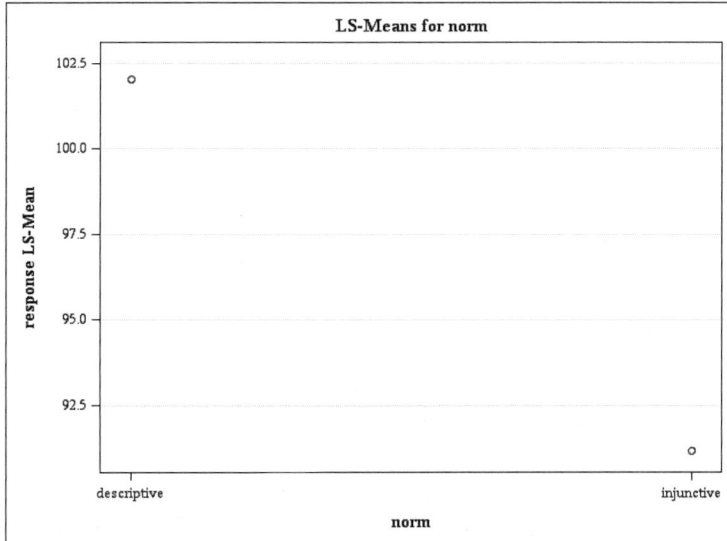

LS-Means for norm

Under the header *norm response LSMEAN H0:LSMean1=LSMean2 Pr > |t|*, you will find again that the main effect of *norm* has a significant p-value (p-value is smaller than 0.0001). Moreover, this table indicates that the mean donation amount given by the people who received the descriptive treatment is 102.04 euros, while it is only 91.16 euros for the people who received the injunctive treatment. These figures are found in the *LSMEAN* column. This difference is significant. The graph with the title *LS-MEANS for norm* visualizes these figures.

Adjustment for Multiple Comparisons: Tukey

donation_amount	response LSMEAN	H0:LSMean1=LSMean2 Pr > |t|
average	90.900000	<.0001
maximum	102.300000	

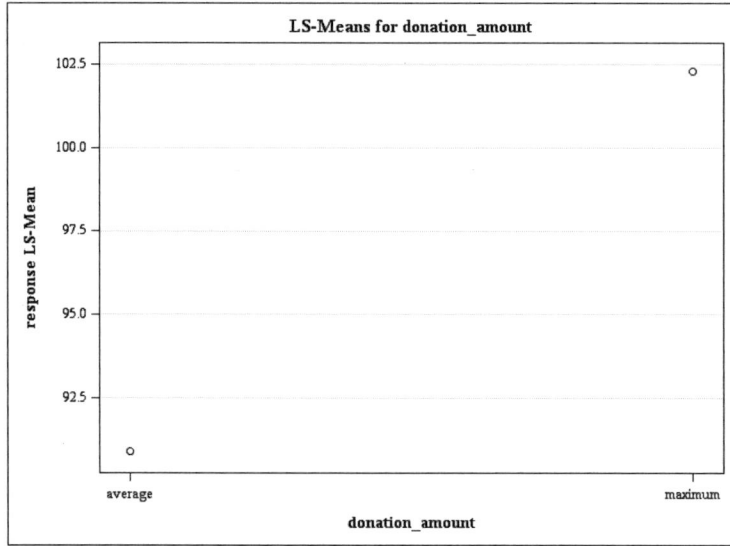

Under the header *donation_amount response LSMEAN H0:LSMean1 =LSMean2 Pr > |t|*, you see again that the main effect of the framing dimension of *donation amount* is significantly impacting the donation behaviour (check the p-value is smaller than 0.0001). Furthermore, you can conclude that framing the maximum donation amount ever donated in the advertisement is the most effective on the real donation behaviour, because the mean maximum donation amount is 102.30 euros, while mentioning the average donation amount in the advertisement results in a mean donation amount of 90.90 euros. The graph entitled *LS-MEANS for donation_amount* gives a visual representation of this result.

Adjustment for Multiple Comparisons: Tukey

norm	donation_amount	response LSMEAN	LSMEAN Number
descriptive	average	97.000000	1
descriptive	maximum	107.080000	2
injunctive	average	84.800000	3
injunctive	maximum	97.520000	4

Least Squares Means for effect norm*donation_amount
Pr > |t| for H0: LSMean(i)=LSMean(j)
Dependent Variable: response

i/j	1	2	3	4
1		0.0173	0.0030	0.9985
2	0.0173		<.0001	0.0259
3	0.0030	<.0001		0.0019
4	0.9985	0.0259	0.0019	

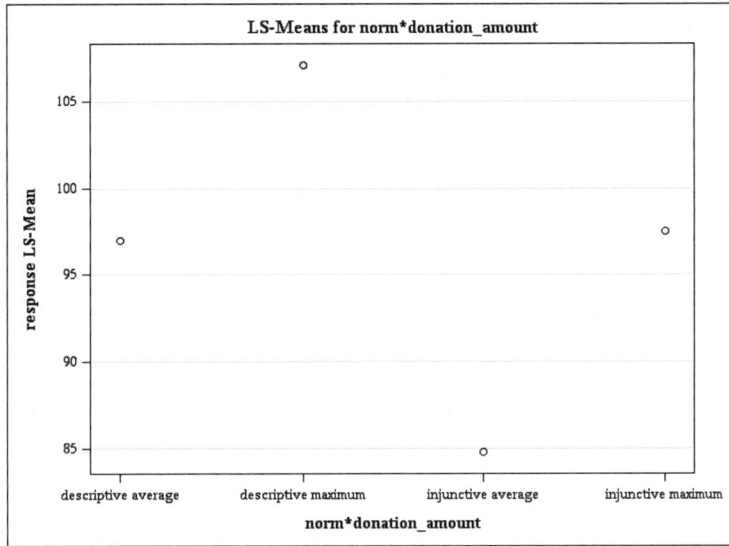

Verifying the different combinations of the interaction between the *norm* and *donation_amount* variables is not necessary given the p-value that indicates a non-significant effect (see supra). The p-values for every mutual combination between *norm* and *donation_amount* are listed under the header *Least Squares Means for effect norm*donation_amount Pr > |t| for H0: LSMean(i)=LSMean(j)*. When the interaction effect is significant, one should interpret it.

Managerial Recommendations

Based on the above results, we advise the company to opt for a descriptive norm framing or to mention the maximum amount ever donated by the donators. The donation amount collected after using these framing options resulted in the highest donation amounts by the donators.

5.1.5. ANALYSIS OF COVARIANCE (ANCOVA)

Keywords: k samples, independent samples

An ANCOVA is a parametric statistical hypothesis test that compares whether the means of more than two independent samples (described by one or more factors) are equal after removing the variance(s) for which the covariate(s) account(s).

Managerial Problem

Public decision makers are aware that investing in an effective promotion campaign that stimulates individuals to eat healthy food is a crucial element in today's society. In an earlier stage of their communication project (see section 5.1.2), they identified that threat appeals were the most effective to motivate consumers to eat fruit and vegetables. Nevertheless, scientific researchers in social marketing communication warned them that the type of threat (whether one focuses on *social* threat, the risk of social rejection; *aesthetical* threat, the risk linked to beauty; or *health* threat, for instance the risk of cardiovascular diseases) could significantly impact the effectiveness of the advertisement. Furthermore, these researchers also emphasized that any other element that may influence the amount of healthy food consumed should be taken into account.

Consequently, the health department decided to push forward the study of the threat appeal effectiveness. They appointed researchers to compare three different types of threats. The impact of the three types of threats on the consumption of healthy food is to be verified in a controlled experiment. Furthermore, participants' attitude towards strawberries prior to the experiment has to be measured and taken into consideration in the analysis. One could indeed argue that the more one likes strawberries, the more likely one will be to consume them, regardless of the quality of the promotion campaign that stimulates eating strawberries. Therefore, in order to be able to infer that the increase of healthy consumption is a result of the advertising campaign, one has to control for that effect too.

Translation of the Managerial Problem into Statistical Notions

The managerial problem is translated into statistical notions by statistically comparing the effectiveness of the three threat advertisements by means of the quantities of strawberries consumed. In this case, the participants are randomly divided into three groups since there are three types of promotion campaigns and each participant sees only one type of advertisement. The final purpose of this setting is to identify the group(s) for which the average quantity of strawberries consumed is significantly higher. However, the participants' attitudes towards strawberries prior to the advertisement's exposure represents the covariate in this study. A covariate is an additional variable that could influence the impact of the threat appeal on the consumption level of the strawberries and thus not taking into account this variable could bias the results.

Hypotheses

The hypotheses are formulated as follows:

H_0:   There are no significant differences between the three threat advertisements on the mean strawberry consumption taking into account the variance of the prior level of attitude towards strawberries.

H_1:   There is at least one threat advertisement that shows a significant difference on the mean strawberry consumption taking into account the variance of the prior level of attitude towards strawberries.

Dataset Description

The SAS data file to consider is the *Threat.xlsx*. It contains 99 observations. The variables to consider are the following:

- The respondent's identification (*ID*).

- The respondent's gender (*Gender*).

- An indicator for the type of threat to which each individual is assigned to (*Type_of_threat*). The data file contains 34 individuals exposed to a warning of the social type (*social*), 33 respondents saw the healthy type of warning (*health*) and 32 respondents were shown the aesthetical threat (*aesthetical*).

- The participant's prior attitude towards strawberries is the covariate (*Astrawberry_prior*). The construct is a composite measure based on six items. Each item is evaluated on a 5-point Likert-scale. The higher the prior attitude is, the more the individual likes strawberries.

- The weight of strawberries consumed expressed in grams is considered as the dependent variable (*Cstrawberries*).

Data Analysis

In order to run an ANCOVA, an ANOVA with covariate(s), the **Linear Models** task is employed.

1.   Add the *Threat.xlsx* dataset to your SAS Enterprise Guide work environment.

2.   Go to **Tasks** → **ANOVA** → **Linear Models...** to run the ANCOVA model.

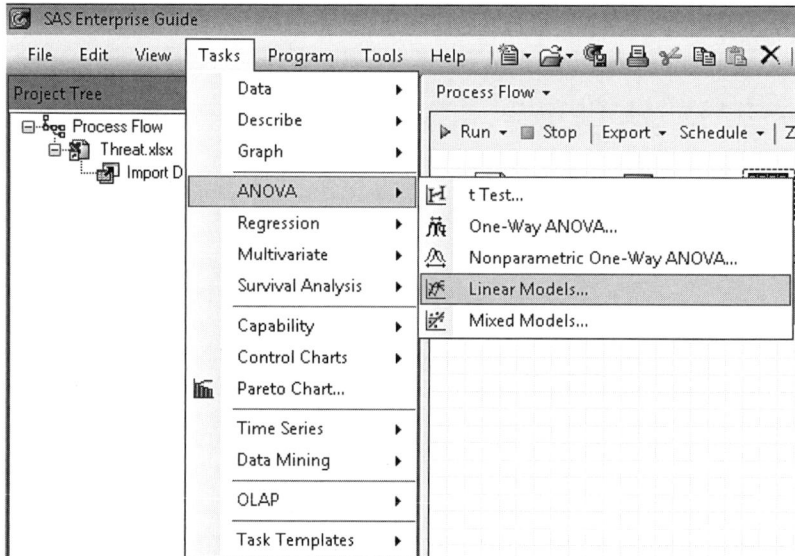

3.   The selection pane opens and under the option pane **Data**, you drag and drop the variable that contains the types of the threat advertisements, the *Type_of_threat* variable, under the **Classification variables** role. The covariate *Astrawberry_prior*, measuring the prior attitude level towards strawberries, is assigned to the role **Quantitative variables**. The dependent variable measuring the amount of strawberries consumed, the *Cstrawberries* variable, is placed under the **Dependent variable** role.

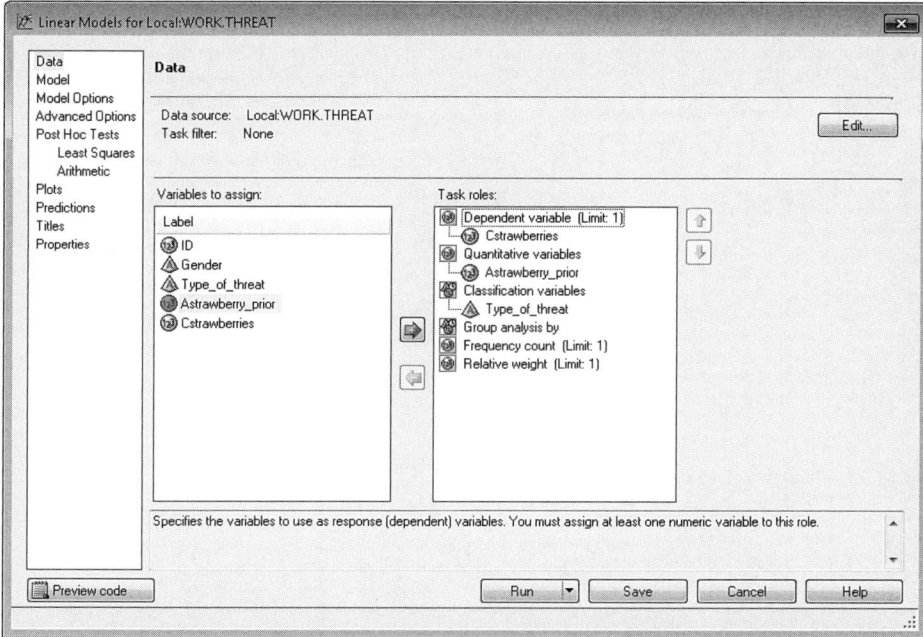

4. In the selection pane, select **Model**. The independent variable and the covariate appear under the **Class and quantitative variables** option. Select both variables, *Astrawberry_prior* and *Type_of_threat*, and click on **Main**, as one wants to check for a main effect of both variables on the strawberry consumption.

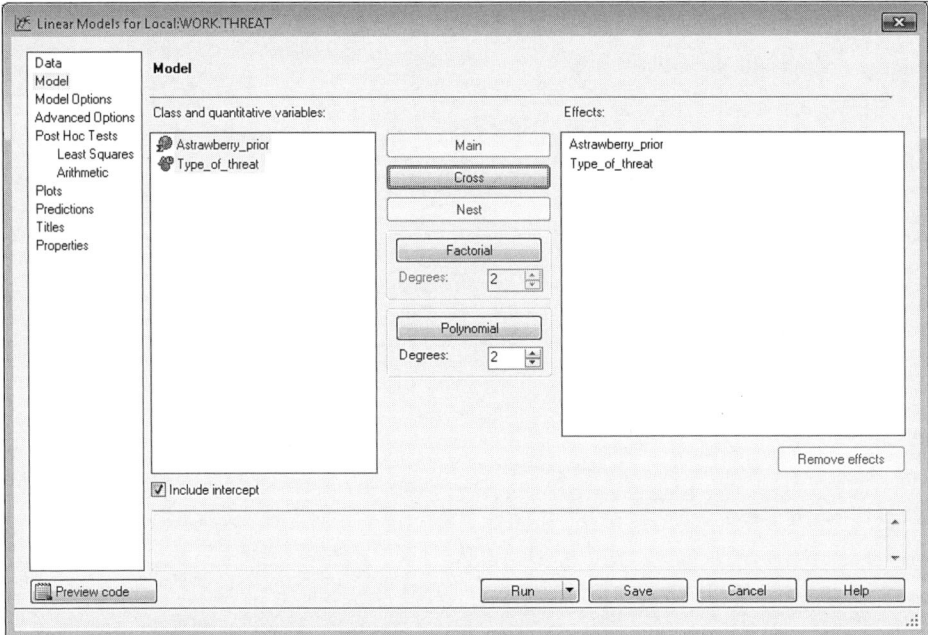

5. Go to **Least Squares** under **Post Hoc Tests** in order to identify where the differences in mean strawberry consumption across the types of advertisement are. Click on the button **Add** if you want to know (i) whether such differences exist across the levels of the independent variable and (ii) where these differences are found. Select the option **True** for the class effect *Type_of_threat* under the option **Class effects to use** for which you would like to test the mean for. Change the **Show p-values for differences** option under the **Comparisons** option in the scrolling pane to **All pairwise differences** to show the p-values for all mutual comparisons on the independent variable. The figure below shows the different options for this research setting.

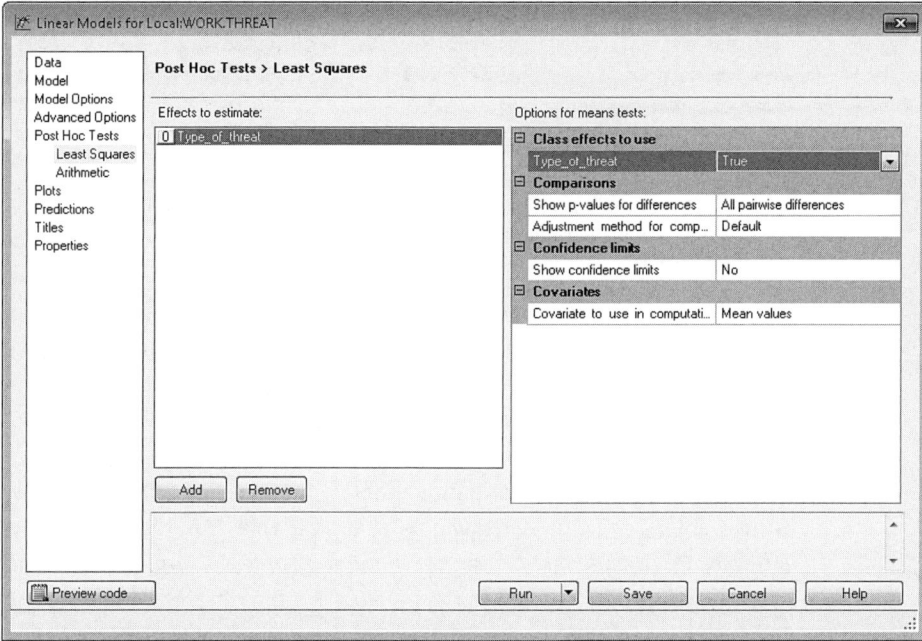

6. Click **Run** to check the results of the ANCOVA under the **Results** tab.

Interpretation

- **Dependent Variable: Cstrawberries**

Source	DF	Sum of Squares	Mean Square	F Value	Pr > F
Model	3	101253.7480	33751.2493	43.99	<.0001
Error	95	72885.5532	767.2163		
Corrected Total	98	174139.3012			

R-Square	Coeff Var	Root MSE	Cstrawberries Mean
0.581453	19.25982	27.69867	143.8159

Source	DF	Type I SS	Mean Square	F Value	Pr > F
Astrawberry_prior	1	45837.03738	45837.03738	59.74	<.0001
Type_of_threat	2	55416.71066	27708.35533	36.12	<.0001

Source	DF	Type III SS	Mean Square	F Value	Pr > F
Astrawberry_prior	1	26896.59263	26896.59263	35.06	<.0001
Type_of_threat	2	55416.71066	27708.35533	36.12	<.0001

Parameter	Estimate		Standard Error	t Value	Pr > |t|
Intercept	94.83604805	B	15.40926570	6.15	<.0001
Astrawberry_prior	3.84994699		0.65022706	5.92	<.0001
Type_of_threat aesthetical	-55.01288781	B	6.87010945	-8.01	<.0001
Type_of_threat health	-45.17802454	B	6.98696623	-6.47	<.0001
Type_of_threat social	0.00000000	B	.	.	.

Note: The X'X matrix has been found to be singular, and a generalized inverse was used to solve the normal equations. Terms whose estimates are followed by the letter 'B' are not uniquely estimable.

This table contains the model p-value for the ANCOVA model. The model F-value and p-value are found under the header *Source DF Sum of Squares Mean Square F Value Pr > F* in the *Model* row. They are respectively equal to 43.99 and smaller than 0.0001. Thus, this p-value is smaller than 0.05. The null hypothesis (H_0) is rejected. This means that there is at least an effect of one of the independent variables, the *Type_of_threat* variable, or the covariate, the *Astrawberry_prior* variable, on the dependent variable, *Cstrawberries*. Under the header *Source DF Type III SS Mean Square F Value Pr > F*, you find the p-values for the different effects in the ANCOVA model. The p-value of *Type_of_threat* indicates that there is a significant difference between the three threat appeals on the amount of strawberries consumed. The p-value is smaller than 0.05. Furthermore, the covariate *Astrawberry_prior* is significant, given its p-value that is smaller than 0.0001. The general model should be interpreted as such: although there is an influence of the prior attitude towards liking strawberries on the amount of strawberries eaten, the type of advertisement influences the consumption.

- **Adjustment for Multiple Comparisons: Tukey-Kramer**

Type_of_threat	Cstrawberries LSMEAN	LSMEAN Number
aesthetical	121.644256	1
health	131.479119	2
social	176.657144	3

Least Squares Means for effect Type_of_threat
Pr > \|t\| for H0: LSMean(i)=LSMean(j)
Dependent Variable: Cstrawberries

i/j	1	2	3
1		0.3355	<.0001
2	0.3355		<.0001
3	<.0001	<.0001	

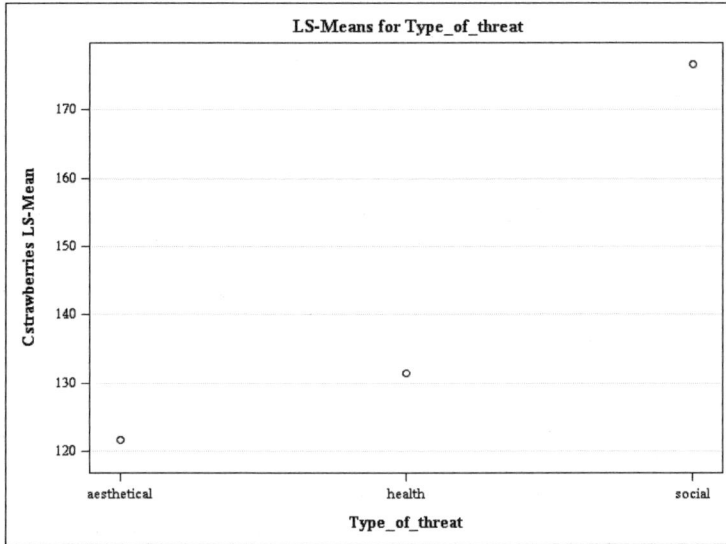

LS-Means for Type_of_threat

These tables give you an insight into the direction of the significant effect of the threat variable. Under the header *Type_of_threat Cstrawberries LSMEAN LSMEAN Number*, one finds under the column *LSMEAN* the mean weight of strawberries consumed per level of *Type_of_threat*. This table indicates that the mean amount of strawberries consumed for the threat *aesthetical* is equal to 121.64 grams, for the *health* threat is equal to 131.48 grams and for the *social* threat is equal to 176.66 grams. Under the following header *Least Squares Means for effect Type_of_threat*, you find the mutual p-values for each and every combination of the different threats of *Type_of_threat*. We note that there is a significant difference between threat number 1 (*aesthetical*) and threat number 3 ($p < 0.0001$) (*social*), while threat 2 (*health*) is also significantly different from threat 3 (*social*) ($p < 0.0001$). These results support the idea that the most effective type of threat is the *social* threat. The graph with the title *LS-MEANS for Type_of_threat* visualizes these figures.

Managerial Recommendations

The ANCOVA model identifies that the social threat message is the most effective type of threat when it comes down to motivating people to increase their consumption of healthy food or strawberries in this case. It is highly recommended that the health department implements an advertising campaign that uses a social threat appeal. This should contribute to make people more aware of the importance of healthy food.

5.1.6. ANOVA WITH REPEATED MEASURES

Keywords: k means, dependent samples

> A repeated measures ANOVA is a parametric statistical hypothesis test that compares whether the means of more than two dependent samples (described by one or more factors) are equal.

Managerial Problem

A broadband Internet provider decided to set up a large-scale, nationwide television advertising campaign that ran for four weeks. The advertisement featured a funny family situation that emphasized technological elements describing the superiority of their service over that of their competitors. The campaign represented an important investment and the advertisement was very different from what the brand had done in the past. To make sure they were on the right track, the management wanted to test how the brand awareness evolved during the four weeks based on specific consumer groups. The company considered that consumers behaved differently according to their gender and their usage (light versus heavy digital TV viewers). The brand awareness measure was measured on a sample of randomly selected viewers, and it was made available for four weeks.

Translation of the Managerial Problem into Statistical Notions

The purpose of this situation is to verify whether the mean value of the brand awareness is statistically different over the four weeks and whether there is a systematic impact of gender and the intensity of television usage. Four samples are considered, one for each week. The measures are *repeated* (the same questions to the same people), over a certain period of time. The samples are dependent, because the same respondents answer the same questions over the four-week period. This is what is called a within-subject study, because the answers coming from the same group of respondents will be analyzed and compared.

Dataset Description

The data collected by the company is available in the Excel 2007 data file *InternetTV. xlsx*. It contains data from 32 viewers and the variables to consider are the following:

- The identification of the viewers (*Subject_ID*).

- The gender of the viewers, male (*M*) or female (*F*) (*Gender*).

- The intensity of television usage of each respondent, heavy (*Heavy*) or light (*Light*) users (*TV_usage*).

- A variable identifying the specific week during which the brand awareness measure has been taken (*Week*). In this column, one will find 1 for the brand awareness measures taken during the first week, 2 for the brand awareness measures taken during the second week, and so on.

- The level of brand awareness is measured on a 5-point Likert-scale. An individual defining its level of brand awareness as low would choose 1, someone with a high brand awareness would tick 5 (*Awareness*). The values referring to the brand awareness in the first week are entered for the respondents next to 1 in the *Week* column. Then, the respondents' data are copied underneath this first set and the values measured for the brand awareness in the second week are encoded in the *Awareness* column next to 2 in the *Week* column, and so on.

Hypotheses

The managerial problem is translated as follows:

H_0:   There is no significantly different impact of gender on the repeated mean measure of brand awareness over the four-week period.

H_1:   There is a significantly different impact of gender on the repeated mean measure of brand awareness over the four-week period.

H_0:   There is no significantly different impact of the level of television usage on the repeated mean measure of brand awareness over four weeks.

H_1:   There is a significantly different impact of the level of television usage on the repeated mean measure of brand awareness over four weeks.

Data Analysis

To run a Repeated Measures ANOVA, the **Mixed Models** task is used.

1. Add the dataset *InternetTV.sas7bdat* to your process flow.

2. Open the Mixed Models task by selecting **Tasks** → **ANOVA** → **Mixed Models...**

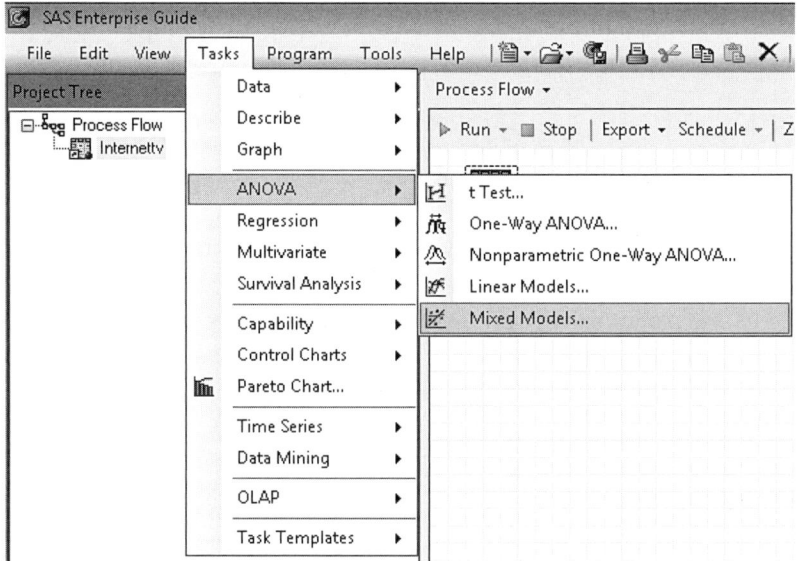

3. The selection pane pops-up and the **Data** pane is shown. The identifier variable (*Subject_ID*), the timing variable (*Week*) and the independent variables (*Gender* and *TV_usage*) must be identified. Assign them all under the **Classification variables** role. The variable of interest, *Awareness*, is assigned under the **Dependent variable** role.

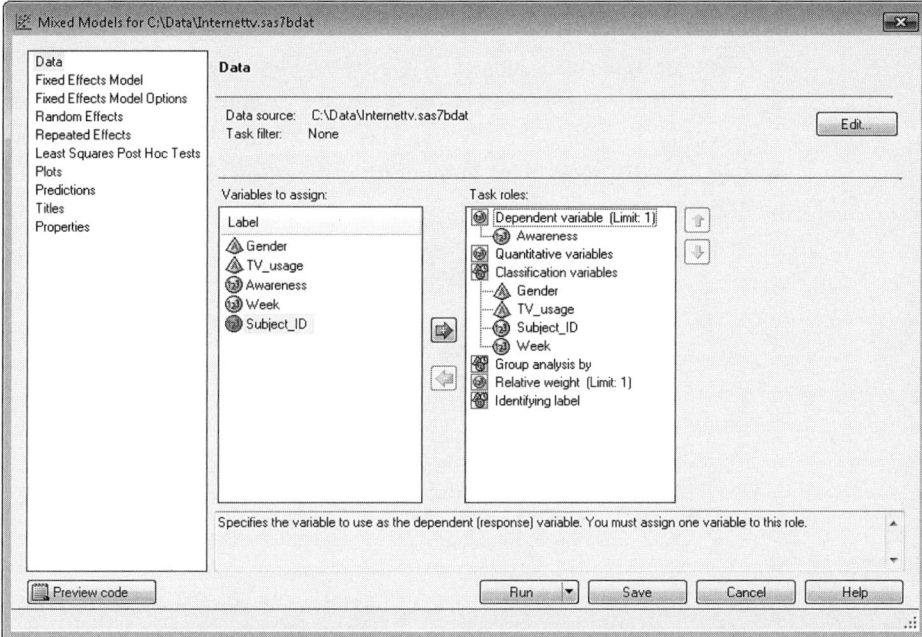

4. In the **Fixed Effects Model** pane, add the variables *Gender* and *TV_usage* as main effects by selecting them first and then by clicking on the <u>**Main**</u> button.

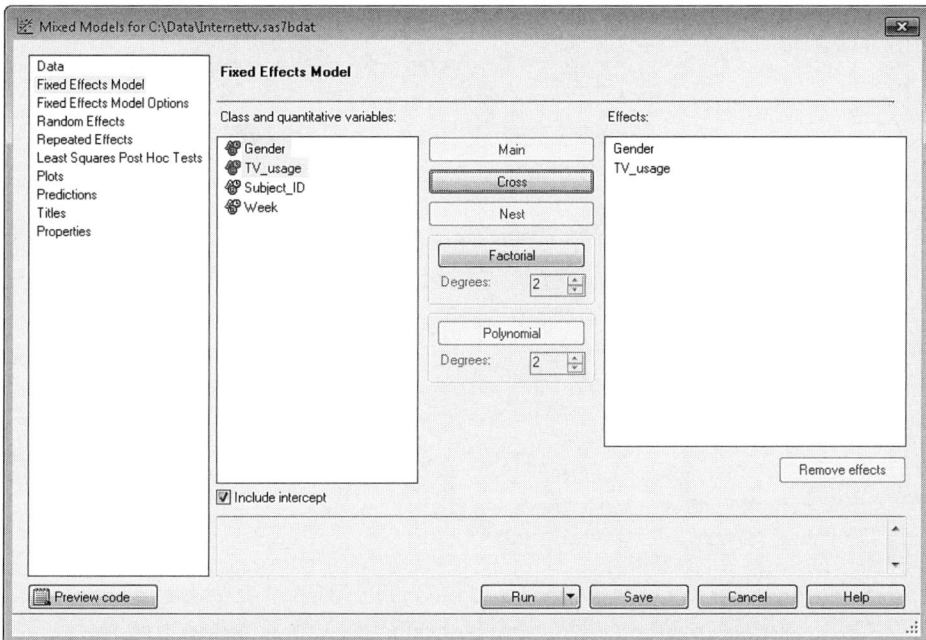

5. In **Model subjects** under the **Repeated Effects** pane, identify the identifier variable by clicking on the **Subject Identifier** option. A pop-up window appears and you select the identifier variable, *Subject_ID*, under **Classification variables**. Finally, you click the button **Main**. The identifier variable appears now under **Subject identifier**. You click **OK** to return to the **Repeated Effect** pane.

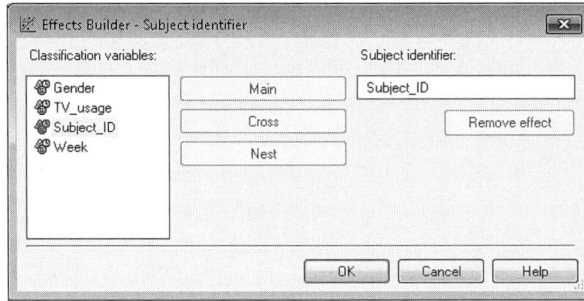

Furthermore, under **Effects to use**, next to the **Within-subjects effect** option, you indicate the time variable in the dataset, the *Week* variable.

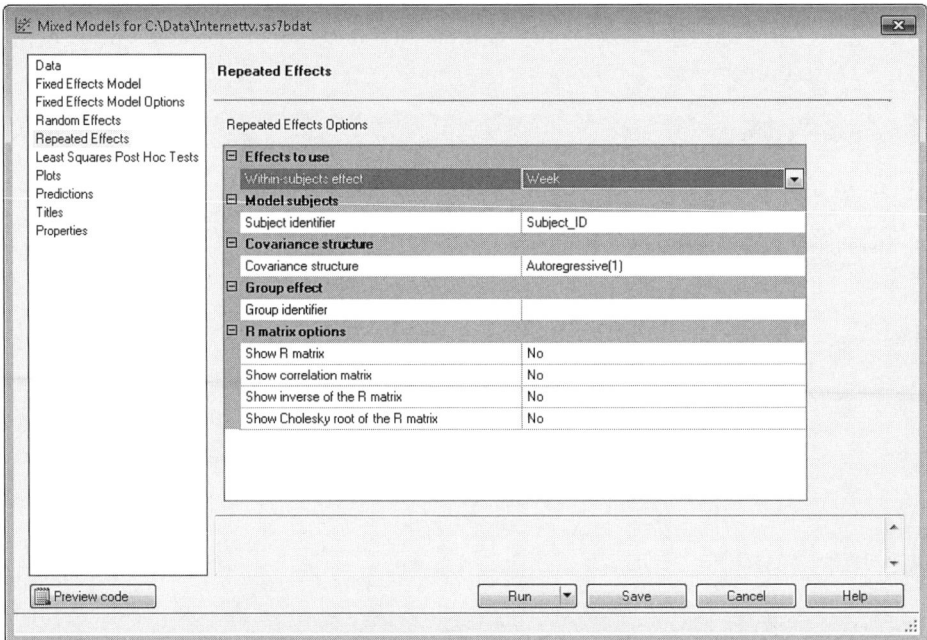

In order to finish the repeated measures ANOVA, you have to change the option **Covariance structure** by ticking the option **Autoregressive(1)**.

6.   Go to **Least Squares Post Hoc Tests** if you want to know whether differences across *Gender* and *TV_usage* exist. Click on the button **Add** if you want to know whether differences exist across the levels of your independent variables and where these differences are found. Select the option **True** for the class effects *Gender* and *TV_usage* under the option **Effects to use** for which you would like to test the mean for. Change the **Show p-values for differences** option under the **Comparisons** option in the scrolling pane to **All pairwise differences** to show the p-values for all mutual comparisons on your independent variables. The figure below shows the different options for this research setting.

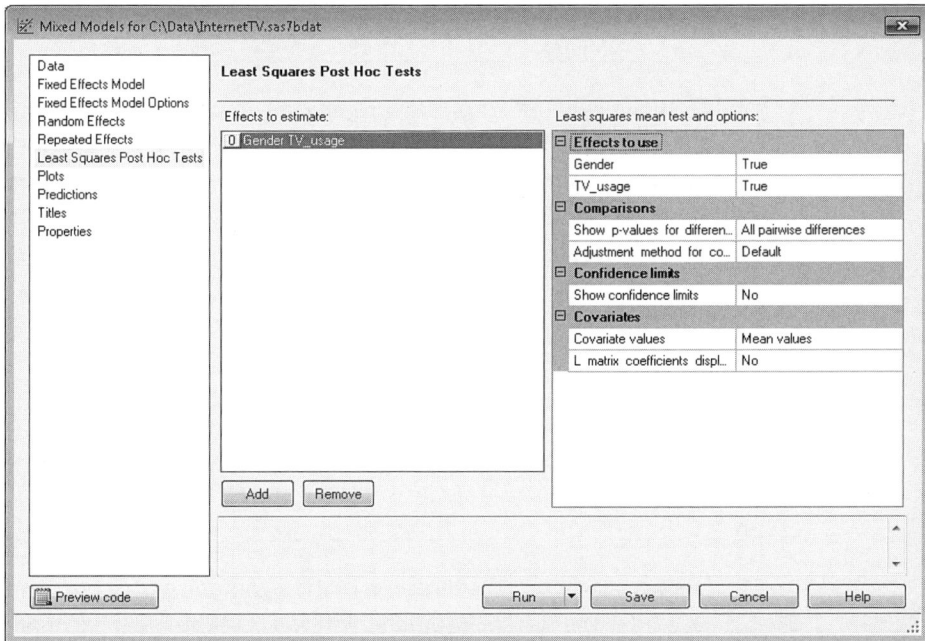

7.   Click **Run** to view the results of these repeated measures ANOVA in the **Results** tab.

Interpretation

* **Null Model Likelihood Ratio Test**

Null Model Likelihood Ratio Test		
DF	Chi-Square	Pr > ChiSq
1	42.94	<.0001

This table indicates whether or not the repeated measures ANOVA is worth doing. The Chi-square value equals 42.94 and the associated p-value is smaller than 0.0001. This is inferior to the significance threshold of 0.05. Consequently, the null hypothesis (H_0) is rejected. This means that there is a significant difference in brand awareness that is explained by the *Gender* and/or *TV_usage* variable.

- **Type 3 Tests of Fixed Effects**

Type 3 Tests of Fixed Effects				
Effect	Num DF	Den DF	F Value	Pr > F
Gender	1	29	26.14	<.0001
TV_usage	1	29	50.46	<.0001

This table shows whether there is a significant impact of *Gender* and *TV_usage* on the brand awareness over time. It shows that both gender (F-value of 26.14 and p-value is smaller than 0.0001) and the television usage (F-value of 50.46 and p-value is smaller than 0.0001) do impact the brand awareness evolution. The null hypothesis (H_0) cannot be accepted.

- **Least Squares Means**

Least Squares Means							
Effect	Gender	TV_usage	Estimate	Standard Error	DF	t Value	Pr > |t|
Gender	F		1.4428	0.1307	29	11.04	<.0001
Gender	M		2.3875	0.1307	29	18.27	<.0001
TV_usage		Heavy	2.5714	0.1307	29	19.68	<.0001
TV_usage		Light	1.2588	0.1307	29	9.63	<.0001

This table gives insight into the direction of the significance of *Gender* and *TV_usage*. Under the header *Estimate*, you will find the mean estimate of the different levels. It is clear from the table that men (*M*) are more influenced than women (*F*), while the heavy (*Heavy*) users are more influenced than the light (*Light*) users.

Managerial Recommendations

In the light of the results obtained, we advise the broadband Internet provider to invest in this advertising campaign as it seems possible to change viewers' brand awareness over time. In order to better target the promotion campaign, time slots with a high number of male viewers and/or heavy viewers are ideal to increase the awareness of the brand over time.

5.2. Non-Parametric Tests

In marketing research, there are situations where the level of measurement of the independent variable is not interval or ratio-scaled or where the data is not normally distributed. These variables may be nominal, ordinal or interval/ratio but not normally distributed. For the sake of clarity, ordinal and interval/ratio data that is not normally distributed is considered as data on the ordinal level. In these cases, non-parametric hypothesis tests have to be used. This section presents the different non-parametric tests in three main sub-sections. The first sub-section is devoted to one sample tests, while the second sub-section explains the tests for independent samples. The last sub-section focuses on dependent samples.

5.2.1. ONE SAMPLE

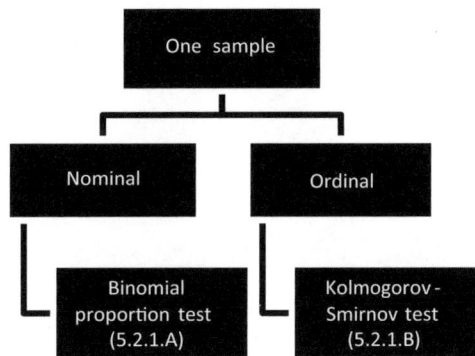

A) Nominal variables: Binomial proportion test

Keywords: one sample, standard

> A binomial proportion test is a non-parametric statistical hypothesis test that compares whether the proportions of a nominal variable deviate from the theoretically expected proportions, the standard.

Managerial Problem

A gas station owner realized that he could increase his fuel prices because consumers were happy with the high quality of service they received in his tanking stations.

For instance, he came to the conclusion that women were more satisfied than men with the new plastic gloves dispensers at their disposal. The gas station owner now considers what he could do to improve the quality of the service in his other gas station, station Z. Will a new plastic gloves dispenser be an option? Before installing the dispenser, he wants to make sure that the proportion of women in station Z is at least equal to the proportion in the main station. He knows that 57 per cent of his consumers in the main station are women and he wants to know if the proportion of women is the same in station Z.

Translation of the Managerial Problem into Statistical Notions

The gas station manager wants to compare the proportion of women in station Z to the known proportion of women in his main station of 57 per cent. He took a two-week clients' sample of station Z and compared the proportion of the gender variable to the known proportion. The binomial proportion test is used for this type of analysis where one compares the proportion of women in station Z to a standard, that is, the proportion of women in the main station.

Dataset Description

The Excel data file *Gas.xlsx* contains the data for this managerial problem. The dataset contains the socio-demographic information relative to the 101 clients who came tanking in the two-week observation period. The variables included in the dataset are listed below.

- The gender identification of each customer during the observation period with *F* for females and *M* for males (*gender*).

- The consumption level of each customer during the observation period (*consumptions*).

Hypotheses

The managerial problem is translated into the following hypotheses:

H_0: There is no significant difference between the proportion of women who tanked at gas station Z and the proportion observed in the main gas station.

H_1: There is a significant difference between the proportion of women who tanked at gas station Z and the proportion observed in the main gas station.

Data Analysis

Running a binomial proportion test comes down to using the **One-Way Frequencies** task in SAS Enterprise Guide.

1. Add the dataset *Gas.xlsx* to your SAS Enterprise Guide process flow.

2. Go to **Tasks** → **Describe** → **One-Way Frequencies...** to let the selection pane pop-up.

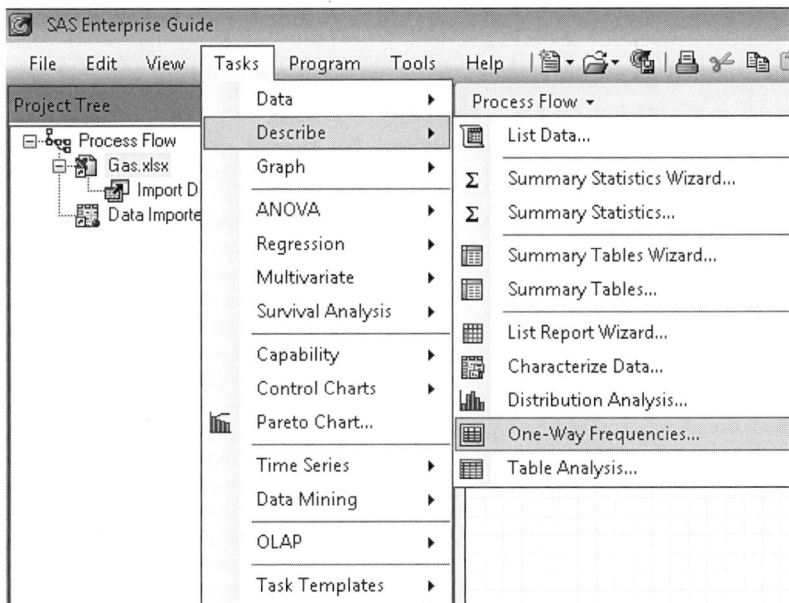

3. In the **Data** pane, drag the variable of interest, in this case *gender*, under the **Analysis variables** role.

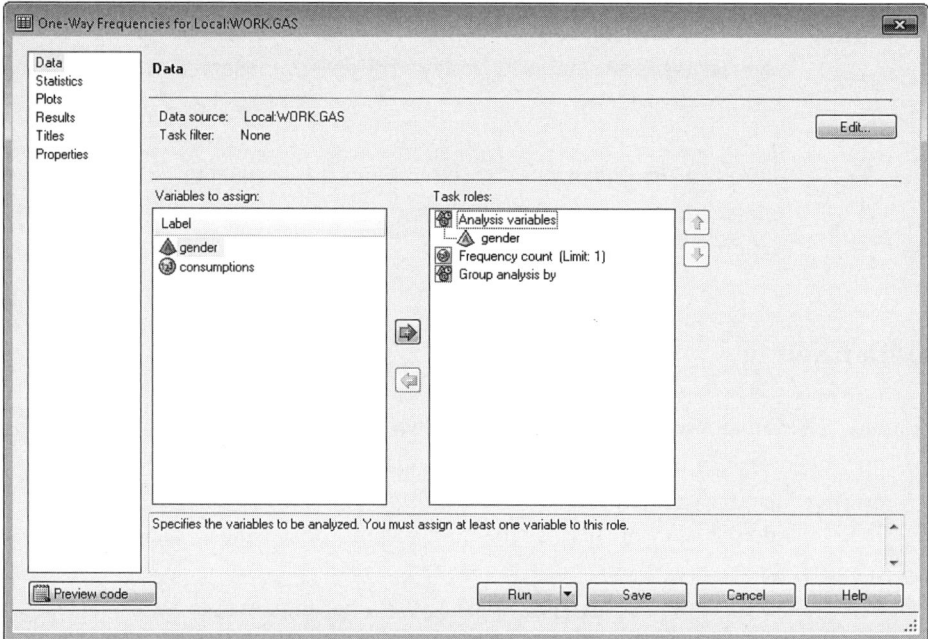

4. Then, select **Statistics** from the selection pane and tick the option **Asymptotic test** under the **Binomial proportions** header. The **Test proportion** box becomes available. Now, you indicate the proportional value towards which the variable of interest is compared, that is, the standard, and the confidence level. In our setting, we would like to compare the proportion of women in station Z to 57 per cent under a 95 per cent confidence level.

The **Asymptotic test** is usually selected in order to provide quick results. However, this statistical procedure only provides an approximation. The **Exact p-values** test provides the exact p-values but requires excessive computing time. This explains why in most cases, the **Asymptotic test** is preferred.

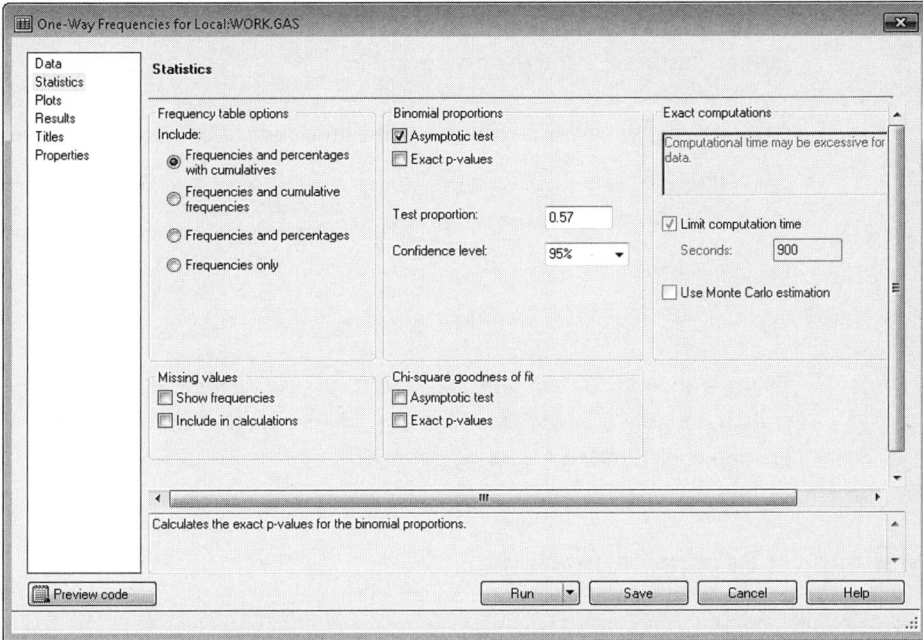

The **Test proportion** option refers to the proportion of the first level of the nominal variable (in other words, the first option) per alphabetical order available for the variable of interest (or the smallest value if coded into 0-1). As the variable gender is coded as F for female and M for male, the **Test proportion** option takes the proportion of the first level in alphabetical order, that is, the females, and thus 0.57 is specified.

5.   Click the **Run** button to get the results in the **Results** tab window.

Interpretation

•   **Test of H0: Proportion = 0.57**

Test of H0: Proportion = 0.57	
ASE under H0	0.0493
Z	0.2874
One-sided Pr > Z	0.3869
Two-sided Pr > |Z|	0.7738

The results indicate that the two-side p-value of the binomial proportion test is 0.7738. This means that the null hypothesis (H_0) cannot be rejected and that there is no significant difference between the proportion of women in station Z and the main station.

- **Gender Frequency Per cent Cumulative Frequency Cumulative Per cent**

Gender	Frequency	Per cent	Cumulative Frequency	Cumulative Per cent
F	59	58.42	59	58.42
M	42	41.58	101	100.00

Taking a look in the column *Per cent*, the empirical distribution of the *gender* variable is specified. This table informs us that the proportion of women in gas station Z is 58.42 per cent.

Managerial Recommendations

If the gas station manager is willing to invest in new dispensers as long as the proportion of women is at least of 57 per cent, the binominal proportion test recommends him to do so. The proportion test did not identify a significant difference in the proportion of women who tanked at station Z compared to the main station. Thus, it appears reasonable to encourage the manager to invest in the well-being of its (female) clients.

B) Ordinal variables: Kolmogorov–Smirnov test

Keywords: one sample, standard

> A one sample Kolmogorov–Smirnov test is a non-parametric statistical hypothesis test that compares the distribution of a sample with the reference probability distribution, that is, the standard.

Given that you want to compare your ordinal data to a standard distribution, the Kolmogorov–Smirnov test is now the appropriate test to use. To find out how to run this test, please refer to section 2.2. Distribution Analysis. The distribution of a variable is there compared to the normal distribution.

5.2.2. INDEPENDENT SAMPLES

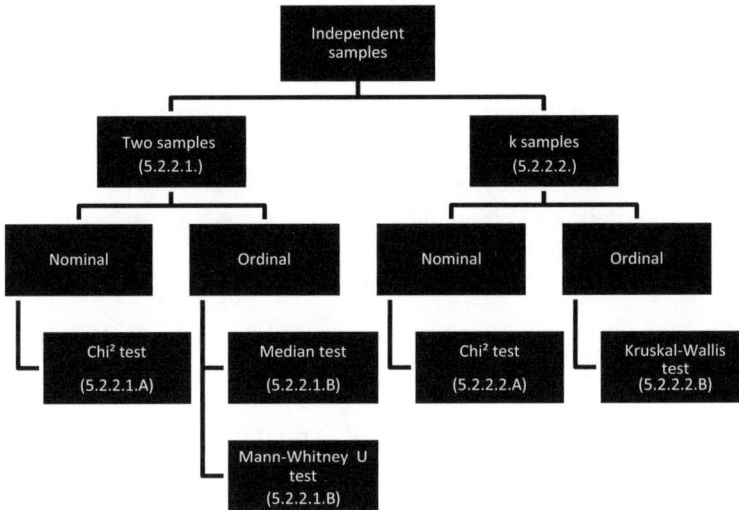

5.2.2.1. Two samples

A) Nominal variables: Chi² test

Keywords: two samples, independent samples

A Chi² test is a non-parametric statistical hypothesis test that compares whether the frequency distribution of two nominal independent samples is equal.

Managerial Problem

IceFarm, an ice cream company, has launched a new cone on to the market. As a special introductory action, the company wants to offer free samples at the entrances of supermarkets. The CEO is convinced that this action will increase brand awareness, and indirectly sales. Nevertheless, he wonders whether or not only women should be targeted for the free sampling. He thinks that women are more sensitive than men to this type of promotional action. Before deciding to run a large-scale free sampling action, he would like to know whether his intuition is correct. In order to check this, students are set in charge. Their task consists of collecting the correct information from consumers in order to make a good decision. In other words, they have to verify, within the group of people who tried the product, whether women are more sensitive to free samples than men.

Translation of the Managerial Problem into Statistical Notions

Students want to identify whether there is a link between the gender of consumers and the purchase of the product after receiving a free sample. Practically, students wrote down: (i) a confirmation that the people interviewed did receive the free sample; (ii) whether or not the respondent bought the product; and (iii) the gender of the respondents. The variables of interest, gender and purchase are measured at the nominal level. The objective is to verify whether there is a significant relationship or dependence between gender and product purchases.

Dataset Description

The data file to consider is *Icecream.sas7bdat*. It proposes a total of 180 observations collected by the students and it represents people who actually tried the product. The variables to consider are the following:

- The gender of these customers, with *F* for female and *M* for male (*Gender*).

- A variable always set to yes, as it confirms that the respondent taken into consideration did receive a sample and tried the product (*Tries*).

- A variable representing whether or not the consumer bought the product: yes (*Y*) or no (*N*) (*Buys*).

Hypotheses

The managerial problem is translated into a null and an alternative hypothesis:

H_0: There is no significant relationship between the gender and the purchase within the group of people who received a sample and tried the new product.

H_1: There is a significant relationship between the gender and the purchase within the group of people who received a sample and tried the new product.

Data Analysis

The Chi² test in SAS Enterprise Guide is run via the **Table Analysis** task.

1. Add the datafile *Icecream.sas7bdat* to your process flow.

2. Select **Tasks** → **Describe** → **Table Analysis...** to build the contingency table. A contingency table or cross tabulation is a visual representation of the frequency distribution of two categorical variables in a matrix format.

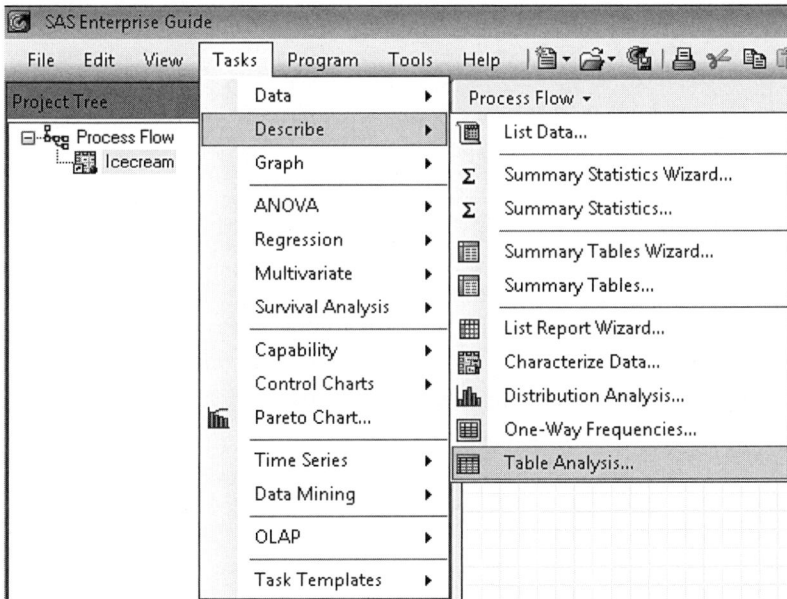

3. The option pane opens at **Data** and you select the correct variables for the contingency table. The variables under consideration, *Gender* and *Buys*, are picked up in the **Variables to assign** box and dropped under the **Table variables** role.

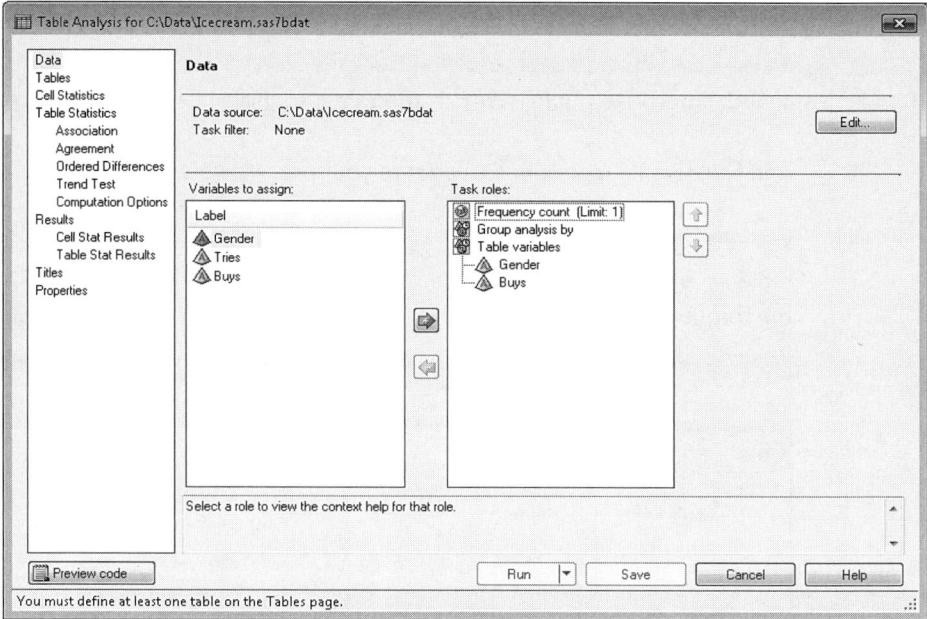

4.   In the selection pane, select **Tables**. The two variables of interest (*Gender* and *Buys*) need to be dropped in the contingency table. Commonly, the independent variable, in our case *Gender*, is placed in the column of the contingency matrix.

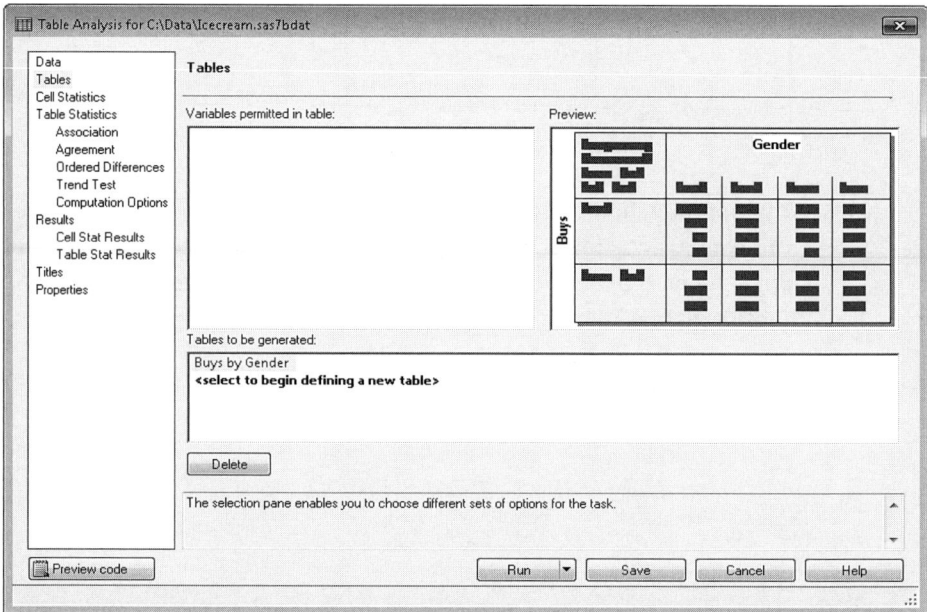

5. Select the **Cell Statistics** pane, and ask for the **Column percentages**, **Cell frequencies** and the **Expected cell frequency** by ticking the respective options.

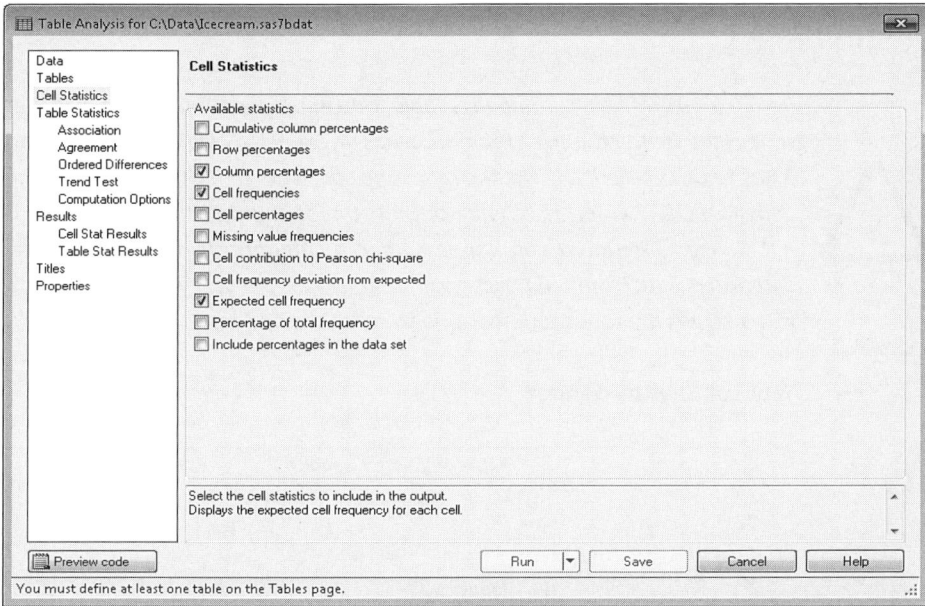

6. Via **Association** under **Table Statistics**, one should now tick the option **Chi-square tests**.

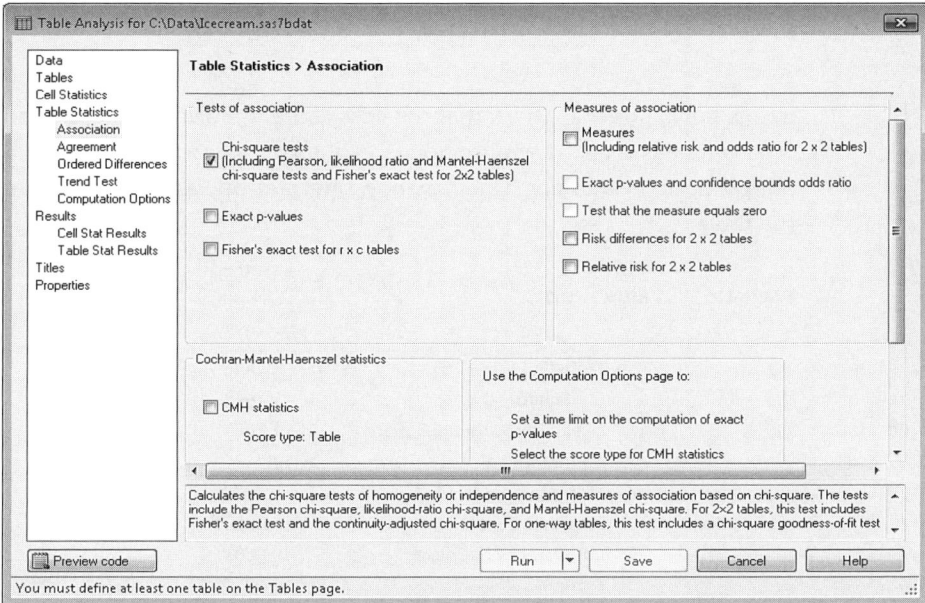

7. Now, click **Run** to see the results in the **Result** tab.

Interpretation

Before interpreting a contingency table, the assumption that less than 20 per cent of the cells of the cross tabulation has an expected frequency of less than 5 has to be checked. If this is the case, one considers that the p-value is valid. Otherwise, SAS Enterprise Guide outputs a warning that this assumption is not fulfilled. The latter can happen when a categorical variable has many categories with a limited number of observations per category. The solution is to merge categories together and to rerun the Chi² test.

• **Table of Buys by Gender**

Table of Buys by Gender				
		Gender		
		F	M	Total
Buys				
N	**Frequency**	80	75	155
	Expected	77.5	77.5	
	Col Pct	88.89	83.33	
Y	**Frequency**	10	15	25
	Expected	12.5	12.5	
	Col Pct	11.11	16.67	
Total	**Frequency**	90	90	180

In this table, one may check that the cells content is always greater than 5. This means that the assumption is verified. SAS Enterprise Guide did not produce the warning. One may now interpret the results provided in the table.

• **Statistic DF Value Prob**

Statistic	DF	Value	Prob
Chi-Square	1	1.1613	0.2812
Likelihood Ratio Chi-Square	1	1.1681	0.2798
Continuity Adj. Chi-Square	1	0.7432	0.3886
Mantel-Haenszel Chi-Square	1	1.1548	0.2825
Phi Coefficient		0.0803	
Contingency Coefficient		0.0801	
Cramer's V		0.0803	

In this table the p-value of the Chi² test is observed. The p-value is 0.2812 and thus the null hypothesis (H_0) cannot be rejected. It appears that there is no significant relationship between the gender and the buying behaviour after receiving a free sample. In other words, the proportion of women who bought after the product trial is not significantly different from the proportion of men who bought. The strength of the link between the variables in the contingency table is valued by the level of the Cramer's V index. It tells us that the relationship between gender and purchase is very weak with an index of 0.0803. A Cramer's V of 1 represents a perfect relationship between the two variables of the contingency table.

*If the p-value of the test had been under the significance level of 0.05, one should have looked into the **Table of Buys by Gender** in order to identify where the difference is. Let's imagine that the output would identify 60 women who did not buy and 30 who did, while the men's scores remained the same, one would have to conclude that women were more sensitive than men to product trial as more women actually bought the product after trying the product.*

Managerial Recommendations

Students report to the company that there is no gender difference as far as sensitivity to sampling is concerned. Men and women demonstrate the same purchase behaviour after receiving a free sample.

B) Ordinal variables: Median Test or Mann–Whitney U test

Keywords: two samples, independent samples

> The Median Test and the Mann–Whitney U test are non-parametric statistical hypothesis tests that compare whether the medians from two independent ordinal samples are equal.

The relative difference between the Median Test and the Mann–Whitney U test is traced back to how the test compares each observation in the sample to the overall median. The Median Test only takes into account the relative position of the observation to the median, that is, lower or higher than the median, while the Mann–Whitney U test additionally takes the ranks of the observations into consideration.

Managerial Problem

Suppose that IceFarm, an ice cream company, wants to find out whether all potential consumers equally rank one of four flavours in their portfolio. They want to know whether both genders equally rank the flavour they intend to propose in a free sampling promotional action, or in other words, whether both men and women equally like the flavour considered for sampling. Indeed, the setting of the sampling action does not enable them to know whether the sample will be given to a woman or a man. The marketing people intend to ask each women and men to rank the four flavours according to the following sequence: 1 for the one they like most and 4 for the one they least like.

Translation of the Managerial Problem into Statistical Notions

Students want to identify whether there is a significant difference in preference between men and women in terms of ice cream flavour. For each flavour there are two samples, men and women, to be compared in terms of preference. Men and women are indisputably two independent samples.

Dataset Description

The data file to consider is *Flavour.xlsx*. It collects a total of 60 observations which represent people who actually gave their ranking order of the four flavours. The variables to consider in this study are the following:

- The gender of the customer, that is, female (*F*) or male (*M*) (*Gender*).

- Customer's ranking for the first flavour (*Flavour_1*).

- Customer's ranking for the second flavour (*Flavour_2*).

- Customer's ranking for the third flavour (*Flavour_3*).

- Customer's ranking for the fourth flavour (*Flavour_4*).

Ranking according to preferences is a typical example of ordinal data, since consumers are asked to order the various options according to their preferences. For each option, the preferences are stated in the following way: *1* is the most liked flavour and *4* the least liked one.

Hypotheses

The managerial problem is translated into the following hypotheses:

H_0:   There is no significant difference in the mean ranking for flavour 1 between males and females.

H_1:   There is a significant difference in the mean ranking for flavour 1 between males and females.

These hypotheses are identical for flavour 2, flavour 3 and flavour 4.

Data Analysis

The **Nonparametric One-Way ANOVA** task is used to run the Median Test or the Mann–Whitney test. The procedure for both tests is the same, but the procedure for the Median Test is shown below.

1.   Add the *Flavour.xlsx* dataset to your SAS Enterprise Guide environment.

2.   The **Nonparametric One-Way ANOVA** task is run via **Tasks → ANOVA → Nonparametric One-Way ANOVA...**

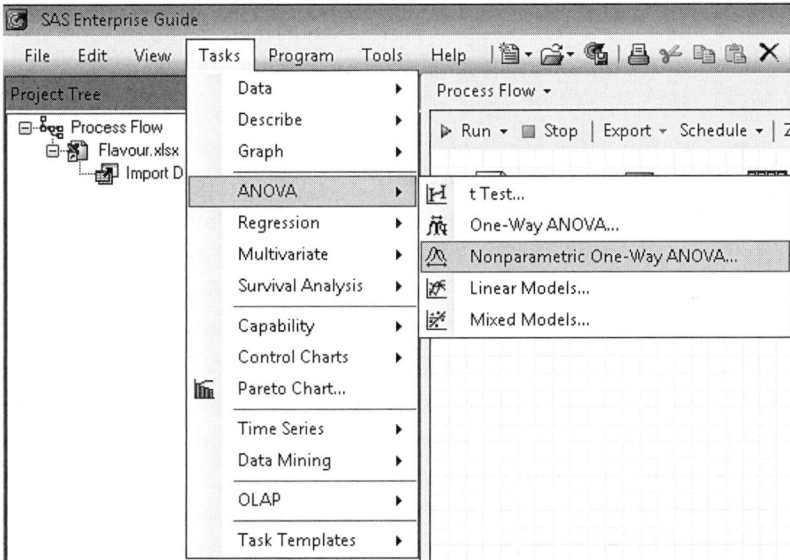

3. Select the variables to be studied in the **Data** pane. The variable of interest or the variable *Flavour_1* is dragged and dropped under the **Dependent variables** role and the independent variable *Gender* is assigned under the **Independent variable** role.

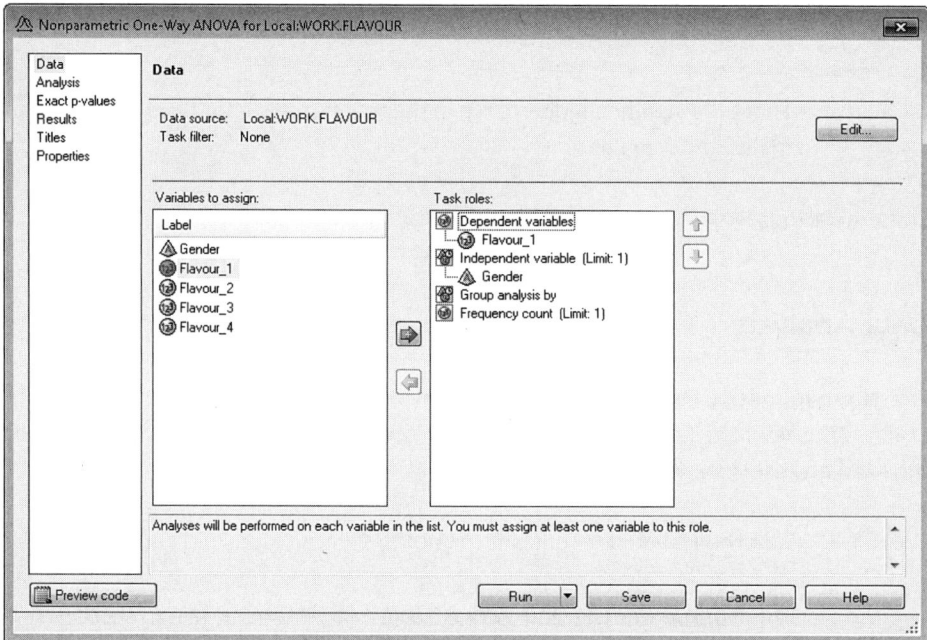

4. In the selection pane, click on **Analysis**. The Median Test is run by clearing the options **Wilcoxon**, **Savage** and **Van der Waerden**.

*The same procedure is followed for the Mann–Whitney U test, but the options **Median**, **Savage** and **Van der Waerden** must be cleared. Only the option **Wilcoxon** is ticked because the Mann–Whitney U test is also known as the Wilcoxon rank-sum test.*

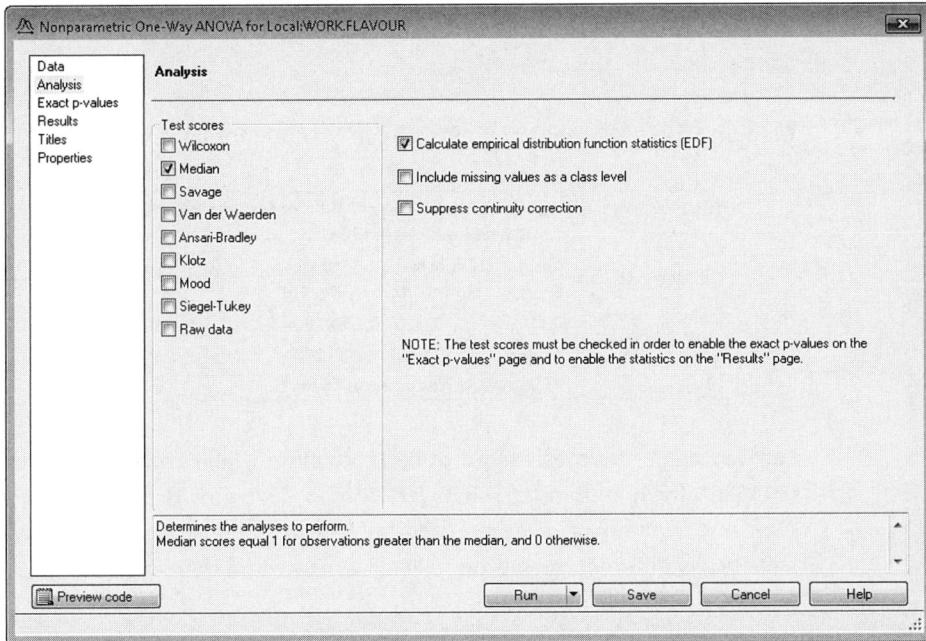

5. Execute the task by clicking **Run** and have a look at the results in the **Results** tab.

Interpretation

- **Median Two-Sample Test**

Median Two-Sample Test	
Statistic	9.6111
Z	-0.7623
One-Sided Pr < Z	0.2229
Two-Sided Pr > |Z|	0.4459

The (two-sided) p-value of the Median Test is equal to 0.4459. This p-value gives sufficient evidence to accept the null hypothesis (H_0). In sum, there is no significant difference in the (median) preference between men and women for the first ice cream flavour.

 *If the managerial problem had consisted in identifying a higher (lower) rank for flavour_1 among women as compared to men (in other words, an hypothesis of superiority (inferiority) and not an hypothesis of difference),*

than one should look at the One-Sided Pr <Z p-value in the Median Two-Sample Test.

- **Median Scores (Number of Points Above Median) for Variable Flavour_1**

Gender	N	Sum of Scores	Expected Under H0	Std Dev Under H0	Mean Score
M	22	9.611111	11.0	1.821904	0.436869
F	38	20.388889	19.0	1.821904	0.536550

Median Scores (Number of Points Above Median) for Variable Flavour_1 Classified by Variable Gender. Average scores were used for ties.

For *Flavour_1*, the mean score to be read under *Mean Score* is equal to 0.436869 for men and 0.536550 for women. This means that although men and women on average ordered *Flavour_1* in a way that is not statistically different, men tend to like it a little more than women.

Managerial Recommendations

It appears that potential customers, whatever their gender is, equally rank the first ice cream flavour. In other words, if Icefarm decides to sample flavour 1, men and women will be equally satisfied with this promotional tasting. This information becomes very valuable in free sampling situations where Icefarm does not really get to know to whom, women or men, the sample is going to be given.

5.2.2.2. K SAMPLES

A) Nominal variables: Chi² test

Keywords: k samples, independent samples

A Chi² test is a non-parametric statistical hypothesis test that compares whether the frequency distribution of more than two nominal independent samples is equal.

The problem here is similar to the Chi² test for nominal variables when having only two samples. The only difference is that in this case three or more samples are considered during the creation of the cross tabulation, and thus during Chi² testing. One should follow the procedure explained in section 5.2.2.1. A. (Two samples, Nominal variables, Chi² test).

B) Ordinal variables: Kruskal–Wallis test

Keywords: k samples, independent samples

> The Kruskal–Wallis test is a non-parametric statistical hypothesis test that compares whether the medians from more than two independent ordinal samples are equal.

The problem is similar to the Mann–Whitney test that compares ordinal variables between two samples. The Kruskal–Wallis test is a generalization of the Mann–Whitney when three or more samples are considered. The same procedure is followed as explained in section 5.2.2.1.B. (Two samples, Ordinal variables: Median Test or Mann–Whitney U test.)

5.2.3. DEPENDENT SAMPLES

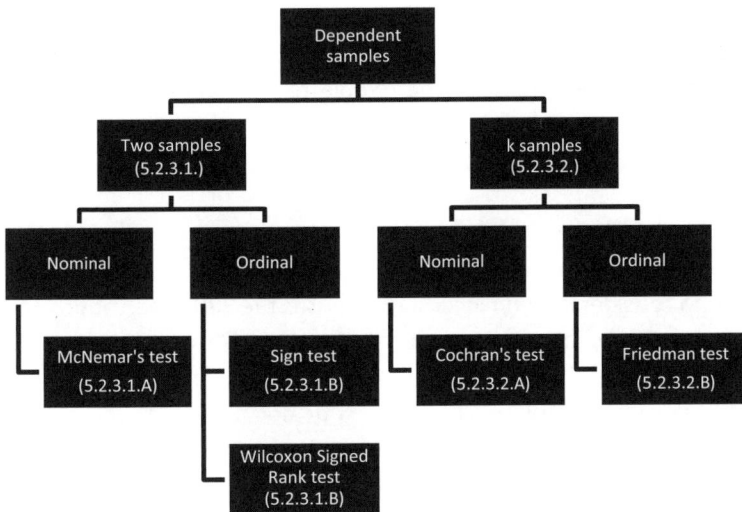

5.2.3.1. Two samples

A) Nominal variable: McNemar's Test

Keywords: two samples, dependent samples

> A McNemar's test is a non-parametric statistical hypothesis test that compares whether the frequency distributions of two nominal dependent samples are equal.

Managerial Problem

IcotU, a famous English company, considers doing free sampling to promote their product on the Spanish market. Although they have been selling it for quite some time in Spain, the marketing people are unsure whether or not distributing free samples is a successful promotional tool in southern European countries. In order to make sound marketing investments, the CEO requests that the marketing researcher tries the free sampling action on a limited number of customers and checks whether the intention to buy before and after the sampling have significantly changed.

Translation of the Managerial Problem into Statistical Notions

The purpose is to statistically compare the buying intentions of a group of people before and after the distribution of the free samples. The intention to buy question is asked to the same group of individuals and thus these two samples (before and after) are dependent. The marketing research agency collected the purchase intentions through a yes–no question, that is, a nominal variable, and these purchase intentions must be compared amongst the same people before and after the free sampling campaign.

Dataset Description

The data file to consider is *Sampling.xls*. It proposes the 380 observations collected by students. The variables to consider are the following:

- Consumers' intentions to buy (*Y*) or not to buy (*N*) the product before sampling (*Buys_before*).

- Consumers' intentions to buy (*Y*) or not to buy (*N*) the product after sampling (*Buys_after*).

- The respondents gender: *M* for males, *F* for females (*Gender*).

Hypotheses

The managerial problem for the McNemar's test is translated in following hypotheses:

H_0: There is no significant difference between the consumers' intentions to buy the product prior to the product trial and after trying the product.

H_1: There is a significant difference between the consumers' intentions to buy the product prior to the product trial and after trying the product.

Data Analysis

The McNemar's test is run using the **Table Analysis** task in SAS Enterprise Guide.

1. Add the *Sampling.xls* dataset to your process flow.

2. Go to **Tasks** → **Describe** → **Table Analysis...** as a contingency table is required to run the McNemar's test. A contingency table or a cross tabulation is a matrix representing the frequencies of respondents per level of the variables under consideration.

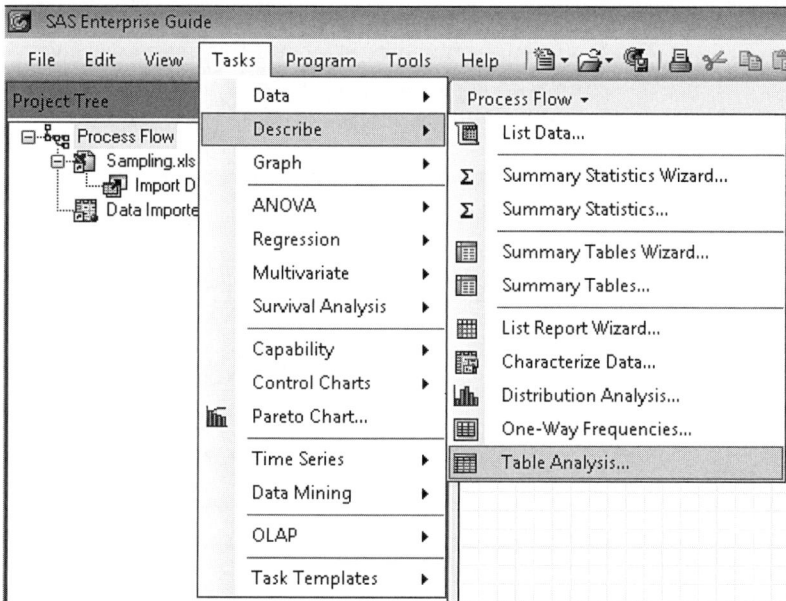

3. The selection pane opens at **Data**. At this stage, one has to drop the variables of interest under the **Table variables** role, that is, *Buys_before* and *Buys_after* in this setting.

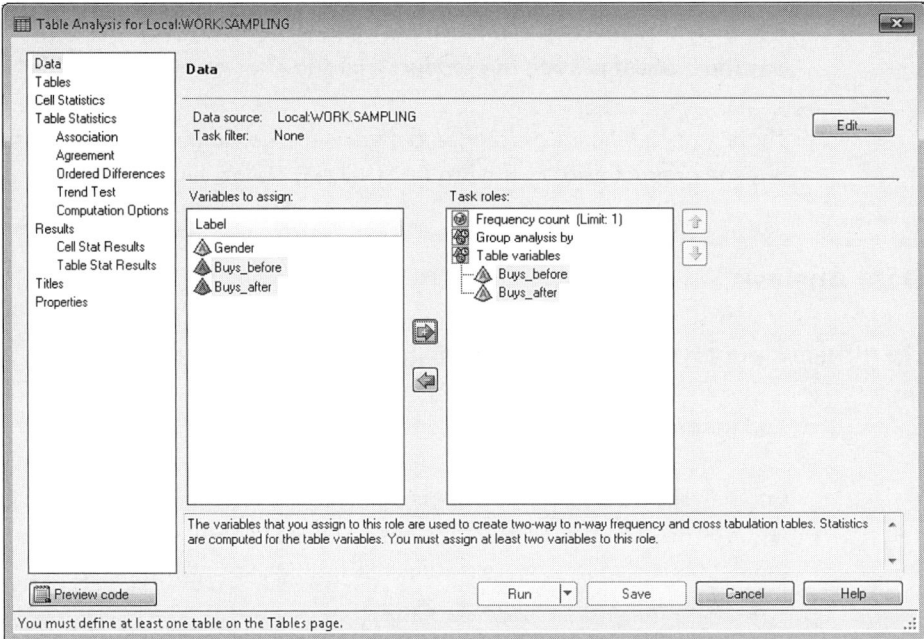

4. The **Tables** pane should be selected. This action will give the analyst the opportunity to construct a contingency table. The *Buys_before* is put in the column and the *Buys_after* is put in the rows.

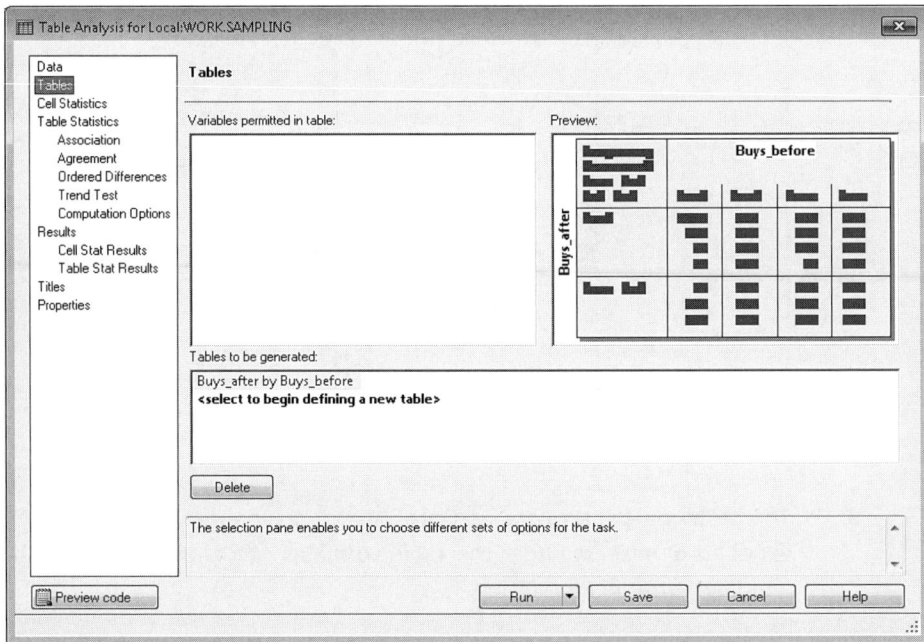

5. In the pane **Agreement** under **Table Statistics**, one ticks the option **Measures** which will run the McNemar's test.

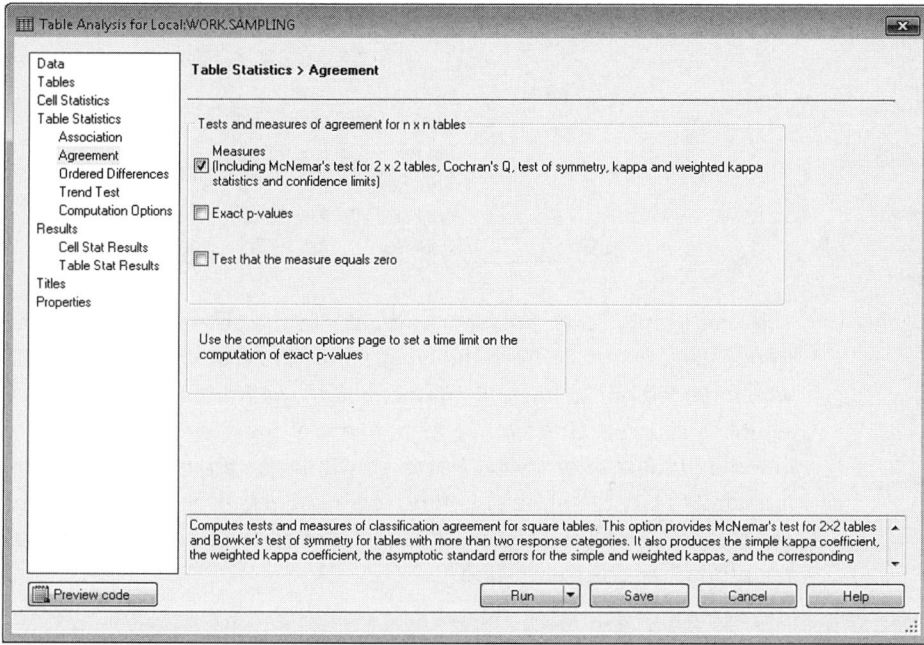

6. Click **<u>Run</u>** to run the McNemar's test. The results are found in the **Results** tab.

Interpretation

- **McNemar's Test**

McNemar's Test	
Statistic (S)	205.7143
DF	1
Pr > S	<.0001

The S-statistic and p-value of the McNemar's test are included in this table. The S-statistic is equal to 205.7143 and the p-value is smaller than 0.0001. This indicates that there is a significant difference. The null hypothesis (H_0) is rejected and thus significant differences exist between the different cells of the contingency table.

- **Table of Buys_after by Buys_before**

Table of Buys_after by Buys_before				
		Buys_before		
		N	Y	Total
Buys_after				
N	Frequency	25	20	45
	Col Pct	8.77	21.05	
Y	Frequency	260	75	335
	Col Pct	91.23	78.95	
Total	Frequency	285	95	380

The contingency table gives more insight into the distribution of the cell frequencies. It is clear from the cross tabulation that within the people who intended not to buy the product before the free sampling, the free sampling action is effective. 91.23 per cent of these people intended to buy the product after trying. However, within the group of people who intended to buy the product before, there is a negative effect of the free sampling action because only 78.95 per cent of these people would buy the product again after testing it.

Managerial Recommendations

Based on these results, the marketing researcher could report to the manager that the product sampling has a very positive effect among the people who never tried the product before the sampling. However, it would be important to state that a proportion of Spanish people do not seem to appreciate this free sampling: they do not want to buy the product anymore. For instance, it is possible that this marketing practice affects their perception of the product image. English products may be perceived as exclusive and the free sampling may damage this perception.

B) Ordinal: Sign test or Wilcoxon Signed Rank test

Keywords: two samples, dependent samples

> The Sign test and the Wilcoxon Signed Rank test are non-parametric statistical hypothesis tests that compare whether the medians from two dependent ordinal samples are equal.

The relative difference between the Sign test and the Wilcoxon Signed Rank test is traced back to how the test compares each observation in the sample to the overall median. The Sign test only takes into account the relative position of the observation to the median, that is, lower or higher than the median, while the Wilcoxon Signed Rank test additionally takes the ranks of the observations into consideration.

Managerial Problem

Suppose that a perfume company wants to invest in a massive communication campaign in women's magazines for the launch of a new scent. However, brand managers hesitate between two types of advertisement. On the one hand, they consider an advertisement that embeds free perfume samples; while on the other hand, they are considering a much cheaper advertisement that does not incorporate free samples. Since the advertisement with the free samples is far more expensive, the company would like to know beforehand whether enabling women to actually smell the perfume will increase their intention to buy it, in comparison to the traditional, cheaper type of advertisement.

Translation of the Managerial Problem into Statistical Notions

One would like to identify whether there is a significant difference in proportion of buying intentions for women who did get an opportunity to smell the perfume, before and after they tried it. In this specific situation, we are comparing the purchase intentions before and after smelling the product, knowing that the intention to buy is measured on an ordinal scale. In this context, dependent samples are considered since the same women are asked to provide their purchase intentions before and after smelling the perfume.

Dataset Description

The data file to consider is the *Perfume.xls*. It contains 143 observations. The variables to consider in the dataset are listed below.

- The intentions to buy before smelling the perfume (with *1* for no, *2* for maybe and *3* for yes) (*Buys_before_trial*).

- The purchase intentions after the product trial (with 1 for no, 2 for maybe and and 3 for yes) (*Buys_after_trial*).

- The difference between the two types of intentions, that is, *Buys_after_trial* – *Buys_before_trial* (*Buys_after_before*). This variable is created for SAS Enterprise Guide to run the test.

Hypotheses

The managerial problem is translated as follows:

H_0:   There is no significant difference in the median of the women's intentions to buy the perfume before and after smelling the perfume.

H_1:   There is a significant difference in the median of the women's intentions to buy the perfume before and after smelling the perfume.

Data Analysis

The procedure of running the Sign test or the Wilcoxon Signed Rank test is the same. For both tests the **Distribution Analysis** task is used.

1.   Add the data file *Perfume.xls* to your SAS Enterprise Guide environment.

2.   Go to **Tasks** → **Describe** → **Distribution Analysis...** to open the selection pane.

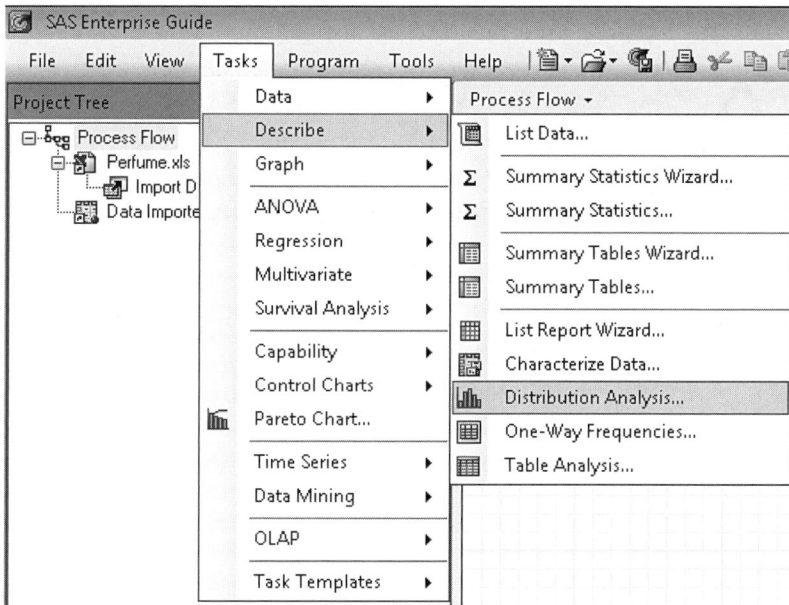

3. The selection pane opens at **Data**. Drag and drop the variable that represents the difference between the purchase intention after the trial and the purchase intention before the trial, that is, the *Buys_after_before* variable, under the **Analysis variables** role.

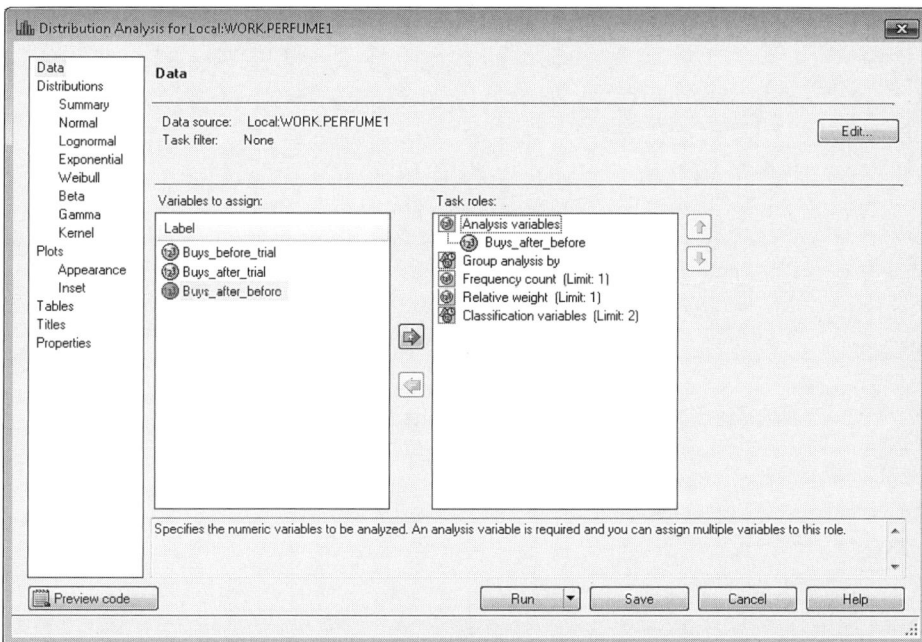

Although the Sign test and the Wilcoxon Signed Rank test compare two dependent samples, SAS Enterprise Guide only expects one variable in the Data Analysis step which represents the difference between the two dependent samples. Depending on one's own dataset, this variable may need to be constructed for the test to be run. Sections 1.6.2 Creating New Variables Using Expressions and 1.6.3 Recoding Variables will help you with that.

4. In the selection pane, select **Tables**. Make sure that the option **Tests for location** is ticked and that the null hypothesis value is set to 0. As such, the sign test and the Wilcoxon Signed Rank test will test whether the median of the difference in purchase intentions before and after the trial is equal to 0, that is, *Buys_after_trial* is equal to *Buys_before_trial*.

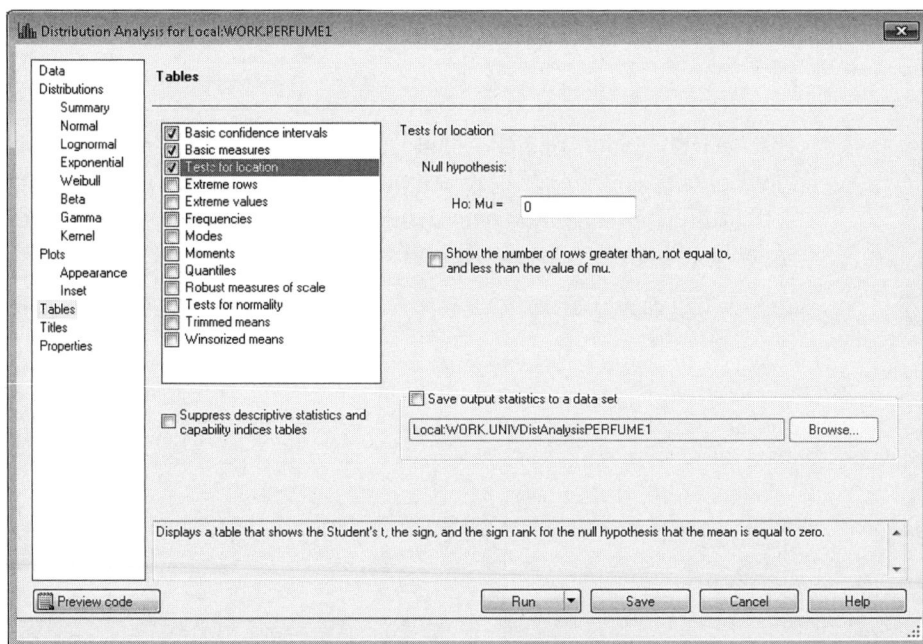

5. Now, click **Run** and check the results in the **Results** tab.

Interpretation

- **Tests for Location: Mu0=0**

Tests for Location: Mu0=0				
Test		Statistic		p Value
Student's t	t	-7.05788	Pr > |t|	<.0001
Sign	M	-23.5	Pr >= |M|	<.0001
Signed Rank	S	-937	Pr >= |S|	<.0001

The table reports the p-values of the Sign test (to be found in the row *Sign*) and the Wilcoxon Signed Rank test (to be found in the row *Signed Rank*). Both tests have a p-value smaller than 0.0001 and thus the null hypothesis is rejected. It indicates that the median of the difference between the two purchase intention measures is different from 0. In other words, this means that *Buys_after_trial* and *Buys_before_trial* are significantly different from one another.

- **Basic Statistical Measures**

Basic Statistical Measures			
Location		Variability	
Mean	-0.58741	Std Deviation	0.99526
Median	0.00000	Variance	0.99054
Mode	0.00000	Range	4.00000
		Interquartile Range	2.00000

The results indicate that an impact exists of letting consumers try the perfume before buying it. The mean value of the difference between *Buys_after_trial* and *Buys_before_trial* to be found in the column *Mean* is negative (-0.58741). This means that the purchase intention before trying the product is bigger than the purchase intention after trying the product.

Managerial Recommendations

The results clearly indicate that the perfume sampling tactic had an impact on the consumer's intention to buy the product. Unfortunately, in this case, the results provided by the mean value of the purchase intentions tell us that the perfume itself does not seem to seduce the people who have been able to try it. As a conclusion, one may advise the company to at least sample the perfume on a larger scale to make sure that it does have commercial potential. For sure, further investigation is needed.

5.2.3.2. k samples

A) Nominal variable: Cochran's test

Keywords: k samples, dependent samples

> A Cochran's test is a non-parametric statistical hypothesis test that compares whether the frequency distributions of more than two nominal dependent samples are equal.

The problem here is similar to the McNemar's test for nominal variables that considers two dependent samples. The only difference is that in this case three or more samples are considered during hypothesis testing. The same procedure is followed as explained in section 5.2.3.1. A. (Two samples, Nominal Variables: Mc Nemar's Test).

B) Ordinal variables: Friedman test

Keywords: k samples, dependent samples.

> The Friedman test is a non-parametric statistical hypothesis test that compares whether the medians from more than two dependent ordinal samples are equal.

Managerial Problem

A company would like to improve the quality of its service. From discussion with their clients, they identify three possible dimensions on which they could provide improvements. However, these three options have a different impact on their cost structure. The first option is the most expensive to implement, the second option and the third option have both a medium rate cost. In order to appropriately choose which option to implement, a quick survey is conducted. The board of directors agrees that there is no need to implement a very expensive solution, if a cheaper option provides the same perceived improvement in service quality. The objective of this study is to identify whether all three options would equally impact the service quality perception.

Translation of the Managerial Problem into Statistical Notions

One wants to identify whether the clients perceive the three options as significantly different. The three options are evaluated by the same clients resulting in the creation of three dependent samples, that is, one for each option. The importance of each service is measured on an ordinal scale, referring to a categorical variable indicating whether an option is important or not important. The final outcome is an ordinal importance measure for the three options evaluated by the same set of clients.

Hypotheses

We can write the managerial problem in the following way:

H_0:   There are no significant differences between the importance levels of the three options.

H_1:   There is at least one option that shows a significantly different importance level.

Dataset Description

The data file *Importance.xlsx* is the result of the data collection. It contains 35 observations, corresponding to the answers of the 35 consumers interviewed. The variables under consideration are the following:

*   The evaluation of option 1's importance measured on an ordinal scale, (with *1* for yes, it is important and *0* for no, it is not important) (*Option1*).

*   The same evaluation on option 2 (*Option2*).

*   The same evaluation on option 3 (*Option3*).

Data Analysis

The Friedman test is run using the **Table Analysis** task in SAS Enterprise Guide.

1.   Add the data file *Importance.xlsx* to your SAS Enterprise Guide environment.

2.   Open the **Table Analysis** task by clicking **Tasks** → **Describe** → **Table Analysis...**

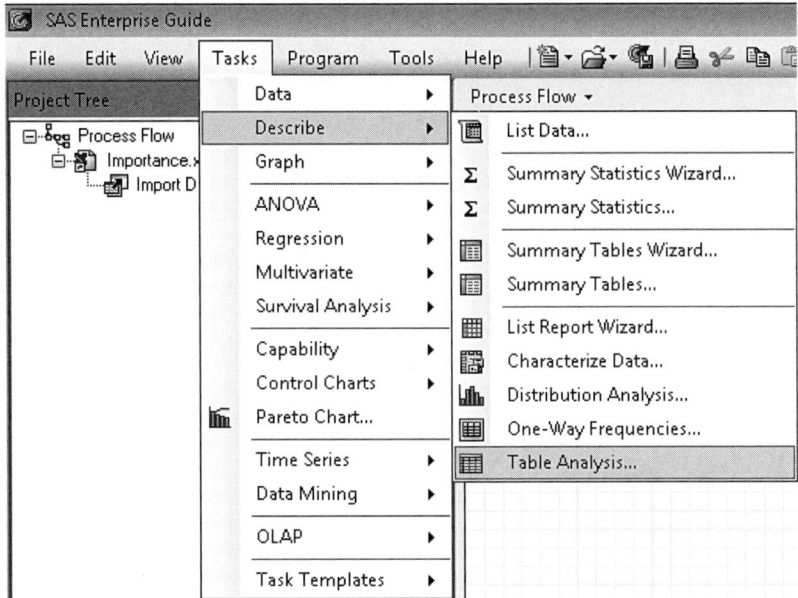

3.   The selection pane opens at **Data**. Drag and drop the variables under consideration, that is, *Option1*, *Option2* and *Option3*, under the **Table variables** role.

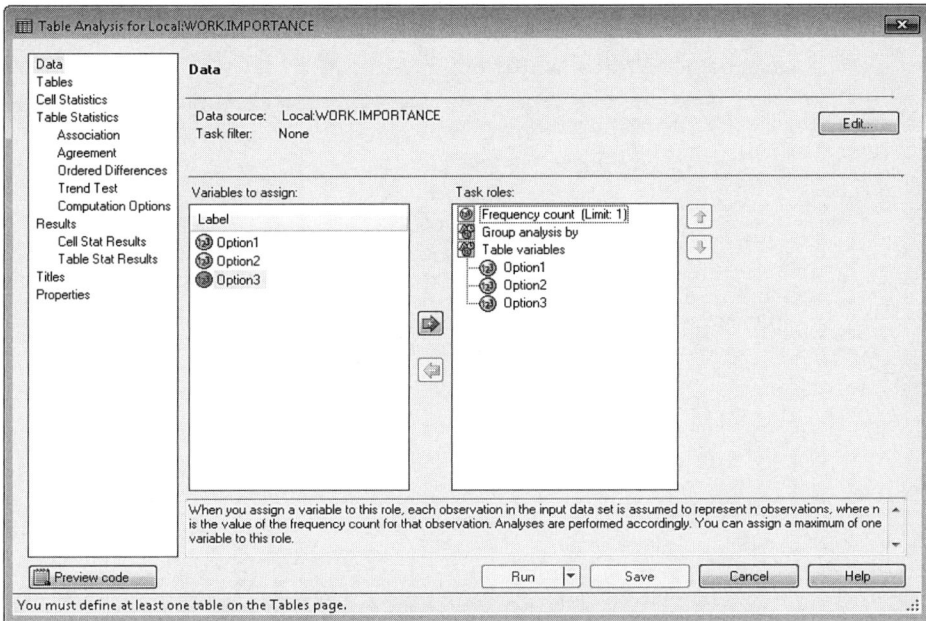

4. In the selection pane, select **Tables**. In the **Variables permitted in table** list, right-click the variable *Option1*. From the pop-up window that appears, select the **Assign to table** option. Repeat this step for the variables *Option2* and *Option3*, respecting that order.

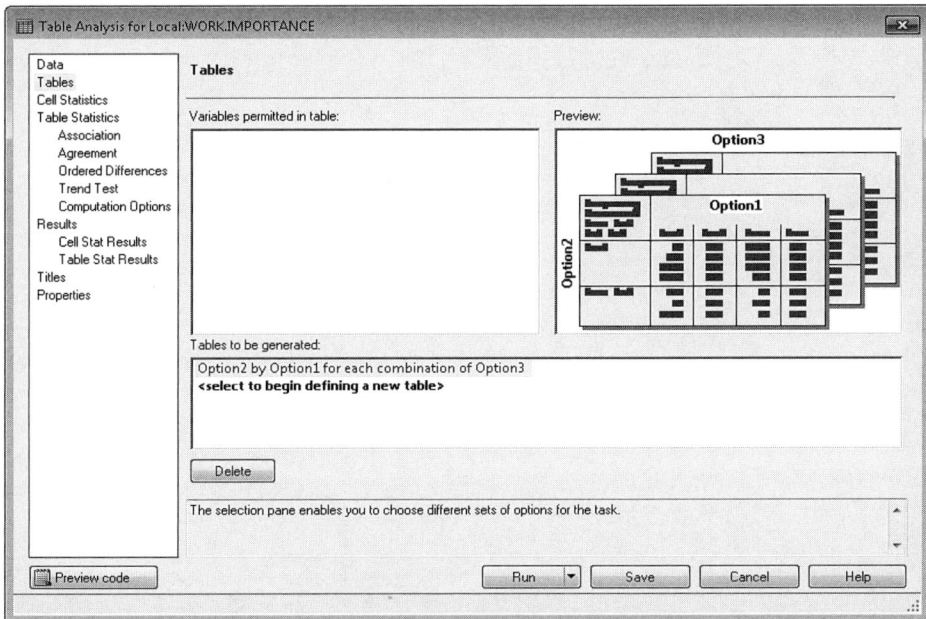

5. In the selection pane, select **Association** under **Table Statistics**. Make sure that the **CMH statistics** option is checked.

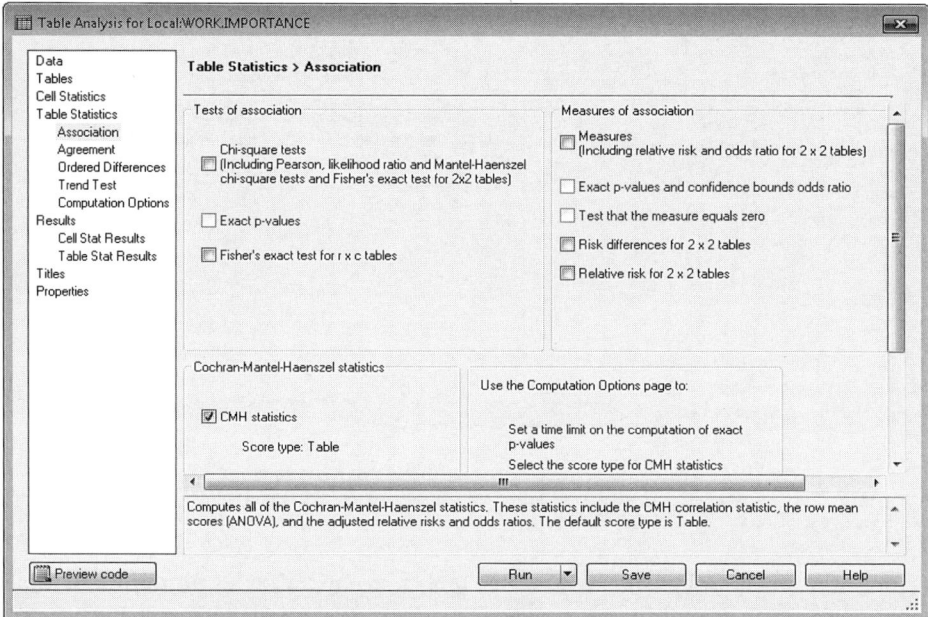

6. Back in the selection pane, select **Computation Options** under **Table Statistics**. Under the option **Score type**, tick the **Rank** option.

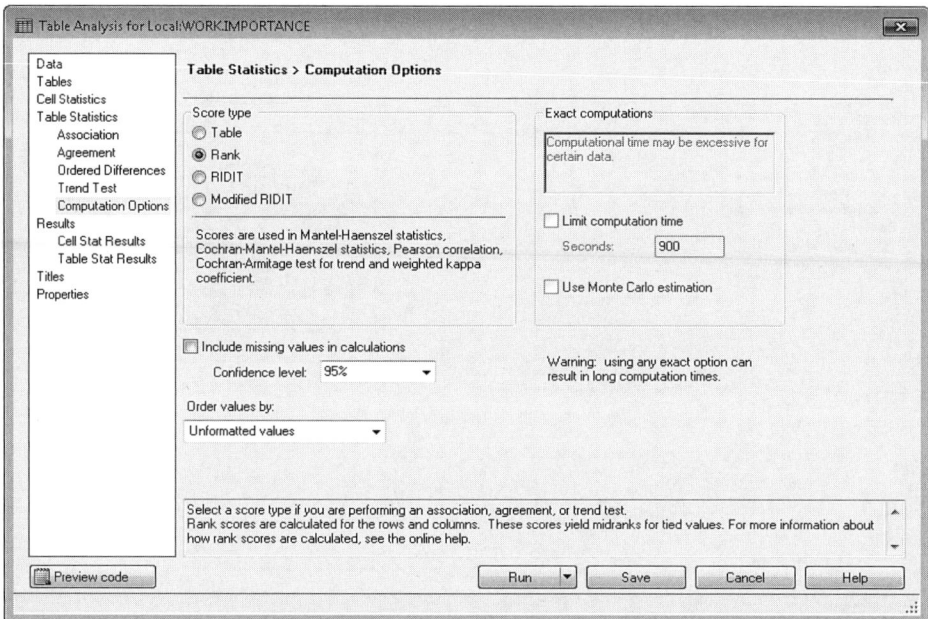

7.   Now, click the **Run** button and check the results in the **Results** tab.

Interpretation

•   **Cochran–Mantel–Haenszel Statistics (Based on Rank Scores)**

Cochran–Mantel–Haenszel Statistics (Based on Rank Scores)			
Statistic Alternative Hypothesis	DF	Value	Prob
1 Nonzero Correlation	1	0.7377	0.3904
2 Row Mean Scores Differ	1	1.0645	0.3022
3 General Association	1	1.6473	0.1993

This table indicates the significance of the Friedman test. In this setting, the results of the Friedman test statistic are identical to the Cochran–Mantel–Haenszel statistic to be read in the row *Row Mean Scores Differ* in the column *Alternative Hypothesis*. The p-value is equal to 0.3022 and thus larger than 0.05. Consequently, the null hypothesis (H_0) is accepted, meaning that no significant differences exist between the three options.

Imagine that the Friedman test did identify a difference between the three options. Unfortunately, the Friedman test does not provide information on where the significant difference exists. In order to statistically identify the difference, one could use the McNemar's test to compare pairs of options.

Managerial Recommendations

It appears reasonable to recommend that the company prioritize the implementation of option 2 or 3 to their service. All options have indeed been identified as equally important by consumers. If the company has limited resources and can only implement one option at a time, it seems strategically wise to recommend the implementation of option 2 or 3 since they are less expensive and perceived as important to consumers as option 1.

Further Reading

Agresti, A. (2002), *Categorical Data Analysis*, Wiley Series in Probability and Statistics, 2nd edition, Wiley-Interscience.

Conover, W.J. (1998), *Practical Non-parametric Statistics*, Wiley Series in Probability and Statistics, 3rd edition, Wiley.

Gibbons, J.D. (1992), *Non-parametric Statistics: An Introduction*, *Quantitative Applications in the Social Sciences*, Sage Publications, Inc.

Gonzalez, R. (2008), *Data Analysis for Experimental Design*, 1st edition, The Guilford Press.

Iacobucci, D. (1994), Analysis of Experimental data, in Bagozzi, R.P. (ed.) (1994), *Principle of Marketing Research*, Blackwell Publishing.

Maxwell, S.E. and Delaney, H.D. (2003), *Designing Experiments and Analyzing Data: A Model Comparison Perspective*, 2nd edition, Routledge Academic.

Sprent, P. and Smeeton, N.C. (2007), *Applied Non-parametric Statistical Methods*, 4th edition, Chapman and Hall/CRC Texts in Statistical Science.

Chapter 6

Correlations

Objectives

1. **Visualize relationships between two variables.**

2. **Understand the difference between the different types of correlation metrics.**

Fundamentals

This chapter gives insight into the relationship of two variables by means of correlation analysis. Indeed, correlations are an ideal tool to discover the association between two variables. A correlation analysis does not only give the analyst an indication whether two variables have a significant relationship, but it also shows whether this relationship is positive or negative.

Different correlation metrics are available to the marketing analyst, and an explanation of the differences as defined by the SAS Enterprise Guide Help is given below:

- **Pearson** calculates Pearson product–moment correlation. This is a parametric measure of association for two continuous random variables. The correlations range from -1 to 1.

- **Hoeffding** calculates the Hoeffding's measure of dependence, D. This is a non-parametric measure of association that detects more general departures from independence. This D statistic scales the range between -0.5 and 1 so that only large positive values indicate dependence.

- **Kendall** calculates Kendall tau-b. This is a non-parametric measure of association that is based on the number of concordances and discordances in paired observations. Concordance occurs when paired observations vary together, and discordance occurs when paired observations vary differently. Kendall's tau-b ranges from -1 to 1.

- **Spearman** calculates Spearman rank–order correlation. This is a non-parametric measure of association that is based on the rank of the data values. The correlations range from -1 to 1.

A correlation analysis differs from a regression analysis in the sense that a correlation analysis does not impose a causal relationship between two variables. Practically, there is no need to define the dependent variable and the independent variable in a correlation analysis. Very often a correlation analysis is used as a preceding step to regression analysis in order to discover the overall trend between two variables. Regression analysis goes a step further than correlation analysis because regression analysis aims at explaining the variation of the dependent variable by another variable called the independent variable.

Managerial Problem

A retail manager recently conducted a survey among 200 customers. Various questions such as the overall satisfaction level and the consumer's emotional responses, that is, the arousal and pleasure level, were asked. Now the retail manager wants to know whether there is a relationship between the satisfaction levels of the customers on the one hand, and their arousal and pleasure level on the other hand. Furthermore, the retail manager would like to understand if the overall store satisfaction varies in the same direction as the arousal and pleasure, that is, whether these relationships are positive. Intuitively, he thinks that the overall satisfaction level is related to the consumers' emotional responses, while he expects to see a positive relationship between the satisfaction level and the pleasure level, and a negative relationship between the arousal level and the satisfaction level.

Dataset Description

This section makes use of the *Correlation.xls* dataset that contains following variables:

- A respondent identifier (*Id*).

- A global store satisfaction index (with 1 = very unsatisfied to 10 = very satisfied) (*GlobalEvalStore*).

- A composite score measuring the level of pleasure experienced during shopping (with 1 = not fun to 5 = very nice) (*Pleasure*).

- A composite index that reflects the level of arousal during the shopping trip (with 1 = relaxed to 5 = excited) (*Arousal*).

Data Analysis

To run a correlation analysis in SAS Enterprise Guide, the **Correlations** task is used.

1.   Add *Correlation.xls* to your SAS Enterprise Guide environment.

2.   Go to **Tasks** → **Multivariate** → **Correlations...**

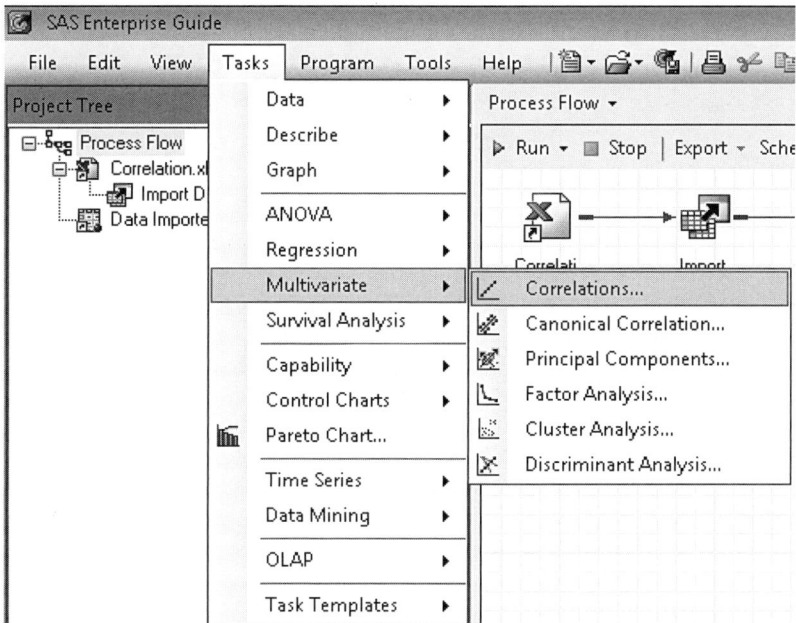

3.   In a next step in the **Data** pane, you should drag and drop the relevant variables to the different **Task roles**. If you drop variables under the **Analysis variables** role, mutual correlations are run for each and every variable under that role. If you drop additionally a variable under the **Correlate with** role, SAS Enterprise Guide runs a correlation analysis between that variable and each and every variable under the **Analysis variables** role. In this example, we are interested to see whether a relationship exists between *GlobalEvalStore* and *Pleasure*, and *GlobalEvalStore* and *Arousal*. So the variable *GlobalEvalStore* is dropped under the **Analysis variables** role, while the *Pleasure* and *Arousal* variables are put under the **Correlate with** role.

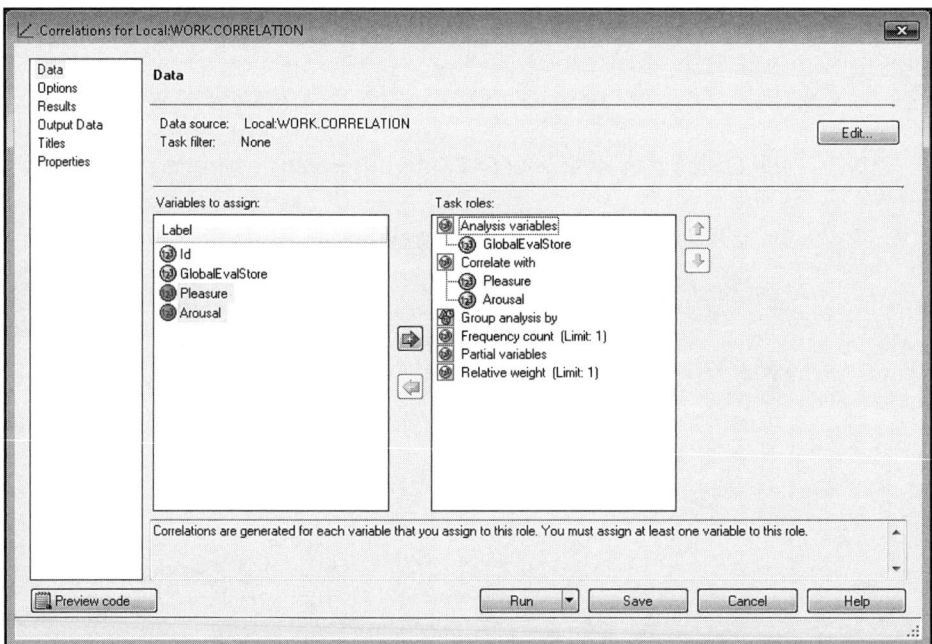

4.   Under the **Options** pane, different correlation types depending on the nature of the variables are considered. In our case, we decide to use the Pearson correlation because the *GlobalEvalStore* and the *Pleasure* and *Arousal* are considered as continuous variables, although both *Pleasure* and *Arousal* are measured on a 5-point Likert-scale.

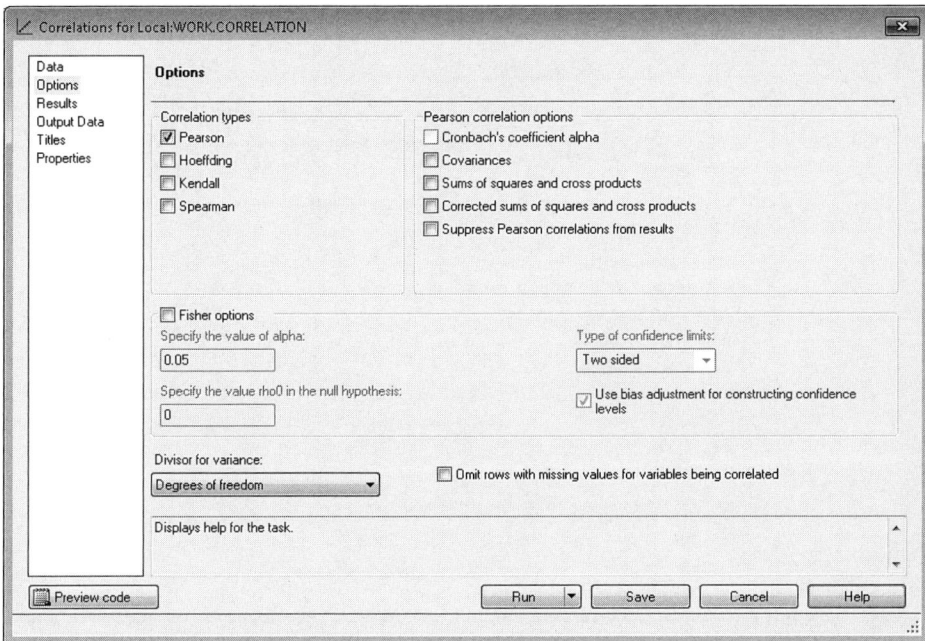

5. In the **Results** pane, the box next to the scatter plot is ticked to create a scatter plot. A scatter plot is a plot where the data is displayed as a collection of points, having the value of the first variable on the X-axis, while having the value of the second variable on the Y-axis. A scatter plot is an ideal way of visualizing the relationship between two variables.

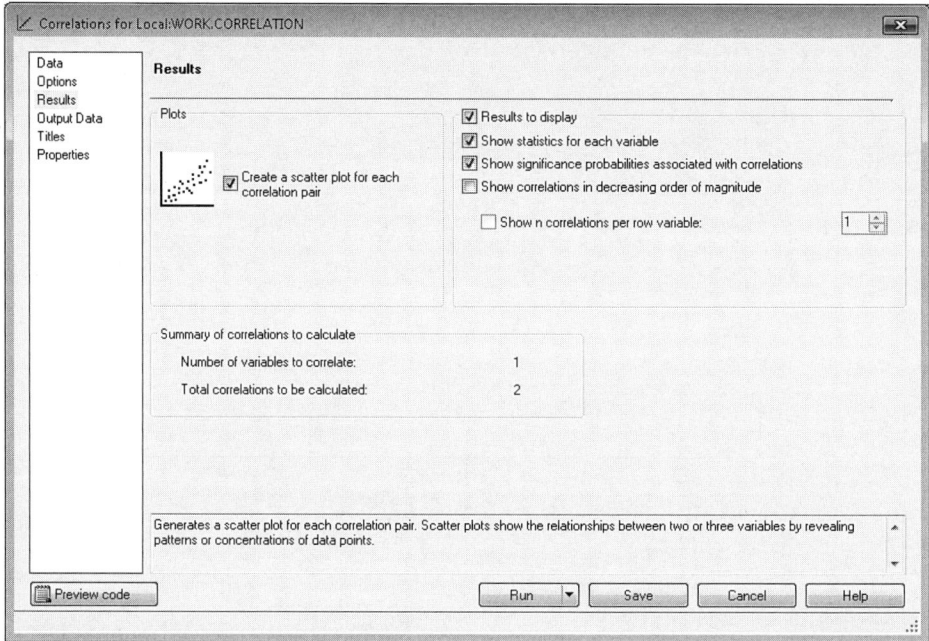

6. Click **Run** to obtain the results. The results are shown in the **Results** tab.

Interpretation

- **Scatter Plot and Scatter Plot Matrix**

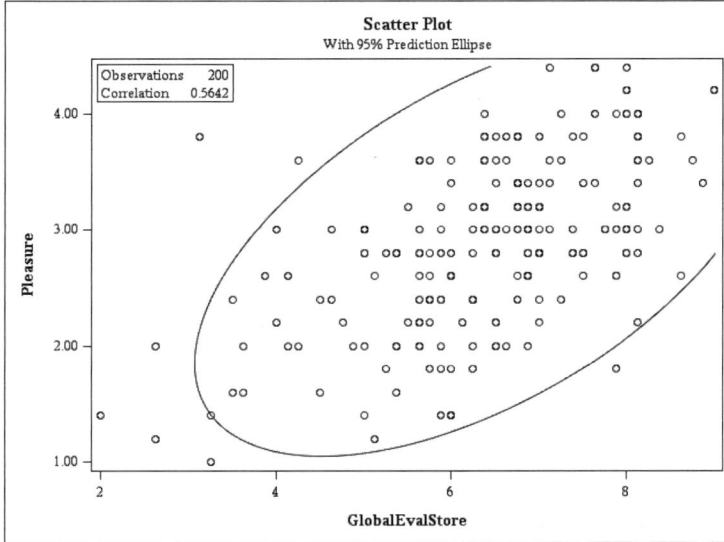

Scatter Plot
With 95% Prediction Ellipse

Observations   200
Correlation   0.5642

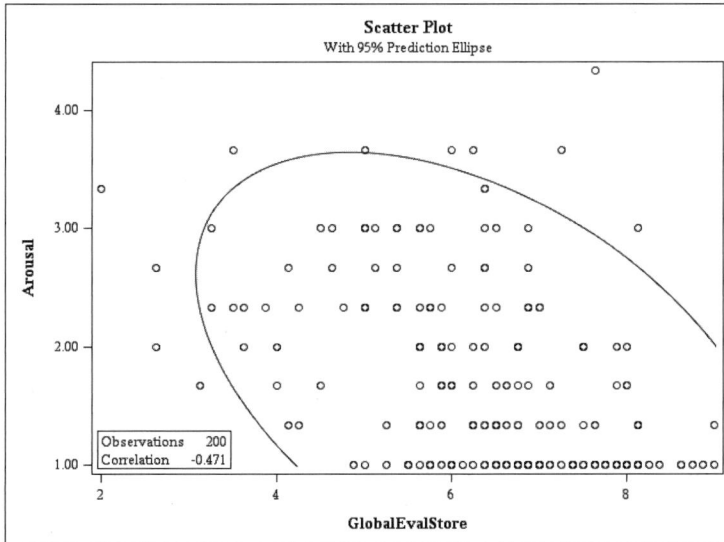

Scatter Plot
With 95% Prediction Ellipse

Observations   200
Correlation   -0.471

Scatter Plot Matrix

GlobalEvalStore

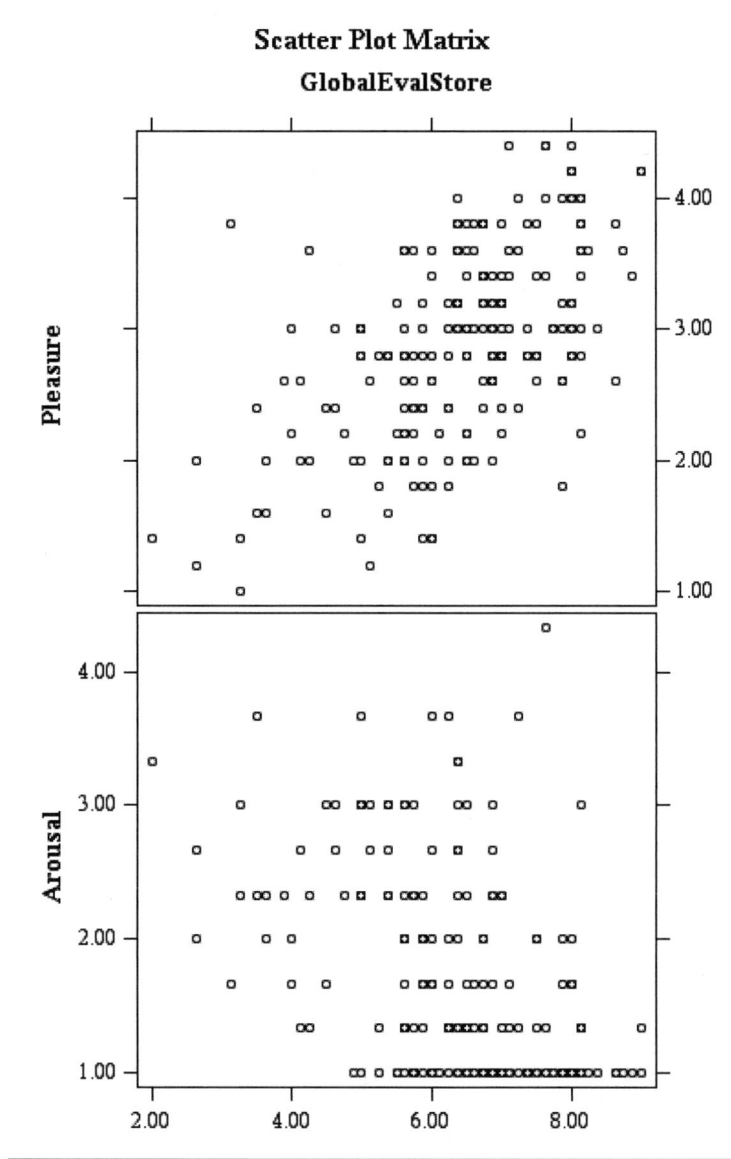

Inspecting the scatter plots, one can conclude that there tends to be a positive relationship between *GlobalEvalStore* and *Pleasure*, while a slightly negative relationship is discovered in the scatter plot between *GlobalEvalStore* and *Arousal*. The prediction ellipses found in the scatter plots help the marketing researcher in discovering the directions of the relationship.

- **Pearson Correlation Coefficients, N = 200**

	Pearson Correlation Coefficients, N = 200 Prob > |r| under H0: Rho=0
	GlobalEvalStore
Pleasure	0.56420 <.0001
Arousal	-0.47115 <.0001

This table statistically tests whether the relationship between two variables is existent or not. For both variables, *Pleasure* and *Arousal*, a significant relationship is found with *GlobalEvalStore*, because the p-value is smaller than 0.05. Furthermore, the direction of the relationships is in line with the conclusions based on the scatter plots. In detail, the correlation coefficient is positive for the relationship between *Pleasure* and *GlobalEvalStore* (correlation coefficient of 0.56420), while it is negative for the relationship between *Arousal* and *GlobalEvalStore* (correlation coefficient of -0.47115).

Managerial Recommendations

The retail manager got track of the fact that a positive relationship exists between the overall satisfaction level and the pleasure level, while the inverse is true for the relationship between the arousal level and the overall satisfaction level. In sum, the correlation results confirm the prior expectations of the retail manager. In the end, the retail manager knows that emotional responses are associated with the store satisfaction. However, this correlation analysis does not inform us about any causal relationship between these variables. Indeed, we cannot conclude that arousal decreases store satisfaction or vice versa. A regression analysis is needed to prove the impact of one variable on another (see Chapter 7 Regression Analysis).

Further Reading

Chen, P.Y. and Popovich, P.M. (2002), *Correlation: Parametric and Nonparametric Measures*, Sage Publications, Inc.

Miles, J. and Shevlin, M. (2001), *Applying Regression and Correlation: A Guide for Students and Researchers*, 1st edition, Sage Publications Ltd.

Thompson, B. (1984), *Canonical Correlation Analysis: Uses and Interpretation*, Quantitative Applications in the Social Sciences, Sage Publications, Inc.

Chapter 7

Regression Analysis

Objectives

1. Understand the aim of linear regression and when it is appropriate to use.

2. Describe specialized variable selection techniques for multiple linear regression analysis.

3. Run a linear regression analysis and interpret the results.

4. Understand the concept of logistic regression and how it differs from linear regression.

5. Understand how to run and interpret a logistic regression model.

7.1. Linear Regression

7.1.1. MULTIPLE REGRESSION WITH CONTINUOUS VARIABLES

Fundamentals

Marketing decisions are sometimes made based on the causal relationship between two or more variables. Often one or several variables are used to explain or to predict another variable. The variable being explained or being predicted is the dependent variable, while the variables being used to explain or to predict the value of the dependent variable are called the independent variables. For instance, from experience, one knows that promotion and advertising affect brand sales. Promotion and advertising are considered to be the independent variables, and brand sales to be the dependent variable. In this case, the manager could use regression analysis to evaluate the strength and the direction of the impact of promotion and advertising expenditures (the independent variables) on brand sales (the dependent variable). Furthermore, the manager could predict the brand sales for a given level of promotion and advertising expenditures.

In sum, regression analysis enables us to evaluate the causal relationship between one dependent variable, and one (simple regression) or more (multiple regression) independent (or explanatory) variables. The dependent variable and the independent variables must be interval- or ratio-scaled variables. However, categorical variables could also be introduced as independent variables, but first they must be transformed into binary or dummy variables (as explained in section 7.1.2. Multiple Regression in the presence of a Nominal Independent Variable (two categories) and 7.1.3. Multiple Regression in the presence of a Nominal Independent Variable (more than two categories)).

In this section, we focus on the multiple regression problem, hereafter referred to as linear regression. The general form of a linear regression model is:

$$Y = \beta_0 + \beta_1 X_1 + \beta_2 X_2 + ... + \beta_p X_p + \varepsilon$$

where Y is the dependent variable, β_0 is the intercept, X_i the independent variable i (for i = 1 to p), β_i the coefficient or parameter estimate of variable i (for i = 1 to p) and ε is the error term. The value of the regression coefficients (β_i) shows the amount of expected variation of Y when X_i is changed by one unit and all other X_i are held constant. More precisely, β_1 represents the expected change in Y when X_1 increases by one unit while X_2 to X_p are held constant.

Assumptions for the Regression Model

There are several assumptions to be verified for the linear regression model.

1. **Causality link.** The linear regression assumes a causal relationship between a dependent variable and one or more independent variables. The decision as to which variable is considered as the dependent variable is inspired by theoretical or intuitive motivations.

2. **Model specification.** The regression model should be properly specified, that is, it must include all relevant independent variables and exclude all irrelevant independent variables.

3. **Linearity**. The relationship between the dependent variable and the independent variables must be linear. In cases where the relationship between the dependent variable and the independent variables is considered as non-linear, mathematical transformations are needed. For instance, adding the polynomial variant of a variable is a common variable transformation to account for non-linearity in regression problems.

4. **The sample size must be large enough**. In order to be able to robustly estimate the regression coefficients, the number of observations must be at least five times the number of independent variables in the regression model.

5. **No multicollinearity.** Multicollinearity is defined as the situation where high mutual correlations between the independent variables exist. This must be avoided because this could heavily impact (i) the strength of the independent variables, and (ii) the direction of the influence of the independent variables.

6. **Residuals**, that is, ε in the regression function, must have the following characteristics:
    a. **Normality** of the error term ε. The error term must be normally distributed.
    b. **Independence** of the error term ε. The error of observations cannot be correlated.
    c. **Homoscedasticity** (homogeneity of variance) of the errors. The variance of errors should be constant across all values of the independent variables.

7. **Outliers**. One must pay attention to outliers, that is, observations showing high or low values for the dependent variable given their values for the independent variables. The presence of outliers might bias the regression estimates. On the one hand, the researcher could decide that the outliers may provide valuable information that must be considered in the regression model. On the other hand, the researcher could decide to remove these observations from the prediction model. However, one must be cautious when discarding outliers in the regression model, because a manipulation of the dataset is often considered as not ethical when it is not based on clear-cut rules.

Managerial Problem

A catering company wants to better grasp what factors related to the restaurant atmosphere influence the customers' evaluation of service quality. According to informal interviews conducted with several customers, the restaurant environment (decor, ambiance and so on) as well as the type of music played strongly influence the customers' perception of service quality. The marketing manager decides to assess the service quality and to determine whether it is affected by the perceived quality of the restaurant environment and/or the congruency of the music with the atmosphere. The results of this study will help the manager to create an appropriate store atmosphere. Data were collected at the exit of several restaurants of the chain. 199 customers agreed to participate in the survey. The questionnaire consists of several questions measuring the service quality, the quality of the restaurant environment and the music congruency with the restaurant atmosphere.

Translation of the Managerial Problem into Statistical Notions

The objective of the marketing manager is to evaluate whether the restaurant atmosphere influences the service quality. The dependent variable is the service quality, whereas environment quality and music congruency are considered as independent variables. The regression analysis is used to determine the causal link between one dependent variable and two independent variables. The regression analysis will determine to what extent the independent variables explain the variation of the dependent variable. The regression analysis can also be used to predict the value of the dependent variable from one or more independent variables. The general form of the linear regression model is the following:

Perceived Service Quality = $\beta_0 + \beta_1$(Music Congruency) + β_2(Environment Quality) + ε

Dataset Description

The Excel file used in this study is named *Service_Quality.xlsx* and it contains 199 observations. It includes the dependent variable (*SQ*) and two independent variables. All these variables are listed below.

- Customer identifier (*ID*).

- Perceived service quality (*SQ*).

- Music congruency (*MC*).

- Environment quality (*EQ*).

SQ, *EQ* and *MC* are composite measures. *SQ* is measured on a 7-point Likert-scale measuring the degree of agreement with eight items ranging from 1 = totally disagree to 7 = totally agree. *EQ* is measured using a 7-point semantic differential scale with seven items. *MC* is measured on two items (7-point Likert-scale ranging from 1 = strongly disagree to 7 = strongly agree). For each variable, the mean over the items is computed after having conducted a factor analysis to verify the unidimensionality of the concepts.

Hypotheses

The null hypothesis of the overall meaningfulness of the linear regression model states that there is no linear relationship between the dependent variable Y and the independent variables X_i.

H_0: $\beta_1 = ... = \beta_p = 0$

H_1: At least one of the $\beta_i \neq 0$

The F test is used to test the null hypothesis (H_0). The F value is equal to the variance explained by the regression model divided by the variance unexplained. The F value follows a F distribution having p degrees of freedom in the numerator and n–p–1 in the denominator, with p equal to the number of variables and n equal to the number of observations in the dataset. SAS Enterprise Guide provides the F test and its corresponding p-value. We reject the null hypothesis (H_0) if the p-value is lower than 0.05, that is, at least one of the model parameters is not equal to 0. However, if we cannot reject the null hypothesis, we cannot conclude that there is a significant relationship between the independent variables and the dependent variable. Consequently, the regression analysis stops at this point.

In addition, to test the overall significance of the model, we can test whether each independent variable contributes to explain the dependent variable. For the independent variables X_i, the following hypotheses are stated:

$$H_0: \quad \beta_i = 0$$

$$H_1: \quad \beta_i \neq 0$$

The t test is used to determine the significance of the relationship between each independent variable and the dependent variable. We test whether the parameter estimated is significantly different from 0. The t test is equal to the estimated parameter divided by its standard deviation. It follows a distribution with $n-p-1$ degrees of freedom, with p equal to the number of parameters and n equal to the number of observations in the dataset. SAS Enterprise Guide provides the p-value associated with the t value. We reject the null hypothesis (H_0) if the p-value is lower than the significance level of 0.05. We conclude that the parameter of X_i is different from 0 or that X_i significantly influences the dependent variable Y.

Data Analysis

A multiple regression is run using the **Linear Regression** task.

1. Add the dataset *Service_Quality.xlsx* to your project.

2. Go to **Tasks** → **Regression** → **Linear Regression...** to open the regression selection pane.

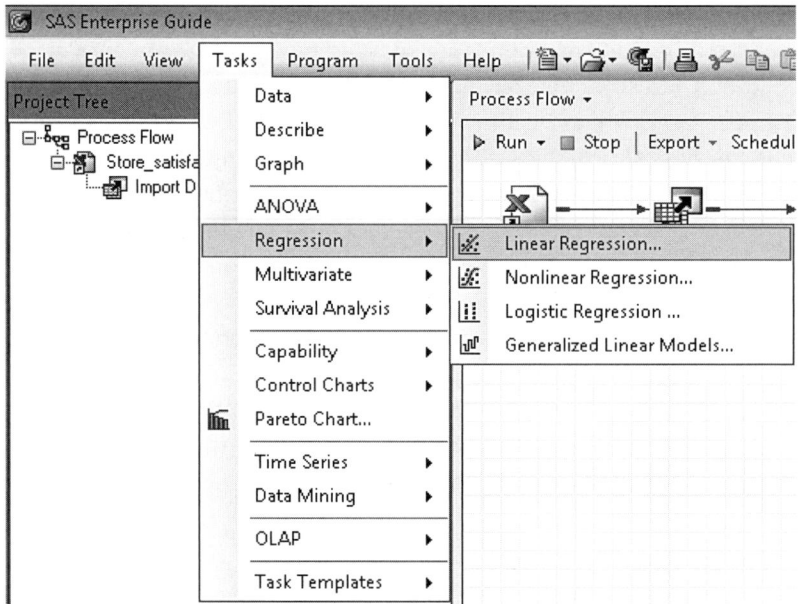

3. In the **Data** pane, drag and drop your variable of interest, that is, *SQ*, to the **Dependent variable** role, while you add the explanatory or independent variables, that is, *MC* and *EQ*, to the **Explanatory variables** role.

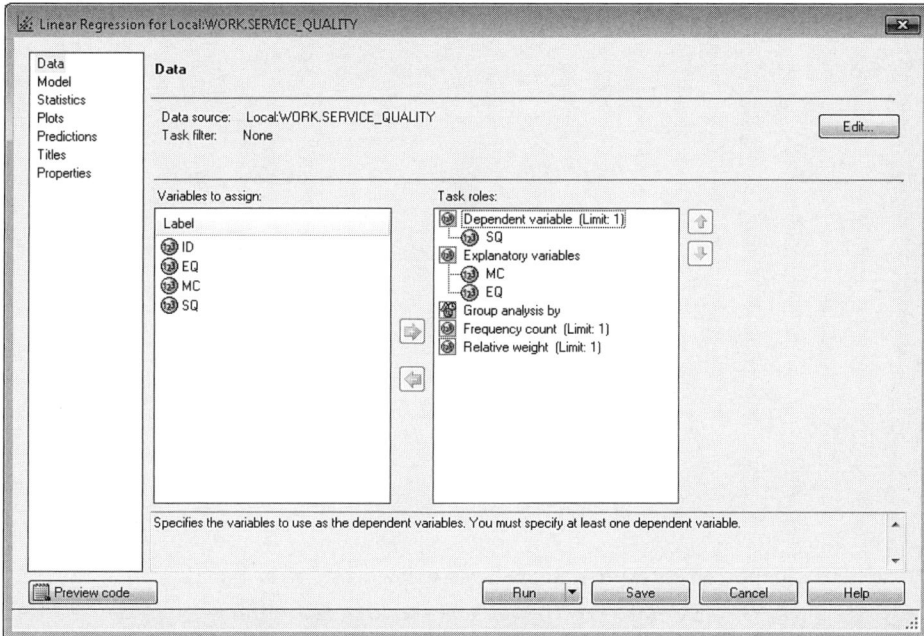

4. Click on **Model** in the selection pane. In this pane one has different options in building a regression model. On the one hand, one could run a regression model that includes all independent variables. This is done by ticking the option **Full model fitted (no selection)**. On the other hand, one could choose a variable selection model. The latter is a regression model that automatically selects the most influential variables based on particular criteria.

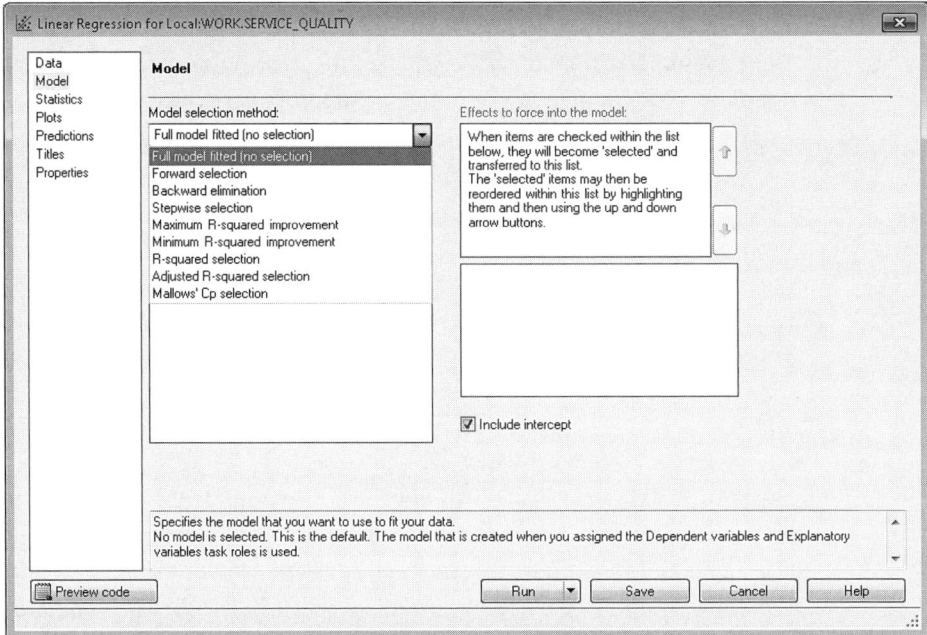

In the SAS Enterprise Guide Help, you will find an explanation of all possible variable selection techniques (Forward selection, Backward elimination, Stepwise selection, Maximum and Minimum R-squared improvement, (Adjusted) R-squared selection and Mallows' Cp selection). Below we only consider the most often used variable selection techniques, that is, Forward selection, Backward elimination and Stepwise selection.

- **Forward Selection**

  The forward selection method begins with no variables in the model. For each of the explanatory variables, this method calculates the variable's contribution to the model as if it should be included. The contribution is expressed by a significance level to be filled in the **To enter the model** text box. The forward selection method adds the most contributing variable to the model. Variables are added to the model as long as the significance level falls below the predefined value. In sum, variables are added one by one to the model until no remaining variable produces a significant test statistic. After a variable is added to the model, it stays there.

- **Backward Elimination**

  The backward elimination method starts by taking all variables into consideration in the model and then deletes variables from the model one by one until all the variables that remain in the model produce test statistics significant at the significance level that is specified in the **To stay** in the model text box. At each step, the variable that shows the smallest contribution to the model is deleted. This method proceeds in the opposite way than the forward selection method.

- **Stepwise Selection**

  The stepwise method is a modification of the forward selection method. It is a method that differs in the way that variables already in the model do not necessarily stay there. As in the forward selection method, variables are added one by one to the model, as long as the variable has a significant contribution (to be specified in the **To enter the model** text box).

  After a variable is added, however, the stepwise method looks at all the variables already included in the model and deletes any variable that does not produce a statistic significant at the significance level that is specified in the **To stay in the model** text box. Only after this check is made and the necessary deletions are accomplished can another variable be added to the model.

  The stepwise process ends when no variable outside the model has a statistic significant at the significance level that is specified to enter the model and every variable in the model is significant at the significance level that is specified to stay in the model, or when the variable to be added to the model is the variable that was just deleted from it.

In this section, the stepwise variable selection procedure is explained. The stepwise variable selection procedure is employed by choosing the option **Stepwise selection** (see figure on next page). Moreover, one should change the enter and stay probabilities to 0.05.

Furthermore in this pane, one could indicate the explanatory variables to be forced into the linear regression model, if needed. You could do this under the **Effects to force into the model** option.

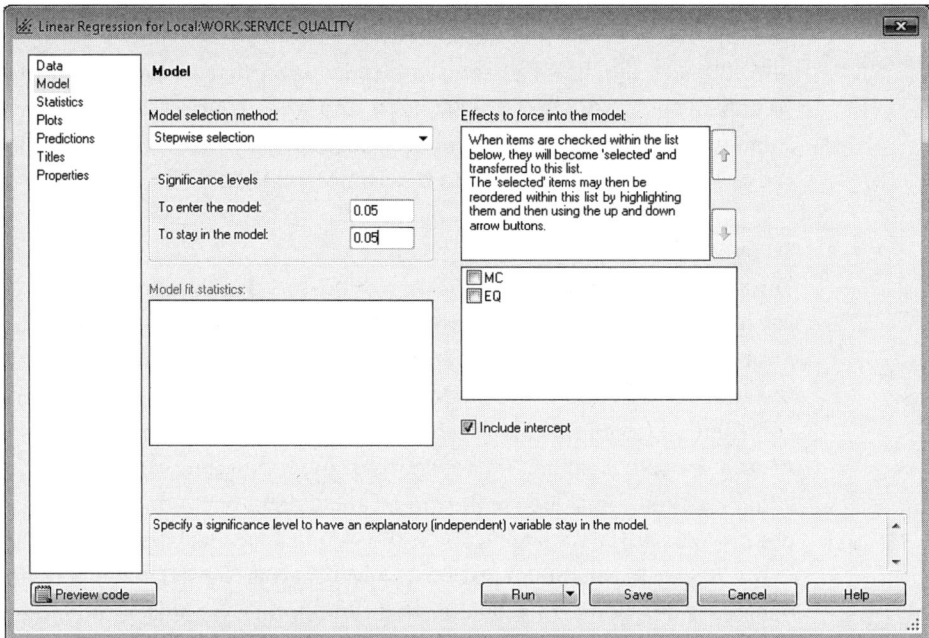

5.   In the **Statistics** pane, you can request additional information about the estimates, the correlation among the variables and the diagnostics concerning the model robustness. Under the header **Details on estimates**, the options **Standardized regression coefficients** and **Correlation matrix of the estimates** are offered. Moreover, under the header **Diagnostics**, the following options are considered:

- **Collinearity analysis** which will give us the eigenvalues, the condition indices and a decomposition of the variances of the estimates in relation to each eigenvalue.

- **Tolerance values for estimates** which is defined as 1-R^2, where R^2 is obtained from regressing the variable on all other variables in the model.

- **Variance inflation values** outputs the reciprocal of the tolerance value.

- The **heteroscedasticity test** which tests whether the variance of the error is constant across all values of the independent variables.

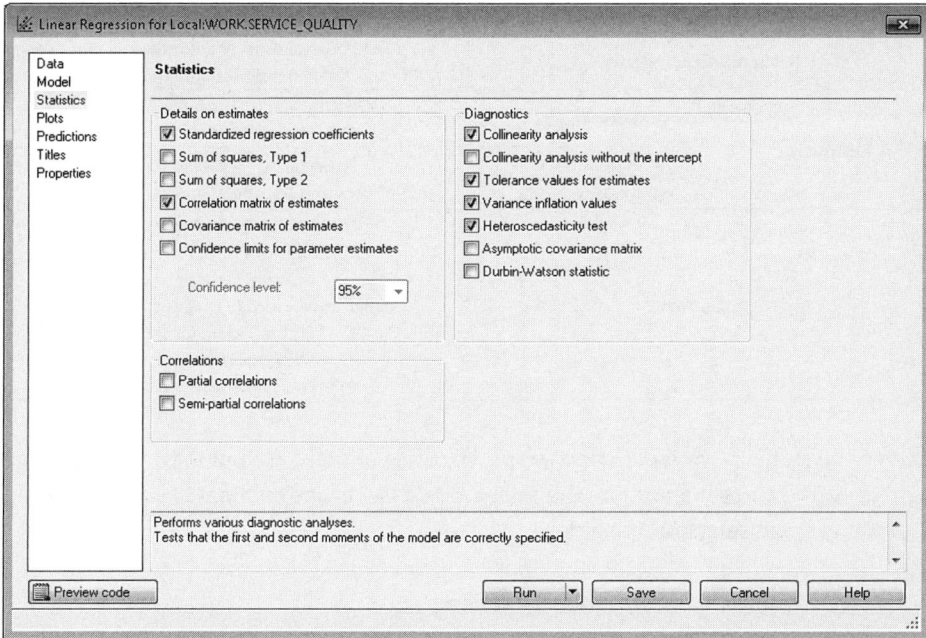

6.   Click **Run** to run the multiple linear regression model. You can explore the results in the **Results** tab.

Interpretation

Before one starts interpreting the usefulness of the linear regression model and its corresponding parameters, the linear regression assumptions must be verified. Assumptions 1 through to 4 (see section Assumptions for the regression model) could be verified without any SAS Enterprise Guide output. A summary table for the assumptions 5 through to 7 and their corresponding headers in the SAS Enterprise Guide outputs appears below.

Assumptions		SAS Enterprise Guide outputs
5. No multicollinearity		Correlation of Estimates Collinearity Diagnostics
6. Residuals	a. Normality	Distribution of Residuals for SQ Q-Q Plot of Residuals for SQ
	b. Independence	Residual by Predicted for SQ
	c. Homoscedasticity	Test of First and Second Moment Specification
7. Outliers		Rstudent by Predicted for SQ Observed by Predicted for SQ Cook's D for SQ Outlier and Leverage Diagnostics for SQ Q-Q Plot of Residuals for SQ Residuals for SQ Influence Diagnostics for SQ

During the stepwise variable selection procedure, variables are put in the balance one by one. In the current situation, the final model selects and retains *EQ* and *MC* in step 2 of the variable selection procedure.

- **Summary of Stepwise Selection**

				Summary of Stepwise Selection				
Step	Variable Entered	Variable Removed	Number Vars In	Partial R-Square	Model R-Square	C(p)	F Value	Pr > F
1	EQ		1	0.2370	0.2370	6.4801	61.20	<.0001
2	MC		2	0.0208	0.2578	3.0000	5.48	0.0202

This table gives an overview of the statistics for the stepwise regression procedure. The following statistics are displayed in the summary of the variable selection process: *Step*, *Variable Entered*, *Variable Removed*, number of variables in the model (*Number of Vars in*), *Partial R-square*, *Model R-square*, Mallow's *C(p)*, the *F Value* and the corresponding probability *Pr>F*.

- **Fit Criteria for SQ**

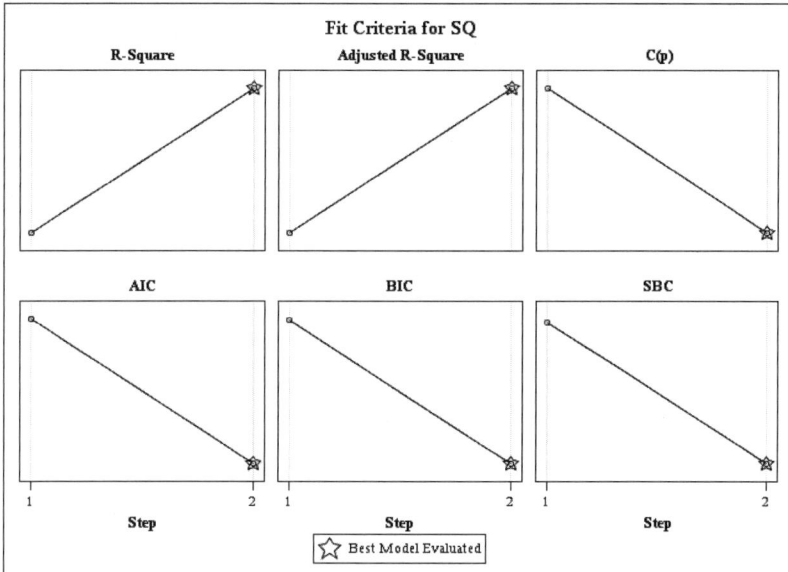

These graphs plot several fit criteria (*R-Square*, *Adjusted R-Square*, *C(p)*, *AIC*, *BIC*, *SBC*) in order to identify how the fit measures evolve during the variable selection procedure. In concrete, the *R-Square* and the *Adjusted R-Square* must be maximized, whereas *C(p)*, *AIC*, *BIC* and *SBC* must be minimized during the selection procedure. In this setting, the final regression model provides the best goodness of fit.

⚠ *The SBC criterion could recommend another solution because it is more influenced by the number of parameters to estimate than other statistics such AIC for example.*

The outputs that are considered for assumption verification are explained in chronological order as output by the SAS Enterprise Guide system. The analysis of variance and the interpretation of the parameter estimates are presented once these linear regression assumptions are checked.

- **Correlation of Estimates**

	Correlation of Estimates		
Variable	Intercept	MC	EQ
Intercept	1.0000	-0.2213	-0.9571
MC	-0.2213	1.0000	-0.0489
EQ	-0.9571	-0.0489	1.0000

This table represents the correlations between the parameter estimates. This table can help to identify multicollinearity problems between the independent variables. The correlation coefficients between the different independent variables must be low to avoid multicollinearity. In this setting, the correlation between *EQ* and *MQ* is pretty low, that is, -0.0489. This indicates that there is no tendency to discover a multicollinearity problem. However, if multicollinearity is present in the dataset, one could make the decision to retrieve one or several independent variables based on the mutual correlations.

- **Collinearity Diagnostics**

		Collinearity Diagnostics			
Number	Eigenvalue	Condition Index	Proportion of Variation		
			Intercept	MC	EQ
1	2.89502	1.00000	0.00140	0.01583	0.00147
2	0.09872	5.41544	0.01793	0.97520	0.02225
3	0.00626	21.50100	0.98066	0.00897	0.97628

When an explanatory variable is nearly a linear combination of other explanatory variables in the model, the estimates of the coefficients in the regression model are unstable, and they will have high standard errors. This table enables to us to identify these multicollinearity problems. A moderate multicollinearity problem arises when the condition index of the final model exceeds 30. The higher the condition index, the heavier the multicollinearity problem is. In the current setting, the condition index of the final model is 21.50. There is no multicollinearity problem in this case.

- **Test of First and Second Moment Specification**

Test of First and Second Moment Specification		
DF	Chi-Square	Pr > ChiSq
5	2.11	0.8332

This table contains the results of a formal statistical hypothesis test for the heteroscedasticity and the independence of the error terms. The hypotheses are formulated as follows:

H_0: There is evidence of homoscedasticity

H_1: There is evidence of heteroscedasticity

The p-value of this heteroscedasticity test is 0.8332, and thus larger than 0.05. This means that the null hypothesis is accepted, and consequently, there is homoscedasticity in the error terms.

- **Distribution of Residuals for SQ**

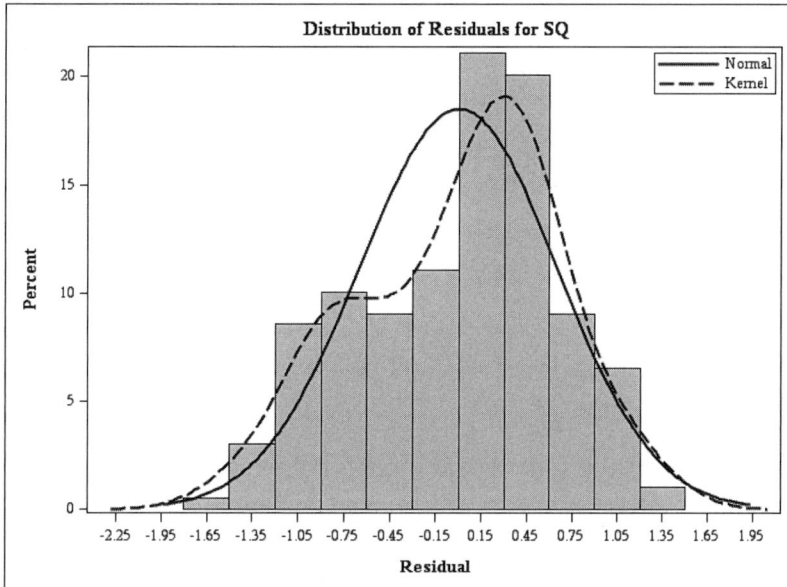

This graph could answer the question whether the error term ε is normally distributed with a mean 0. This graph is a histogram of the residuals of the linear regression model. By comparing the empirical, Kernel distribution (in dotted line) with the theoretical normal distribution, it is possible to verify whether the residuals are normally distributed. When the Kernel distribution follows the theoretical normal distribution, there is an indication that the residuals are normally distributed. The latter is true in the current context, so there is an indication that the residuals are normally distributed.

- **Residual by Predicted for SQ**

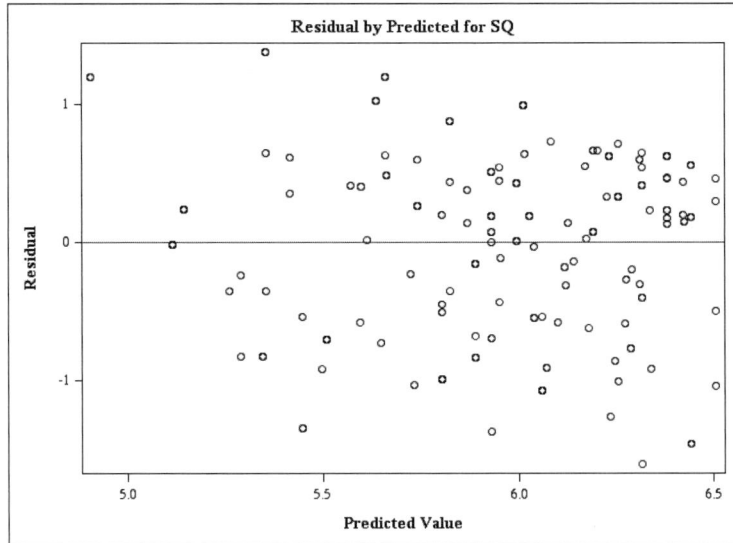

Via this graph one could check the assumptions of the homogeneity of variance of residuals or homoscedasticity. If there is homoscedasticity, no pattern in this plot should be identifiable. In other words, plotting the predicted values for the dependent variable versus the residuals of the linear regression model should produce a distribution of points scattered randomly around 0. However, the homoscedasticity assumption is violated in the following two situations:

- the residuals increase or decrease along the predicted values. In other words, the residual distribution forms a funnel in the plot;
- the points in the plot lie on a curve around 0 rather than fluctuating randomly.

In these two cases, the variance of the residuals is not homogeneous and there will be heteroscedasticity. Heteroscedasticity can have at least two causes:

- the relationship between the dependent variable and the independent variables is not linear. In this case, it is advised to transform the variables by using the logarithm or the square of the variables;
- one or several independent variables are missing. In this case, one should check whether all relevant variables are included in the model. If not, verify whether they could be made available.

In the current setting, we can see no trend appearing in the plot. The points are randomly shattered, which indicates that heteroscedasticity is not a concern. This result is consistent with the test of first and second moment specification described above.

- **Rstudent by Predicted for SQ**

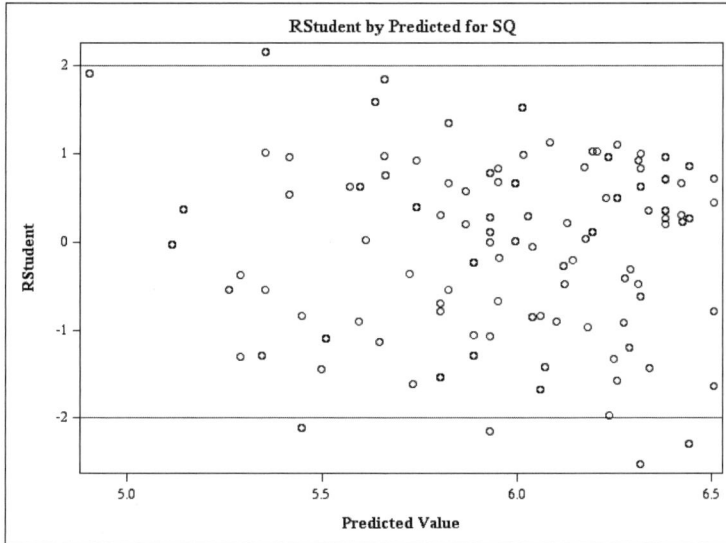

The Rstudent is the externally studentized residual. This is a studentized residual in which the error variance for the ith observation is estimated as being the error variance without this ith observation, where the studentized residual is defined as the division of the residual by an estimate of its standard deviation. This graph gives a representation of the predicted value of an observation versus its Rstudent. One should start worrying about an observation when the absolute value of the studentized residual exceeds 2. When studentized residuals exceed +2.5 or -2.5, one should be cautious about these observations, because they could indicate potential outliers. In the current setting, some observations fall below -2 or above 2. These observations could be considered as potential outliers, but because these observations are not exceeding the absolute value of 2.5, there is a small chance that they are real outliers. For that reason, these observations stay in the dataset.

• **Observed by Predicted for SQ**

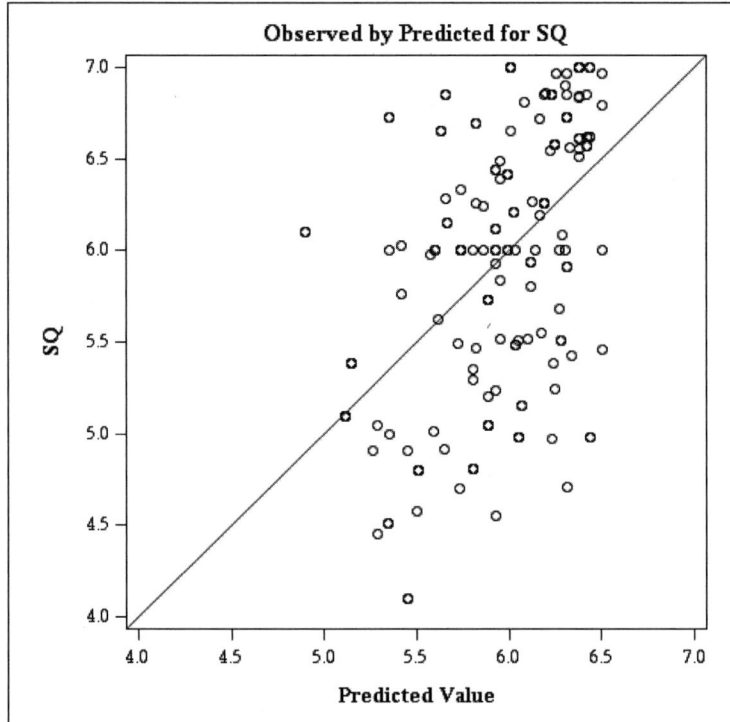

Observed by Predicted for SQ

By plotting the observed values for *SQ* to the predicted values of *SQ*, the marketing analyst is able to discover discrepancies in the complete set of data points. Observations represented as dots in the graph that widely deviate from the 45-degree line could indicate potential outliers. In the current setting, very few points heavily deviate from the 45-degree line and therefore no real outlier candidates are drawn to our attention.

- **Cook's D for SQ**

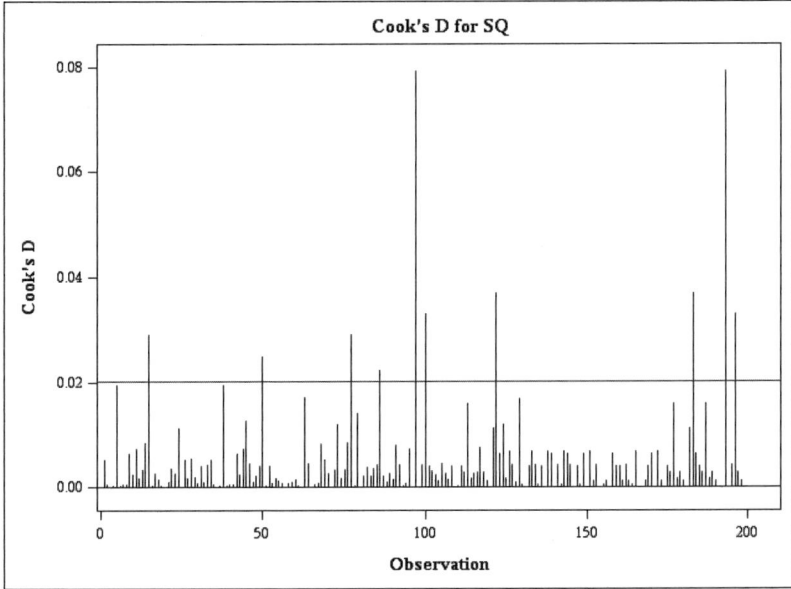

This graph gives a visual representation of the Cook's D statistic, a measure to identify influential observations. Cook's D for an observation measures the change to the estimates that results from deleting that observation. An observation with a Cook's D bigger than $4/n$, with n equal to the number of data points in the sample, should be further investigated. SAS Enterprise Guide outputs a graph that makes it easy to spot influential observations by plotting the observation number versus its Cook's D statistic. In this case, the critical Cook's D is 4/199 or 0.020. By having a look at the plot, several influential observations could be detected, because the Cook's D for these observations is higher than 0.020.

• **Outlier and Leverage diagnostics for SQ**

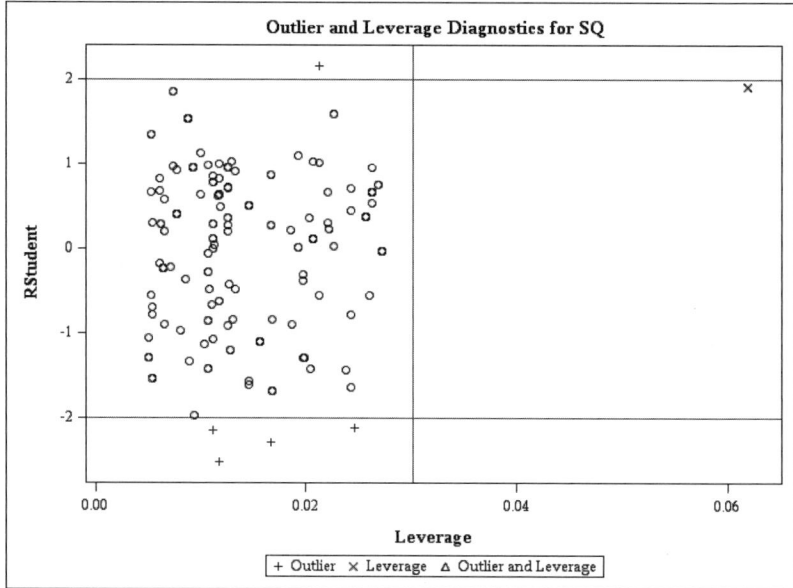

Outlier and Leverage Diagnostics for SQ

It is important to consider the observations in the dataset which are labelled as outliers or leverage points or both. An outlier is defined as a point that has a large residual, which means that there is a huge discrepancy in the relationship between its dependent-variable value and its values for the independent variables. The Rstudent, the externally studentized residual, for the ith observation is a studentized residual in which the error variance is estimated when the ith observation is removed. One should examine an observation as being an outlier when the absolute value of the studentized residual exceeds the absolute value of 2.5.

The leverage is a statistic that indicates how far an observation is away from the centroid of the data in the space of the explanatory variables. Observations far from the centroid are potentially influential in fitting the regression model. Observations whose leverage values exceed $2p/n$ are high leverage points, with p the number of parameters estimated in the model (intercept included), and n the number of observations used to estimate the regression model. In this particular case, the cut-off value is therefore 0.0302 with n equal to 199 and p equal to 3 (that is, two independent variables in addition to the intercept).

The plot of RStudent versus Leverage shows two horizontal lines that indicate the potential outlier thresholds, and it has a vertical line that indicates the threshold for high leverage points. In the current setting, five potential outliers and one observation with a leverage statistic higher than expected could be detected. Based on these results, one may discard these observations and one could rerun the model to verify their impact on the regression model. However, based on a qualitative inspection of these data points, these observations stay in the current dataset as they do represent real consumer behaviour.

- **Q-Q plot of Residuals for SQ**

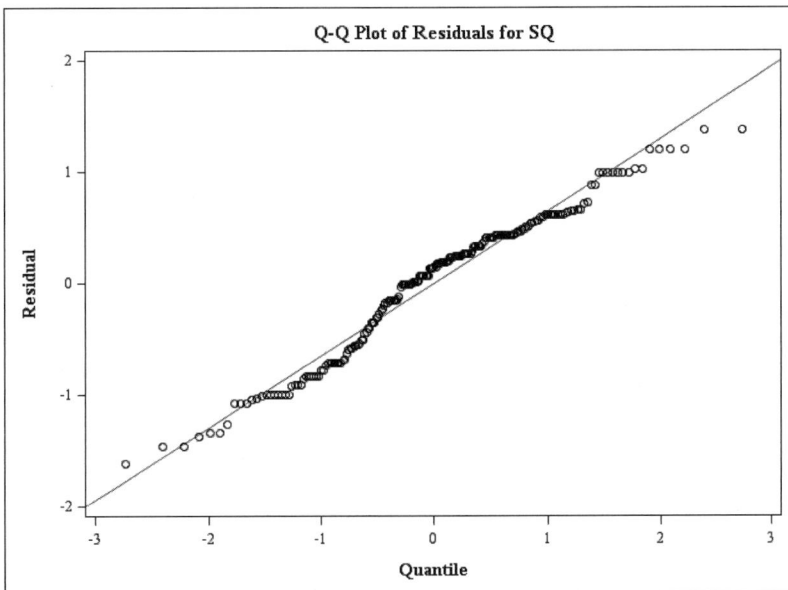

The Q-Q plot is useful for testing the normality of residuals and for identifying potential outliers. The Q-Q plot plots the quantiles of the theoretical normal distribution against quantiles of the empirical distribution of the residuals. If the scatter trend follows the 45-degree line, there is an indication that the distribution of the residuals is normal. In the current setting, the Q-Q plot displays that the residuals are approximately normally distributed, because the scatter plot follows the 45-degree line. Furthermore, when particular observations show extremely large positive or negative values, this could indicate that these observations are outliers. In sum, outliers are considered as points that are far away from the overall pattern of points. In this setting, very few observations could be considered as an outlier.

- **Residuals for SQ**

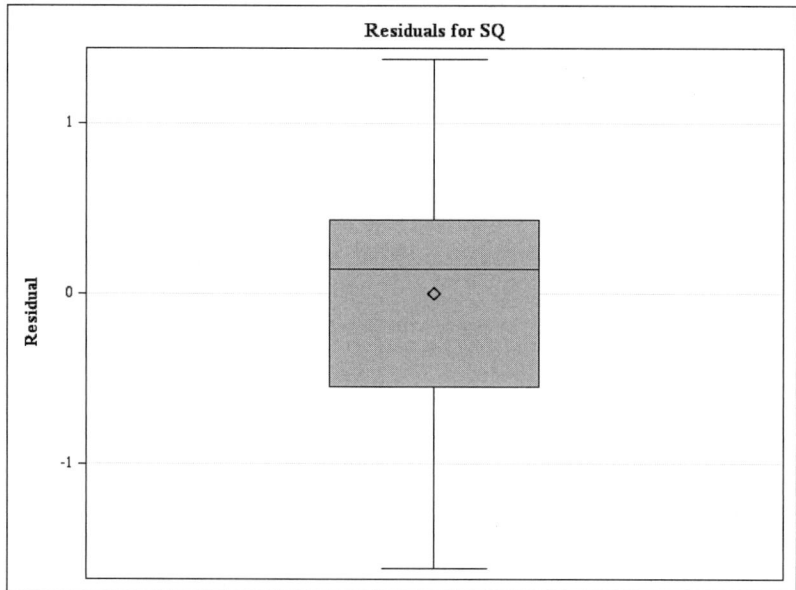

The box plot enables us to identify potential outliers, that is, extreme values within 1.5 times the inter-quartile range from the upper or lower quartile. These outliers are plotted as individual points in the box plot. In the current setting, there is not a single outlier identified within the box plot.

- **Influence Diagnostics for SQ**

Two additional diagnostics for discovering influential observations could be considered, that is, the DFFITS and DFBETAS (see figures below). Both measures are complementary to the Cook's D measure. DFFITS is very similar to the Cook's D statistic and the cut-off point is set to $2\sqrt{p/n}$, while the cut-off point for DFBETAS is set to $2/\sqrt{n}$ with p the number of parameters in the model and n equal to the number of observations in the dataset. Values of DFFITS and DFBETAS exceeding these thresholds indicate possible influential observations.

Influence Diagnostics for SQ

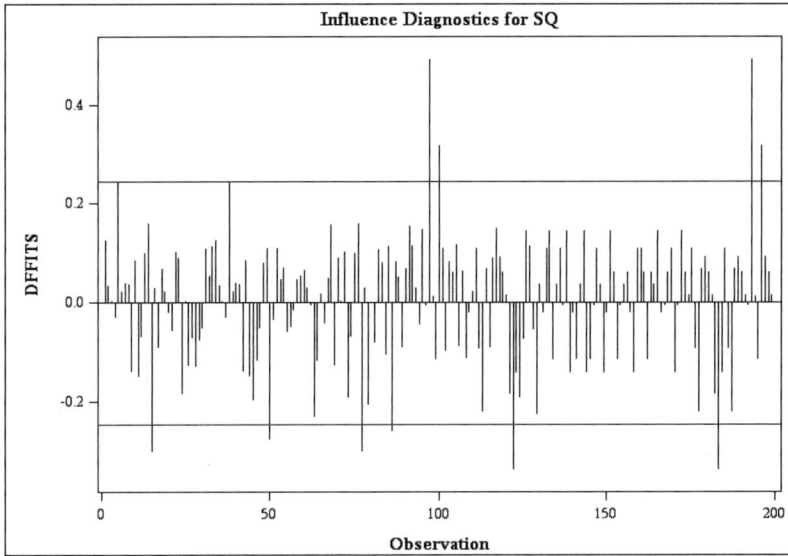

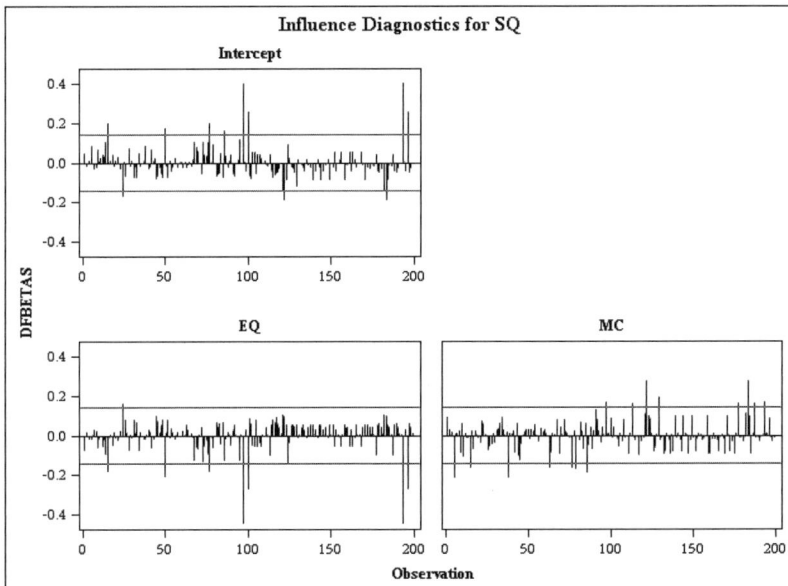

By now, the assumptions are verified and no serious problems could be discovered. Consequently, the marketing analyst could start exploring the output of the regression. Two subsequent steps are necessary. First, one should check the model's meaningfulness by exploring whether at least one of the variables of the regression has a significant impact on the dependent variable. If this is the case, one should further investigate which of the variables are significant and what the direction of the impact is.

• **Analysis of Variance**

Analysis of Variance					
Source	DF	Sum of Squares	Mean Square	F Value	Pr > F
Model	2	28.75959	14.37979	34.04	<.0001
Error	196	82.80782	0.42249		
Corrected Total	198	111.56740			

Root MSE	0.64999	R-Square	0.2578
Dependent Mean	5.91531	Adj R-Sq	0.2502
Coeff Var	10.98828		

This table gives an indication of the meaningfulness of the linear regression model. The F test is used to test the null hypothesis (H_0), that is, none of the variables has a significant impact on the dependent variable. The F statistic is equal to the variance explained by the regression model (the value under the *Mean Square* column in the row *Model*) divided by the unexplained variance (the value under the *Mean Square* column in the row *Error*). The F value for the regression model is 34.04 with p degrees of freedom in the numerator and $n-p-1$ in the denominator, with p equal to the number of variables, 2, n equal to the total number of observations in the dataset, 199. The p-value associated with the F test is smaller than 0.0001, and thus smaller than 0.05. It rejects the null hypothesis (H_0), which means that there is at least one parameter estimate different from 0.

The R-Square or the coefficient of determination is used to assess the goodness of fit of the estimated regression equation. It is the percentage of variance explained in the dependent variable by the estimated regression model. In our setting, the R-square is equal to 25.78 per cent. The higher the R-square, the better the regression model. An R-square of 70 per cent or higher is most often considered as good. However, when the regression model tries to explain consumers' perception or real behaviour, lower R-squares are considered as acceptable.

The Adjusted R-Square is an adapted version of the traditional R-Square, because it takes into account the number of variables in the model. For instance, suppose that you have two linear regression models each explaining 40 per cent of the variance. Suppose further that the first model has only one independent variable, while the second regression model has eight independent variables. In such a situation, the first model is preferred because it explains the same variance, but with less independent variables. So correcting the original R-Square for the number of variables in the model is useful and this is summarized in the Adjusted R-Square measure. The latter is used to compare the goodness-of-fit of multiple models with a different number of variables.

- **Parameter Estimates**

		Parameter Estimates						
Variable	DF	Parameter Estimate	Standard Error	t Value	Pr > |t|	Standardized Estimate	Tolerance	Variance Inflation
Intercept	1	2.46894	0.42108	5.86	<.0001	0	.	0
MC	1	0.06322	0.02700	2.34	0.0202	0.14423	0.99761	1.00240
EQ	1	0.51349	0.06594	7.79	<.0001	0.47980	0.99761	1.00240

This table shows the estimates of the regression model, that is, the intercept β_0 and the regression coefficients β_1 and β_2 associated with each independent variable (that is, *EQ* and *MC*) (*Parameter Estimate*). For each coefficient, SAS Enterprise Guide provides the standard error (*Standard Error*), the *t* value (*t Value*) and the *p*-value (*Pr>|t|*). As we run a stepwise linear regression with the enter and stay probability equal to 0.05, all variables are significantly different from 0. The variables *EQ* and *MC* significantly influence the customers' perception of service quality, because the *p*-value associated with the *t* test for each of these two variables is lower than 0.05.

Next, the direction of the impact of the independent variables on the dependent variable must be discovered. This is done via the signs of the regression coefficients. In the column *Parameter Estimate*, you see that both variables, *MC* and *EQ*, have positive signs. Therefore, when *EQ* and *MC* increase, the perceived service quality increases as well.

Subsequently, the question of which variable has the largest impact on explaining the dependent variable arises. The answer to this question is found in the column *Standardized Estimate*. By scaling the variables to the same scale (standardization), the parameter estimates become comparable. In the current setting, it is clear that *EQ* has the largest impact on explaining the perceived quality, because its standardized estimate is 0.4798 compared to the standardized estimate of *MC* which is 0.1442.

The columns *Tolerance* and *Variance Inflation* give an indication of the multicollinearity in the regression model. A tolerance value of less than 0.20 or a variance inflation index of more than 5 indicates a multicollinearity problem. In this case, the values of both statistics indicate that no multicollinearity problem is observed.

Finally, the parameter estimates can also be used for prediction purpose. Indeed, based on the estimated regression model, one can forecast what the service quality perception in a store would be with *MC* and *EQ* known. Let us assume that *EQ* is equal to *4* and *MC* is equal to *6*. Using the following equation, one can easily derive *SQ*:

$$SQ=\beta_0+\beta_1 MC+\beta_2 EQ$$

or

$$SQ=2.469+0.063*4+0.513*6 = 5.799$$

Consequently, the regression model can be used to predict the effect of the environment design and the choice of the music played in the restaurant on the perceived service quality.

Managerial Recommendations

This linear regression shows that both variables, environment quality and music congruency explain the customers' perception of service quality. Restaurant managers should not neglect the atmosphere as well as the music played in their restaurants. The music must be selected so that it fits well with the restaurant atmosphere, while the restaurant environment must be comfortable, bright, attractive and pleasant. However, if budgets are too limited to change both aspects of perceived service quality, the restaurant manager must first focus on refurbishing the restaurant environment, while afterwards investments could be made to implement an audio system to play good quality music consistent with the restaurant atmosphere.

7.1.2. MULTIPLE REGRESSION IN THE PRESENCE OF A NOMINAL INDEPENDENT VARIABLE (TWO CATEGORIES)

Managerial Problem

A retail company wants to better understand customers' store loyalty. The company offers its customers a loyalty card and it wants to assess to what extent loyalty card holders are more loyal to the store than non-holders. Furthermore, the marketing manager believes that their own private label products, which have the same brand name as the store, also generate store loyalty. The marketing manager conducted a survey to evaluate to what extent store loyalty can be explained by store satisfaction, retailer brand loyalty and loyalty card ownership.

Translation of the Managerial Problem into Statistical Notions

The regression model includes a dependent variable, that is, the store loyalty, and three independent variables that are the customers' store satisfaction, their loyalty to the store brand and their loyalty card ownership. These variables are measured on an interval scale, except the loyalty card ownership variable which is a nominal variable containing two categories. The values of the nominal variable are 1 if the customer is a loyalty card holder, and 2 if the customer is not enrolled in the loyalty programme. To include a nominal variable in the regression, the nominal variable must preferably be recoded as a dummy variable with values 0 and 1. Therefore, the loyalty card ownership variable is recoded as follows: 0 if the customer is not enrolled in the loyalty programme and 1 if the customer is enrolled in the loyalty programme. Recoding the nominal variable is only needed if the initial values of the nominal variable are not 0 and 1.

Dataset Description

The Excel file used in this study is named *Store_loyalty.xls*. It summarizes the responses of 278 customers. Moreover, it contains the following variables:

- Loyalty to the store as the dependent variable (*STORE LOYALTY*).

- Satisfaction level with the overall store experience (*STORE SATISFACTION*).

- Loyalty towards the store's private label products (*RETAILER BRAND LOYALTY*).

- A binary indicator for the possession of a loyalty card with *1* as a holder for a loyalty card and *0* for a non-holder of the loyalty card (*LOYALTY CARD*).

- Three dummy-variables indicating the age group a customer belongs to. These variables are used in section 7.1.3. Multiple Regression in the Presence of a Nominal Independent Variable (more than two Categories).

All variables except *LOYALTY CARD, AGE1, AGE2, AGE3* are measured on 5-point Likert-scales.

Hypotheses

The general form of this linear regression model is the following:

$$\text{STORE LOYALTY}=\beta_0+\beta_1(\text{STORE SATISFACTION})+\beta_2(\text{RETAIL BRAND LOYALTY})+\beta_3(\text{LOYALTY CARD})+\varepsilon$$

First, the overall meaningfulness of the model is checked. This null hypothesis states that there is no linear relationship between the dependent variable Y and the independent variables X_i.

H_0: $\beta_1=\beta_2=\beta_3=0$

H_1: At least one of the $\beta_i \neq 0$

The F test is used to test the null hypothesis (H_0). In addition, to test the overall significance of the model, we could test whether each independent variable contributes to explain the dependent variable. For the independent variable X_i, the following hypotheses are tested:

H_0: $\beta_i=0$

H_1: $\beta_i \neq 0$

The t test is used to determine the significance of the relationship between each independent variable and the dependent variable.

Data Analysis

A multiple regression with a nominal independent variable is run using the **<u>Linear Regression</u>** task.

1. Add the dataset *Store_loyalty.xls* to your project.

2. Go to **<u>Tasks</u>** → **<u>Regression</u>** → **<u>Linear Regression...</u>** to open the regression selection pane.

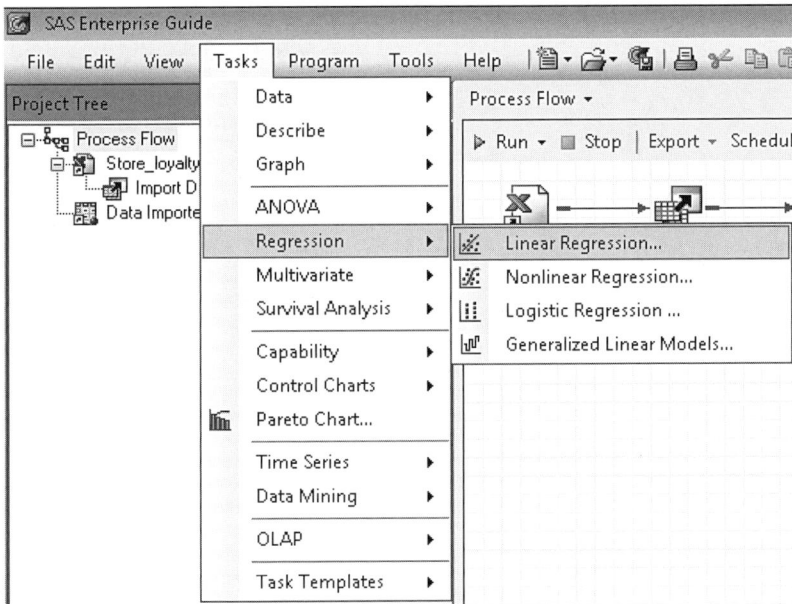

3. In the **Data** pane, drag and drop your variable of interest, that is, *STORE LOYALTY*, to the **Dependent variable** role, while you add the explanatory or independent variables to the **Explanatory variables** role.

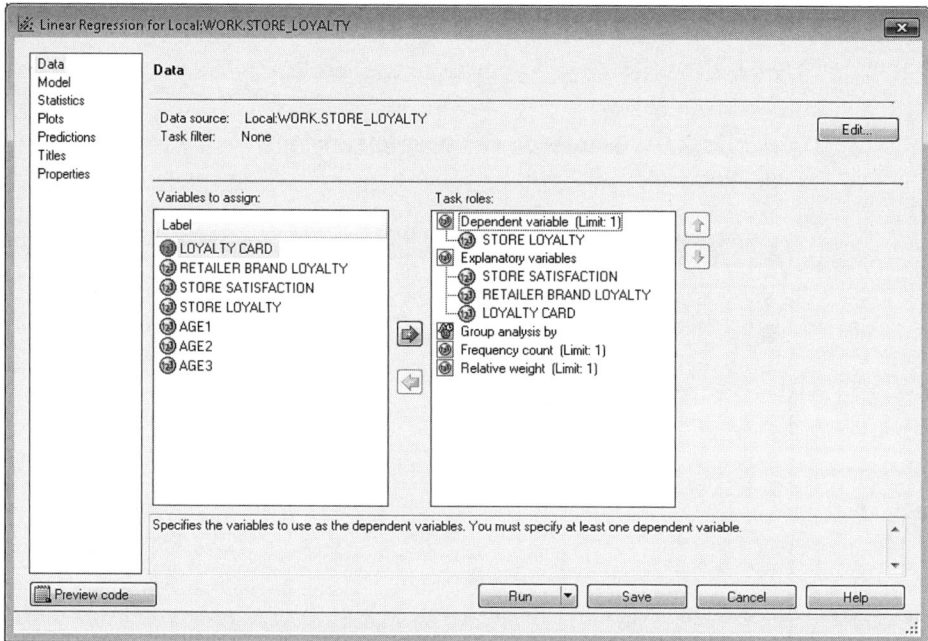

4. By clicking on **Model** in the selection pane, different options appear to build a regression model. Either a full model could be run, that is, a regression model that includes all independent variables, or a variable selection model could be run, that is, a regression model that automatically selects the most influential variables based on particular criteria (see section 7.1.1. Multiple Regression with Continuous Variables for more information about the variable selection methods or click on **Help** to open the SAS Enterprise Guide Help). This section employs a stepwise variable selection regression model with entry and stay significance levels equal to 0.05. This is done by ticking the option **Stepwise selection** under the **Model selection method** header. Furthermore, one could tick the explanatory variables to be forced in the model, if needed. You could do this under the **Effects to force into the model** header.

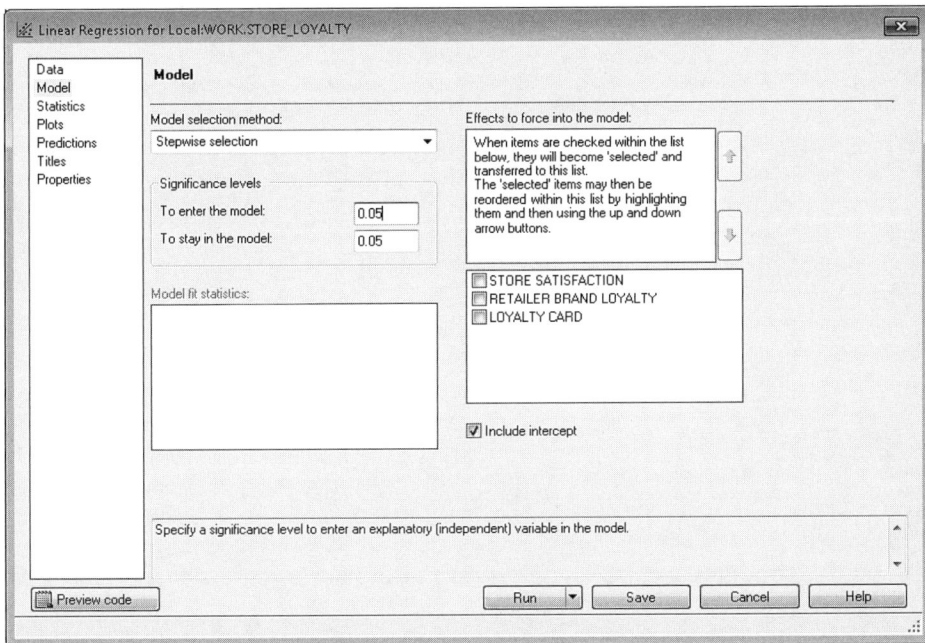

5.   In the **Statistics** pane, more information could be asked for the parameter estimates, the correlation among the variables and the diagnostics for model robustness. Under **Details on estimates**, we asked for **Standardized regression coefficients** and a **Correlation matrix of the estimates**. Moreover, we ask for a **Collinearity analysis**, **Tolerance values for estimates**, **Variance inflation values** and the **Heteroscedasticity test** (see section 7.1.1. Multiple Regression with Continuous Variables for an explanation of these options or click **Help** to open the SAS Enterprise Guide Help).

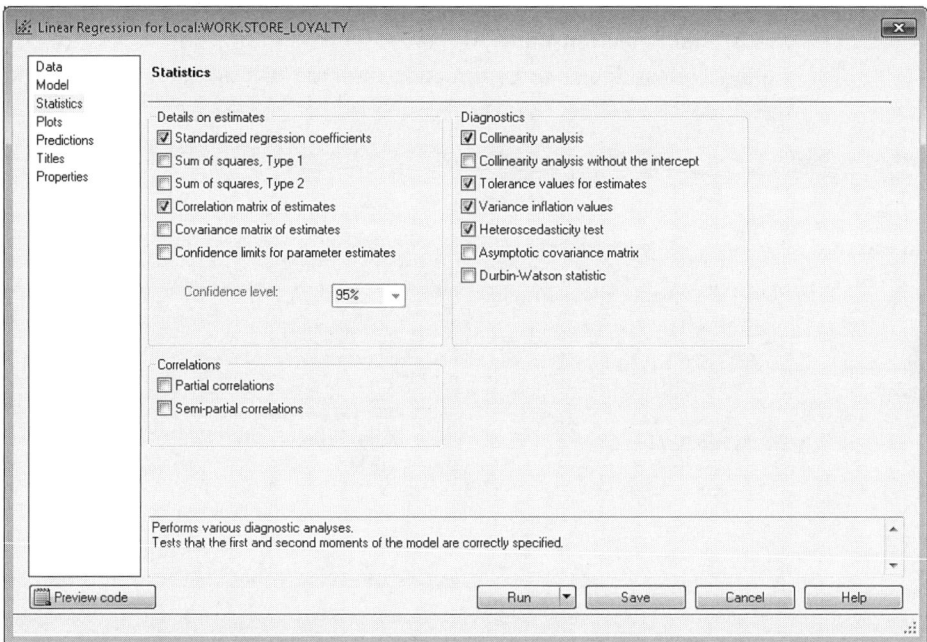

6.   Click **Run** and explore the results of this linear regression in the **Results** tab.

This section focuses on the interpretation of the overall meaningfulness of the model and the significance of the independent variables. All output related to the stepwise variable selection process and the assumption testing process is omitted.

Interpretation

The stepwise variable selection method selects the significant variables and adds them one by one to the model. Variables that are selected and retained in the last step (step 3) of the stepwise regression model are *STORE SATISFACTION*, *RETAILER BRAND LOYALTY* and *LOYALTY CARD*.

- **Analysis of Variance**

Analysis of Variance					
Source	**DF**	**Sum of Squares**	**Mean Square**	**F Value**	**Pr > F**
Model	3	58.73742	19.57914	44.66	<.0001
Error	274	120.12028	0.43840		
Corrected Total	277	178.85770			

Root MSE	0.66211	R-Square	0.3284	
Dependent Mean	3.09712	Adj R-Sq	0.3210	
Coeff Var	21.37837			

This table gives insight into the overall significance of the linear regression model. The F test is used and its estimated value is 44.66 with *3* degree of freedom in the numerator and *274 (278-3–1)* in the denominator. The p-value associated with the F value is smaller than 0.0001, and thus lower than 0.05. Consequently, the null hypothesis (H_0) is rejected, meaning that at least one parameter estimate is significantly different from 0.

As mentioned earlier, the R-Square measures the explained percentage of variance in the dependent variable and it is often used to evaluate the goodness of fit for regression equations. In our situation, it is equal to 32.84 per cent. Guidelines tell us that an R-square of 70 per cent or higher is most often considered as good. However, in marketing, we consider acceptable lower R-Squares when the regression model explains consumers' behaviour or intentions observed on empirical survey data.

Furthermore, the Adjusted R-square is an adaptation of the traditional R-Square measure, because it takes into account the number of variables in the model. This measure is often used to compare several linear regression models having a different number of variables.

- **Parameter Estimates**

Parameter Estimates

Variable	DF	Parameter Estimate	Standard Error	t Value	Pr > |t|	Standardized Estimate	Tolerance	Variance Inflation
Intercept	1	-0.32019	0.30278	-1.06	0.2912	0	.	0
STORE SATISFACTION	1	0.67192	0.07797	8.62	<.0001	0.44178	0.93269	1.07217
RETAILER BRAND LOYALTY	1	0.22821	0.04822	4.73	<.0001	0.23891	0.96167	1.03986
LOYALTY CARD	1	0.21317	0.09457	2.25	0.0250	0.11366	0.96390	1.03746

This table shows the parameter estimates for the linear regression model, that is, the intercept and the regression coefficients associated with each independent variable. For each coefficient, one can find the *Parameter Estimate*, the *Standard Error*, the *t Value* and the p-value (*Pr>|t|*). In our setting, all the variables are significantly different from 0, that is, the p-values associated to the t test are all lower than 0.05. It is logical because we use the stepwise method. Thus, only significant variables are included in the final model. However, if one does not select the stepwise method, it is important to check that all p-values are lower than 0.05.

Furthermore, it is important to identify the direction of the relationship. All three independent variables show a positive relationship with the dependent variable, because their estimates are positive. The interpretation of coefficients is slightly different between continuous variables, *STORE SATISFACTION* and *RETAILER BRAND LOYALTY*, and categorical dummy variables like *LOYALTY CARD*. For the continuous variables, a higher *STORE SATISFACTION* (*RETAILER BRAND LOYALTY*) is associated with higher levels of *STORE LOYALTY*. This interpretation is a little bit different for the binary variable *LOYALTY CARD* which is equal to *1* when customers hold a loyalty card, and *0* otherwise. The estimated coefficient for the variable *LOYALTY CARD* (β_3= 0.21317) is interpreted as follows: loyalty card holders are more loyal to the store than non-holders, because their store loyalty increases on average with 0.21317.

In order to check the variable with the highest impact on the dependent variable, one has to check the standardized estimates in the *Standardized Estimate* column. Standardized estimates of different variables are comparable to one other, and they are an ideal tool for an impact analysis. In the current setting, it is clear that *STORE SATISFACTION* has the largest impact with a standardized estimate of 0.44178, followed by *RETAILER BRAND LOYALTY* (0.23891) and *LOYALTY CARD* (0.11366).

Managerial Recommendations

The linear regression model demonstrates that loyalty to the retail brand products and the overall store satisfaction positively influence the store loyalty. Moreover, it is shown that loyalty card holders are more loyal to the store than non-holders. The store loyalty for customers enrolled in the loyalty programme is 0.21317 points higher than that of customers not enrolled. Loyalty towards retail brand products and the loyalty card usage should be used to enhance customers' overall level of loyalty. For instance, the retailer could induce retail brand purchases by providing extra rewards to loyalty card holders.

7.1.3. MULTIPLE REGRESSION IN THE PRESENCE OF A NOMINAL INDEPENDENT VARIABLE (MORE THAN TWO CATEGORIES)

Managerial Problem

The managerial problem is similar to the previous one. The retail company wants to better grasp customers' store loyalty. Specifically in this setting, the company wants to check whether customers' age explains the loyalty level in addition to satisfaction and the loyalty to the retail brand products. The marketing manager conducted a survey to evaluate to what extent store loyalty can be explained by store satisfaction, retailer brand loyalty and customers' age.

Translation of the Managerial Problem into Statistical Notions

The regression model includes a dependent variable, that is, the store loyalty, and three independent variables that are the customers' store satisfaction, their loyalty to the store brand products and the customers' age. All these variables have interval properties except the customers' age that is a nominal variable with three categories. When a nominal variable is introduced into the regression model, the nominal variable must be recoded into one or several dummies. The number of dummy variables is equal to the number of categories. Suppose that we want to include customers' age in the regression model as an independent variable. Three categories are considered for the variable age; 18–35 years, 36–55 years and older than 55 years. We create three dummy variables: *AGE1*, *AGE2* and *AGE3*. These variables are coded as follows:

Dummy variable	18–35 years	36–55 years	>55 years
AGE1	1	0	0
AGE2	0	1	0
AGE3	0	0	1

In detail, *AGE1* is equal to *1* if the consumer falls in the category *18–35 years*, and *0* if not. *AGE2* is equal to *1* if the individual is in the category *36–55 years*, and *0* if not. *AGE3* is equal to *1* if the individual belongs to the category *>55 years*, and *0* if not.

In the regression analysis, all these dummy variables cannot be included at once. One must always omit one dummy variable to estimate the regression model, because otherwise a linear combination of variables is included in the model. Suppose that we do not include *AGE1* but we do include *AGE2* and *AGE3*, we can evaluate whether the customers' loyalty of *AGE2* and *AGE3* differs from *AGE1*. Similarly, if we omit *AGE3* and we include *AGE1* and *AGE2*, we could assess the loyalty difference between *AGE3* and the two other groups.

Dataset Description

The Excel file used in this study is named *Store_loyalty.xls*. It summarizes the responses of 278 customers. Moreover, it contains the following variables:

- Loyalty to the store as the dependent variable (*STORE LOYALTY*).

- Satisfaction level with the overall store experience (*STORE SATISFACTION*).

- Loyalty towards the store's private label products (*RETAILER BRAND LOYALTY*).

- A binary indicator for the possession of a loyalty card with *1* as a holder for a loyalty card, and *0* as a non-holder of the loyalty card (*LOYALTY CARD*).

- Three dummy-variables indicating the age group a customer belongs to. These variables are used in this section (*AGE1, AGE2, AGE3*).

All variables except *LOYALTY CARD, AGE1, AGE2, AGE3* are composite variables (that is, means of several items measured on 5-point Likert-scales (ranging from 1 = totally disagree to 5 = totally agree).

Hypotheses

Suppose dummy variables *AGE1* and *AGE2* are included in the linear regression model, then the general form of the linear regression model is the following:

$$\text{STORE LOYALTY} = \beta_0 + \beta_1(\text{STORE SATISFACTION}) + \beta_2(\text{RETAIL BRAND LOYALTY}) + \beta_3(\text{AGE1}) + \beta_4(\text{AGE2}) + \varepsilon$$

On the other hand if we decide to include the variables *AGE2* and *AGE3*, the following linear regression is obtained:

$$\text{STORE LOYALTY} = \beta_0 + \beta_1(\text{STORE SATISFACTION}) + \beta_2(\text{RETAIL BRAND LOYALTY}) + \beta_3(\text{AGE2}) + \beta_4(\text{AGE3}) + \varepsilon$$

The null hypothesis of the overall meaningfulness test states that there is no linear relationship between the dependent variable Y and the independent variables X_i.

H_0: $\beta_1 = \beta_2 = \beta_3 = \beta_4 = 0$

H_1:   At least one of the $\beta_i \neq 0$

The F test is used to test the null hypothesis (H_0). In addition, to test the overall significance of the model, we can test whether each independent variable contributes to explain the dependent variable. For the independent variable X_i, the following hypotheses are stated:

H_0: $\beta_i = 0$

H_1: $\beta_i \neq 0$

The t test is used to determine the significance of the relationship between each independent variable and the dependent variable.

Data Analysis

A multiple regression with a nominal variable with more than two categories is run using the **Linear Regression** task.

1.   Add the dataset *Store_loyalty.xls* to your project.

2. Go to **Tasks** → **Regression** → **Linear Regression...** to open the regression selection pane.

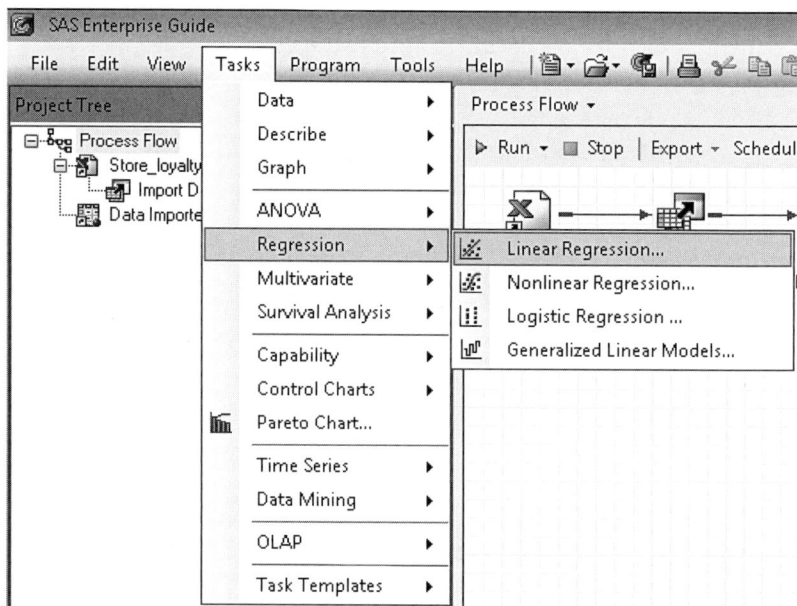

3. In the **Data** pane, drag and drop your variable of interest, that is, *STORE LOYALTY*, to the **Dependent variable** role, while you add the explanatory or independent variables to the **Explanatory variables** role. In detail, only two of the three dummy variables, *AGE1* and *AGE2*, are added to the regression model in addition to *STORE SATISFACTION*, *RETAILER BRAND LOYALTY*. This imposes that the third age category is considered as the reference group.

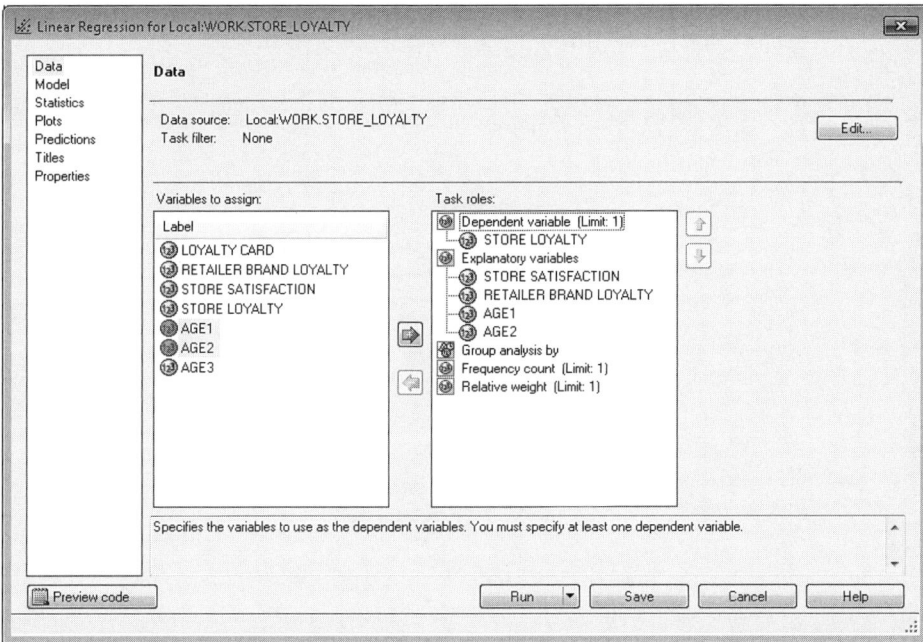

4. Click on **Model** in the selection pane. In this pane one has different options in building a regression model. Either one could run a full model, that is, a regression model that includes all independent variables, or a variable selection model, that is, a regression model that selects the most influential variables based on particular criteria (see section 7.1.1. Multiple Regression with Continuous Variables for more detailed information on the variable selection procedures or click **Help** to open the SAS Enterprise Guide Help). In this example, no variable selection technique is employed, so the **Full model fitted (no selection)** option is ticked.

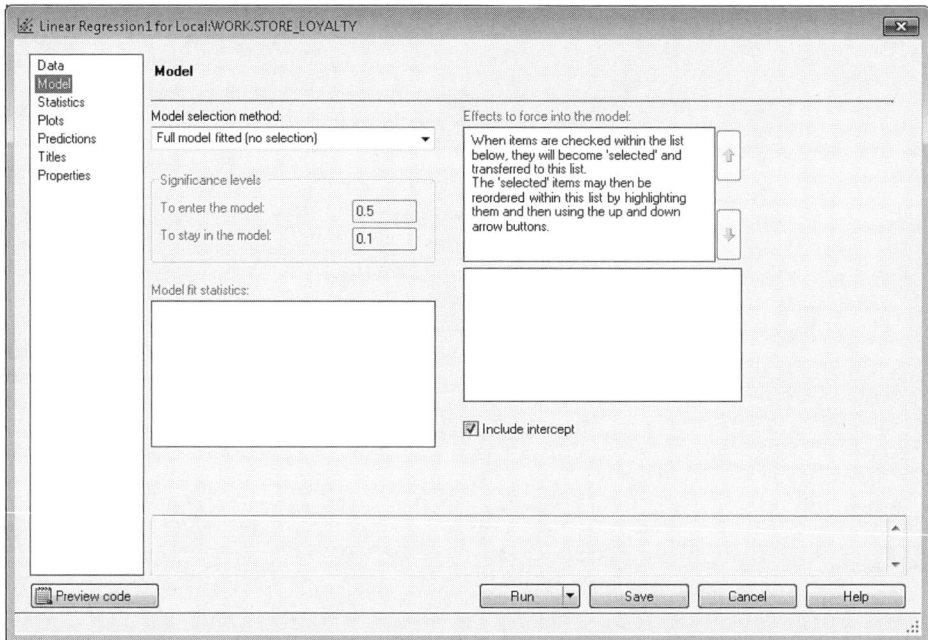

5. In the **Statistics** pane, you have the possibility to ask more information for the parameter estimates, the correlation among the variables into the model and the diagnostics for model robustness. Under **Details on estimates**, we ask for **Standardized regression coefficients** and a **Correlation matrix of the estimates**. Moreover, we ask for a **Collinearity analysis, Tolerance values for estimates, Variance inflation values**, the **Heteroscedasticity test** under the header **Diagnostics** (see section 7.1.1. Multiple Regression with Continuous Variables for more information on the options selected or click **Help** to open the SAS Enterprise Guide Help).

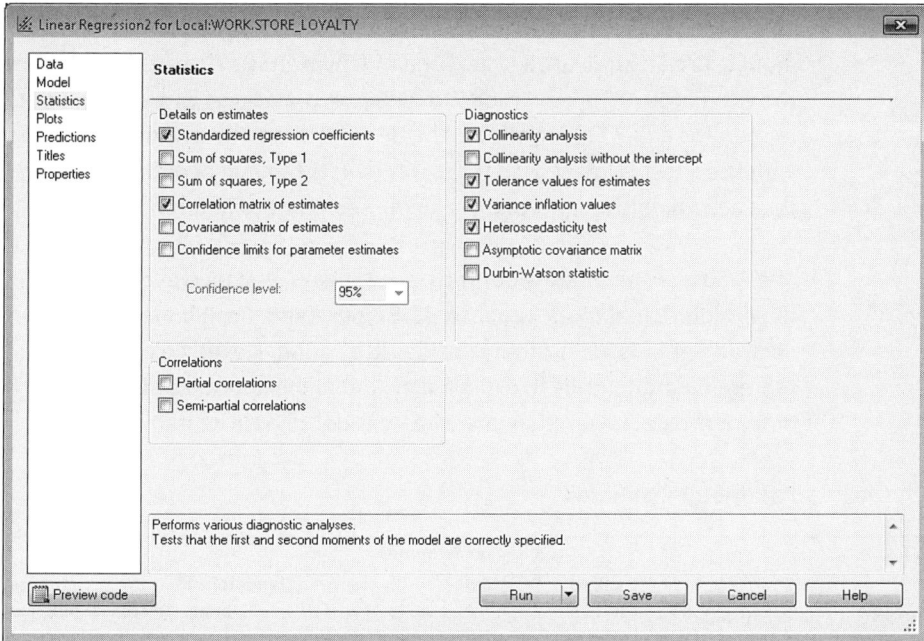

6. Click the **Run** button to run the multiple regression. Verify the results in the **Results** tab.

⚠️ *This section focuses on the interpretation of the overall meaningfulness of the model and the significance of the different independent variables. All output related to the assumption testing is omitted. The interpretation of the assumption outputs have already been discussed in section 7.1.1. Multiple Regression with Continuous Variables.*

Interpretation

- **Analysis of Variance**

Analysis of Variance					
Source	DF	Sum of Squares	Mean Square	F Value	Pr > F
Model	4	58.25473	14.56368	32.97	<.0001
Error	273	120.60297	0.44177		
Corrected Total	277	178.85770			

Root MSE	0.66466	R-Square	0.3257	
Dependent Mean	3.09712	Adj R-Sq	0.3158	
Coeff Var	21.46047			

This table gives insight into the meaningfulness of the linear regression model. The F test is used to test the null hypothesis (H_0). The F-value for the estimated regression model is 32.97 with *4* degree of freedom in the numerator and 273 (*278-4-1*) in the denominator. The p-value associated with the F test is lower than 0.05. This rejects the null hypothesis (H_0) and thus accordingly at least one parameter estimate is different from 0.

The R-Square, an indicator of the percentage of variance explained of the dependent variable, is equal to 32.57 per cent. An R-square of 70 per cent or higher is most often considered as good. Nevertheless, when the regression model tries to explain consumers' perception or behaviour on empirical data, lower R-squares are considered as acceptable as well.

- **Parameter Estimates**

Parameter Estimates								
Variable	DF	Parameter Estimate	Standard Error	t Value	Pr > |t|	Standardized Estimate	Tolerance	Variance Inflation
Intercept	1	-0.21624	0.31263	-0.69	0.4897	0	.	0
RETAILER BRAND LOYALTY	1	0.24601	0.04898	5.02	<.0001	0.25755	0.93940	1.06451
STORE SATISFACTION	1	0.69534	0.07716	9.01	<.0001	0.45717	0.95969	1.04200
AGE1	1	-0.14806	0.11427	-1.30	0.1962	-0.08915	0.52177	1.91657
AGE2	1	0.02879	0.13306	0.22	0.8289	0.01477	0.53028	1.88578

This table shows the estimated regression model, that is, the intercept and the regression coefficients associated with each independent variable. For each coefficient, SAS Enterprise Guide provides the *Parameter Estimate*, the *Standard Error*, the *t Value* and the p-value (*Pr>|t|*). If we consider a p-value of 0.05 during significance testing, *RETAILER BRAND LOYALTY* and *STORE SATISFACTION* significantly impact the customers' loyalty. The higher the *RETAILER BRAND LOYALTY* (*STORE SATISFACTION*) is, the higher the STORE LOYALTY is. However, none of the age variables, *AGE1* and *AGE2*, are significant. Given that *AGE3* is not included in the regression model, customers who fall in the categories *AGE1* have the same level of loyalty as customers in the category *AGE3* and it also holds for *AGE2*. Or the influence of age on the store loyalty is the same for categories *AGE1* and *AGE2* compared to *AGE3*.

In the previous analysis, we have not included *AGE3*. Consequently, we compare the influence of *AGE1* and *AGE2* on customers' loyalty to the influence of *AGE3* on consumers' loyalty. We still need to evaluate whether the influence of *AGE2* on customers' loyalty differs from the influence of *AGE1*. We rerun the regression analysis with the following independent variables: *RETAILER BRAND LOYALTY*, *STORE SATISFACTION*, *AGE2* and *AGE3*. Repeat steps 1 till 6 of the *Data Analysis* part and interpret the **Parameter Estimates** table as shown below.

Parameter Estimates								
Variable	DF	Parameter Estimate	Standard Error	t Value	Pr > |t|	Standardized Estimate	Tolerance	Variance Inflation
Intercept	1	-0.36430	0.30677	-1.19	0.2361	0	.	0
RETAILER BRAND LOYALTY	1	0.24601	0.04898	5.02	<.0001	0.25755	0.93940	1.06451
STORE SATISFACTION	1	0.69534	0.07716	9.01	<.0001	0.45717	0.95969	1.04200
AGE2	1	0.17685	0.10001	1.77	0.0781	0.09070	0.93879	1.06520
AGE3	1	0.14806	0.11427	1.30	0.1962	0.06675	0.93071	1.07445

Only if we consider a critical significance level of 0.10, *AGE2* contributes to the linear regression model. In this case, this means that *AGE2* significantly influences the customers' loyalty. More specifically, customers belonging to *AGE2* are more loyal than customers in the category *AGE1*. Customers from 36 to 55 years old are more loyal to the store than younger customers, that is, *AGE1* with 18–35 years old.

Managerial Recommendations

On the basis of the regression model estimation, the retail company knows that store satisfaction and loyalty to their own branded products contribute to explain store loyalty. Moreover, customers' store loyalty also depends on customers' age, only if the significance level is relaxed to 0.10. In that case, the results demonstrate that customers from 36 to 55 years old are more loyal to the retail store than young adults. The retailer's efforts to improve customers' loyalty could preferably focus on young adults (*AGE1*) and consumers older than 55 years (*AGE3*).

7.2. Logistic Regression

Fundamentals

Binary logistic regression, hereafter referred to as logistic regression, investigates the relationship between a binary dependent variable, that is, a categorical variable that only contains two categories, and a set of independent variables that can be continuous and/or categorical. It is a useful analysis technique for modelling problems where the objective is to discriminate between two groups represented by two categories of the dependent variable. The main difference with linear regression is that binary logistic regression handles a binary categorical variable, while linear regression assumes that the dependent variable is continuous.

The purpose of a traditional logistic regression is twofold. First, logistic regression can be used to discover the underlying trends of a binary response variable. Knowing which independent variables have an impact on certain customer behaviour is a first crucial step in better understanding the research problem. Discovering the direction of the impact, that is, a positive or negative relationship, on the dependent variable is vital when one wants to draw relevant managerial conclusions. Second, logistic regression can be conducted to predict customer behaviour summarized in a binary dependent variable, for instance the preferred type of mobile subscription, that is, whether it is a pre-paid or post-paid subscription. Practically, the dependent variable used within logistic regression is coded as 0-1, that is, the preferred type of mobile connection could be coded as 1 if the customer prefers a post-paid subscription and 0 otherwise. The category coded as 1 is called the event, while the other category is considered as the non-event. The independent variables in this case could be the customers' age, the gross income per month and the intensity of mobile phone usage. In a prediction context, the logistic regression is used to estimate the probability that the customer will choose the post-paid subscription given a particular set of values for the independent variables.

Statistically speaking, the probability that the dependent variable Y equals 1 given the multiple logistic regression model is given by the following equation:

$$E(Y) = P(Y=1 \mid X) = \frac{e^{\beta_0 + \beta_1 X_1 + \beta_2 X_2 + \beta_3 X_3 + \ldots + \beta_n X_n}}{1 + e^{(\beta_0 + \beta_1 X_1 + \beta_2 X_2 + \beta_3 X_3 + \ldots + \beta_n X_n)}}$$

with E(Y) equal to the expected value of Y; P(Y = 1|x) the probability that Y equals 1 given the independent variables vector $X_1, X_2, X_3, \ldots, X_n$; X_i the value of the independent variable i and β_i the coefficient to be estimated for variable i.

The optimization of a logistic regression model comes down to estimate the β_i as accurately as possible using the maximum likelihood criterion. In other words, the final model is built so that the likelihood of reproducing the original dependent variable given a set of explanatory variables is at maximum. During the optimization process, the logistic regression builds different logistic regression models with different values of β_i and the parameter set that gives the best fit to the data is retained. Once the parameters of the regression model are obtained, they are used to construct the logit or $\beta_0 + \beta_1 X_1 + \beta_2 X_2 + \beta_3 X_3 + \ldots + \beta_n X_n$. Afterwards the logit transformation makes sure that the value of $P(Y = 1|X)$ ranges from 0 to 1. 0 means that the probability of expecting $Y = 1$ given X is non-existent based on the logistic regression model, while a value of 1 indicates the certainty of expecting $Y = 1$.

Managerial Problem

A music downloading company wants to identify what drives certain customers not to renew their downloading subscription. Furthermore, they want to assign a probability that their actual customers will not renew their subscription at the end of their subscription period. The objective of this company is to predict on an individual customer level whether the subscription will/will not be renewed after the maturity date. The music downloading company collected data about its customers' subscription base for the last four years. The company considers that a customer is a churner when his/her subscription is not renewed within one week after the expiry date. The independent variables contain information covering a 36-month period returning from every individual renewal point. The independent variables contain information about interactions between the customers and the company, socio-demographic information and subscription-describing information.

In this specific context, we plan to use logistic regression to determine the effects of the explanatory variables on the probability that customers will not renew their music downloading subscription. The dependent variable is the subscription renewal variable. It takes the value *1* if the customer does not renew his/her subscription within a week after the maturity date, and *0* otherwise. The independent variables are calculated taking into account 36 months of customer information.

Dataset Description

Two SAS datasets are considered in this section, that is, *Subscription1.sas7bdat* and *Subscription2.sas7bdat*. *Subscription1.sas7bdat* contains data of 1,000 customers with 50 per cent of the people renewing their music subscription and 50 per cent of the customers who did not. *Subscription2.sas7bdat* is a smaller sample of 200 customers. *Subscription1.sas7bdat* is used to build the logistic regression model and to identify the impact of the variables on the renewal variable, while *Subscription2.sas7bdat* is used to demonstrate how to assign a churn probability to customers not used during the logistic regression building phase. The following variables are included in the dataset:

- Customer identifier (*id*).

- Variable indicating whether a customer renewed his/her subscription, with *1* equal to a churner, and *0* otherwise (*RENEWAL*).

- The number of times a customer was in contact with the music downloading service (*CONTACT*).

- The elapsed time since last contact (*CONTACT_RECENCY*).

- The number of complaints (*COMPLAINT*).

- The amount of money spent during the last 36 months with the company, also called the monetary value (*MON_VAL*).

- The length of relationship expressed in days (*LOR*).

- A dummy variable indicating the gender, with *1* equal to male and *0* equal to female (*GENDER*).

- The age of the customer (*AGE*).

Hypotheses

First, we test the overall significance of the logistic regression model in a similar way to the multiple linear regression case. The null hypothesis states that none of the independent variables is making a significant contribution in explaining the dependent variable:

H_0: $\beta_1 = \beta_2 = \beta_3 = \ldots = \beta_i = 0$

H_1:   At least one of the $\beta_i \neq 0$

For a binary logistic regression model, SAS Enterprise Guide displays the likelihood ratio test that tests whether the fit of the final logistic regression models is different from the fit of the null model, that is, a logistic regression model without the independent variables. The test statistic of the likelihood ratio test follows a chi-square distribution with $p-1$ degrees of freedom, with p the parameters in the final regression model including the intercept. When the p-value is lower than the significance level of 0.05, the null hypothesis (H_0) is rejected and we conclude that the logistic regression model is meaningful.

In addition, to test the overall meaningfulness of the model, we can test whether each independent variable contributes to the logistic regression model. For the independent variable X_i, the following hypotheses are tested:

H_0: $\beta_i = 0$

H_1: $\beta_i \neq 0$

For each independent variable, SAS Enterprise Guide provides the chi-squared Wald test, and its associated p-value. The Wald statistic is the value of the estimated coefficient divided by its standard error. When the p-value is lower than the expected significance level of 0.05, we conclude that the independent variable is impacting the dependent variable.

Data Analysis

To run a logistic regression model, the **Logistic Regression** task is used.

1. Add the dataset *Subscription1.sas7bdat* to your process flow.

2. Open the logistic regression task by clicking **Tasks** → **Regression** → **Logistic Regression...**

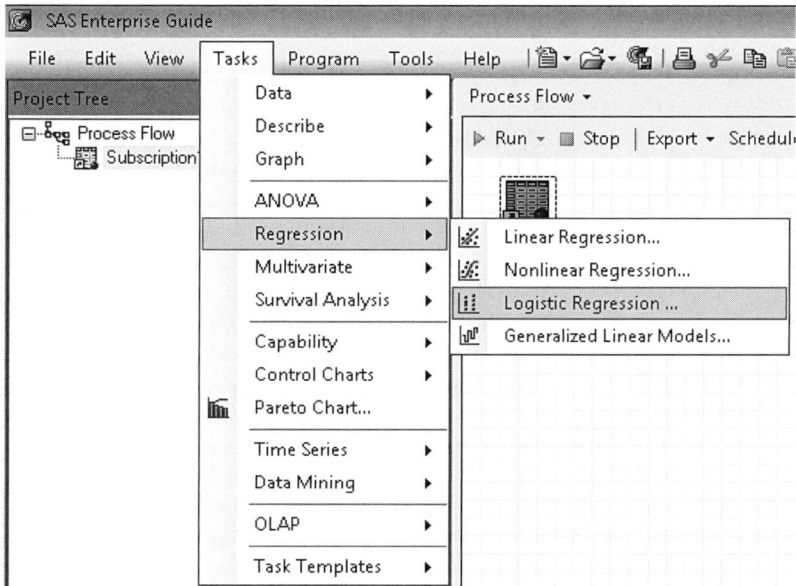

3.   In the **Data** pane, select the variable of interest, that is, the *RENEWAL* variable, and drop it under the **Dependent variable** role. All continuous independent variables are put under the **Quantitative variables** role, while the categorical variables are put under the **Classification variables** role.

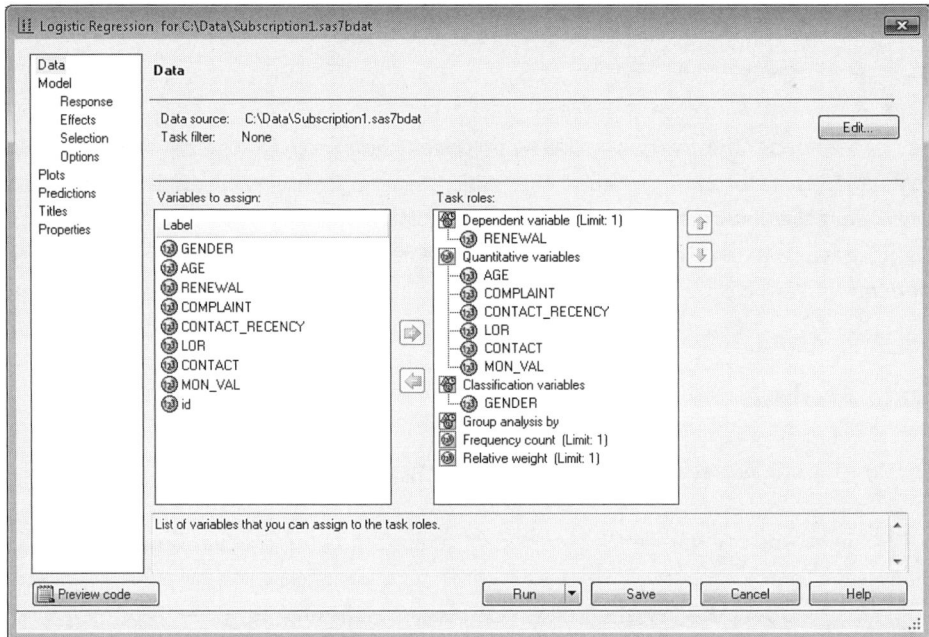

4.   Under **Response** in the **Model** pane, select the **Response type** of your dependent variable. Three different types of logistic regression models exist:

- if your dependent variable has only two options, the response type will automatically propose the label **Binary**, that is, a binary logistic regression model;
- when your dependent variable has more than two values, the researcher has the choice to run an **Ordered** or an **Unordered** model, that is, an (un)ordered multinomial logistic regression model.

In our setting, the option **Binary** is chosen, because only two categories in the dependent variable are present.

This section focuses on the binary logistic regression model, but it will pinpoint the main differences in option choices for the multinomial logistic regression models.

Under the option **Type of model**, you have the choice to run a logit or probit model, or a complementary log-log model. Choose here the option **logit** to opt for a traditional logit link model.

The response levels for the dependent variable are automatically shown next to the **Response levels for RENEWAL** option.

*If you previously selected **Ordered**, then you can specify the order of response levels by clicking on the arrows.*

The last option is the **Fit model to level** option that specifies to which level of the dependent variable one has to fit the model. Because the **Binary** option is selected, you select the category of your dependent variable you are interested in. In our setting, we are interested in building a logistic regression model that outputs estimates and probabilities for the people who did not renew their subscription, that is, Y=*1*.

*If you selected **Ordered** as a response type, there will appear a drop-down list to specify the order of the responses. If you select the first ordered value, then the response categories are ordered as they appear in the **Response levels for RENEWAL** box. If you select the last ordered value, then the response categories are set in reverse order.*

5. Under **Effects** in the **Model** pane, the analyst has to select the independent variables or effects he wants to include into the final logistic regression model. You have the choice to only add main effects (the **Main** button), to manually add interaction effects by selecting the relevant variables under the **Class and quantitative variables** role and by clicking on the button **Cross**, to automatically add all main and *X* degree interaction effects of the selected variables (the **Factorial** button), or to add polynomial terms like the square of a variable (the **Polynomial** button). In this example, we only add main effects of all independent variables under consideration. This is done by selecting all independent variables under the **Class and quantitative variables** role, and then by clicking the button **Main**.

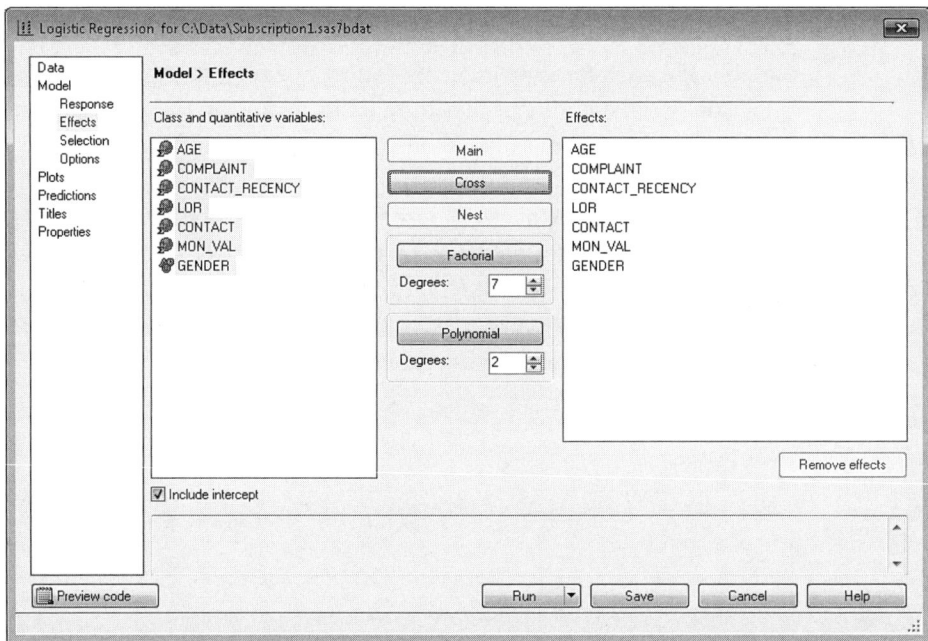

6. In the **Selection** pane under **Model**, you have to specify the model selection method. A model selection method is a method that automatically builds a robust logistic regression model by including only the independent variables that show a significant impact on the dependent variable. Under the **Model selection method** option, you have two choices; either you apply no variable selection at all, that is, the **Full model fitted (no selection)** option, or you apply an automatic variable selection technique. Below you will see an overview of the different variable selection options available as explained by the SAS Enterprise Guide help.

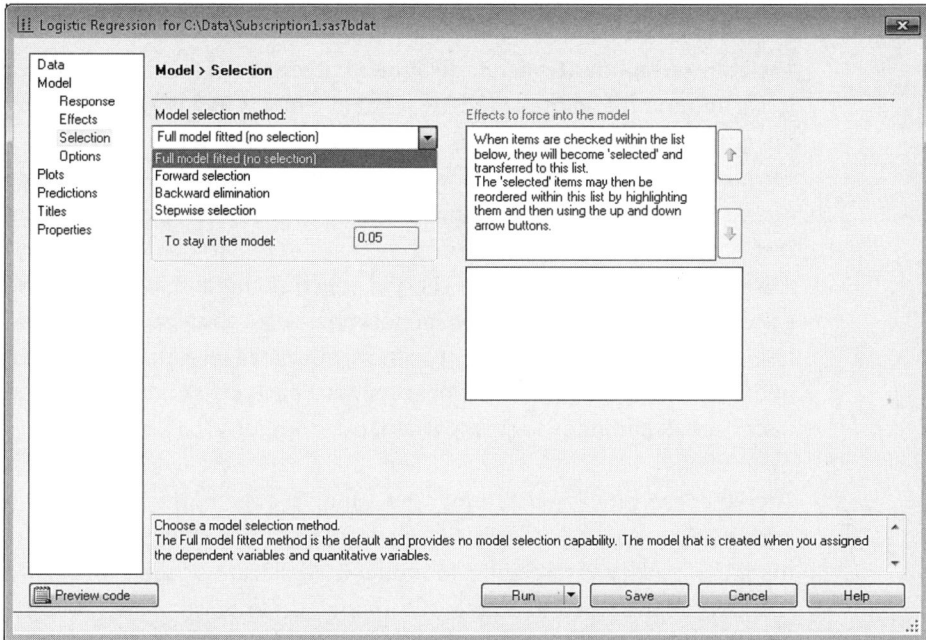

- **Forward Selection**

   The forward selection method begins with no variables in the model. For each of the explanatory variables, this method calculates the variable's contribution to the model as if it should be included. The contribution is expressed by a significance level to be filled in the **To enter the model** text box. The forward selection method adds the most contributing variable to the model. Variables are added to the model as long as the significance level falls below the predefined value. In sum, variables are added one by one to the model until no remaining variable produces a significant test statistic. After a variable is added to the model, it stays there.

- **Backward Elimination**

   The backward elimination method starts by taking all variables into consideration in the model and then deletes variables from the model one by one until all the variables that remain in the model produce test statistics significant at the significance level that is specified in the **To stay in the model** text box. At each step, the variable that shows the smallest contribution to the model is deleted. This method can be considered as opposite to the forward selection method.

- **Stepwise Selection**

  The stepwise method is a modification of the forward selection method. It is a method that differs in the way that variables already in the model do not necessarily stay there. As in the forward selection method, variables are added one by one to the model, as long as the variable has a significant contribution (to be specified in the **To enter the model** text box).

  After a variable is added, however, the stepwise method looks at all the variables already included in the model and deletes any variable that does not produce a statistic significant at the significance level that is specified in the **To stay in the model** text box. Only after this check is made and the necessary deletions are accomplished, can another variable be added to the model.

  The stepwise process ends when no variable outside the model has a statistic significant at the significance level that is specified to enter the model and every variable in the model is significant at the significance level that is specified to stay in the model, or when the variable to be added to the model is the variable that was just deleted from it.

If you choose a variable selection method, you have the choice to force an independent variable into the model. This is accomplished by ticking the box next to the variable under the **Effects to force into the model** option.

In this study, a stepwise variable selection method is used by selecting the **Stepwise selection** option under the **Model selection method** header. The enter and stay probabilities are set to 0.05.

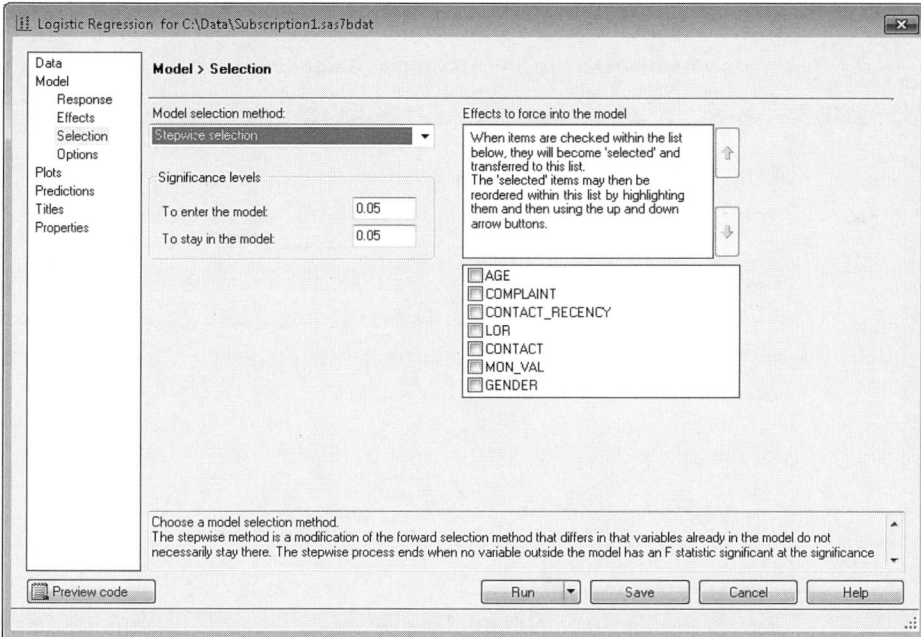

7.	In the pane **Model** under **Options**, you can choose different statistics to be output by SAS Enterprise Guide. It is interesting to see how well the model estimates and classifies the observations. Under the **Classification table** option, one asks for a classification table by ticking the option **Show classification table**. This is a table that summarizes the classification of the cases in the dataset based on a user-defined threshold on the posterior probabilities. In a binary classification context having a balanced sample on the dependent variable, a cut-off point of 0.5 is a logical choice. This means that a customer is considered as a churner when the posterior churn probability is higher than 50 per cent, and as someone who renews otherwise. A classification table gives a visual representation of the discrepancy of the predicted classification and the observed classification of the cases in the dataset. The probability threshold must be set to 0.5 under the **Critical probability values (cutpoints)** option. Under the **Model fit assessment** option, you could ask for fit measures of the estimated model. Only tick the option **Generalized R-squared** to obtain a proxy for the traditional R^2 which approximates the amount of variance explained. If needed, confidence interval information on the estimates and the odds ratios could be asked in the **Confidence limits** options.

More information on the other options could be obtained via the **Help** button which opens the SAS Enterprise Guide Help.

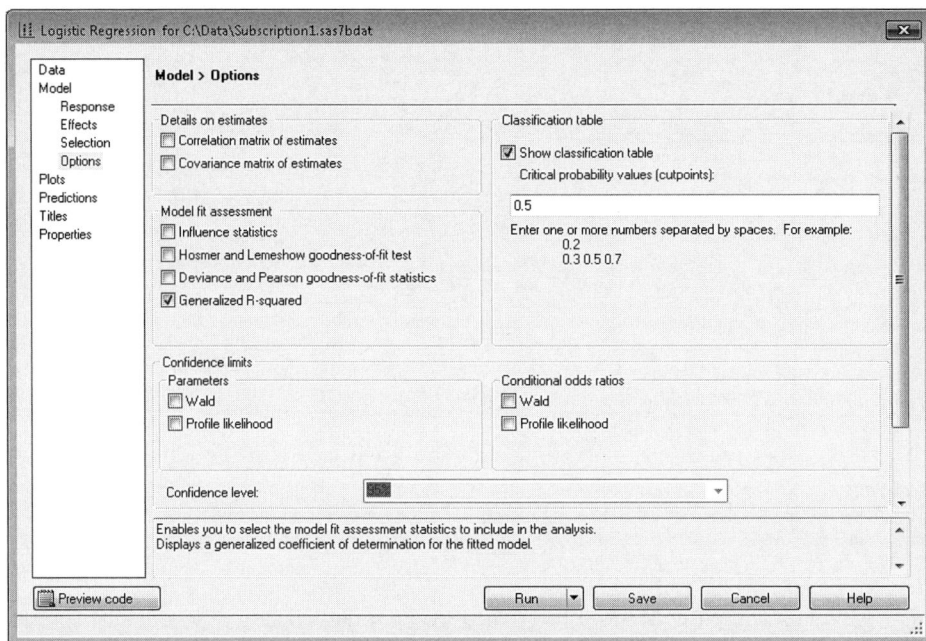

8. In order to facilitate the interpretation of the output, there are no plots asked as they have already been discussed in section 7.1.1. Multiple Regression with Continuous Variables. This is done by clicking the **Plots** pane, and by clearing the option **Show plots for regression analysis**

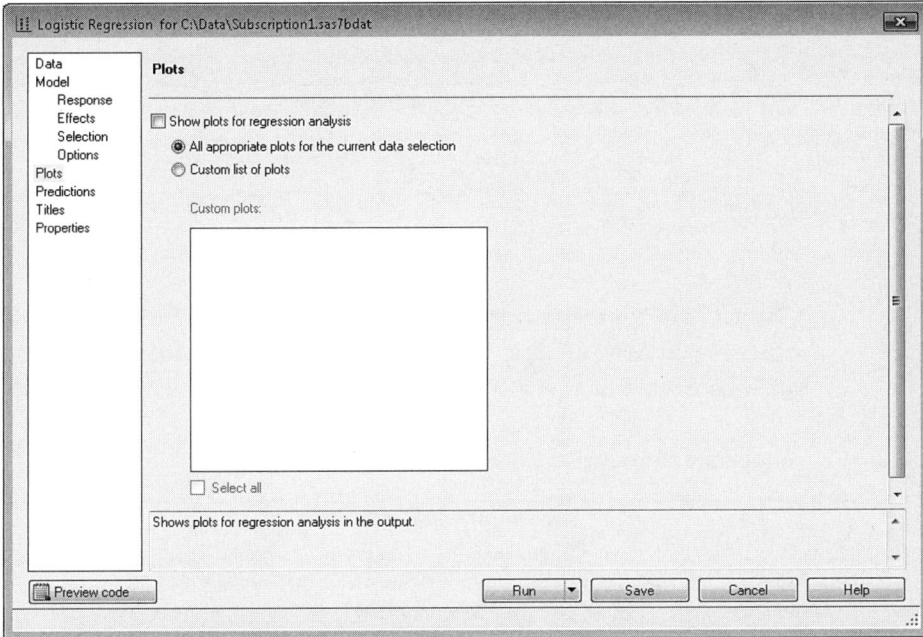

9.   One clicks **Run** to run the logistic regression model. Check the results in the **Results** tab.

Interpretation

*   **Response Profile**

Response Profile		
Ordered Value	RENEWAL	Total Frequency
1	0	500
2	1	500

This table summarizes the distribution in the dependent variable. We see that the sample under consideration is balanced, meaning 500 customers who did not renew their subscription, and 500 customers who did renew it.

- **Class Level Information**

Class Level Information		
		Design
Class	Value	Variables
GENDER	0	1
	1	-1

This table shows the recoding scheme for the categorical variable(s). For the variable *GENDER*, it is shown that females are recoded as 1, while males are recoded as -1.

- **Summary of Stepwise Selection**

	Effect			Number	Score	Wald		Variable
Step	Entered	Removed	DF	In	Chi-Square	Chi-Square	Pr > ChiSq	Label
1	LOR		1	1	29.9897		<.0001	
2	CONTACT		1	2	7.6840		0.0056	
3	GENDER		1	3	7.0692		0.0078	GENDER

The variable selection process consists of three steps and a summarization of the stepwise selection process is given in this table. For instance, you see that three variables are included in the final stepwise logistic regression model, that is, *LOR*, *CONTACT* and *GENDER*, while no variables were removed once entered the stepwise logistic regression model.

As the stepwise variable selection is used, basic fit statistics are included for each and every step in the variable selection process. In order to start interpreting the final model when using a variable selection method, one has to look at the statistics in the last step of the selection procedure, in our case Step 3.

- **Testing Global Null Hypothesis: BETA=0**

Testing Global Null Hypothesis: BETA=0			
Test	Chi-Square	DF	Pr > ChiSq
Likelihood Ratio	45.4490	3	<.0001
Score	44.2793	3	<.0001
Wald	42.1503	3	<.0001

To verify the overall usefulness of the model, one should look in this table. In the row *Likelihood Ratio*, you will find whether or not the likelihood ratio test is significant. It is a statistical test that compares the fit of two logistic regression models, that is, the null model (or the baseline model without inclusion of the independent variables) and the alternative model (or the logistic regression with the independent variables included). This test compares how many times more likely the data is approximated under the alternative model versus the null model.

If one uses a variable selection technique, this table is output in the final step statistics. In our setting, we consider the output of this table under the header Step 3. Effect Gender entered. If no variable selection technique is employed, the relevant table is output within the overall output.

In our setting, we see that the p-value is smaller than 0.0001, and thus smaller than 0.05. This means that the model obtained in the last step of the stepwise selection procedure (step 3) is meaningful.

- **Analysis of Maximum Likelihood Estimates**

Analysis of Maximum Likelihood Estimates					
Parameter	DF	Estimate	Standard Error	Wald Chi-Square	Pr > ChiSq
Intercept	1	0.5997	0.1139	27.7199	<.0001
LOR	1	-0.00305	0.000588	26.9259	<.0001
CONTACT	1	-0.0485	0.0182	7.0783	0.0078
GENDER 0	1	0.1813	0.0683	7.0431	0.0080

This table gives an indication whether there is an impact of an independent variable on the dependent variable. When a variable shows a significant impact, the direction of the relationship needs to be explored.

Given the fact that a stepwise selection procedure is used in this example, all independent variables will have a significant impact on the dependent variable, that is, having a p-value smaller than 0.05.

Consequently, the direction of the relationship between the independent variables and the dependent variable is explored. The table shows that the *LOR* has a negative sign, this means that the longer the length of relationship of the customer is, the lower his probability that he will not renew his subscription. The same interpretation is valid for the *CONTACT* variable. The variable *Gender* on the other hand is a dummy variable, that is, a categorical variable with two categories. The impact of this variable is positive, meaning that women have a higher probability of churning than men.

In concrete the change in logit or $\beta_0 + \beta_1 X_1 + \beta_2 X_2 + \beta_3 X_3 + ... + \beta_n X_n$ is given by the estimate in the table. For instance, the estimate of *LOR* is -0.00305. This means that if the length of relationship increases by one day, the logit value will decrease by -0.00305.

• **Odds Ratio Estimates**

Odds Ratio Estimates			
		95% Wald	
Effect	Point Estimate	Confidence Limits	
LOR	0.997	0.996	0.998
CONTACT	0.953	0.919	0.987
GENDER 0 vs 1	1.437	1.099	1.879

Furthermore, the impact of the independent variables on the dependent variable could also be explored in terms of the odds ratio. The logit (or log odds) is equal to $\beta_0 + \beta_1 X_1 + \beta_2 X_2 + \beta_3 X_3 + ... + \beta_n X_n$. The log odds are defined as:

$$\text{log odds} = \text{Log} \frac{\text{the probability of an event (Y=1)}}{\text{the probability of a non-event (Y=0)}}$$

Consequently, the odds are defined as:

$$\text{odds} = \frac{\text{the probability of an event (Y=1)}}{\text{the probability of a non-event (Y=0)}}$$

So the odds ratio for a particular variable is defined as the factor with which the odds will change considering a one unit increase for that variable. If the parameter estimate is larger (smaller) than 0 then the odds ratio will be bigger (smaller) than one. An odds ratio of 1 results in a parameter estimate that is equal to 0. For instance, for the variable *Contact*, the conversion from male to female increases the odds with a factor of 0.953.

The link between the estimates, the probability of a (non)-event, the odds and the odds ratio is represented below for a change from female to male (*Gender*), considering a constant length of relationship of 100 days and four contact points.

	Males (*GENDER = -1*)		Females (*GENDER = 1*)
Logit	$0.5997 + (-0.00305) * 100 + (-0.0485)$ $* 4 + 0.1813 * -1 = -0.080$	Logit	$0.5997 + (-0.00305) * 100 + (-0.0485)$ $* 4 + 0.1813 * 1 = 0.282$
P(Y=1)	$e^{-0.080}/1+e^{-0.080} = 0.480$	P(Y=1)	$e^{0.282}/1+e^{0.282} = 0.570$
P(Y=0)	1-0.480 = 0.520	P(Y=0)	1-0.570 = 0.430
Odds	0.480/0.520 = 0.923	Odds	0.570/0.430 = 1.326
Odds ratio	1.326/0.922 = 1.437		

By comparing the odds ratios of the different variables in the model, one is able to rank the variables in terms of their effect size on the dependent variable. In our setting, it is for instance clear that the variable *GENDER* has the highest impact on the churning behaviour because the deviation of the odds ratio from one is the largest.

- **Classification Table**

Classification Table									
	Correct		Incorrect			Percentages			
Prob Level	Event	Non-Event	Event	Non-Event	Correct	Sensitivity	Specificity	False POS	False NEG
0.500	317	268	232	183	58.5	63.4	53.6	42.3	40.6

Furthermore, the performance of your logistic regression model could be assessed by the prediction capacity of the model. The logistic regression outputs posterior probabilities of churning for each and every customer in the dataset. By setting a threshold on the posterior probabilities, one is able to classify the customers into churners and non-churners. For instance, in our case we set it to 0.5, meaning that if the probability of churning assigned to a customer by the model is higher than 50 per cent, that customer is classified as a churner and as a non-churner otherwise. At this stage, one is able to compare the classification of the customers based on the model with their real churning behaviour summarized in the dependent variable. Classification results are often summarized in a confusion table as shown below.

		Real renewal behaviour (Y)	
		1	0
Predicted renewal behaviour	1	True Positives (TP)	False Positives (FP)
(P(Y=1| X))	0	False Negatives (FN)	True Negatives (TN)

If TP are the number of actual churners that are correctly identified by the algorithm (*Correct Event*), FP are the number of actual non-churners that are classified by the logistic regression model as churner (*Incorrect Event*), FN are the number of actual churners that are classified by the churn model as non-churner (*Incorrect Non-Event*), and TN are the number of actual non-churners that are classified as non-churner (*Correct Non-Event*). Then, for the cut-off value of 0.5 on the posterior probabilities:

- *Sensitivity* or the true positive rate is (TP/(TP+FN)): the proportion of actual churners that are predicted to be churner among all actual churners.
- *Specificity* or the true negative rate is (TN/(TN+FP)): the proportion of actual non-churners that are classified as non-churners among all actual non-churners.
- *False POS* or false positive rate is (FP/(FP+TP)): the proportion of actual non-churners that are classified as churners among all customers predicted to be churners.
- *False NEG* or false negative rate is (FN/(FN+TN)): the proportion of actual churners that are classified as non-churners among all customers predicted to be non-churners.

The purpose is that the sensitivity and the specificity are as high as possible, while the false positive rate and the false negative rate must be as small as possible. In our setting there is not that much differentiation between the sensitivity and the specificity on the one hand, and the false positive rate and false negative rate on the other hand. This indicates a limited prediction power of this logistic regression setting. This conclusion is confirmed when having a look at the column *Correct* that contains the accuracy of the prediction model or the number of cases which are correctly classified, that is, (TN+TP)/(TN+TP+FN+FP). In our setting, it is clear that the logistic regression is only able to predict 58.5 per cent of the cases correctly.

Once your final logistic regression model is built and you know the estimates β_i for each significant variable, it is possible to predict the probability of Y = *1* by plugging in the values of the respondents and applying the following formula:

$$E(Y)=P(Y=1\,|\,X) = \frac{e^{\beta_0+\beta_1X_1+\beta_1X_1+\beta_2X_2+...+\beta_nX_n}}{1+e^{(\beta_0+\beta_1X_1+\beta_1X_1+\beta_2X_2+...+\beta_nX_n)}}$$

In order to assign predicted probabilities to a sample of customers not used for model building, one has to execute the following procedure:

1. Go to the **Results** tab of the logistic regression analysis and click on **Modify Task**.

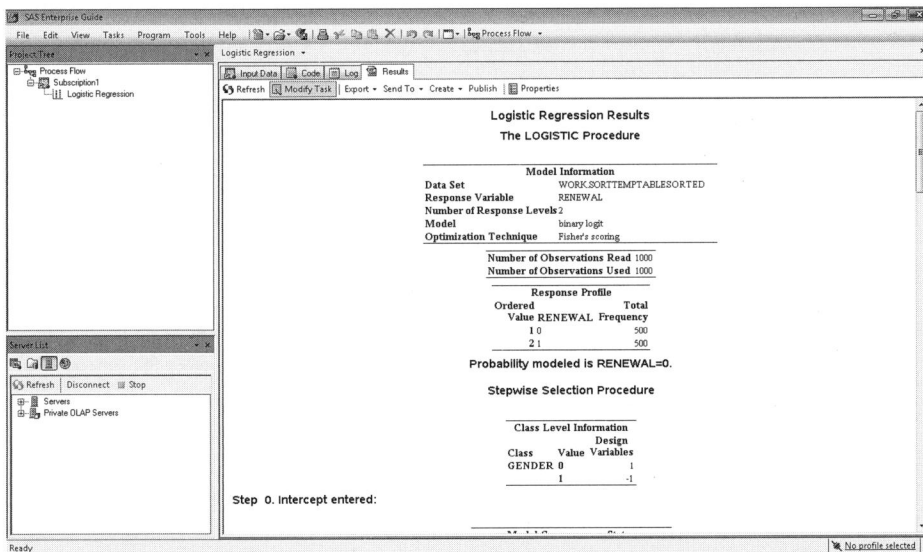

2.   In the selection pane, select **Predictions**. Under the option **Data to predict**, you can choose to add predictions to the dataset which is used during model building (**Original sample**), or you can add predictions to a new dataset that is not used for model building (**Additional data**). Tick the latter option and browse for the new dataset *Subscription2.sas7bdat* on your computer. This dataset is found in the library *ECLIB000*. Finally, add it to the SAS Enterprise Guide environment.

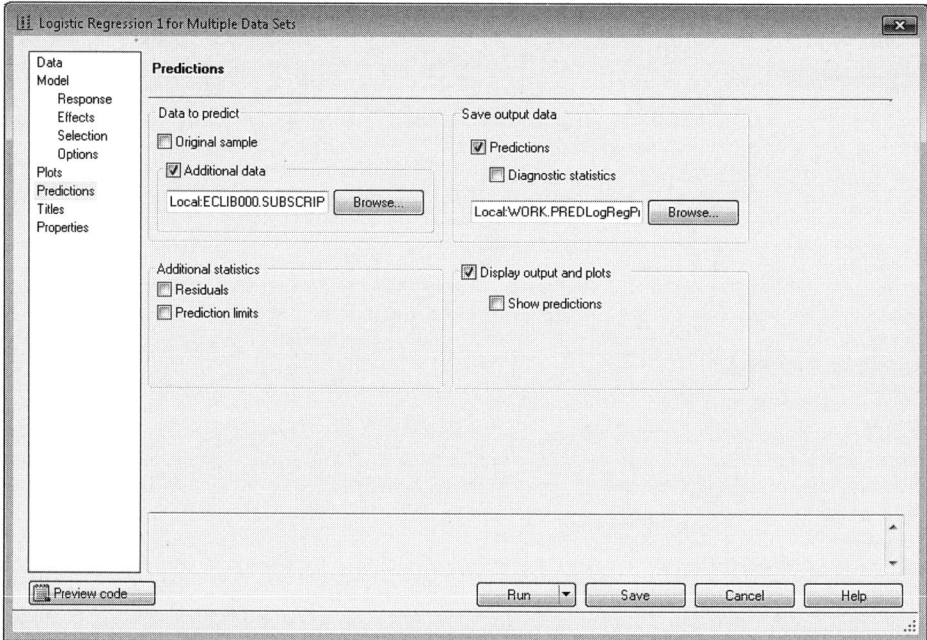

3.   Click **Run** to re-estimate the model and to make predictions for the new dataset.

You can verify the output of this task by going to the **Output Data** tab and you will see that four additional columns are added to the dataset. A column with the original dependent variable, a column with the predicted category of the dependent variable, a column with the predicted probability for RENEWAL=*0* and a last column with the predicted probabilities of RENEWAL=*1*.

Managerial Recommendation

The results indicate that three variables have a significant impact in explaining the renewal behaviour of the customers of the music downloading company. It is shown that the longer a customer has a relationship with the company, the smaller the probability is that the subscription will not be renewed. Furthermore, it is shown that the number of times customers take the initiative to get in touch with the company significantly impacts their churn probabilities. It seems that loyal customers are more likely to contact the firm to discuss things in advance, while non-loyal customers tend to simply end their subscription instead of reporting their concerns to the company. In the end, females tend to have a higher churn probability than men.

Further Reading

Aiken, L.S. and West, S.G. (1991), *Multiple Regression: Testing and Interpreting Interactions*, Sage Publications, Inc.

Berry, W.D. (1993), *Understanding Regression Assumptions*, Quantitative Applications in the Social Sciences, Sage Publications, Inc.

Berry, W.D. and Feldman, S. (1985), *Multiple Regression in Practice*, Quantitative Applications in the Social Sciences, Sage Publications, Inc.

Cohen, J., Cohen, P., West S.G. and Aiken L.S. (2002), *Applied Multiple Regression/ Correlation Analysis for the Behavioral Sciences*, 3rd edition, Routledge Academic.

Hardy, M.A. (1993), *Regression with Dummy Variables*, Quantitative Applications in the Social Sciences, Sage Publications, Inc.

Hosmer, D.W and Lemeshow, S. (2000), *Applied Logistic Regression*, 2nd edition, Wiley Series in Probability and Statistics, Wiley-Interscience.

Menard, S. (2001), *Applied Logistic Regression Analysis*, Quantitative Applications in the Social Sciences, 2nd edition, Sage Publications, Inc.

Schroeder, L., Sjoquist, D. and Stephan P.E. (1986), *Understanding Regression Analysis: An Introductory Guide*, Quantitative Applications in the Social Sciences, Sage Publications, Inc.

Chapter 8

Discriminant Analysis

Objectives

1. Describe the concept of discriminant analysis and its objectives.

2. Discuss the difference between the two-group discriminant analysis and the multiple discriminant analysis.

3. Interpret the discriminant analysis results and determine which predictor variables contribute the most.

4. Evaluate the discriminant solution in terms of predictive capacity.

Fundamentals

Discriminant analysis is an analysis technique used when the dependent variable is categorical containing two or more categories. For instance, the dependent variable may represent whether or not a customer bought the service after being sent a promotion leaflet. When the dependent variable has only two categories, the technique is called two-group discriminant analysis. When more than two categories are considered in the dependent variable, the technique is known as multiple discriminant analysis.

The application area of discriminant analysis is twofold. First, it can investigate the impact of one or more predictor variables or independent variables on a dependent variable. Second, discriminant analysis can classify individuals based on the discriminant function(s) estimated. Suppose that we want to classify new customers into several groups based on their interest in several products categories. Based on a dataset that contains the customers' group membership, the dependent variable, as well as their appeal and interest in several product categories, the independent variables, the discriminant analysis task builds a discriminant model based on the appeal variables that best classify customers into one of the customer groups. Once the discriminant function is built, it can be used to classify new customers into the existing groups.

Statistically speaking, discriminant analysis is an analysis technique that combines independent variables into a linear combination of the following form:

$$D = \beta_0 + \beta_1 X_1 + \beta_2 X_2 + ... + \beta_n X_n$$

where D is equal to the discriminant score, X_i is equal to independent variable i, β_0 is the intercept and β_i equals the weight or discriminant coefficient of variable i. A discriminant function is built and optimized so that the weights given to the independent variables discriminate as much as possible between the categories of the dependent variable. This occurs when the ratio of the between-group sum of squares to the within-group sum of squares for the discriminant scores is at maximum. In other words, the discriminant scores of individuals belonging to one category must be as different as possible from the discriminant scores of individuals belonging to the other categories. Discriminant analysis estimates a number of discriminant functions equal to the number of categories in the dependent variable minus one.

Discriminant analysis is interchangeable with the formerly explained logistic regression approach. However, there are situations where the logistic regression is preferred over the discriminant analysis and vice versa. On the one hand, logistic regression is more robust in situations where the assumption that the set of independent variables is distributed multivariate normal with a common variance-covariance matrix is not satisfied. Furthermore, logistic regression can handle both continuous as well as categorical independent variables, whereas discriminant analysis can only handle continuous variables. On the other hand, discriminant analysis can handle dependent variables with more than two categories, whereas a traditional binary logistic regression model can only handle a dependent variable with two categories. In this situation, the alternative to logistic regression when more than two categories are considered is called multinomial logistic regression.

Managerial Problem

A retail company has segmented its customers into three categories according to their loyalty card membership status. Three different profiles of customers are identified, that is, the loyalty card holders, the loyalty card non-holders with a positive intention to adoption and the loyalty card non-holders with no intention to adopt.

The retailer wants to better understand the differences between these three groups. A random sample of the retailer's customers has recently participated in a survey. The questionnaire included several questions about the consumers' perception of the loyalty card such as the loyalty card relative advantages, the loyalty card risk (privacy concern), the complexity of usage, the influence of others in their decision to adopt the loyalty card and the effort required to obtain the loyalty card. Furthermore, other variables such as their emotional attachment to the store, their share of wallet (SOW) and their share of visit (SOV), their apathetic and economic orientation, and the number of loyalty cards held were also recorded. The retailer's objective is to identify the variables that best discriminate the three different loyalty card profiles. The research questions are as follows:

- What are the variables that enable the retailer to differentiate the three consumer groups?

- Is it possible to classify customers into the three loyalty card groups based on the survey information available?

Translation of the Managerial Problem into Statistical Notions

In this setting, the dependent variable is a variable indicating the loyalty card membership, that is, the loyalty card holder, the non-holder with an intention to become enrolled and the non-holder with no intention to adopt the loyalty card. The independent variables that could explain the differences between the categories are the survey variables. Statistically speaking, the purpose of discriminant analysis is to find linear discriminant functions of the survey variables X_n that give different discriminant scores to individuals belonging to the different loyalty card segments.

In this particular example, three categories in the dependent variable are considered, and thus two discriminant functions are needed to separate them.

Dataset Description

The dataset *Loyalty_card_adoption.sas7bdat* includes 480 respondents classified in three classes according to their membership level. The variables in the dataset are:

- An identification of the respondent (*CODE_REP*).

- A loyalty card membership indicator with *1* for holder, *2* for non-holder with intention to adopt and *3* for non-holder with no intention to adopt (*CLASS*).

- The loyalty card relative advantage (*LC_RA*).

- The loyalty programme complexity (*COMPLEXITY*).

- The risk related to loyalty card adoption and usage linked to privacy concerns (*RISK*).

- The influence of relatives in the adoption process (*OTHER_INFLUENCE*).

- The effort required to get enrolled in the programme (*EFFORT*).

- Customer's emotional bond with the store (*STORE_ATTACHMENT*).

- The customer's economic orientation (*ECONOMIC*).

- The customer's apathetical orientation (*APHATHIC*).

- The number of loyalty cards held by the customer (*LC#*).

- The share of wallet based on store expenditures is defined as the amount of money spent by the customer in the retail store per year divided by the total amount of money that this customer spent in all the stores considered per year (*SOW*).

- The share of visit based on store patronage frequency is defined as the patronage frequency to the retail store for the customer on a yearly basis divided by the total number of visits to all the stores considered for that customer per year (*SOV*).

Data Analysis

A discriminant analysis is run using the **Discriminant Analysis** task.

1. Add the dataset *Loyalty_card_adoption.sas7bdat* to your SAS Enterprise Guide environment.

2. Go to **Tasks** → **Multivariate** → **Discriminant Analysis...**

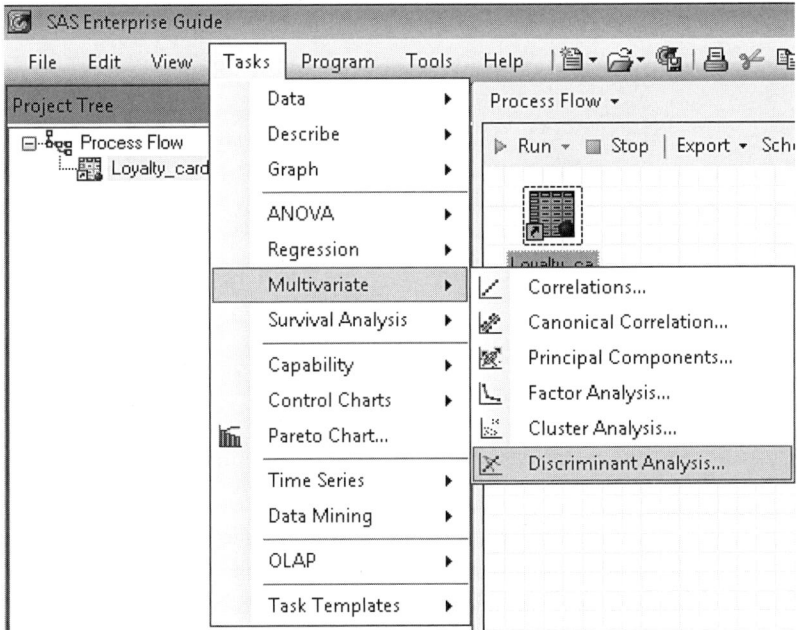

3. The selection pane opens and in the **Data** pane, you drag and drop the dependent variable containing the class labels, that is, *Class*, to the **Classification variable** role, while you put the independent variables under the **Analysis variables** role.

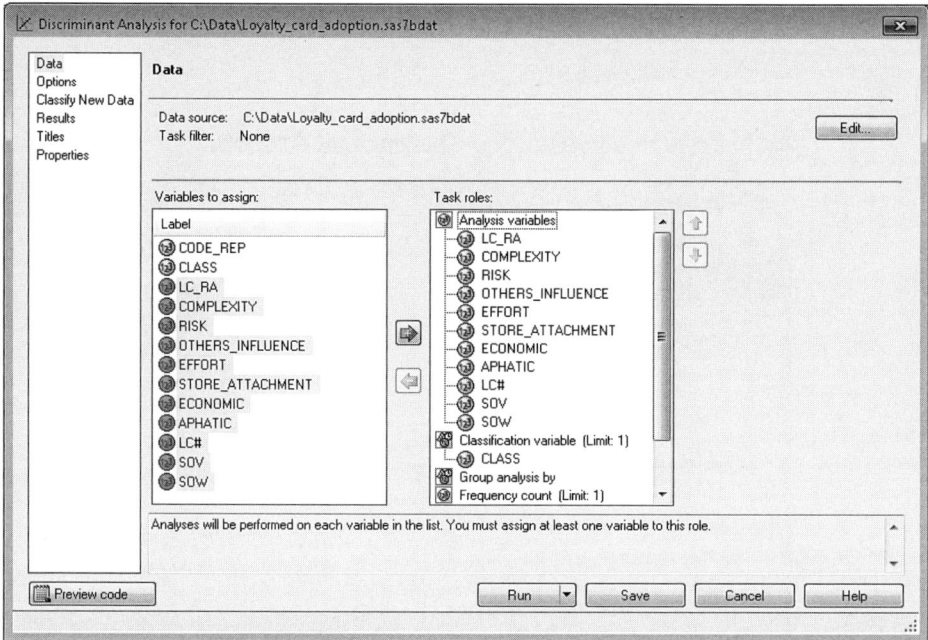

4.   In the **Options** pane, you have to make sure that you tick the options **Univariate test for equality of class means** in order to obtain the significance tests of the independent variables, and **Multivariate tests for equality of class means** in order to be able to test the overall meaningfulness of the discriminant analysis. Furthermore, ticking the option **Performs canonical discriminant analysis** will make it possible to explore the canonical structure. The canonical structure represents correlations of the observed variables and the unobserved latent discriminant functions. This will help to identify which variable(s) has (have) the most important impact on the dependent variable.

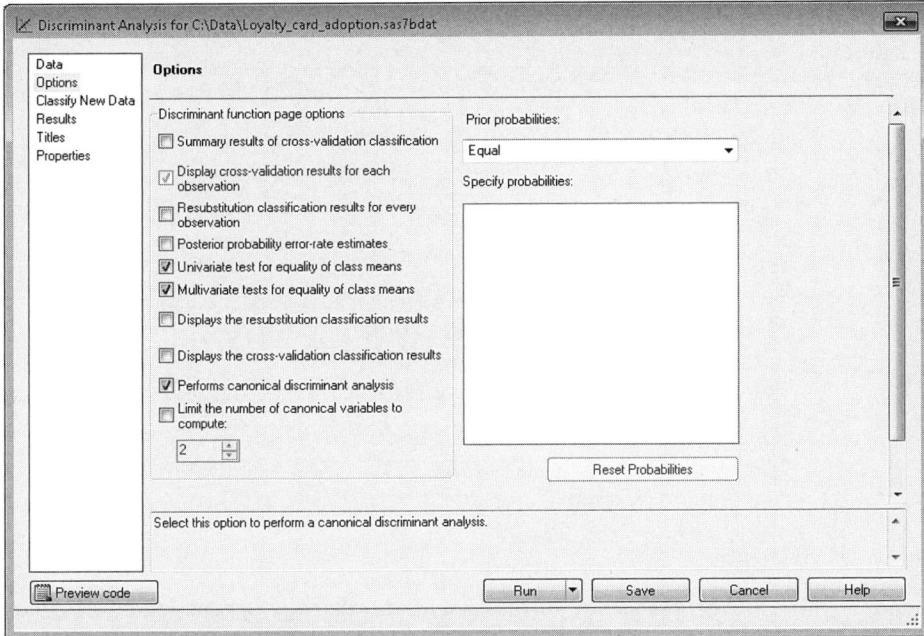

5. Click **Run** to execute the task. You can check the results of the discriminant analysis in the **Results** tab.

Interpretation

- **Class Level Information**

	Class Level Information				
CLASS	Variable Name	Frequency	Weight	Proportion	Prior Probability
1	1	399	399.0000	0.831250	0.333333
2	2	43	43.0000	0.089583	0.333333
3	3	38	38.0000	0.079167	0.333333

This table contains information about the distribution of the different categories of your dependent variable. In detail, it is clear from the table that 83.13 per cent of the respondents have a loyalty card (class 1), 8.96 per cent of the respondents do not have a loyalty card but show an interest to adopt it (class 2), and 7.92 per cent of the respondents are non-holders of a loyalty card with no clear intention to adopt it (class 3).

- ## Multivariate Statistics and F Approximations

Multivariate Statistics and F Approximations S=2 M=4 N=232.5					
Statistic	Value	F Value	Num DF	Den DF	Pr > F
Wilks' Lambda	0.56204466	14.17	22	934	<.0001
Pillai's Trace	0.46734398	12.97	22	936	<.0001
Hotelling–Lawley Trace	0.72692923	15.40	22	796.5	<.0001
Roy's Greatest Root	0.64598493	27.48	11	468	<.0001
NOTE: F Statistic for Roy's Greatest Root is an upper bound.					
NOTE: F Statistic for Wilks' Lambda is exact.					

This table contains the output of statistical tests that verify whether the estimated discriminant functions are statistically different. It would not be meaningful to start interpreting the other output tables if the estimated discriminant functions were not statistically different. The following hypotheses are considered:

H_0: The means of the discriminant function in all groups considered are equal.

H_1: The means of the discriminant function in all groups considered are different.

In the column *Statistic* in the row *Wilks' Lambda*, the p-value is shown to be smaller than 0.0001. H_0 is rejected and we are sure that interpreting the significance tests of the independent variables is meaningful.

- ## Univariate Test Statistics

Univariate Test Statistics F Statistics, Num DF=2, Den DF=477							
Variable	Total Standard Deviation	Pooled Standard Deviation	Between Standard Deviation	R-Square	R-Square /(1-RSq)	F Value	Pr > F
LC_RA	0.7261	0.6951	0.2624	0.0872	0.0956	22.80	<.0001
COMPLEXITY	0.6558	0.5922	0.3477	0.1878	0.2313	55.16	<.0001
RISK	1.0457	1.0293	0.2401	0.0352	0.0365	8.71	0.0002
OTHERS_INFLUENCE	1.1063	1.0946	0.2148	0.0252	0.0258	6.16	0.0023
EFFORT	0.9143	0.8557	0.3996	0.1276	0.1463	34.89	<.0001
STORE_ATTACHMENT	0.9315	0.8875	0.3533	0.0961	0.1063	25.36	<.0001
ECONOMIC	1.1811	1.1825	0.0608	0.0018	0.0018	0.42	0.6556
APHATIC	0.5912	0.5912	0.0470	0.0042	0.0042	1.01	0.3644
LC#	1.1995	1.1206	0.5308	0.1308	0.1505	35.90	<.0001
SOV	0.2854	0.2697	0.1163	0.1110	0.1248	29.77	<.0001
SOW	0.2413	0.2384	0.0492	0.0277	0.0285	6.80	0.0012

The p-values in this table indicate whether or not a variable has a significant impact in discriminating the different categories from one other. It is clear from the table that all independent variables used to discriminate the three categories appear to have a significant impact, except the variables *ECONOMIC* and *APHATIC*. For all the significant variables, the p-value is smaller than 0.05.

- **Linear Discriminant Function for CLASS**

Linear Discriminant Function for CLASS			
Variable	1	2	3
Constant	-81.80799	-74.83586	-68.85726
LC_RA	7.58251	7.81475	6.97791
COMPLEXITY	12.68474	10.94532	11.54355
RISK	4.47320	4.24589	4.37417
OTHERS_INFLUENCE	0.24536	0.61041	0.29635
EFFORT	3.87034	4.47310	4.69654
STORE_ATTACHMENT	2.62393	3.02679	1.90731
ECONOMIC	2.61501	2.69070	2.54154
APHATIC	11.75189	11.93880	11.52015
LC#	2.19194	1.09034	0.69792
SOV	7.12640	3.19185	2.33869
SOW	3.73781	3.08512	2.47658

This table gives an overview of the discriminant coefficients or weights for the independent variables within the discriminant function for each category in the dependent variable *CLASS* (with *1* for holder, *2* for non-holder with intention to adopt and *3* for non-holder with no intention to adopt). The interpretation of the discriminant coefficient is similar to that in multiple regression analysis. The value of the coefficients is dependent on the other independent variables included into the discriminant model, while the signs of the different β_n indicate whether there is a positive or a negative relationship. For reasons of clarity, the variable *Constant* is β_o, that is, the intercept, in the discriminant functions. The values in this table are not standardized, meaning that comparing the absolute raw values do not reveal anything, because the variables are measured on different measurement scales.

- **Pooled Within Canonical Structure**

Pooled Within Canonical Structure		
Variable	Can1	Can2
LC_RA	0.325670	0.578261
COMPLEXITY	0.595224	-0.173355
RISK	-0.214585	-0.289103
OTHERS_INFLUENCE	-0.114054	0.463935
EFFORT	-0.475440	0.058191
STORE_ATTACHMENT	0.300646	0.769481
ECONOMIC	-0.006506	0.146815
APHATIC	-0.069526	-0.117575
LC#	0.480810	-0.120549
SOV	0.435761	0.163788
SOW	0.194930	0.221731

This table represents the canonical structure, also known as the canonical loadings or discriminant loadings, that represents the correlations between the observed values of the independent variables and the unobserved discriminant functions. The values in this table are comparable and represent normal correlation coefficients ranging from -1 to 1. By inspecting the absolute height of a variable on the unobserved discriminant function, you discover its impact on the canonical discriminant function. For instance, *COMPLEXITY, EFFORT, LC#* and *SOV* load high for the first canonical discriminant function, while *LC_RA, OTHERS_INFLUENCE* and *STORE_ATTACHMENT* load high on the second canonical discriminant function. The same strengths are confirmed when exploring the table **Pooled Within-Class Standardized Canonical Coefficients**, that contains the standardized canonical discriminant function coefficients. These standardized discriminant coefficients are interpreted as traditional standardized estimates in multiple linear regression.

- **Number of Observations and Per cent Classified**

	Number of Observations and Per cent Classified into CLASS			
From CLASS	1	2	3	Total
1	324	56	19	399
	81.20	14.04	4.76	100.00
2	9	22	12	43
	20.93	51.16	27.91	100.00
3	2	8	28	38
	5.26	21.05	73.68	100.00
Total	335	86	59	480
	69.79	17.92	12.29	100.00
Priors	0.33333	0.33333	0.33333	

	Error Count Estimates for CLASS			
	1	2	3	Total
Rate	0.1880	0.4884	0.2632	0.3132
Priors	0.3333	0.3333	0.3333	

This table gives an overview of the classification performance of the discriminant functions. In the rows under the header *From CLASS*, you will find the original distribution of respondents belonging to category 1, 2 or 3, while in the columns under the header *Into Class*, you find the number of respondents who are predicted to be in category 1, 2 or 3 based on the discriminant analysis. The correct predictions are listed in the diagonal line. For instance, you will notice that from the 399 respondents originally belonging to the first category, the discriminant analysis is able to predict 324 respondents correctly, that is, 81.20 per cent. In sum, you find in the table that 374, that is, 324+22+28, of the total 480 respondents are correctly classified in the three consumer groups. This corresponds to a hit rate of 77.91 per cent. Hit rates of more than 75 per cent obtained on empirical data are considered as acceptable. Furthermore, the cells which do not appear diagonally represent the misclassifications of the respondents based on the model. The misclassifications per category are further specified in the table **Error Count Estimates for CLASS**. For instance, 18.80 per cent of the respondents originally belonging to category 1 are misclassified to category 2 or 3.

Managerial Recommendations

The managerial conclusions for the loyalty adoption case are twofold. First, one is able to explain the loyalty adoption process based on the survey carried out by the company. In detail, all independent variables have a significant impact on the adoption process, except the variables *ECONOMIC* and *APHATHIC*. Furthermore, the results indicate that *COMPLEXITY, EFFORT, LC#, SOV, LC_RA, OTHERS_INFLUENCE* and *STORE_ATTACHMENT* are amongst the best explaining variables. Second, the obtained discriminant functions are able to make a good prediction of the current customer base. 77.91 per cent of all customers are correctly classified in one of the three categories of the dependent variable!

Further Reading

Huberty, C.J. and Olejnik, S. (2006), *Applied MANOVA and Discriminant Analysis*, Wiley Series in Probability and Statistics, 2nd edition, Wiley-Interscience.

Klecka, W.R. (1980), *Discriminant Analysis, Quantitative Applications in the Social Sciences*, Sage Publications, Inc.

McLachlan, G.J. (2004), *Discriminant Analysis and Statistical Pattern Recognition*, Wiley Series in Probability and Statistics, Wiley-Interscience.

Index